European Socialism

European Socialism

A Concise History with Documents

William Smaldone

ROWMAN & LITTLEFIELD PUBLISHERS, INC.
Lanham • Boulder • New York • Toronto • Plymouth, UK

Published by Rowman & Littlefield Publishers, Inc.
A wholly owned subsidiary of The Rowman & Littlefield Publishing Group, Inc.
4501 Forbes Boulevard, Suite 200, Lanham, Maryland 20706
www.rowman.com

10 Thornbury Road, Plymouth PL6 7PP, United Kingdom

British Library Cataloguing in Publication Information Available

Library of Congress Cataloging-in-Publication Data

Smaldone, William.
European socialism : a concise history with documents / William Smaldone.
pages cm
Includes bibliographical references and index.
ISBN 978-1-4422-0907-7 (cloth : alk. paper) — ISBN 978-1-4422-0908-4 (pbk. : alk. paper) —
ISBN 978-1-4422-0909-1 (electronic)
1. Socialism—Europe—History. I. Title.
HX236.5.S6293 2014
335'.109—dc23
2013012883

∞™ The paper used in this publication meets the minimum requirements of American
National Standard for Information Sciences Permanence of Paper for Printed Library
Materials, ANSI/NISO Z39.48-1992.

Printed in the United States of America

Contents

Acknowledgments

Many people have helped me write this book. I especially wish to thank Bill Duvall and Lars Stiglich for their close reading of the manuscript, good conversations, and many useful suggestions. I am also grateful to the students in my course on modern socialism with whom I used the manuscript in a test run. In particular, I want to thank Maureen Lavelle, Peter Adamson, Jordis Miller, Patrick Atack, and Linda Kelly for their thoughtful comments. As always, the librarians at Willamette's Hatfield Library were extremely helpful in procuring necessary materials, and I appreciate very much Willamette University's readiness to provide the sabbatical that allowed me to complete the manuscript. I am also indebted to Susan McEachern for her sound advice during the writing process and to my anonymous peer reviewers for their careful reading and many excellent suggestions. Finally, I am most grateful to Jennifer Jopp, who, as usual, read every word and was generous with her wisdom and patience.

A Note on the Text

This aim of this book is to provide introductory students and general readers with a compact overview and analysis of European socialism's complex history from the mid-eighteenth century to the present. To that end, I have organized the work around five core chapters that trace the evolution of various socialist currents as they emerged in the context of rapid socioeconomic, political, and cultural change. In addition to the narrative text, I have also appended a selection of documents to each chapter. These are not meant to be comprehensive but rather aim to illustrate the range of socialist approaches to the remaking of the world, to highlight core issues, and to stimulate classroom discussion. This type of work is by nature synthetic, and for reasons of space I have used footnotes only in reference to direct quotations. Instead of a comprehensive bibliography, I have provided suggestions for further reading organized by chapter.

Abbreviations

ADAV	General German Workers' Association
CC	Central Committee
CDU	Christian Democratic Union
CGT	Confédération général du Travail (General Confederation of Trade Unions)
Cheka	Extraordinary Commission for Combating Counter-Revolution and Sabotage
CIS	Commonwealth of Independent States
CNT	Confederación National de Trabajo (National Workers' Confederation)
COMECON	Council for Mutual Economic Assistance
Cominform	Communist Information Bureau
Comintern	Communist International
CPRF	Communist Party of the Russian Federation
CPSU	Communist Party of the Soviet Union
CSDSD	Czech Social Democratic Party
DC	Italian Christian Democrats
DNA	Norwegian Labor Party
ECSC	European Coal and Steel Community
EEC	European Economic Community
ELP	European Party of the Left
ETUC	European Trade Union Confederation
EU	European Union
FDP	Free Democratic Party
GATT	General Agreement on Tariffs and Trade
GCTU	Grand National Consolidated Trades Union
GDR	German Democratic Republic
GULAG	Soviet system of forced-labor camps

ILP	Independent Labor Party
IMF	International Monetary Fund
ISB	International Socialist Bureau
IU	United Left
IWSP	Italian Workers' Socialist Party
Kadets	Russian Constitutional Democrats
KGB	Committee for State Security
KPD	German Communist Party
KSC	Czechoslovak Communist Party
MECW	Marx-Engels Collected Works
MRC	Military Revolutionary Committee
NATO	North Atlantic Treaty Organization
NEP	New Economic Policy
NES	New System of Economic Planning and Management
NKVD	People's Commissariat for Internal Affairs
NSDAP	National Socialist German Workers' Party (Nazi Party)
NSF	National Salvation Front
OEEC	Organization for European Economic Cooperation
OPZZ	All-Polish Alliance of Trade Unions
PASOK	Panhellenic Socialist Movement
PCE	Spanish Communist Party
PCF	French Communist Party
PCI	Italian Communist Party
PDS	Party of Democratic Socialism
PES	Party of European Socialists
POB	Belgian Workers' Party
PS	Parti Socialiste (French Socialist Party)
PSI	Italian Socialist Party
PSOE	Spanish Socialist Party
PUWP	Polish United Workers' Party
RC	Rifondazione Communista (Party of Communist Refoundation)
RSDLP	Russian Social Democratic Labor Party

SAP	Swedish Workers' Party
SDAP	German Social Democratic Workers' Party
SDF	Social Democratic Federation
SdRP	Social Democracy of the Republic of Poland
SED	Socialist Unity Party
SFIO	French Section of the Workers' International
SLD	Polish Democratic Left Alliance
SPD	German Social Democratic Party
SPÖ	Austrian Social Democratic Party
SRs	Russian Socialist Revolutionaries
SYRIZA	Coalition of the Radical Left
TUC	Trades Union Congress
UGT	Unión General de Trabadores (General Union of Workers)
UP	Union of Labor
USPD	German Independent Social Democratic Party
VDAV	Federation of German Workers' Associations
WEA	Workers' Educational Association

ONE

Introduction

SOCIALISM AND THE LEGACY OF THE FRENCH REVOLUTION

On 6 February 2009, almost twenty years after the fall of the Berlin Wall and eighteen years after the collapse of the Soviet Union, *Newsweek* published a cover story that stunned many Americans. Titled "We Are All Socialists Now," its author, Jon Meacham, claimed that the United States, despite almost three decades of free market economics and a political culture highly suspicious of government, was well on its way to becoming a "modern European state." Indeed, it was the conservative Republican president George W. Bush who had created the largest expansion of the welfare state in thirty years by passing a prescription drug program for the elderly, but even more dramatically, as the Great Recession of 2008 set in, he had effectively nationalized the banking and mortgage industries and pumped $700 billion into the collapsing financial sector. With the stock market plummeting, unemployment rising, and home foreclosures accelerating, Bush's successor, centrist Democrat Barack Obama, planned even larger fiscal outlays to stem the decline. Economic realities demanded government action regardless of which party was in office, and the same thing was true for meeting the medical needs of an aging population, the challenge of global warming, and other pressing issues. The government's enhanced role indicated that "we are heading in a more European direction" and toward a "mixed economy."[1]

Meacham did not argue that George W. Bush or Barack Obama was a "socialist," a claim for which there is no evidence. Both men certainly would deny it and could point to predecessors, such as Franklin Delano Roosevelt, who forcefully used state power to save capitalism from itself rather than to supplant it. But Meacham's assertion that moving in a European direction means that we are becoming socialists raises impor-

1

tant questions. Did not the disappearance of the Soviet Union and the transition to capitalism in China mark the end of socialism as a viable alternative to capitalism? Of course, by "Europe," Meacham is referring primarily to the richer industrial states of the West and North, but are these not capitalist societies in which private property, the market, and large transnational corporations flourish? Government's role in the economies of these societies certainly is important, but does this mix of state and market make them "socialist"?

In a society in which many (if not most) people regard socialism and its ideologically close relative communism as something to be feared and combated, Meacham's essay generated a good deal of debate. Unfortunately, much of the discussion was based more on myth than on a clear understanding of the history of European socialism and the movement's role in the contemporary world. Matters became even more confusing after 2009. President Obama's reform of the American health care system and his efforts to balance the federal budget by reducing spending and raising taxes on the richest Americans led some critics to label him a communist, a socialist, and also a fascist. Such accusations have little to do with the reality of Obama's politics, but they illustrate well the continued strength of anticommunism and the depth of ideological confusion in American political discourse.

One of the aims of this book is to help clarify matters by providing a brief, accessible history of European socialism from the French Revolution to the present. By socialism, I am referring to a set of related but often conflicting political and social movements that share a particular set of ideals. Instead of a society dominated by competition among individuals and groups, socialists emphasize the importance of planning, cooperation, workplace democracy, and mutual responsibility. To establish social equality, they strive to replace the capitalist economy, based on the ownership of private property, with one based on social or public ownership. Socialists also have aimed to build a world in which social solidarity is achieved through the realization of individual freedom and legal and social equality. As it matured into a mass movement, socialism propagated an ideal of universal human emancipation that would overcome all forms of exploitation and discrimination based on class, race, religion, or gender.

Many of the basic tenets of socialist thought may be traced back to the Greco-Roman and Judeo-Christian traditions of the ancient world. Greek philosophers, such as Plato and Aristotle (and, of course, Jesus Christ and his interpreters), all lived in societies wracked by violence, crass social inequality, and brutal exploitation and spent much of their time thinking about how to overcome these problems. In the *Republic*, for example, Plato suggests abolishing private property and the family to undercut the tendency for individuals and groups to selfishly accumulate wealth and power. In their place, he calls for the creation of a society led by virtuous philosopher kings. Old Testament prophets, too, were routinely indignant about the increasing social inequalities that accompanied foreign domination and Israel's deepening integration into the cosmopolitan world of the eastern Mediterranean. They urged a return to a simpler, more virtuous life based on egalitarian and pastoral values. Many early Christians argued similarly, and their assertion that the poor, along with all social outcasts, could achieve salvation more easily than the rich flew in the face of the dominant Greco-Roman aristocracy's aesthetic and moral norms and formed the ideological basis for early Christian communist societies, which eschewed private property and elevated community needs over those of the individual.

As the Christian church became the dominant institution of the Roman world, it gradually pushed these egalitarian tendencies into the background, but they never entirely disappeared, as the proliferation of monasteries and nunneries in the Middle Ages clearly illustrated. The contradiction between the wealth, power, and hierarchy in the church and its more egalitarian ideological roots was an ever-present tension that helped fuel the Reformation and also stimulated a wide range of thinkers to contemplate models of a better world. Sir Thomas Moore's *Utopia* (1516), written firmly in the Christian tradition, stands out among many early modern works that juxtaposed an idealized, more perfect society with the less-than-perfect contemporary one.

Although it is important to recognize that socialist ideas have deep roots in the ancient, medieval, and early modern worlds, this work focuses on the development of *modern* socialism, the origins of which are located in three largely secular transformative movements of the eighteenth century: the Enlightenment, the industrial revolution, and the rise of liberalism. The Enlightenment represented a new way of understanding the human condition based on the use of reason and the scientific method. Enlightenment thinkers, or philosophes, believed that the natural and social worlds could be understood and changed through the application of reason rather than religious faith. They assumed that history consisted of a series of progressive stages in which people steadily improved their understanding of the world and possessed universal, natural rights based on their humanity rather than belonging to any particular religion or social caste. There was great variation in the degree to which Enlightenment thinkers believed and applied these approaches, but their general outlook represented a new point of departure for those who wished to change the world. Religious beliefs would always remain an important motivating force among socialists, but they eventually took second place to a more secularized worldview.

Writing for European elites, philosophes such as Montesquieu (Charles-Louis de Secondat; 1689–1755), Voltaire (François-Marie Arouet; 1694–1778), Jean-Jacques Rousseau (1712–1778), Adam Smith (1723–1790), and Immanuel Kant (1724–1804) incisively criticized a wide range of institutions and practices that they considered anachronistic and in need of reform. They condemned torture, religious fanaticism and intolerance, censorship, arbitrary government, and state control over the economy while promoting changes that they believed would benefit all people rather than just privileged elites. Many of their ideas form the basis of modern approaches to politics and economics, for example, that people should be governed by laws, not arbitrary rulers; that powers within government should be separated to limit the concentration of authority; that the people are sovereign, that is, that the government's authority rests on the consent of the ruled or should at least serve their interests; that the government was responsible for the welfare of the population; and that individuals should be able to pursue their economic interests largely unfettered by state controls (laissez-faire).

The philosophes opposed the transformation of their societies through popular revolution. Indeed, many were mistrustful of the masses, viewed them as irrational and fickle, and, like Voltaire, preferred "enlightened despots" as the most effective agents of positive change. Still, by assuming that all individuals with enough education and material wherewithal could learn to assess their needs and those of the community, the philosophes laid the intellectual foundations for those who wished to challenge the established order. In that sense, as their ideas percolated through European society, they became revolutionary.

The intellectual energy unleashed by the Enlightenment intersected with the advent of the industrial revolution, which began in Great Britain around 1750, and with the rise of liberalism, which spawned political revolutions first in the United States in 1776 and then in France in 1789. This "Dual Revolution," to use Eric Hobsbawm's term, marked the beginning of the end of the old socioeconomic and political order and the advent of the modern world.

The term "industrial revolution" describes the transition from an economy in which most goods are produced on farms or by hand in small shops to one in which they are produced on a larger scale using increasingly sophisticated machinery. The onset of industrialization was part of a long process in which rising agricultural productivity, a growing population, and increasing commercial activity within and between states promoted the accumulation of capital surpluses that could be invested in manufacturing. Although many among Western Europe's traditional elites participated in these developments, it was the middle classes—commonly referred to as the bourgeoisie—who benefited most. Increased commercial activity created new opportunities for merchants and manufacturers as well as for the many urban professionals who serviced them. The accumulation of wealth made it easier for rich bankers, merchants, and industrialists to climb the social ladder, and it also gave them the wherewithal to promote their interests in societies in which hitherto birth rather than merit had most easily opened the doors to power and wealth.

While industrialization increased the social and political stature of the middle classes, for workers in town and country it often meant economic dislocation and loss of status. The reorganization of agricultural and artisanal production and the introduction of machinery in one sector of the economy after another undercut the value of unskilled as well as artisanal labor and led to growing insecurity among wide swaths of the population. Some workers were able to take advantage of new opportunities that also arose, but for many the sweeping changes that accompanied industrialization fueled intense anxiety and spawned different forms of resistance, such as strikes, machine smashing, and unionization. As historians such as Peter Stearns have observed, by the early nineteenth century some workers and intellectuals in Western Europe also began seeking alternatives to the new industrial capitalist order. It was from this effort that "socialism," which was both an ideology and a social and political movement, emerged.

An essential precursor to the rise of socialism, however, was liberalism. During the late eighteenth century, many middle-class people, along with some members of the aristocracy and clergy, had became sharply critical of the traditional social and political order and increasingly attracted to an ideology that embodied many the Enlightenment's core ideals. Devotees of what later came to be called "liberalism" were concerned primarily with the concept of liberty or freedom, which they saw as the key to individual fulfillment and social progress. Liberals chafed at what they perceived as arbitrary, irrational obstacles to liberty and strove for a society in which citizens enjoyed freedom of assembly, speech, and the press; elected representative government; and equality before the law. Liberals looked to government to protect private property and order, but they also desired freedom of trade and a system that encouraged rather than hindered individual competition. Liberals believed that material success rested on a person's own ingenuity and diligence, and they generally ascribed failure to personal inadequacy rather than impersonal forces outside of an individual's control.

Liberal ideals did not "cause" the French Revolution, but, as in the American colonies, they provided an intellectual framework and a clear set of goals for critics of the established order willing to take action. The absolutist French monarchy collapsed in 1789 because it had gradually lost legitimacy in the eyes of many of its subjects, who viewed it as rigid, arbitrary, and incompetent. Many of those anxious to reform or overthrow it stemmed from the rising middle class or bourgeoisie, as well as the peasant and working classes, but a substantial number also came from disgruntled elements of the privileged orders. By the end of the 1780s, the regime's failure to grapple with long-standing and widespread poverty, its hesitation to contemplate major legal and social reforms, deepening fiscal insolvency, and looming famine precipitated a crisis from which the government could not extricate itself. Desperate to address the state's impending bankruptcy, Louis XVI's decision to summon the Estates General in the spring of 1789 inadvertently facilitated the mobilization of forces opposed to the status quo and opened the door to popular upheaval.

From 1789 until 1793, France experienced an increasingly radical revolution in which successive elected governments, pressured by the rural and urban masses, carried out fundamental and largely "liberal" reforms. Public anger initially centered on the king, whose actions in the summer of 1789 fueled open rebellion in Paris, culminating in the seizure of the Bastille on 14 July. Violence soon spilled over into the countryside, too, as long-suffering peasants vented their pent-up fury at the aristocracy by burning down chateaux and destroying manorial records delineating their feudal dues. On 4 August, radical elements of the Estates General, reorganized as the National Assembly, abolished the feudal order on which the Old Regime rested. With the monarchy and formerly privileged classes in retreat, France was in the throes of a full-blown political *and* social revolution.

The National Assembly quickly followed up its abolition of feudalism by promulgating the Declaration of the Rights of Man and Citizen, which established the general principles of the new order. Derived from Enlightenment thought, classical models, and the ideas embedded in the American Declaration of Independence, this powerful document asserted that "men are born and remain free and equal in rights." It stressed the centrality of individual freedom, of civic equality, and of the right of free expression on all matters, including religion. Sovereignty derived from "the nation" made up of individual citizens endowed with rights regardless of social class. Following Rousseau, the Declaration described law as "the expression of the General Will" and foresaw a representative legislative system. Individuals were no longer subject to arbitrary arrest, nor could the state take their "inviolable" and "sacred" property unless public necessity required it. Focusing on the legal rather than material equality of individuals, the Declaration enshrined the liberty to pursue wealth and status regardless of birth. Although it referred frequently to "mankind," the document was silent about the status of women and slaves.

Over the next two years, the National Assembly carried out a program of extensive reforms in which its own power superseded the monarch's. The state seized the Catholic Church's extensive landholdings, abolished the religious orders, and transformed Church officials into salaried public servants subject to government control. It granted citizenship and civil rights to Protestants and Jews and abolished slavery in France though not in the colonies. In the economic sphere, it rationalized and liberalized the tax code for the whole country and swept away most impediments to free enterprise by abolishing guilds and other corporate or monopolistic entities thought to impede commerce.

The Constitution of 1791 formalized the implementation of these changes and created a constitutional monarchy. The new system was more democratic than the old one, but its reforms benefited the bourgeoisie more than any other group. It gained not only from the economic legislation promoting commercial activity and breaking the power of the craft guilds but also from gender and property qualifications that excluded most people from the franchise. Thus, wealthier males became "active" citizens who dominated the legislative process, while women and the poor were relegated to "passive" status. The language of the constitution implied that the people had the right and duty to overthrow any government that did not serve its citizens. Many would remember this as it became clear that, despite the revolution's call for universal "liberty, equality, and fraternity," a new system of wealth-based privilege was emerging.

Indeed, as political and economic conditions declined, mass unrest brought more radical changes. The royal family's failed effort to flee in June 1791 strengthened the hand of republican forces in the new Legislative Assembly elected that fall. Organized in the Jacobin Club, republican leaders such as Maximilian Robespierre (1758–1794) and Georges-Jacques Danton (1759–1794) believed that only a republic could fully guarantee the people's liberties. By April 1792, the republican "left" (so-called due to the location of its seats in the Legislative Assembly) was stronger that the monarchist "right" and was prepared to launch a revolutionary war against France's monarchist neighbors, who had threatened to intervene on behalf of the king. A string of defeats early in the war, coupled with soaring bread prices and fear of domestic counterrevolutionaries, sparked new waves of revolutionary action that resulted in the mobilization of volunteers for the front, the replacement of the Parisian city government with a new radical authority known as the Commune, the violent seizure of the royal family, and, in the fall of 1792, the convocation of a new national assembly, the Convention. This body, elected by universal manhood suffrage, abolished the monarchy, tried and executed the king, and wrote a new, far more democratic constitution granting the franchise to all adult males.

Under the pressure of foreign wars, civil war, and a deepening economic crisis, the Jacobins split into two warring factions. Robespierre's radical Montagnards pushed for political equality regardless of social origin, supported economic measures to protect the poor, and demanded the centralization of government authority against domestic and foreign opponents; the more moderate "Girondins," headed by Danton, resisted the concentration of power in the national government and advocated a more laissez-faire approach to the economy. Backed by the Parisian poor, by 1793 the Montagnards dominated the Convention and implemented mass terror against perceived enemies of the revolution, including the Girondins. Governing through special committees, such as the infamous Committee of Public Safety, they never put the Constitution of 1793 into practice. Nevertheless, its passage marked the high point of the revolution's democratic tide, and, as conservative forces began to reassert themselves the following year, it became a polestar for many radicals. Although it did not resolve the problem of economic inequality, many saw it as an important political step in that direction.

Thus, the industrial and democratic revolutions of the late eighteenth century embodied deep contradictions. Industrialization made possible the creation of more wealth and the promise of a richer life for all, but it also led to increasing social insecurity and widespread distress. The French Revolution, like its American predecessor, inspired generations of later democratic activists who believed that the people could take charge of their own history and change the world. At the same time, however, it fueled a split between those democrats who reveled in its liberal achievements and those who felt that it had failed to live up to its principles. For later socialists, it was these revolutions' egalitarian promise and their creation of a new hierarchical social and political order based on unequal wealth that stood at the center of their critique. In its essence, the story of socialism is nothing more than the effort to resolve this contradiction.

NOTE

1. Jon Meacham, "We are All Socialists Now," *Newsweek* (6 February 2009).

TWO

Socialist Ideals and Imaginings, 1789–1830

On the morning of 27 May 1797, French officials in the small town of Vendôme, about 150 miles southwest of Paris, escorted the freshly convicted traitors François-Noël "Gracchus" Babeuf (b. 1760) and Augustin Darthé (b. 1769) to the Place des Armes and guillotined them. Both men were grievously wounded after failing to commit suicide by stabbing themselves in the courtroom immediately after being sentenced. Their three-month trial, which had been transferred from Paris for security reasons, had been a momentous one. Along with sixty-two associates in their Society of Equals, Babeuf and Darthé were accused of conspiring to overthrow the government and to restore the democratic Constitution of 1793, which the French state had earlier abrogated. Both men, aware of the symbolic power of a martyr's death, hoped that, by dying heroically, they would rally support to their cause. Their hopes came to naught as conservative forces crushed their movement. In the long run, however, generations of revolutionaries would look back at Babeuf's moment as an inspirational and defining one in the history of socialism.

BABEUF AND THE CRITIQUE OF PRIVATE PROPERTY

The mid-1790s were years rife with conspiracy as the corrupt and unpopular French government, the Directory, clung to power. Among the broad array of the Directory's opponents, what set Babeuf and his compatriots apart was their radical politics, which went beyond the Jacobin call for a return to the Constitution of 1793 with its promise of universal male suffrage regardless of wealth. Babeuf and disciples such as Philippe-Michel Buonarrati (1761–1837) and Sylvain Maréchal (1750–1803)

9

also concluded that the only way to achieve true social justice was to abolish private property. "By its origins," Babeuf argued to the court, "the land belongs to no one and its fruits are for everyone." The introduction of private property was "a surprise foisted upon the mass of simple and honest souls. The laws of this institution must necessarily bring about the existence of the fortunate and the unfortunate, of masters and slaves."[1] Thus, Babeuf threw down the gauntlet to those who saw the legal equality proclaimed by the Declaration of the Rights of Man and Citizen (1789) as the French Revolution's penultimate achievement. Without material equality, equality before the law meant little.

The circumstances that led Babeuf to reach this conclusion are instructive. With the onset of the industrial revolution in England and the democratic revolutions of the United States, France, and Haiti, Europeans experienced enormous social and political changes that transformed the ways in which people thought, lived, and governed themselves. Babeuf was swept up in this maelstrom, in which he, like many others, also became an agent of change.

Born in the small town of Saint-Quentin in Picardy, Babeuf was the son of a poor tax collector. Although he received no formal education, he learned to read and write and eventually became a *feudiste*, an official who managed the archives of feudal estates and provided aristocrats with the legal grounds for the dues and taxes they exacted from peasants living on their lands. This profession became increasingly important as rising commercial pressures and social expectations led the nobility to seek means of increasing their income. As a professional, Babeuf gained a degree of status, and access to estate libraries allowed him to further his self-education by reading Voltaire, Plato, Aristotle, and Rousseau, among others. By 1787, he was a regular correspondent with the secretary of the Arras Academy, Ferdinand Dubois de Fosseux. Nevertheless, his opportunities remained limited, and he chafed at the condescension of his aristocratic clients and at being denied honorary membership in the Academy.

Babeuf's job revealed to him the ruthlessness with which the nobility and clergy exploited their tenants and the injustice disturbed him. He made his discomfort explicit in July 1787 in a letter to Dubois commenting on two reform projects that the secretary had recently described to him. One dealt with the establishment of a communist utopia, while the other addressed the establishment of a uniform civil code. The liberal Dubois took the latter project seriously but poked fun at the former and referred to its author as "the reformer of the whole world." Babeuf, on the other hand, asserted that reforming the civil code so that "men of all classes . . . would be accorded the same rights in the order of succession to property . . . *would be very good* . . .[but] obtain[ing] for all individuals, without distinction, an absolutely equal portion of all the goods and advantages that can be enjoyed in this mean world . . . *would be even better*."[2]

Babeuf pointed out that the nobility had established its rule by force and maintained it by using law to legitimize the pillage of wealth that belonged to others. While agreeing with Rousseau's contention that the first man to enclose a plot of land and declare "this is mine" was the initial author of all the evils that afflicted humanity,[3] he also believed that "the reformer of the whole world" had a much more workable solution to the problem than that of the noble Jean Jacques, who, in the end, accepted private property. Ten years later, Babeuf would find himself defending the reformer's solution before the tribunal; only then, it was no longer an academic question.

The abolition of feudalism ended Babeuf's career as a *feudiste*. Quickly joining the revolutionaries in Picardy, he attempted to earn his living as a journalist and pamphleteer, but by casting himself in the role of a popular tribune on the issues of unjust taxation and arbitrary government, he ran afoul of the old local elite straining to hold on to its authority. Arrested as an incendiary in May 1790, support from patriots in high places secured his release. Then, after being appointed to a minor post in charge of selling off national properties, in August 1793 he was convicted of fraud and sentenced to twenty years' imprisonment. He escaped to Paris just as the Terror moved into high gear and, with the help of his friend Maréchal, found a post in the bureaucracy charged with provisioning the capital. In November, however, the provincial authorities tracked him down. After eight miserable months in prison, the efforts of Maréchal and a sympathetic judge, a Jacobin from his hometown, finally won his release in July 1794.

At the beginning of the revolution, Babeuf had associated himself with the radical Jacobins based on his reading of Rousseau. Although he had argued for the abolition of property in his correspondence with Dubois, it took time before he came to see communism as the single practicable solution to injustice. In his early revolutionary writings, Babeuf expressed sentiments similar to those of the Jacobin firebrand St. Just (1767–1795). Babeuf asserted that every household had the right to an equal portion of France's productive land, and he proposed other redistributive policies to create a minimum standard of living for all and give everyone access to a range of government services. Such a model of reform had little to do with "communism" but was, rather, a call for expanded small peasant proprietorship. Babeuf, like St. Just, wanted to create a republic of virtue by reforming institutions. That goal meant purging the aristocracy and the clergy and using the state as an instrument to redistribute, not eliminate, property. To bring the recalcitrant into line with the "General Will," he was willing to use force. This was a radical approach, but it was not communism.

Babeuf changed his mind as the revolution unfolded. He was in Paris at the apotheosis of Jacobinism in 1793, when, under popular pressure, the Convention created a radical democratic constitution and empowered the Committee of Public Safety to root out counterrevolution at home and mobilize the nation's resources to defeat France's enemies abroad. Led by Maximilian Robespierre (1758–1794), the committee pursued justice via the use of mass terror, but it also sought to minimize the suffering of the poor by controlling prices, requisitioning needed products, and imposing rationing. Babeuf helped implement the latter and became convinced that it was possible for the state to redistribute commodities as a means of achieving absolute equality.

The overthrow of Robespierre's faction in July 1794 was followed by the conservative "Thermidorian" Reaction. The Convention ended the terror and established the Directory, which limited the franchise, suppressed its opponents, and, despite severe economic misery, reversed economic and social policies protecting the poor. Babeuf, calling himself "Gracchus" (after the Gracchi brothers, who died fighting for radical land redistribution in ancient Rome), vehemently opposed this counterrevolutionary turn and sought to rally outcast Jacobins and radical egalitarian supporters against it. In his *People's Tribune*, he called for a return to the Constitution of 1793 and elaborated a new economic model that would lead to true equality. In a "Manifesto of the Plebeians," he advocated the creation of a state that would suppress private property and put all men to work according to talent or trade. The products produced by individuals would be kept in a "common storehouse" to be rationed by the state administration "according to the most scrupulous equality."[4] Here we see the core of Babeuf's new program, which had gone beyond the radical redistribution of private property and now called for the latter's elimination.

As a first step toward this goal, Babeuf organized a conspiracy to seize power and restore the Constitution of 1793. Control and planning for action was in the hands of a small central committee, whose agents were to carry out propaganda among civilians and soldiers, organize insurgent cells, and gather arms. In April, the committee published a radical manifesto summarizing its egalitarian program. At its peak, it may have had a few thousand active supporters, drawn largely from among discontented artisans and shopkeepers, some of whom adhered mainly to the Jacobin ideals of 1793, while others enthused over Babeuf's radical egalitarianism. In early May, as the "Conspiracy of Equals" prepared for action, the police, having infiltrated its ranks, arrested its leadership and effectively smothered the movement in its cradle.[5]

Babeuf's life and political activities are important for many reasons. Born into a society experiencing rapid change, during the Revolution he used his talents and energy to take advantage of new opportunities that gave him substantial influence. However, when he carried the ideological principle of equality from the political into the economic and social realms, the effort conflicted with a new order in which equality before the law rested on the basis of an economic system predicated on inequality.

Babeuf's economic model had little in common with those of most nineteenth- and twentieth-century socialists or communists. He provided no systematic analysis of social development, and his recognition of private property as the key determinant of who ate well and who did not was in keeping with the views of other preindustrial champions of equality. Unlike later socialists, who saw the potential for liberation brought about by the machine age, his ascetic and static communism was based on what he knew: the artisanal and peasant production of the past.

More modern were the techniques that the Babouvists employed to organize their conspiracy under a political regime intent on destroying them. Such methods stressing secrecy, centralized decision making, discipline, and the preparation of revolutionary activists, reappeared repeatedly in the nineteenth and twentieth centuries under such leaders as Auguste Blanqui (1805–1881) in France and V. I. Lenin (1870–1924) in Russia. From the beginning, they also raised questions about the nature of the postrevolutionary order. Babeuf believed that it was the duty of leaders to keep an eye on those in power and to rouse the people against injustice and tyranny. He, too optimistically, thought that his efforts would culminate in a mass insurrection and that, once in power, the people would serve as a check on those seeking to dominate others. Like the Jacobins, he was not averse to the use of terror if it were necessary to realize the General Will and set the hesitant on the road to happiness, though he hoped that the radical transition could be brought about through peaceful persuasion. The tensions in this line of thinking would be a constant presence among the revolutionaries who followed him.

PAINE, CONDORCET, AND THE SEARCH FOR SOCIAL SECURITY

Babouvism was a revolutionary response to the political and social contradictions that resulted from the establishment of a new republican order based on equality before the law, private property, and commercial competition. In a society in which most people either were or aspired to become independent artisans, shopkeepers, or small farmers, Babeuf's attack on private property, despite the existence of widespread social misery and political unrest, did not resonate widely. Yet he certainly was not alone in his feeling that the moment had come for society to address the problem of socially created poverty. Other intellectuals, such as English journalist Thomas Paine (1733–1809) and the French mathematician Antoine-Nicholas de Condorcet (1743–1794), also believed that economic and political conditions had emerged that made it possible for society to create equal opportunity and social security for all citizens.

Much of Paine's thought exemplified that of the democratic radicals of the late eighteenth century. His many lines of work—as an artisan, a minor British official, a shopkeeper, a tutor, and finally a journalist—

were typical of those pursued or aspired to by urban workers and middle-class people of his day. They also formed the bulk of the new reading public, and Paine, an excellent writer, understood their lives of hard work and insecurity and knew how to articulate their feelings. An ardent defender of the American and French revolutions, Paine saw in them the realization of the great potential for improving the human condition associated with the Enlightenment. Grounding his views on reason, he favored the expansion of democratic rights to all adult males and attacked corrupt and arbitrary government, the established church, and social privileges based on birth and wealth. These views earned him the enmity of conservatives, but he never challenged private property or the intensifying commercialization of economic life.

In the *Rights of Man* (1792) and *Agrarian Justice* (1797), Paine explicated proposals designed to promote individual independence and security within a democratic republic equipped with institutions that functioned according to the application of reason rather than tradition. He believed that, in the past, the monarchy's wealth—mostly wasted in war and useless offices—had generated the people's poverty via a system of landownership, inheritance, and heavy taxation on those who could least afford it. A reorganized and rational democratic government could eliminate the vast amount of waste and reprioritize expenditures to ameliorate want and abolish unfair taxes on the poor. He proposed yearly grants to families to aid in the raising of children, the creation of a universal pension system, and the allocation of resources so that all children could attend school. He urged benefits for veteran soldiers, small grants to new mothers and newly married couples, and even a grant to defer funeral expenses of people who, while traveling for work, die far from home. To pay for such policies, he advocated repeal of myriad indirect and direct taxes that hurt the poor and the introduction of progressive taxes "to extirpate the unjust and unnatural law of primogeniture, and the vicious influence of the aristocratical system."[6]

Operating in the French context at about the same time, Condorcet thought along similar lines. A member of the French nobility, the Jesuit-educated marquis made his mark first as a mathematician and then in politics. Elected to the Academy of Sciences at age twenty-six, he later became permanent secretary of both it and the French Academy. When his friend the philosophe A. R. Turgot (1727–1781) was appointed to the powerful post of controller general in the government of Louis XVI, he made Condorcet the inspector general of the Paris Mint. Condorcet sympathized with the ideals of the American Revolution, favored the abolition of slavery, and supported equal rights for women. He welcomed the French Revolution and in 1791 won a seat in the Legislative Assembly, in which he associated himself primarily with the Girondin faction. A leader in the debates over the new constitution, in October 1793 he fell afoul of Robespierre's Montagnards, was declared a traitor, and went into hiding. Over the next eight months, he wrote *Sketch for a Historical Picture of the Progress of the Human Mind*, his most famous work. Caught in March, he died mysteriously in prison soon afterward.

To his last breath, Condorcet was a forceful exponent of the idea of progress, a concept rooted in the Enlightenment and given its first concrete expression in Turgot's *A Philosophical Review of the Successive Advances of the Human Mind* (1750). Condorcet agreed with Turgot's basic propositions that it could be empirically demonstrated that human society had advanced from dark, primitive origins to the enlightened present and that this movement had gained such momentum that it could not be reversed. Human history, Condorcet believed, was in no way related to any divine plan; it was, rather, an autonomous process that could be observed and understood with the tools of science. Its results were cumulative and predictive: "What happens at any particular moment," he wrote, "is the result of what has happened at all previous moments, and itself has an influence on what will happen in the future."[7] Society had already moved through nine stages involving tenacious struggle between the forces of reason and the "prejudices" of philosophers, of the unenlightened lower classes, and of those with vested interests in suppressing the truth. The labors of the most recent stages, he believed, had "done much for the honor of man, something for his liberty, but so far almost nothing for his happiness."[8] But the period from Descartes to the French Revolution had now established the material and intellectual groundwork for a major change. "Everything tells us," he asserted confidently, "that we are now close upon one of the great revolutions of the human race."[9]

Condorcet believed that the tenth stage of human development would witness "the abolition of inequality between nations, the progress of equality within each nation, and the true perfection of mankind." To achieve such equality, humanity had to overcome what he called "imperfections of the social art." The final end of the latter, he asserted, would be "real equality . . . in which even the effects of the natural differences between men will be mitigated and the only kind of inequality to persist will be that which is in the interests of all and which favors the progress of civilization, of education, and of industry, without entailing either poverty, humiliation or dependence." In such a society, "everyone will have the knowledge necessary to conduct himself in the ordinary affairs of life, according to the light of his own reason," and will be able, "through the development of his faculties, to find the means of providing for his needs." It followed that "misery and folly will be the exception and no longer the habitual lot of a section of society."[10]

The Anglo-Americans and the French people were in the forefront of this movement, in which all peoples would participate. Since humankind, in the form of priests, despots, and economic monopolists, not nature, threw up obstacles to progress around the world, fundamental change was possible as the American and French revolutions showed. Condorcet envisioned a world without slavery or racial prejudice, in which colonies became independent nations and free trade displaced the corrupt monopolies of mercantilism. With the assistance of their European brothers, the "large tribes" of Africa and Asia would learn the principles and practice of liberty, knowledge, and reason and thus enter the realm of civilization.[11] As Gareth Stedman Jones has noted, various currents of "progressive opinion" expressed by thinkers such as Montesquieu and Adam Smith shared these views. Where Condorcet differed was in his proposals to reduce inequality within each nation.[12]

According to Condorcet, "The necessary cause of inequality, of dependence, and even of misery" was the majority's lack of access to land or capital. Even in the most advanced countries of Europe, a great number of individuals were "almost entirely dependent for the maintenance of themselves and their family either on their own labor or on the interest from capital invested so as to make their labor more productive." Since "both these sources of income depend . . . on the health of the head of the family. . . . They provide what is rather like a life annuity, save that it is more dependent on chance."[13] Thus, Condorcet concluded, the lives of people relying on their own labor were subject to constant risk, while those living mostly on revenue from their lands or from capital investments were much more secure.

This problem could be addressed, argued Condorcet, "by guaranteeing people in old age a means of livelihood produced partly by their own savings and partly by the savings of others who make the same outlay, but who die before they need to reap the reward." The same principle could be applied to ensure the security of widows and orphans, and all children could be supplied "with the capital necessary for the full use of their labor, available when they start work and found a family, a capital which increases at the expense of those whom premature death prevents from reaching this age." These types of social insurance schemes, Condorcet felt, were eminently practical and required only a clear understanding of probability. Either public or private associations could administer them.

Greater equality could also result from "making industrial progress and commercial activity more independent of the existence of the great capitalists." Condorcet put the most emphasis on the provision of education. The latter's goal, he wrote, should be "to exclude all dependence, either forced or voluntary." With the proper syllabus and methods, "we can teach the citizen everything one needs to know in order to be able to manage his household, administer his affairs, and employ his labor and his faculties in freedom." Students would learn to know their rights and how to exercise them, they would grasp their duties and how to fulfill them, and they would learn to judge their own and other people's actions according to their own lights.[14]

Condorcet's central point was not to promote *absolute* equality among individuals. He was not opposed to private property, and he believed that people's various natural talents and inborn attributes would make some superior to others. To create a better world, however, he believed it essential to give all individuals the tools they needed to avoid dependency and thus be able to build their own lives. Together, a well-directed education system, good laws that remedy "natural" inequality in material wealth, and constitutionally regulated liberty would create a foundation that would ensure "all men enjoyment of the common rights to which they are called by nature."[15]

Both Paine and Condorcet recognized that poverty and insecurity flowed from unequal access to means of subsistence, such as land and tools. Unlike Babeuf, however, neither saw the need to abolish private property. Equal opportunity and democratic freedoms were essential to the pursuit of happiness but not absolute equality. To go down that road, noted Condorcet, "would be foolish and dangerous." It would introduce "even more fecund sources of inequality" and strike "more direct and fatal blows at the rights of man."[16]

Condorcet and Paine were deeply engaged with the intellectual discourse of the Enlightenment, and their approach to poverty derived partly from their readings of such figures as Adam Smith. Like John Locke (1632–1704) much earlier, Smith recognized that the growth of the eighteenth-century English economy was accompanied by a general improvement in economic opportunity and the standard of living. He also saw the parallel development of an increasingly complex division of labor and growing economic insecurity. The democratic revolutions in the United States and France opened the door to popular participation in governance that was previously the sinecure of the rich and privileged. For thinkers like Condorcet and Paine, the democratic breakthrough represented an opportunity to address the problem of rising social insecurity through political action. Taken together, their ideas represented a second major current of thought—what later socialists would label a social democratic one—in the socialist tradition. In contrast to Babeuf's call for a revolutionary democratic state that would abolish private property and the market and take over the management of the economy, they believed that a democratic state could provide a framework for a redistribution of wealth without undermining private property or the functions of the market.

LIMITS TO RADICAL CHANGE

Babeuf, Condorcet, and Paine were thinkers and activists who called for changes designed to improve the lot of ordinary people. Each paid a terrible price for his efforts. Condorcet, the great exponent of progress, equality, and tolerance, was a victim of Jacobin terror, while Babeuf's opposition to the Thermidor and private property cost him his head. Paine, a truly international revolutionary democrat, managed to die in his American bed in 1809, but only after his political popularity in England, France, and the United States had evaporated in the face of the wave of conservatism that swept all three countries. Of the three, Paine enjoyed the greatest following—in England, for example, hundreds of thousands read his *Rights of Man*, and democratic associations sprang up in over twenty townships in 1792—but his ideas, too, were suppressed.[17] What caused this temporary eclipse of radical democratic politics? Why did ordinary people not rally to their support, or, if they did, why were they defeated?

The answers to these questions varied from place to place. In England, Paine's critique of the monarchy, support for the Revolution in France, and his popularity petrified and angered the aristocracy and many middle-class property holders. The government suppressed Paine's books, drove him into exile, and, after convicting him in absentia for sedition and libel, organized loyalist mobs to burn him in effigy. Loyalists also set up 1,500 associations to combat sedition, which meant rooting out the so-called British Jacobins, especially after war broke out with France in 1793.

In England, the term "Jacobin" was used to blacken the reputation of those reformers who aimed to democratize England's corrupt parliamentary government, dominated by a small landed elite. Drawing on contemporary notions of the "rights of man" and the need for government based on reason, the reformers also looked to the English past to argue that those with landed wealth had usurped the popular sovereignty embodied in such documents as the Magna Carta (1215) and the Bill of Rights (1689). The reformers were primarily people of modest means, such as artisans and shopkeepers. Excluded from parliament, they promoted change not through violent revolution but rather through mass education. They published pamphlets, organized public meetings, and established political discussion clubs, such as the London Corresponding Society, founded in 1792 by men such as Thomas Hardy (1752–1832), a shoemaker, and John Frost (1750–1842), an attorney. Reform organizations also arose in Scotland and Ireland, where different cultural and political contexts shaped their outlook, but their basic goals were the same. In December 1792, a Convention in Edinburgh brought together representatives of eighty reform societies to demand universal male suffrage and annual parliaments.

The reformers' efforts alarmed the British state. Hardy was tried for treason, and, though he was acquitted, the remarks of the presiding judge, Lord Chief Justice Eyre, made the government's attitude clear. Eyre asserted that such activity "might degenerate and become unlawful in the highest degree. . . . A few well meaning men . . . assemble together to deliberate on the means of obtaining redress. The number increases, the discussion grows animated, eager, and violent. A rash measure is proposed, adopted and acted upon. Who can say when this will stop."[18] The government was determined to shut down reformers' activities.

Between 1794 and 1799, Britain's protracted war against France, food riots, unrest in Scotland and Ireland, and mutinies in the Royal Navy intensified Prime Minister Pitt's efforts to crush perceived disloyalty. The government suspended habeas corpus, outlawed secret organizations and corresponding societies, restricted press freedoms, and forbade employee and employer unions. Many reform leaders, such as the Scotsman Thomas Muir (1765–1799), were tried and shipped off to remote places like Botany Bay. With state-sanctioned "Church and King" mobs harassing active reformers, the latter's organizations rapidly lost members and fell apart. Although a few radicals in different regions attempted to go underground and organize violent resistance, they found little support. Government repression was effective, and, in the context of war, most people rallied to the flag. The patriotic context, along with economic growth and the spread of Methodism, which urged workers to accept their lot in life, temporarily undercut the movement for democratic reform. At that time, the option of democratic revolution appealed to very few.

In France, too, support for universal suffrage and state action to combat poverty ebbed following Robespierre's fall. During the early days of the Revolution, the government had made grappling with widespread indigence or "mendacity" a priority. In January 1790, it created a committee to assess the situation and suggest remedies. After estimating that one out of eight Frenchmen were beggars, the committee asserted that charity could not resolve a situation caused by social inequality. Assuming that "every man has the right to subsistence through work, if he is able-bodied, and to free assistance if he is unable to work," the committee saw it as a responsibility of the nation to end destitution, which fueled violence and promoted submissiveness among the poor. It proposed a series of measures similar to many of those suggested by Paine and Condorcet. In 1793–1794, the Convention transformed some of these ideas, such as pensions for the aged and infirm and allowances for poor families, into law.[19]

Implementation, however, was another matter. Wartime expenses, falling tax revenues, the flight of the rich, the outbreak of famine, and the collapse of paper currency in 1795 essentially bankrupted the state. The Directory's assumption of power then brought with it new economic priorities that aimed to promote commercial interests rather than support the poor. It abrogated the Convention's legislation and reimposed the system of indirect taxes favored by the monarchy. Largely disarmed and exhausted by the terror, seemingly endless war, and material deprivation and facing a Directory backed by the propertied and alert to Jacobin and royalist threats, the Parisian poor, the sansculottes, who earlier had driven the radical democratic forces forward, were in no position to reassert themselves.

During the Napoleonic Wars and the decade of conservative reconstruction that followed, movements for radical democratic reform in Britain and France made little headway. A landed aristocracy dominated British society and government, while post-Napoleonic France saw the return of the Bourbons to the throne and the partial restoration of noble privilege. Conservative forces were successful in stemming political reform, but change remained in the offing as capitalist development continued to transform working people's lives. Not only did they have to endure the miseries of war, but they also had to grapple with the increasing effects of commercialization and industrialization. Facing changes that both threatened their economic survival and offered new opportunities, the ways in which working people mobilized to promote their interests had long-lasting ramifications for the development of socialism.

INDUSTRIALIZATION AND ITS EARLY CRITICS

England in the late eighteenth century had the most advanced economy in Europe. The feudal economy, dominated by lords extracting rents in goods, labor, or cash from serfs bound to the soil, had disintegrated there at least two centuries before and been replaced by a system centered on production not for use but for sale on the market. No longer legally tied to the manor, the often-landless peasants were now "free" to move about and sell their ability to work in return for wages. Data from 1688 show that most people lived in the countryside, where the aristocracy and non-noble "gentry" held sway over large estates worked by a vast army of poor and landless peasants, but there were many independent peasants as well as small, independent "yeoman" and tenant farmers. Meanwhile, the cities and towns housed a vast array of artisanal producers, unskilled laborers, professionals, merchants, shopkeepers, soldiers, clergy, and government officials. Over the next 150 years, landed estate holders consolidated and enlarged their holdings by "enclosing" common lands essential to the survival of smallholders and removing many of the latter from their properties. These now landless people either stayed in the countryside and worked for wages on the farms or moved to the city. There, they formed a huge pool of cheap, largely unskilled labor and a growing market for sellers of farm products and artisanal goods. The establishment of a growing overseas empire that, following mercantilist principles, imported cheap raw materials and exported high-value finished goods supplemented this expanding British home market.

Enclosure and new agricultural techniques increased landowners' ability to exploit rural laborers. Simultaneously, a colonial policy based on conquest, forced labor, slavery, unequal exchange, and taxes brought increased wealth to the country. Higher output sustained a growing population that increased from 9 million in 1700 to 16.5 million a century later, and profits made from resultant demand promoted capital accumulation and reinvestment in new production capacity or new enterprises. After 1750, British entrepreneurs, drawn from the banking and merchant bourgeoisie, owners of larger (artisanal) manufacturing enterprises, and some lords, began investing in newly invented, large-scale machinery driven first by water and later by coal-fired steam power, which transformed production initially in cotton textiles and then in iron goods. Although it took well over a century, eventually mechanization would extend into all sectors of production.

The process unfolding in England soon spread to the Continent, though development in each country had its own particularities. In France, for example, strong elements of feudalism remained intact throughout the eighteenth century even as the capitalist sector of the economy expanded. The French Revolution, launched in the name of free trade as well as individual liberty, swept away feudal impediments to capitalist growth, which, after a delay during the Napoleonic Wars, accelerated, though at a slower pace than in Britain. We cannot dwell here on the factors that caused the rise of capitalism and of the industrial revolution in Europe. It is essential, however, to recognize that the changes they brought about were crucial to the growth of the socialist movement in the nineteenth century. Commercialization and industrialization transformed the social hierarchy and the world of work. As a society comprised largely of lords, serfs, independent peasants, and craftsmen gave way to a new one dominated by rural and urban capitalists and dependent wage laborers, workers had to assert their interests by drawing on past experience and developing new means of struggle.

The social transformation of Europe occurred slowly. For decades after the turn of the nineteenth century, the aristocracy remained politically ascendant and economically powerful. The clergy, too, remained a powerful social and political group with close ties to the state. While serfdom ended in France and much of central Europe during the Napoleonic period, feudal and semifeudal relations remained the norm in southern and Eastern Europe, especially in Russia, where serfdom dominated until 1861. Capitalist development, first in England and France and then across the Continent, reshaped this social order as the owners of merchant and productive capital became more numerous and economically powerful and the number of wage-dependent workers expanded in both rural and urban settings. Although wage laborers eventually became the majority, traditional urban artisans—working in small shops or larger manufactories—dominated in the production of nonagricultural goods until the late nineteenth century. It was their world that Adam Smith described in the *Wealth of Nations* (1776), not that of the factory dominated by machine production.

For centuries, urban artisans had promoted their social, economic, political, and cultural interests by organizing in guilds. These associations regulated production methods, the quality and quantity of goods, and the relationships between the masters and their dependent journeymen and apprentices. The guilds provided social insurance for members, saw to it that they behaved in socially acceptable ways, and organized cultural events. Guilds often competed with one another for local political power, and violent conflict among them was not uncommon. Violators of guild rules faced fines or expulsion from the craft. Guilds promoted a type of regulated capitalism dominated by small producers focused on local markets. The rise of larger, less regulated regional and national markets in which buyers and sellers functioned outside guild control undermined their ability to protect the masters' economic interests. This process was most advanced in England, where the guilds had essentially disintegrated by the end of the eighteenth century. Viewing such workers' organizations as a hindrance to commerce and a political threat, the French National Assembly abolished them in 1791.

The guilds' loss of control over the labor market resulted in intensified competition among small producers who could now enter the field at will. It did not, however, undercut the techniques of craft production itself. The introduction of large workshops in which individual craftsmen, once responsible for the entire product, now were assigned ever-simpler tasks initiated that process. But the death knell of artisanal production came with the advent of large-scale machine production. It was the workers in the textile industry who first encountered the contradictions that flowed from mechanization.

Until the late eighteenth century, the production of woolen and cotton cloth in England was largely a rural affair carried out in the homes of cottagers who may have had a substantial garden but did not have enough land to subsist. Some weavers' households were fully independent enterprises. The weavers owned their own looms and purchased the raw material that all members of the family helped clean, spin, weave, and sell in a process they controlled. More common, however, were households dependent on merchants for their operations. Avoiding urban guilds and taking advantage of the family's access to food production, merchants could pay low wages as they supplied families with raw materials and sometimes rented them necessary equipment. The merchants then collected the cloth and sent it on for dying or sale. The disadvantage of this system for capitalists was that it was difficult to control the pace of work or to manage a labor force not wholly dependent on wages. Machine production and the concentration of the workforce in factories solved those problems.

The invention of the spinning jenny in 1764 along with the water frame and an improved steam engine in 1769 made it possible for workers to increase the number of spindles they could operate from one to eighty and eventually far more. The enormous increase in the production of woolen and cotton thread in factories powered by water and then by steam increased the demand for skilled hand-loom weavers, whose numbers grew along with their wages and status. After 1785, however, the introduction of the power loom began to undermine their position. Improved machinery simplified and sped up workers' individual output and opened the door to less skilled competition.[20]

This example illustrates several key impacts of the industrial revolution. The use of machinery shifted the locus of production from the home or small shop to the factory, which transferred the workers' ability to organize the work process and control its tempo to the capitalist. Workers, who had earlier devoted part of their time to farming or who had owned their own looms, now were fully divorced from the means of production and completely dependent on wages. In addition, machine production undercut the value of some workers' skills, such as the spinners, while increasing that of others, like the weavers. It also created new fields of skilled work, such as machine building.

In response to the pressures brought by the changing economy, English workers set up associations or unions to defend their interests. During the eighteenth century, following the example of their forebears in the guilds, they organized along craft lines. Conflicts with employers over wages and working conditions often resulted in strikes, boycotts, riots, employer lockouts, and, on occasion, collective bargaining agreements. Some unions were local; others, such as the Society of Weavers on Lancashire, operated regionally and attempted to bring workers' grievances to the government's attention. During the 1790s, ironworkers in Sheffield, paper workers in Kent, and millwrights in Norwich and London, to name a few examples, also began to press their demands, which frightened manufacturers and fueled the suspicious state's willingness to outlaw workers' organizations in 1799.

The ban on unions and the denial of political representation left workers with few meaningful options to express their grievances. In spite of the law, workers organized clandestinely and tried to use legal methods, such as parliamentary petitions, to defend their interests, but with no success. Frustration intensified as parliament repealed the last remaining regulations in the cotton and woolen industries. As unskilled workers flooded into the crafts, wages collapsed and hardship increased. In 1812, when petitions and efforts to bargain brought no redress, workers in textile centers such as Lancashire, Yorkshire, and the East Midlands proclaimed: "We petition no more that won't do fighting must."[21] Beginning in Nottingham in late 1811, for the next two years they wrecked power looms and other equipment not in uncontrolled riots but through organized direct action. Marching under the banner of the mythical "Ned Ludd," these so-called Luddites used secrecy and solidarity to effectively mobilize supporters and destroy over 1,000 machines. To restore order, the British government brought in 12,000 troops and declared machine smashing a capital offense.

Luddism was more than "collective bargaining by riot." The Luddites were not pursuing political revolution, nor were they opposed to techno- logical innovation. Theirs was an effort to protect what remained of a way of life that was on the threshold of being destroyed by capitalism. Their struggle against a new system of domination revealed the contra- dictions of the "progress" that was at the core of the emerging capitalist order. That they could resist effectively and flout the forces of order was a challenge that the state could not ignore. Hence, it moved quickly and brutally—making use of the hangman's noose and transportation—to suppress them. At the same time, legions of political economists mobi- lized to defend the interest of capital and praise the introduction of ma- chinery as the key to social progress.

The British authorities crushed the Luddites, but workers' organizing efforts continued. Along with underground union building, by 1815 al- most 1 million artisans, tradesmen, and laborers were members of self- managed "friendly societies," which provided benefits against sickness, unemployment, and funeral expenses. In addition, the widespread mis- ery caused by the economic depression following the Napoleonic Wars sparked a revival of the movement for political reform. The government viewed these developments as seditious and responded with spies, agent provocateurs, and violence. For example, at St. Peter's Field outside of Manchester in August 1819, cavalry units, consisting in part of volunteers drawn from the local bourgeoisie, attacked a crowd of 60,000 workers peacefully demonstrating for reform. Eleven were killed and hundreds wounded in this "Peterloo Massacre," which exemplified the ferocity of class conflict in Britain. It also failed to halt the efforts of many workers and middle-class people to pursue reform, which, as we will see, contin- ued unabated.

Between 1760 and 1830, Britain became the world's leading industrial power. It was responsible for about "two-thirds of Europe's industrial growth of output," and its share of the world's manufacturing produc- tion rose from 1.9 to 9.5 percent. By 1850, more than half of its people lived in towns and cities, and ten years later, when it reached the zenith of its economic power relative to the rest of the world, it was producing 53 percent of the world's iron and 50 percent of its coal and consuming almost half of its raw cotton. As we noted in the case of the textile indus- try, such development brought with it enormous social changes. New "middle-class" groups controlled and managed capital, while wage- dependent factory hands, drawn from the declining crafts, unskilled ur- ban workers, and rural migrants, became increasingly important. As peo- ple's lives changed, so did their sense of identity. In Britain, many work- ers found themselves living in overcrowded, unsanitary, urban commu- nities in which they relied on capital to earn their living. Excluded from participation in government, they also faced repression when they sought to organize. Many workers began to consider themselves not as members of separate and competing crafts but increasingly as a group or class with its own interests. The development of this "working-class consciousness" was a key factor in the growth of the labor and socialist movements.

On the Continent, industrial transformation occurred differently from one locale to another. In France, where it developed more slowly and enterprises tended to be smaller and to focus on high-quality specialized goods, artisans were able to shape the process in the interest of their craft traditions. After the Bourbon restoration, for example, it was the journeymen—not the masters—who took the lead in reestablishing corporate organizations in virtually all the skilled trades. The journeymen used these institutions to defend their interests in labor disputes with the masters but not to challenge the traditional hierarchy of the workshop. At that time, they were still thinking mainly along craft rather than "class" lines. As William H. Sewell has noted, this outlook did not change until, in the context of the struggle following the July Revolution of 1830 (see chapter 2), French workers appropriated the language and the vision of 1789 for themselves.[22]

In politically divided "Germany," as was true in most of Europe, French occupation under Napoleon swept away many feudal obstacles to capitalist development. Although these changes undercut the guild system in many areas, artisanal production remained dominant well into the nineteenth century. There were pockets of industrial development, for example, in the Rhineland and Silesia, but economic changes occurred slowly. Germany remained divided into more than three dozen separate states in which Austria and Prussia vied for power. After the Vienna Congress of 1815, it was difficult for any groups to pursue political change, as reactionary monarchism and social and cultural conservatism dominated Europe. Using harsh legislation, secret police forces, and, when necessary, the military, the monarchs of Austria, Prussia, and Russia oversaw the suppression of liberal democratic, republican, and nationalist movements everywhere. Culturally, this period experienced revived church influence and religious feeling. Conservative romanticism dominated the arts and letters as intellectuals and artists idealized the corporatist world of the Middle Ages and elevated spirit and emotion over what they saw as the cold mechanistic rationalism and selfish individualism of the Enlightenment.

Despite the strength of the conservative reaction, it failed to completely snuff out voices favoring change. Indeed, this period also gave rise to some of the most innovative social thinking of the nineteenth century as Europeans grappled with the spreading effects of industrialization. The "dark satanic mills" of industrialism described by poet William Blake in 1803 certainly repelled people from all walks of life. Many conservatives reviled the damage done to the rural landscape and saw in it the embodiment of liberalism's threat to their ideal political and social order. Other critics, however, were not interested in restoring the old world; their criticisms of rising capitalism aimed to clear the ground for wholly different models of social development. Unlike the competitive, chaotic, and socially polarized society emerging under capitalism, these models aimed to establish a society that was more rational, cooperative, egalitarian, and harmonious. Charles Fourier (1772–1837) and Claude Henri de Saint-Simon (1760–1825) in France and Robert Owen (1771–1858) in England were three of the most important of these early nineteenth-century thinkers. Although later socialists, such as Karl Marx (1818–1883) and Friedrich Engels (1820–1895), disparaged their approaches as "utopian," many of their ideas strongly influenced the socialist vision in the second half of the nineteenth century.

Charles Fourier was an eccentric figure possessed of an extraordinary imagination. Some of his notions were so bizarre that some observers have thought him mad. Whatever the state of his mind, however, there is no doubt that he was a prescient thinker willing to challenge many accepted maxims of his day. Fourier grew up in the small town of Besancon in the home of a successful cloth merchant who died when he was nine. Despite his "despotically prudish and narrow-minded" mother, he reveled in the joys of life, such as flowers, sweets, and playing the violin.[23] Basically a loner, Fourier developed a fondness for order and symmetry that would be reflected in his later stress on harmony in music, mathematics, and social relations.

To receive his father's substantial inheritance, Fourier was required to enter into the cloth trade. After high school, he reluctantly completed an apprenticeship in Lyon, where he witnessed the deep poverty of the city's poor and the frequent strife between the silk workers and dominant merchants. Drafted into the cavalry in 1794, he served eighteen months before returning to commerce as a cloth salesman engaged with businesses in Marseilles, Lyon, and Bordeaux. After losing all his inheritance in the tumult of revolution, he eked out a living on the lower rungs of commerce. From that perch, he observed the corruption of business and politics that informed his critique of "civilization."

According to Fourier, commerce was merely a "mode of exchange in which the seller has the right to defraud with impunity and to determine by himself . . . the profit which he ought to receive."[24] Commerce "allowed deceit and plunder to triumph," but manual labor as practiced in civilized society was no better. He attacked the bourgeois work ethic and the capitalist division of labor, which forced workers to toil for long hours at the same activity day in and day out, as dehumanizing. Organized in a chaotic system of competition that impoverished producers and enriched dishonest, unproductive merchants, he concluded that "civilized industry is at the antipodes of reason; it is a world gone wrong, a faulty mechanism."[25]

To replace it, Fourier proposed reorganizing society into small cooperative communities called phalanxes, in which residents would strive to establish harmony. Life would be organized according to what he called the Law of Passionate Attraction, or "the drive given to us by nature prior to any reflection; it is persistent despite the opposition of reason, duty, prejudice, etc."[26] Fourier identified twelve basic passions that shaped human relations: five of the senses (touch, hearing, sight, taste, and smell), four of the soul (friendship, love, ambition, and parenthood), and three that he labeled "distributive." When combined in various ways, they produced a total of 810 different personality types. Optimally, a phalanx would have two of each type for a total of 1,620 residents.

Fourier envisioned the phalanx as a largely self-sufficient community based on artisanal and agricultural production in which all, including children, would work, but work would become a form of play in which change and variety were a part of the daily experience and people could follow their own inclinations. Self-fulfillment was essential, for women as well as men, in love as well as in work. He was a radical feminist who believed that women should have an equal role in administering the community and sharing in its joys. He viewed marriage, patriarchy, and monogamy as means of subjugating women. The phalanx would tolerate all forms of sexual relations that were not coerced or violent, and it would exclude no one who wished to participate. Fourier did not believe that women were in all ways equal to men but saw in gender differences part of the symmetrical balance in nature. Like his contemporaries Mary Wollstonecraft (1759–1797) in England and Olympe de Gouges (1748–1793) in France, he was in the forefront of those who saw women's liberation as an essential element in the creation of a free society.

Fourier did not favor absolute material equality. Members of the phalanx would be remunerated in accordance with the amount of their investment and the type of work they performed. He envisioned a community in which the poorest would be comfortable, but there would be no "community of goods" as Babeuf proposed. Scarred by the experience of the French Revolution, he also opposed the use of violence to bring about change.

For decades, Fourier worked at his trade and spent his spare time filling thousands of notebook pages with his ideas. Some of his works, such as *The Theory of the Four Movements* (1808), appeared in his lifetime but attracted little attention. Many of his writings, especially on sexual matters, went unpublished until much later. Hoping to attract financial backing, he sent copies of his books and advertisements to government officials, leading businesspeople, philanthropists, and intellectuals. Few deigned to reply. For years, he insisted on returning home each day at noon just in case a rich investor might appear; none ever came.

Fourier did have a few admirers who discovered his books and sought him out. In 1833, they attempted to construct a phalanx, but the effort soon collapsed due to lack of capital. Despite this setback, these disciples did much to promote their master's ideas. Shortly after his death, so-called Fourierist groups appeared and founded communities drawing on some of his ideas in France and North America. Although these failed, the efforts to create them made Fourier's ideas an important current in socialist thought after 1840.

While Fourier saw the spread of small cooperative communities as the solution to the problems of civilization, his fellow Frenchman Count Claude Henri de Saint-Simon (1760–1825) aimed to remake society by harnessing the advances of modern science and industry. Descended from the famous Duke de Saint-Simon, whose memoirs bore witness to life in the court of Louis XIV, the ambitious count instructed his valet to wake him each day with the reminder, "Remember, Monsieur le Comte, you have great things to do."[27] Certainly, Saint-Simon's early life was filled with adventure. Commissioned as an officer at age seventeen, in 1779 he was part of the French expedition to aid England's rebellious American colonies in their war of independence. Acquitting himself well at Yorktown, he later fell into British hands—after being stunned by a cannonball—in the Caribbean. Eventually freed from internment in Jamaica, he made his way to the court of the Viceroy of Mexico, to whom he vainly proposed a plan to link the Atlantic and Pacific via a canal through Lake Nicaragua. Like Babeuf, Condorcet, Paine, and Fourier, Saint-Simon felt that the challenges of the day, be they economic, social, or political, required large-scale solutions; the viceroy's rebuff in no way dampened his enthusiasm for big ideas.

After returning to France, Saint-Simon soon left the army and went to Holland, where in 1786 he became involved in an abortive Dutch and French plan to drive the English out of India. Returning to France in 1789, he supported the Revolution and commuted between his ancestral estates, where he was involved in legislative and military matters, and Paris. He also became a land speculator, which brought him into contact with many shady types as well as the full gamut of political movers and shakers. Renouncing his title in September 1793 did not save him from arrest as the Committee of Public Safety moved to round up many of his associates in November. Released after Robespierre's fall, he returned to his speculative activities and made a fortune, only to then lose it all and sink into poverty by 1805. Hospitalized after a nervous breakdown in 1813, he recovered within a year and returned to Paris, where he received a post in the library of the Arsenal.

For Saint-Simon, science was the key to humanity's future. His first book, *Letters from an Inhabitant of Geneva* (1803), called for the establishment of a scientific and artistic elite whose members, given wealth via subscription and power via public appointment, would use their skills to end the strife caused by the warring classes and to address society's most pressing problems. Unlike Condorcet, who stressed the accumulation of knowledge over time as the basis of progress, Saint-Simon looked at the ways in which ideas and social groups were linked together and changed over time. He applied this historicist approach to analyze the function of institutions, such as the church, and different classes, such as the clergy and aristocracy, during different phases of historical development.

With the advent of science and industry, the nobility and clergy had become useless and parasitical. Clinging to power, they hindered the rise of a new order dominated by what Saint-Simon regarded as the "productive" majority (*les industriels*), which included industrialists, scientists, artists, technicians, managers, and workers. Saint-Simon favored doing everything possible to facilitate the rational mobilization of these productive elements. Planning and cooperation were better suited to that task than reliance on "anarchic" competition among individual scientists or the capitalist marketplace. In that regard, Saint-Simon set himself apart from liberal economists like Smith, who placed more emphasis on market mechanisms to deploy resources.

As Albert Lindemann has observed, Saint-Simon was an exponent of modernism rather than a socialist. He emphasized productivity, organization, innovation, and technological discovery but was elitist. Workers were valuable as producers but needed the guidance of the industrial, scientific, and artistic elite. Saint-Simon also rejected social and economic equality as a solution to class conflict. More effective would be the creation of a rational, planned system that overcame individualism and gave people the opportunity to work for the common good; such a system required hierarchy and authority.[28]

For most of his life, Saint-Simon maintained a secular outlook, but his last major work, published in 1825, advocated the creation of a "new Christianity" modeled on the early or "primitive" church. Led by priest-scientists according to the principle that "all men are brothers," the main goal of renewed Christianity would be "to ameliorate the condition of the poorest class."[29] Saint-Simon insisted that the new Christians adhere to strict pacifism, and he hoped that the new order could be introduced gradually. He called on the princes of Europe to "listen to the voice of God" and convert.[30]

It is debatable whether Saint-Simon turned to religion out of conviction or the recognition that, in the context of the spiritual revival under the Restoration, religion was popular. What is clear, however, is that during the last decade of his life, he attracted a following of young intellectuals, such as August Comte (1798–1857), later high priest of positivism, and the future historian Augustín Thierry (1795–1856). While these two soon left him, others, such as Barthélemy-Prosper Enfantin (1796–1864) and Saint-Amaud Bazard (1791–1832), remained his loyal disciples. Following his death, they used the new religious departure as a means of building a sect, which, despite splits and a government ban, claimed 40,000 adherents by 1840.

Unlike Fourier, who derived his chief experiences from the long-established cloth trade, and Saint-Simon, whose influence initially stemmed from his noble pedigree, Robert Owen was a product of the new industrial world. The son of an ironmonger and saddle maker, he left home at age ten and worked his way up from a draper's apprentice to become, at age twenty-eight, co-owner of New Lanark Mills, the largest cotton-spinning establishment in Britain. Owen found a community similar to others he had experienced. "Ignorance and ill training," he wrote, had given the people "habits of drunkenness, theft, falsehood, and lack of cleanliness." Divided by "sectarian feelings, [and] strong national prejudices both political and religious," they opposed "all attempts to improve their condition."[31] Within a few years, however, Owen was able to turn the situation around. New Lanark became a model enterprise that made him rich and transformed him into a national figure.

Owen was a paternalistic and often patronizing entrepreneur who did little to encourage democratic habits among his employees. What set him apart from most of his fellow capitalists, however, was his conviction that people were a product of their environment. If one altered the conditions in which they lived and worked and provided them with educational opportunity, one could also alter their behavior. Owen raised wages; improved working conditions; built housing, schools, and day care facilities; ended child labor; and created social insurance programs that markedly improved life in New Lanark, but he regarded ending ignorance as the key element of the whole project. Making the world a better place required a material and moral transformation. The land and workforce to achieve the former was already at hand, and education, his "revolution by reason," would ensure the latter.

New Lanark's reforms attracted thousands of visitors, and Owen worked hard to convince Britain's economic and political elites to apply them across the land. At first, he received a respectful hearing, especially from conservative Tories, who agreed with his critique of the factory system and apparent support for the preindustrial moral economy. This support evaporated, however, as Owen became more openly critical of Christianity and the family and as his economic ideas became more radical. As an alternative to the market and private property, he urged the creation of small, self-sustaining, agricultural Villages of Cooperation that would absorb the unemployed, provide a range of services, and outcompete private enterprises. Already suspect in the minds of his fellow industrialists, such proposals, which required substantial investment, were stillborn; Owen had burned his bridges with the upper-class supporters he had hoped to convince.

In 1824, Owen sold his stake in New Lanark and invested almost his whole fortune in a property at New Harmony, Indiana, which became the first of sixteen Owenite communities founded in the United States. This experiment, like the others, quickly ran into trouble. Squabbles between selfless Owenite and more self-interested settlers, as well as the lack of preparedness for the rigors of rural life among many middle-class recruits, were among just a few of the problems that arose. Although well respected, Owen was unable to control the situation in New Harmony as he had with his own business in Scotland. By 1828, the community had collapsed, and he was back in Britain.

Much had changed during his absence. The repeal of the Combination Acts in 1826 resulted in a resurgence of trade union activity. Many of Owen's ideas for social reform had also attracted a following among workers who founded the London Co-Operative Society to promote them. Its *London Co-Operative Magazine* was the first to use the term "socialism" in discussions about whether capital held privately or in common best served the public good. Owen quickly joined this working-class movement and, at its peak in 1834, became leader of the trade unions' national organization.

But this was a role that could not last. Like Fourier and Saint-Simon, Owen abhorred class conflict and the possibility of violent struggle or revolution. To realize his goals he, too, sought elite support. When they ignored him, he was willing to ally himself with workers, but his project always remained one of education, not radical action. When, by the early 1830s, many workers insisted on using other methods to bring about change, Owen had to go his own way. He would spend the remainder of his long life preaching his "revolution by reason" to ever-fewer listeners.

As we have seen, radical English and French intellectuals responded to the challenges brought forth by the Dual Revolution in a variety of radical or reformist ways. Few of their ideas, however, circulated much beyond the literate artisans or the middle and upper classes; they had little resonance among the poor and unskilled. At the same time, we observed how the workers of the preindustrial world struggled against and adapted to rising capitalism. By the late 1820s, many of the radical thinkers' ideas, which were increasingly referred to as "socialist," were percolating among these workers, some of whom saw them as reasonable solutions to the concrete problems of their world. A new movement was in the process of being born.

DOCUMENT 2.1. ANALYSIS OF THE DOCTRINE OF BABEUF (1796)

In April of 1796 Babeuf's followers pasted up placards around Paris outlining Babeuf's basic ideas. The text below is a condensed version of its assertions. Although Babeuf was not the author, he endorsed them.

1. Nature has given every man an equal right to the enjoyment of all its goods.
2. The goal of society is to defend this equality, often attacked in the state of nature by the strong and the wicked, and to add to common happiness by the working together of all.
3. Nature has imposed on everyone the obligation to work; no one can, without committing a crime, shirk labor.
4. Labor and pleasures should be in common.
5. Oppression exists when there is one who wears himself out at work and lacks everything, while another swims in abundance while doing nothing.
6. No one can, without committing a crime, exclusively expropriate the goods of the earth or of industry.
7. In a real society, there should be neither rich nor poor.
8. The rich who don't renounce their excess in favor of the indigent are enemies of the people.
9. No one can, through the accumulation of all means available, deprive another of the instruction necessary for his happiness. Instruction must be for all.
10. The goal of the revolution is to destroy inequality and restore the common welfare.
11. The Constitution of 1793 is the true constitution of the French; because the people solemnly accepted it [and] the Convention did not have the right to change it. . . .

Source: Philip Buonarroti. *La conspiration pour l'égalité*, Editions Sociales, Paris. 1957. Translated for marxists.org by Mitchell Abidor. CopyLeft: Creative Commons (Attribute & ShareAlike) marxists.org 2004.

DOCUMENT 2.2. THE PROGRESS OF THE HUMAN MIND: THE TENTH STAGE (1793)

Antoine-Nicolas de Condorcet

All the causes that contribute to the perfection of the human race, all the means that ensure it must by their very nature exercise a perpetual influence and always increase in their sphere of action. . . . We may conclude then that the perfectibility of man is indefinite. . . .

Organic perfectibility or deterioration amongst the various strains in the vegetable and animal kingdom can be regarded as one of the general laws of nature. This law also applies to the human race. No one can doubt that, as preventative medicine improves and food and housing become healthier, as a way of life is established that develops our physical powers by exercise without ruining them by excess, as the two most virulent causes of deterioration, misery, and excessive wealth, are eliminated, the average length of human life will be increased and a better health and a stronger physical constitution will be ensured. The improvement of medical practice, which will become more efficacious with the progress of reason and of the social order, will mean the end of infectious and hereditary diseases and illnesses brought on by climate, food, or working conditions. It is reasonable to hope that all other diseases may likewise disappear as their distant causes are discovered. Would it be absurd then, to suppose that this perfection of the human species might be capable of indefinite progress; that the day will come when death will be due only to extraordinary accidents or to the decay of the vital forces, and that ultimately the average span between birth and decay will have no assignable value? Certainly man will not become immortal, but will not the interval between the first breath that he draws, and the time when, in the natural course of events, without disease or accident, he expires, increase indefinitely? . . .

Finally, may we not extend such hopes to the intellectual and moral faculties? May not our parents, who transmit to us the benefits of disadvantages of their constitution, and from whom we receive our shape and features as well as our tendencies to certain physical affections, hand on to us also that part of the physical organization which determines the intellect, the power of the brain, the ardor of the soul or the moral sensibility? Is it not probable that education, in perfecting these qualities, will at the same time influence, modify and perfect the organization itself? Analogy, investigation, of the human faculties and the study of certain facts, all seem to give substance to such conjectures which would further push back the boundaries of our hopes.

These are the questions with which we shall conclude this final stage. How consoling for the philosopher who laments the errors, the crimes, the injustices which still pollute the earth and of which he is often the victim in this view of the human race, emancipated from its shackles, released from the empire of fate and from that of the enemies of its progress, advancing with a firm and sure step along the path of truth, virtue and happiness! It is the contemplation of this prospect that rewards him for all his efforts to assist the progress of reason and the defense of liberty. He dares to regard these strivings as part of the eternal chain of human destiny; and this persuasion he is filled with the true delight of virtue and the pleasure of having done some lasting good which fate can never destroy by a sinister stroke of revenge, by calling back the reign of slavery and prejudice. . . .

Source: Antoine-Nicolas de Condorcet. *Sketch for a Historical Picture of the Progress of the Human Mind.* Translated by June Barraclough with an introduction by Stuart Hampshire (Westport, CT: Hyperion Press, 1979, reprint of 1955 edition), 199–202.

DOCUMENT 2.3. LETTERS FROM AN INHABITANT OF GENEVA TO HIS CONTEMPORARIES (1803)

Claude Henri Saint-Simon

This excerpt from Saint-Simon's first book sets out his initial ideas for reorganizing the social hierarchy. Although he later moved away from Enlightenment rationalism, he retained the fundamental idea on the need for a new elite to guide social development throughout his life.

I am no longer young, I have observed and reflected actively all my life and your happiness has been the end to which all my work has been directed; I have thought of a project which I think might be useful to you and I now propose to tell you about it.

Open a subscription in honour of Newton's memory: allow everyone, no matter who he may be, to subscribe as much as he wishes.

Let each subscriber nominate three mathematicians, three physicists, three chemists, three physiologists, three authors, three painters and three musicians.

The subscriptions and nominations should be renewed annually, although everyone should be completely free to renominate the same people indefinitely.

Divide the amount of the subscriptions between the three mathematicians, the three physicists, etc., who have obtained the most votes.

Invite the President of the Royal Society in London to receive the subscriptions for the first year. In subsequent years, entrust this honourable duty to whomsoever has given the highest subscription.

Make it a proviso that those who have been nominated should accept no posts, honours or money from any special group, but leave each man absolutely free to use his gifts as he wills.

Men of genius will in this way enjoy a reward which is worthy of themselves and of you; this reward is the only one which will supply them with the means to give you all the service of which they are capable; it will become the object of the ambition of the most active minds and will deflect them from anything which might disturb your peace of mind.

Finally, by doing this you will be providing leaders for those who are working for the progress of your enlightenment; you will be endowing these leaders with great prestige and you will be placing considerable financial resources at their disposal.

Source: The Political Thought of Saint-Simon (London & New York: Oxford University Press, 1976), reproduced at http://www.marxists.org/reference/subject/philosophy/works/fr/st-si-mon.htm.

—————

DOCUMENT 2.4. DEGRADATION OF WOMEN IN CIVILIZATION

Charles Fourier

In addition to his radical critique of commerce and the capitalist division of labor, Fourier was convinced that women in France and England were essentially enslaved. In his view, the degree of women's equality was an important measure of a society's progress toward a better life for all.

Is there a shadow of justice to be seen in the fate that has befallen women? Is not a young woman a mere piece of merchandise displayed for sale to the highest bidder as exclusive property? Is not the consent she gives to the conjugal bond derisory and forced on her by the tyranny of the prejudices that obsess her from childhood on? People try to persuade her that her chains are woven only of flowers; but can she really have any doubt about her degradation, even in those regions that are bloated by philosophy such as England, where a man has the right to take his wife to market with a rope around her neck, and sell her like a beast of burden to anyone who will pay his asking price? Is our public opinion on this point much more advanced than in that crude era when the Council of Mâcon, a true council of vandals, debated whether or not women had a soul and decided in the affirmative by a margin of only three votes? English legislation, which the moralists praise so highly, grants men various rights that are no less degrading for the sex [women], such as the right of a husband to sue his wife's recognized lover for monetary indemnification. The French forms are less gross, but at bottom the slavery is always the same. Here as everywhere you can see young women languishing, falling ill and dying for want of a union that is imperiously dictated by nature but forbidden by prejudice, under penalty of being branded, before they have been legally sold. Such incidents, though rare, are still frequent enough to attest to the slavery of the weaker sex, scorn for the urgings of nature, and the absence of all justice with respect to women.

Among the signs that promise the happy results to come from the extension of women's privileges, we must cite the experience of other countries. We have seen that the best nations are always those that accord women the greatest amount of liberty; this can be seen as much among the Barbarians and Savages as among the Civilized. The Japanese, who are the most industrious, the bravest, and the most honorable of the Barbarians, are also the least jealous and the most indulgent toward women; this is so true that the Magots of China travel to Japan to deliver themselves up to the love that is forbidden them by their own hypocritical customs.

Likewise the Tahitians were the best among the Savages; given their relative lack of natural resources, no other people have developed their industry to such an extent. Among the Civilized, the French, who are the least inclined to persecute women, are the best in that they are the most flexible nation, the one from which a skillful ruler can get the best results in any sort of task. Despite a few defects such as frivolity, individual presumptuousness, and uncleanliness, however, the French are the foremost civilized nation owing to this single fact of adaptability, the trait most alien to the barbarian character.

Likewise it can be seen that the most corrupt nations have always been those in which women were most completely subjugated . . .

As a general thesis: *Social progress and historic changes occur by virtue of the progress of women toward liberty, and decadence of the social order occurs as the result of a decrease in the liberty of women.*

Other events influence these political changes, but there is no cause that produces social progress or decline as rapidly as change in the condition of women. I have already said that the mere adoption of closed harems would speedily turn us into Barbarians, and the mere opening of the harems would suffice to transport the Barbarians into Civilization. In summary, *the extension of women's privileges is the general principle for all social progress.*

Source: "Degradation of Women in Civilization," *Théorie des Quatre Mouvements et des Destinées Générales* (The Theory of the Four Movements and of the General Destinies), 3rd ed. (originally published in 1808, this ed. 1841–1848). Republished in *Oeuvres Complètes,* I (Paris, 1966), pp. 131–33, 145–50. Reprinted in Susan Groag Bell and Karen M. Offen, eds., Karen M. Offen, trans., *Women, the Family, and Freedom: The Debate in Documents, Volume One, 1750–1880* (Palo Alto, CA: Stanford University Press, 1983), 40–41.

DOCUMENT 2.5. AN ADDRESS TO THE INHABITANTS OF NEW LANARK (1816)

Robert Owen

But, my friends, if what has been done, what is doing, and what has yet to be done here, should procure the benefits which I have imperfectly enumerated, to this village, to our neighborhood, and to our country, only, I should be greatly disappointed; for I feel an ardent desire to benefit all my fellow-men equally. I know not any distinction whatever. Political or religious parties or sects are everywhere the fruitful sources of disunion and irritation. My aim is therefore to withdraw the germ of all party from society. As little do I admit of the divisions and distinctions created by any imaginary lines which separate nation from nation. Will any being, entitled to the epithet intelligent, say that a mountain, a river, an ocean, or any shade of color, or difference of climate, habits, and sentiments, affords a reason sufficient to satisfy the inquiries of even a well-trained child, why one portion of mankind should be taught to despise, hate, and destroy another? Are these absurd effects of the grossest ignorance never to be brought to a termination? Are we still to preserve and encourage the continuance of those errors which must inevitably make man an enemy to man? Are these the measures calculated to bring about that promised period when the lion shall lie down with the lamb, and when uninterrupted peace shall universally prevail? — peace, founded on a sincere goodwill, instilled from infancy into the very constitution of every man, which is the only basis on which universal happiness can ever be established? I look, however, with the utmost confidence to the arrival of such a period; and, if proper measures shall be adopted, its date is not far distant. . . .

The principles on which the practical system I contemplate is to be founded, are now familiar to some of the leading men of all sects and parties in this country, and to many of the governing powers in Europe and America. . . . They have been subjected to the minute scrutiny of the most learned and acute minds formed on the old system, and I am fully satisfied of their inability to disprove them. These principles I will shortly state.

Every society which exists at present, as well as every society which history records, has been formed and governed on a belief in the following notions, assumed as *first principles:*

First, — That it is in the power of every individual to form his own character.

Hence the various systems called by the name of religion, codes of law, and punishments. Hence also the angry passions entertained by individuals and nations towards each other.

Second, — That the affections are at the command of the individual.

Hence insincerity and degradation of character. Hence the miseries of domestic life, and more than one-half of all the crimes of mankind.

Third, — That it is necessary that a large portion of mankind should exist in ignorance and poverty, in order to secure to the remaining part such a degree of happiness as they now enjoy.

Hence a system of counteraction in the pursuits of men, a general opposition among individuals to the interests of each other, and the necessary effects of such a system,-ignorance, poverty, and vice.

Facts prove, however —

First, — That character is universally formed *for*, and not *by*, the individual.

Second, — That *any* habits and sentiments may be given to mankind.

Third, — That the affections are *not* under the control of the individual.

Fourth, — That every individual may be trained to produce far more than he can consume, while there is a sufficiency of soil left for him to cultivate.

Fifth, — That nature has provided means by which population may be at all times maintained in the proper state to give the greatest happiness to every individual, without one check of vice or misery.

Sixth, — That any community may be arranged, on a due combination of the foregoing principles, in such a manner, as not only to withdraw vice, poverty, and, in a great degree, misery, from the world, but also to place *every* individual under circumstances in which he shall enjoy more permanent happiness than can be given to *any* individual under the principles which have hitherto regulated society.

Seventh, — That all the assumed fundamental principles, on which society has hitherto been founded, are erroneous, and may be demonstrated to be contrary to fact. And

Eighth, — That the change which would follow the abandonment of those erroneous maxims which bring misery into the world, and the adoption of principles of truth, unfolding a system which shall remove and for ever exclude that misery, may be effected without the slightest injury to any human being.

Here is the groundwork, — these are the data, on which society shall ere long be re-arranged; and for this simple reason, that it will be rendered evident that it will be for the immediate and future interest of every one to lend his most active assistance gradually to reform society on this basis. I say *gradually*, for in that word the most important considerations are involved. Any sudden and coercive attempt which may be made to remove even misery from men will prove injurious rather than beneficial. Their minds must be gradually prepared by an essential alteration of the circumstances, which surround them, for any great and important change and amelioration in their condition. They must be first convinced of their blindness: this cannot be effected, even among the least unreasonable, or those termed the best part of mankind, in their present state, without creating some degree of irritation. This irritation must then be tranquillized before another step ought to be attempted; and a general conviction must be established of the truth of the principles on which the projected change is to be founded. Their introduction into practice will then become easy, — difficulties will vanish as we approach them, — and, afterwards, the desire to see the whole system carried immediately into effect will exceed the means of putting it into execution.

The principles on which this practical system is founded are not new; separately, or partially united, they have been often recommended by the sages of antiquity, and by modern writers. But it is not known to me that they have ever been thus combined. Yet it can be demonstrated that it is only by their being *all brought into practice together* that they are to be rendered beneficial to mankind; and sure I am that this is the earliest period in the history of man when they could be successfully introduced into practice. I do not intend to hide from you that the change will be great. "Old things shall pass away, and all shall become new."

But this change will bear no resemblance to any of the revolutions, which have hitherto occurred. These have been alone calculated to generate and call forth all the evil passions of hatred and revenge: but that system which is now contemplated will effectually eradicate every feeling of initiation and ill will which exists among mankind. The whole proceedings of those who govern and instruct the world will be reversed. Instead of spending ages in telling mankind what they ought to think and how they ought to act, the instructors and governors of the world will acquire a knowledge that will enable them, in one generation, to apply the means which shall cheerfully induce each of those whom they control and influence, not only to think, but to act in such a manner as shall be best for himself and best for every human being. And yet this extraordinary result will take place without punishment or apparent force.

Source: Owen, R. (1816) *An Address to the Inhabitants of New Lanark*, London. Available in *the informal education archives*: http://www.infed.org/archives/e-texts/owen_new_lanark.htm.

NOTES

1. "Babeuf's Defense (From the Trial at Vendome, February–May, 1797)," reprinted in *Socialist Thought: A Documentary History*, ed. Albert Fried and Ronald Sanders (New York: Columbia University Press, 1992), 63.
2. "Babeuf to Dubois de Fosseux, July 8, 1787," in Fried and Sanders, *Socialist Thought*, 46 (emphasis in the original).
3. Jean Jacque Rousseau, "Discourse on the Origins of Inequality among Men (1757)," reprinted in Fried and Sanders, *Socialist Thought*, 33.
4. R. Rose, *Gracchus Babeuf: The First Revolutionary Communist* (London: E. Arnold, 1978), 211.
5. David Thomson, *The Babeuf Plot* (Westport, CT: Greenwood Press, 1975), 37–40; Rose, *Gracchus Babeuf*, 264.
6. Thomas Paine, "Rights of Man. Part II," in *Collected Writings*, ed. Eric Foner (New York: Library of America, 1995), 598, 642–43.
7. Antoine-Nicolas de Condorcet, *Sketch for a Historical Picture of the Progress of the Human Mind*, trans. June Barraclough (Westport, CT: Hyperion Press, 1955), 4.
8. Condorcet, *Sketch*, 169.
9. Condorcet, *Sketch*, 12.
10. Condorcet, *Sketch*, 174.
11. Condorcet, *Sketch*, 175–77.
12. Gareth Stedman Jones, *An End to Poverty? A Historical Debate* (New York: Columbia University Press, 2004), 19.
13. Condorcet, *Sketch*, 180–81.
14. Condorcet, *Sketch*, 182.
15. Condorcet, *Sketch*, 184.
16. Condorcet, *Sketch*, 179–80.
17. Jones, *An End to Poverty?*, 67.
18. Quoted in Malcolm I. Thomis and Peter Holt, *Threats of Revolution in Britain, 1789–1848* (Hamden, CT: Archon, 1977), 14.
19. Jones, *An End to Poverty?*, 111–18; Alan Forrest, *The French Revolution and the Poor* (New York: St. Martin's Press, 1981).
20. Phyllis Deane, *The First Industrial Revolution*, 2nd ed. (Cambridge: Cambridge University Press, 1979), 89–91.
21. Quoted in Thomis and Holt, *Threats*, 32.
22. William H. Sewell, "Artisans, Factory Workers, and the Formation of the French Working Class, 1789–1848," in *Working Class Formation: Nineteenth Century Patters in Western Europe and the United States*, ed. Ira Katznelson and Aristide R. Zolberg (Princeton, NJ: Princeton University Press, 1986), 56–59.
23. Jonathan Beecher, *Charles Fourier: The Visionary and His World* (Berkeley: University of California Press, 1986), 23.
24. Jonathan Beecher and Richard Bienvenu, eds., *The Utopian Vision of Charles Fourier: Selected Texts on Work, Love, and Passionate Attraction* (Columbia: University of Missouri Press, 1983), 114.
25. Beecher and Bienvenu, *Utopian Vision*, 127–28.
26. Beecher and Bienvenu, *Utopian Vision*, 216.
27. Quoted in Fried and Sanders, *Socialist Thought*, 74.
28. Albert Lindemann, *A History of European Socialism* (New Haven, CT: Yale University Press, 1984), 48–50.
29. Saint-Simon, "The New Christianity," in Fried and Sanders, *Socialist Thought*, 82.
30. Saint-Simon, "The New Christianity," 101.
31. Robert Owen, *A New View of Society* (1818; reprint, New York: AMS Press, 1972), 3.

THREE

Socialist Ideology amid Reform and Revolution, 1830–1870

The decades between the outbreak of the French Revolution of 1830 and the Paris Commune in 1871 witnessed the growth and transformation of European socialism. Excluded from political power, workers during the 1830s increasingly came to view their interests as separate from those of middle-class people, who not only enjoyed a more comfortable and relatively secure way of life but also were able to expand their role in the political systems of the Western European states. At the same time, as industrialization advanced, the composition of the working class slowly changed as wage-earning, dependent workers began to supplant independent artisans in the production process. Artisans remained the dominant political force among workers throughout this period but found themselves under increasing economic pressure not only due to competition from factories but also as a result of restructuring within the crafts in which mechanization lagged. This situation helped fuel intense social and political unrest, culminating most pointedly in the European Revolutions of 1848. The failure of the various political currents within the labor movement to achieve even their most basic political and economic demands then forced workers and their leaders to rethink their aims and approaches to political power. The conclusions they drew shaped the development of the socialist movement well into the twentieth century.

THE RISE OF CHARTISM IN BRITAIN

During the late 1820s, a new economic slump in Britain resulted in rising unemployment, falling wages, and declining living conditions for many rural and urban workers. One reaction was the "Swing Riots" of rural workers in southern and eastern England who, in late 1830, attacked new threshing machines that threatened their livelihood. This movement, like its Luddite predecessor, was ruthlessly crushed. Another response, especially from the recently legalized and growing union movement, was the renewed call for parliamentary reforms giving male workers the right to vote and to stand for election. Events across the English Channel buoyed hopes for change. At the end of July 1830, in a three-day popular uprising, Parisians swept the reactionary Charles X (1756–1836) from the French throne and replaced him with a more liberal cousin, Louis Philippe (1773–1850), the Duke of Orléans. The revolution then triggered successful liberal rebellions in Belgium, which won its independence from the Netherlands in 1831, and Switzerland, where democratic forces pushed the Federal Diet to eliminate press restrictions, grant universal male suffrage, and limit clerical influence. Although liberal and nationalist revolts in Spain, Poland, and Italy failed, the revolutionary wave frightened the British upper classes and made them amenable to limited reforms.

Even before the July Revolution, the Tory-led British government had sought to ease domestic tensions with new legislation such as the repeal of the anti-union Combination Acts as well as laws preventing non-Anglicans, especially Catholics, from holding office or serving in parliament. Working-class leaders, such as the Owenite cabinetmaker William Lovett (1800–1877), now hoped for further gains. They were joined in this sentiment by middle-class supporters of the Whig Party, who hoped to increase their representation in a parliament largely dominated by wealthy landowners. Most Whigs were not interested in extending the suffrage to workers but aimed primarily to reform an electoral system rigged to favor the rural gentry at the expense of the rapidly growing industrial towns where the middle classes were strongest. Thus, middle-class leaders were willing to join forces with workers to press for change, but not of the kind that would directly enhance workers' political power. On the contrary, they used the mass mobilization of workers as a means of sending a dire message to the landed elite: only by broadening the franchise to the middle class will the state hold back the revolutionary mob.

In 1830, the Whigs won a slim majority in the House of Commons, but it took two more years of intense campaigning, including huge street rallies and violent outbreaks in districts under the control of reform opponents, as well as complex parliamentary machinations, to push the Reform Bill through the reactionary House of Lords. The final product increased the number of those qualified to vote from 220,000 to 670,000, about 20 percent of the adult male population. This arrangement greatly strengthened the parliamentary power of the rising commercial and industrial classes but left the workers out in the cold. Although the new Whig majority banned slavery in the empire in 1833 and instituted some minimal restrictions on child labor, it also rejected a bill limiting the workday to ten hours, and in 1834 it passed the New Poor Law, which ended the traditional parish-based system of out-relief for the indigent. Those who could not find work now had the choice of either starving or entering the "workhouse," where family members were separated and adults performed hard labor in return for miserable bed and board. By undercutting local support for the impoverished, the law created a nationwide labor market to serve the burgeoning capitalist economy. And, as the later Chartist leader James Bronterre O'Brien (1865–1864) noted, it also "helped to open the people's eyes as to who are the real enemies of the working classes."[1]

In the face of political exclusion and growing economic insecurity, many workers became increasingly conscious of themselves as a separate group with their own interests. They set about building their own institutions and finding their own solutions to pressing problems. Many became more open to socialist ideas. This process was already under way well before the campaign for reform. Between 1828 and 1832, the number of Owenite cooperative societies increased from four to 500. Spread throughout the country, they promoted cooperative retail stores "to circumvent the principles of capitalist trading" and founded "labor exchanges," where artisans attempted to recoup the full value of their labor by trading goods priced in units of labor time (i.e., the amount of labor time embodied in their production) rather than in currency.[2] Many of these enterprises, especially the labor exchanges, were undercapitalized or suffered from intractable practical problems that made them short lived, but they also illustrated the energy and optimism of the labor movement.

This vibrancy was especially true of the expanding trade unions. In the decade following their legalization, new craft unions emerged in sectors ranging from weaving to the building trades, and these attempted to create umbrella organizations to promote their joint interests. In early 1834, they formed the Grand National Consolidated Trades Union (GCTU), in which Owen played a leading role. Aiming not only to improve wages and working conditions, the GCTU also intended "to bring about *a different order of things*" in which the "undue control" of the "ignorant, idle, and useless parts of society" will be replaced by a system in which "the really useful and intelligent part of society . . . shall have direction of its affairs."[3] These ambitious goals made clear that the union's long-term vision, however vague, went well beyond the immediate improvement of workers' lives and that change was to be achieved not as Owen had initially hoped, through the actions of society's elites, but rather from the bottom up.

Within a few months, the GCTU recruited over 500,000 workers to its banners, but it simultaneously had to grapple with ongoing strikes and a wave of new labor actions that quickly overwhelmed its resources. Employers responded to union organizing by forcing workers to sign documents pledging not to join, and the state began arresting and exiling unionists for "administering illegal oaths." Owen was also soon at odds with other GCTU leaders over how to move forward. He rejected harsh criticism of employers and the idea of class struggle. Although he dreamt of a great work stoppage that would bring the elites to their senses, in the summer of 1834 he preferred to shut down the GCTU's press rather than support a wave of new strikes. In August, with its membership hemorrhaging and its leadership in disarray, a GCTU delegate congress dissolved the organization.

Owenite cooperatives, labor exchanges, and trade unions won mass support because people saw them as a means of achieving a variety of aims. Denied the franchise, their press hindered by exorbitant stamp taxes, and their livelihood undercut by low wages, unemployment, and poor working conditions, many workers fumed at a system of wealth, power, and privilege that the radical democrat William Cobbet (1763–1835) called "The Thing."[4] The dissolution of the GCTU was a blow to the construction of a nationwide union organization, but organizing continued, and Owenism remained a strong influence among workers, who continued to cast about for new means to achieve their ends.

In 1836, radical democratic activists led by William Lovett founded the London Working Men's Association for the political education of skilled workers. Two years later, Lovett penned the "Great Charter," which laid out six key demands for the democratization of the country: universal male suffrage, abolition of property qualifications for members of parliament, annual parliaments, equal electoral districts, the secret ballot, and salaries for parliamentarians. These "Chartist" demands were not in themselves "socialist," but many viewed their realization as an essential step toward establishing social justice. Within a year, supporters of the Charter built a nationwide mass movement that for a decade seemed poised to transform Britain's entire political order.

Chartism aimed to achieve reform through mass education and parliamentary petition. Although at times noisy segments of the movement advocated insurrection as a last resort, such sentiments garnered little support among workers who, despite frustrations, largely believed that major changes in Britain could be had without violent revolution. Chartist-supported mass demonstrations, strikes, and militaristic drilling, along with fiery rhetoric from top leaders, such as the charismatic orator Feargus O'Connor (1794–1855), sometimes created a very radical impression, but in the end the Chartists stepped back from the revolutionary brink.

Chartism, argues Dorothy Thompson, drew its strength from constituencies rooted in Britain's growing but still small and relatively homogeneous industrial communities, in which state and church authority was weak. These areas had their own traditions in regulating economic and other affairs, were close knit, and had a generally unified sense of purpose. A wide range of skilled workers, factory operatives, and small shopkeepers backed the movement, which was also very much a family affair. Although patriarchal mores dominated the working-class milieu, Chartism encouraged the participation of women in its rituals and demonstrations, recognized their contributions to the family economy, and accepted their signatures. There were few female public speakers, but women organized Chartist schools, created important ancillary organizations to support the cause, and, with their husbands frequently under arrest, often faced managing their families on their own. Women's relative inclusion was a direct challenge to the norms of the Victorian middle classes and reflected the radical democratic outlook of the overall movement.

Chartism benefited from a wide array of local workers' organizations that rallied around the six points. These were linked together by an extensive press, the flagship of which was O'Connor's *Northern Star*. Working together, the press, traveling orators, and local organizations could mobilize mammoth demonstrations of hundreds of thousands of people, as they did in support of petitions presented to parliament in 1839 (1,280,000 signatures), 1842 (3,315,000 signatures), and 1848 (1,975,000 signatures). Parliament's summary dismissals of these petitions usually then precipitated intense infighting among Chartist leaders about how to respond. Tensions arose among factions led by such men as Lovett, a worker-intellectual interested mainly in organizing elite craftsmen and using an incremental, "moral force" approach to reform; O'Connor, a firebrand who spoke to the unskilled, opposed socialism, but also wielded the rhetoric of violent insurrection; and the journalist James Bronterre O'Brien, an Owenite socialist who, anticipating Marx, held that "the 'Working Classes' are the slave populations of the civilized countries." He feared that only a violent upheaval could bring their oppression to an end but hoped for peaceful change and was open to building alliances with middle-class supporters. O'Brien and O'Connor initially worked together but split over the latter issue and over a risky scheme of O'Connor's to resettle workers on the land.[5]

Such divisions weakened Chartism's ability to respond to the government's intransigent and often repressive policies. Following parliament's rejection of the petition in 1839, for example, a local uprising in Newport created a pretext for the police to arrest 450 Chartist leaders, including O'Connor and O'Brien. Decapitated, the movement went underground but revived in 1840 with the formation of the National Charter Association, which soon had 40,000 members. Following the failure of the petition of 1842, the Chartists were again paralyzed. When wage reductions precipitated massive strikes in Lancashire, Yorkshire, and the Midlands, they backed the strikers and paid a heavy price as the army occupied the region and arrested 1,500 people.

Support for Chartism ebbed but revived in the wake of the economic crisis of 1846–1847. O'Connor's election to parliament signaled the onset of renewed activity. A new petition campaign again included impressive mass demonstrations, and in the spring of 1848, as revolutions swept across Europe, Britain appeared headed for civil war. Amidst the talk of possible insurrection, however, the government remained unmoved. When the Chartists planned a giant demonstration to accompany the delivery of the new petition to parliament on 10 April, it mobilized such a show of armed force that the Chartist leaders, who were able to turn out only 30,000 followers at Kennington Common, backed down. Continued agitation over the summer resulted in widespread arrests. The movement then slipped into decline and disappeared by the mid-1850s.

Chartism arose primarily as a means for craft workers in tightly knit, smaller industrial communities to protect their institutions and way of life from the advance of laissez-faire capitalism. It also embodied workers' aspirations for greater political and social equality in a world increasingly dominated by the newly enfranchised bourgeoisie. The movement declined in part as a result of demoralization following repeated defeats, police repression, infighting among its leaders, and the national organization's bankruptcy in the wake of O'Connor's failed land resettlement scheme. But it also waned as its context changed. After 1850, Britain's industrial expansion created a more complex, less homogeneous urban world in which the traditional cultures of craft work gave way to newly emerging ones shaped by wage labor. At the same time, parliament's repeal of the Corn Laws (1845), which lowered the grain tariff and the cost of food, and the Ten Hours Bill (1847), which limited working hours in certain sectors, convinced many workers of the efficacy of gradual reform. Many came to see trade unions as a more viable alternative. Not forgotten, the aims of Chartism would be achieved within different community settings and via different institutional means.

THE REVOLUTION OF 1830 AND THE EMERGENCE OF FRENCH SOCIALISM

While Britain's constitutional monarchy proved flexible enough to avoid revolution in the early nineteenth century, the same cannot be said of its less democratic counterparts across the English Channel. Following the defeat of Napoleon in 1815, the victorious powers (Russia, Austria, Prussia, and Great Britain) reconstructed Europe's political order along conservative dynastic lines. In France, they restored the Bourbon dynasty to power, and the elevation of Louis XVIII also meant the revived influence of the church and the nobility. In Portugal, Spain, and central and southern Europe, the powers also restored monarchical governments, which did everything they could to exorcise the influence that French occupation had brought in the legal, administrative, and cultural spheres. The old elites everywhere reasserted their dominance by erecting political systems that excluded the mass of the people from participation. When dissent threatened, they could rely on domestic police and military forces. As a last resort, they could look to the armies of the Holy Alliance (Russia, Austria, and Prussia) to intervene on their behalf.

As John Merriman has observed, these efforts to restore the old order "resembled the Dutch boy gamely trying to dam the deluge by plugging up the holes in the dike with his fingers."[6] Immediately following the Vienna Congress in 1815, liberal and nationalist forces challenged its effort of restoration in a series of revolts in Portugal, Spain, and Italy. These rebellions failed and put other reactionary governments on the alert. In 1819, for example, alarmed Austrian and Prussian officials in the German Confederation responded to widespread student support for a united Germany by issuing the Karlsbad Decrees, which muzzled the press, banned fraternities, and blacklisted teachers. But it was beyond the powers of even the most ruthless states to completely snuff out liberal and nationalist ideas. The Greek revolt in 1821 against Turkish domination won support across Europe putting pressure on Britain, France, and Russia to back the rebels and thus contradict their own conservative principles. Meanwhile, in Russia, though Tsar Nicholas I (1796–1855) easily crushed a liberal revolt in December 1825, the "Decembrist" uprising showed that forces advocating change were active even in Europe's most reactionary state.

The French monarchy was one of the first to crumble in the face of pressure from below. The restoration in France was less thorough than Louis XVIII (1755–1824) had desired because to secure his throne, he had to recognize key achievements of the revolution. These included the centralized state bureaucracy, Napoleon's Civil Code, the sale of nationalized church and aristocratic lands, and the titles, decorations, and pensions dispensed under Napoleon. Catholicism again became France's official religion, but in accordance with Napoleon's Concordat with the Papacy, it was subject to state controls, and the Civil Code granted toleration to Protestants and Jews. Louis's personal power was extensive but limited by terms spelled out in the Charter that he promulgated after Napoleon's fall. It guaranteed legal equality and freedom of the press and established an Assembly consisting of a Chamber of Deputies elected from a very narrow, property-based franchise and a Chamber of Peers appointed by the king (peerage was lifelong and hereditary). The king chose the government's ministers, who were responsible to him, not the Assembly, but taxes required the latter's consent.

These arrangements made few people happy. Archconservatives thought the system too democratic and sought to strengthen the authority of the Crown and Catholic Church. At the same time, middle-class merchants and industrialists chafed at their exclusion from a parliament controlled by the landed elites. Tensions escalated after the reactionary Charles X assumed the throne in 1825. In the midst of an economic downturn, he not only rejected liberal demands to broaden the franchise but, in late July 1830, also abrogated the Charter and disenfranchised three-quarters of those already qualified to vote. The result was a popular uprising in Paris that forced Charles to abdicate on 2 August and brought his liberal cousin, Louis Philippe, to the throne. He promised to respect the Charter and extended the franchise to include the upper echelons of the bourgeoisie. This act doubled the electorate from about 100,000 to 200,000, or about 3 percent of the adult population.[7]

Louis Philippe's government denied the franchise to most middle-class people, but its pursuit of laissez-faire economic policies and its ethos, reflected in Prime Minster Guizot's admonition to the middle class to "enrich yourselves" and the king's habit of dressing like a bourgeois and surrounding himself with businessmen, made clear that it supported bourgeois interests. Indeed, under this "bourgeois monarch," France experienced substantial economic development, but many middle-class people remained alienated, and the workers, who had done most of the fighting in July, were particularly aggrieved. Following the "three glorious days," Parisian artisans had expected the government to ameliorate the impacts of the industrial depression and to recognize their right to control their trades. They called for higher wages, shorter working hours, public works to help the unemployed, and restrictions on mechanization. The government's response, however, disappointed them. It rejected their demands as attacks on "the liberty of industry" and forcibly suppressed demonstrations and strikes.[8]

Without access to the franchise and still subject to laws that punished union organizing and strikes with heavy fines and prison terms, French workers found themselves in a situation similar to that of their British counterparts following the passage of the Reform Bill. Over the course of the 1830s, however, many French artisans, who dominated productive industry, drew much more radical conclusions than the British. A substantial minority became convinced that neither the monarchy nor laissez-faire capitalism served their social or political interests and sought new means of organizing and asserting themselves in both economics and politics. Through their own experience and through their interaction with republican militants and newly emerging socialist thinkers, many artisans supported the idea of replacing destructive, competitive, private production with cooperative producers' associations in which workers collectively owned the means of production. In monarchical France, where private property was sacrosanct, radical workers' connections with republicanism and their idea of associative production put them on a collision course with the state and with the majority of property-owning Frenchmen.

French artisans did not have to start from scratch as they organized to promote their aims. As noted earlier, despite the 1791 ban on guilds, journeyman workers continued to operate traditional corporate institutions, such as the *compagnonages*, which were secret societies that provided shelter, placement, and training for men undertaking their Tour de France. Tolerated after the Restoration, their hierarchies, costumes, and rituals strongly shaped the identities of the tradesmen, and they also provided journeymen with an organizational basis to defend themselves, using partial or total work stoppages, when conflicts arose with the masters. In addition to the *compagnonages*, craftsmen established mutual aid or friendly societies that provided benefits in case of sickness, death, or disability. Contrary to law, these institutions also functioned as centers from which tradesmen could oversee wages and working conditions and take action when necessary. In Paris alone, there were hundreds of such societies during the 1830s.[9]

Workers' efforts to control their trades encountered not only the hostility of the state but also that of the masters, who resisted any interference with their use of private property. Initially, journeymen did not view their activities as means of supplanting the latter since the dream of every artisan was to have his own shop, but over time that began to change. As William H. Sewell has argued, the constant struggles between workers and capitalists over control of the production process, which actually led to major, ruthlessly suppressed uprisings in Lyon and Paris in 1831, 1832, and 1834, ultimately propelled a significant minority to conclude "that collective control over their trades was impossible without collective ownership of the means of production."[10]

The idea of moving toward an economy based on collective ownership was rooted in craftsmen's objection to the masters' appropriation of the products of their labor for their own profit. In the fall of 1830, Parisian printers began publishing *l'Artisan*, a journal expressing the conviction that, as the producers of all wealth, workers were the only productive class. Seeing mechanization under capitalism as a means for the masters to undercut their rivals by reducing labor costs, they proposed pooling resources and forming cooperative associations so that machinery could be used to ease their burdens and raise productivity from which all would benefit. This simple and straightforward analysis of the problem of exploitation and its solution formed the starting point for the trade socialism movement, which expanded rapidly over the next two decades.

Workers were not alone in exploring new means of addressing their problems. As we have seen, by the 1830s the ideas of Owen, Fourier, and Saint-Simon were widely circulated, but their analyses of exploitation and the means of ending it were rather different from those of the French workers. Many of their disciples, however, soon gravitated toward trade socialism. The physician Philippe Buchez (1796–1865), for example, was a former Saint-Simonian who had left the movement after its turn to religion. He agreed that, in industries in which skilled artisans (not factory hands, who needed outside control) predominated, workers did not require the aid of a capitalist master. To establish collectively owned shops, he suggested the creation of public credit banks that would provide start-up capital to new enterprises that would then be organized in cooperative trade associations.

This idea won the support of many Parisian workers, such as the tailors, box makers, chair makers, and glove makers, who in 1833 set up new associations or "national workshops" to employ striking workers and to put pressure on employers, and quickly spread among artisans in provincial cities such as Lyon, Marseilles, and Bordeaux. Although the government tried to suppress such efforts, they continued to spread. Republican groups, such as the Society of the Friends of the People and the Society of the Rights of Man, and the newspaper *La Tribune* (*The Tribune*) also began to advocate for cooperative production and public credit banks. Urging workers to join in the struggle against the monarchy, they asserted that "the essential duty of the republic will be to furnish proletarians with the means of forming . . . cooperative associations and exploiting industry themselves."[11]

Perhaps the figure that best embodied this emerging socialist republican outlook was the lawyer and journalist Louis Blanc (1811–1882), whose book *The Organization of Work* (1840) argued that state aid could establish a system of "national workshops," or ateliers, run by the workers themselves. Blanc believed that capitalism exploited workers and prevented full employment. Influenced by Saint-Simon, he thought that the state could provide the legal framework and the capital, via a publicly owned credit bank, to create a rationally organized and more productive economy. His reading of Fourier, however, also convinced him that the state should not run the system. Instead, he envisioned urban workers managing industrial enterprises on their own with their cooperative associations supervising the distribution of a wide range of welfare benefits. In the countryside, where most people lived, he foresaw a system of modern collective farms and industrial centers displacing isolated peasant producers. Unlike Saint-Simon, Blanc placed democracy, in the form of universal manhood suffrage, at the heart of this system, which would guarantee employment, facilitate the organization of work, and ensure adequate wages and good working conditions. Rejecting class conflict and violent revolution as a means of achieving socialism, he optimistically hoped for change through reasoned discourse and broad-based social consensus.

Other socialist republicans, such as Auguste Blanqui (1805–1881), saw matters rather differently. Blanqui was the prototype of the nineteenth-century professional revolutionary. As a sixteen-year-old Parisian student, he joined the Carbonari, a clandestine movement seeking constitutional or republican governments in Italy, France, Spain, and Portugal.

Wounded in the Revolution of 1830, the young journalist then took part in the failed republican rising of 1832. Tried for his writings, when asked his profession, he replied "proletarian," an answer pointing to the social aspect of his revolutionary perspective. The term "proletarian" was originally used in the ancient world to describe the very poorest layers of society. Babeuf had revived the term and used it in the classical sense. Blanqui used it, however, in reference to the newly emerging class of wage laborers and factory workers. He identified with this emerging group, but having read Buonarrati's popular history of Babeuf's conspiracy, published in 1828, Blanqui also sympathized with his forebear's egalitarian aims and conspiratorial methods. A participant or leader in the insurrections of 1830, 1839, 1848, and 1871, he spent his entire adult life, thirty-three years of it in prison, struggling to implement them.

Blanqui differed from Babeuf in that he put great store in progress and science, and his writings, while unsystematic, engaged the assumptions of contemporary political economy, but the conclusions he drew were similar. Private property was illegitimate because a few individuals had "seized upon the common earth by ruse or by violence . . . and established by laws that it is to be their property forever." They used control over property to force others into various states of dependence as slaves, serfs, or wage-earning factory workers. The latter had no freedom "but that of choosing their masters" and were more expendable than slaves, who represented a larger investment. Wage laborers faced "incessant toil, barely providing today's pennies, constant uncertainty about tomorrow, and famine, if a caprice of anger or of fear" should result in their unemployment. Meanwhile, the privileged owners enjoyed "absolute autocracy" and ultimately "the right of life or death" over their workers.[12]

The struggle between workers and "idlers" was at its root an irreconcilable "duel to the death between profit and wage." The only way out, Blanqui was convinced, was the establishment of a communist society, one that he did not describe in detail but that would be based on "principles of association" worked out in the future. In order to achieve this aim, he insisted that it was necessary to clandestinely organize a small group of trusted revolutionaries who would seize power and establish a republic headed by a dictatorial committee of public safety that would then undertake gradually to create the new world. Blanqui expected workers to rally to the new regime en masse and thus secure it from counterrevolution. As events showed, that was his great miscalculation.

Blanqui became the master of insurrectionary planning. In 1835, he organized an underground Society of Families, so named from its secret structure based on small groups. As it plotted to seize power and amassed arms, the police infiltrated its ranks and arrested Blanqui and other leaders. After a year in jail, they were amnestied and immediately set up a new conspiratorial group, the Society of Seasons, which used the seasonal calendar to organize its hierarchy. Consisting mostly of workers but also some students, it also hoped to win over soldiers to its cause. On 12 May 1839, Blanqui showed that his organization was well disciplined and capable of action. Taking the authorities by surprise, he and about 600 men seized Paris's City Hall and proclaimed a republic. To their chagrin, however, the workers did not rally to the cause. Within a short time, government forces regrouped and crushed the rebels. Tracked down a few months later, Blanqui received a death sentence that was commuted to life in prison. The conditions of his incarceration were so brutal, however, that his health collapsed, and, thought to be on the verge of death, he was released in 1847. He recovered just in time to participate in the Revolution of 1848.

Blanqui's actions inspired many other radicals yet showed them the foolhardiness of insurrectionary politics divorced from mass support. Many other socialist leaders, including Marx, Engels, and Lenin, sharply criticized his focus on the technique of seizing power without having built closer connections with the people.

The workers' muted response to Blanqui's insurrection did not mean that revolutionary sentiment was lacking; there was much ferment among artisanal trade socialists, republican activists, and socialist intellectuals following the July Revolution. Another sign of mass support for radical change was the popularity of the "communist" teachings of Etienne Cabet (1788–1856), a lawyer who, after participating in the July Revolution and serving as a government official and a member of the Chamber of Deputies, became a sharp critic of the lack of democracy. Exiled to England between 1834 and 1839, he was strongly influenced by Owenism, radical trade unionism, and his reading of Thomas Moore's *Utopia* (1516). After returning to France, he published a popular novel, *Voyage en Icarie* (1840), depicting a communist society of absolute equality in which a democratically controlled state managed the production and distribution of goods. Cabet's ideas were not original, and his attempts to found communist communities in France and, after 1848, in the United States failed like so many other, similar efforts. His importance, however, stemmed from his recruitment of thousands of followers among distressed craft workers in many regions, mainly through skillful use of newspapers such as *Le Populaire*, founded in 1841. Cabet's ability to speak to workers won him widespread respect even among critics. As Amédée Dunois put it, "The Cabet who counts for history is . . . the founder and leader of one of the first proletarian groupings, of a veritable workers' party."[13]

Many skilled workers turned to the ideas of men like Cabet because of perceived threats to their way of life. Like their twenty-first century counterparts, early nineteenth-century craftsmen viewed work as more than simply a way to earn money. They certainly sought employment to achieve economic security, but they also reveled in their autonomy as independent producers, in the creativity of the labor process, and in their ability to strive for mastery in turning out high-quality goods. It was the spread of large-scale manufactories in which wage-earning artisans carried out increasingly repetitive, simplified tasks in a more complex division of labor (later amplified through the introduction of machinery) that threatened their future and steered many into radical politics. As we have seen, some viewed collective property as a means of preserving their control over the trades. But others rejected this solution and sought, instead, alternatives that would preserve small property. Among the most important of their spokesmen was the autodidact and printer Pierre Proudhon (1809–1865).

Proudhon was at heart a social conservative with deeply held antifeminist, anti-Semitic, anticommunist, and antihomosexual views who wished to preserve the patriarchal social order of preindustrial France. His reputation as a "socialist," however, grew out of the analysis in his most important book, *What Is Property?*, published in 1840. His answer, "It is theft!," made him famous but was also less sweeping than it sounded. Proudhon did not mean all property, only that permitting someone to live without working. Opposed to the inequality that accompanied the rise of large-scale industry, he wished to abolish the established system of credit and exchange and create one that supported small communities of cooperative, family-run enterprises supporting one another through mutual aid (e.g., credit cooperatives and insurance societies). Proudhon regarded the state as an oppressive institution intricately bound up with the exploitive economic system. Rejecting violent revolution and, more inconsistently, participation in parliamentary politics, he argued for replacing the centralized state with a decentralized federal system. This opposition to the state made Proudhon one of the founders of what some call "libertarian socialism" or anarchism. Overlapping with and rivaling more state-centered socialist movements, it became a strong force in southern European politics until late in the century.

Thus, Paris in the 1840s was a center of social, political, and ideological ferment. Growing worker unrest, intensifying criticism of the monarchy, and wide-ranging debates about the society of the future made the city a magnet for intellectual dissidents from across the Continent. Among the most important of the foreigners to arrive in those years were Karl Marx (1818–1883) and Friedrich Engels (1820–1895), who, like many of their countrymen, were escaping the repressive absolutism of Prussia and its allies. Their impact on the development of socialism was of central importance, and it is to their story that we now turn.

MARX, ENGELS, AND THE COMMUNIST MANIFESTO

Few intellectual and political partnerships have been as powerful and long lasting as that of Marx and Engels; their ideas not only contributed to the emergence of socialism as a mass movement but also were essential to the founding of the modern social sciences. As theorists and activists, both men created a large body of work based on certain approaches to philosophy, history, economics, and politics, but they were also flexible thinkers capable of changing their views in light of new evidence. As a result, those influenced by their general outlook have frequently disagreed about how to interpret what they meant on many specific issues. As we shall see, such debate often led to the enrichment of intellectual discourse on a wide range of subjects (e.g., our understanding of economic and social development); at other times, however, especially in the realm of politics, such divisions had powerful and sometimes deleterious consequences.

Marx and Engels came from very different backgrounds. Marx grew up under comfortable circumstances in Trier, a beautiful old Roman city on the Moselle River near the French border. Stemming from a line of rabbis who long had led the small Jewish community in the largely Catholic town, his father, Hirschel, broke with tradition and became a lawyer. France's annexation of Trier in 1793 and the introduction of French law improved the status of the city's Jews, but after Prussia occupied the town, it reimposed discriminatory legislation against them. In order to practice law, Hirschel converted to Protestantism; the rest of the family soon followed.

Hirschel (now Heinrich) Marx was loyal to Prussia, but his enthusiasm for the ideas of the French Enlightenment permeated the household. Karl received a humanistic education focusing on the centrality of reason as a means of improving society. At the same time, however, he was strongly influenced by his father's liberal aristocratic friend, Baron Ludwig von Westphalen (1770–1842), who, aside from being the father of Marx's great love, Jenny, whom he married in 1843, also infused him with a deep attachment to romantic literature (e.g., Homer, Shakespeare, and Goethe). Marx's thinking, as David Priestland asserts, often reflected the tensions between the Enlightenment's rationalism and romanticism's passion for heroic struggle. Marx, the political economist, fully understood what it meant to undertake disciplined, evidence-based empirical study, but Marx, the philosophical and political revolutionary, hated routine and was ready to cast aside order and take risks.

After graduation from the local Gymnasium, Marx went to the University of Bonn to study law, but after a year of beer drinking, dueling, and other distractions, he transferred to the University of Berlin. He soon fell under the spell of G. W. F. Hegel (1770–1831), who, at the time of his death in 1831, had been Prussia's leading exponent of philosophical idealism. Living in a world deeply shaken by the French and industrial revolutions, Hegel sought to understand the meaning of these changes for individuals and society through an analysis of the role of reason, which he called the World Spirit, the Idea, or the Absolute, in history. The evolution of the World Spirit was expressed in the human search for truth and resulted in the progressive evolution of society in which ideas, social relations, and institutions moved toward an ever more harmonious condition. Historical changes were driven forward "dialectically" through the continual conflict of opposites in the ideological and social realms. From such conflicts emerged new syntheses or solutions that immediately encountered their opposite in a continuous process of transformation. Conveniently for Hegel's job security, he concluded that the Prussian state was the World Spirit's complete and final manifestation.

Hegel's ideas inspired much controversy among his intellectual heirs, and Marx quickly joined the fray. Unlike those who accepted the master's conservative conclusions, Marx was drawn to those "Young Hegelians" who saw the subversive potential in Hegel's system of change and the need to subject orthodox ideas and institutions to criticism. They began in the sphere of religion by suggesting that if Christianity arose in response to the needs of ancient society, it was no longer sufficient for meeting the needs of the modern world. David Friedrich Strauss's explosive *Life of Jesus* (1835) used historical analysis to challenge traditional Christian axioms rooted in faith. Six years later, Ludwig Feuerbach's *Essence of Christianity* argued that "the personality of God" is not a manifestation of the World Spirit; it is rather "nothing else than the projected personality of man."[14] Feuerbach (1804–1872), like Hegel, was concerned about man's alienation (estrangement) from his community and from himself. Unlike Hegel, however, he thought that religion, as a projection of humanity's own essence, deepened this alienation. For humans to achieve their creative potential and to be truly free, they had to return to themselves by dispensing with God and by recognizing their own godlike powers.

Marx found Feuerbach's materialist critique of religion compelling but, as we will see, soon concluded that one must also extend it into the contradictions of the real world. He reached this conclusion as a result of his own experiences and further study. Having finished his PhD in philosophy in early 1841, Marx initially hoped for an academic post, but the Prussian government, having soured on Hegel's progeny, made that impossible. Alternatively, he turned to journalism and in 1842 took a job as editor of the *Rheinische Zeitung* (*Rhenish Gazette*) a liberal newspaper published in Cologne. Reporting on the major political and social questions of the day forced Marx to grapple with a number of concrete issues that earlier he had only observed from afar. Marx succeeded in expanding the paper's circulation considerably, but his radical democratic politics, reflected in the paper's editorials criticizing censorship and new laws forbidding peasants from gathering wood for fuel from private lands, soon led to conflict with the authorities. In January 1843, they closed the paper.

Seeing no future in Germany, Marx and his new bride, Jenny von Westphalen (1814–1881), headed to Paris, where they settled in the large German exile community. Marx mingled with German and French artisans, met Proudhon and other leading socialists, befriended the radical German poet Heinrich Heine, and read widely in socialist literature. Aiming to carry out "the ruthless criticism of everything existing," he and the Young Hegelian Arnold Ruge (1802–1880) set out to publish a new radical periodical, the *Deutsch-Französisische Jahrbücher* (*German and French Annals*), in which Marx published two important essays.[15] In "On the Jewish Question," he criticized the views of his former friend Bruno Bauer (1809–1882), a Young Hegelian who had opposed the emancipation of the Jews because he believed that, unless the Christian state were fully secularized, discrimination against Jews would continue. Marx held that secularization did not go far enough. He asserted that the existence of religion as such is a defect whose source "can only be sought in the nature of the state itself" and that the latter had to be viewed in terms of its relationship to the question of human emancipation.[16] Human emancipation could not be achieved in the civil society created by the French Revolution, which consisted of atomized mutually hostile individuals based on private property. Rather, it could occur only when man recognized himself as a communal being, a "species being," and "when he has recognized and organized his own powers and social powers, so that he no longer separates this social power from himself as political power."[17]

Thus, Marx, like Feuerbach, was concerned with man's "return to himself" as the basis of full emancipation, but he soon moved beyond the critique of religion. In his second contribution, he asserted that the only way to overcome a world in which "man is an abased, enslaved, abandoned, and contemptible being" was through a total transformation carried out by a new social class that exists "in civil society but not of civil society, a class that is the dissolution of all classes, a sphere of society that has a universal character because its sufferings are universal . . . in short [it is] the total loss of humanity . . . which can only recover itself by a complete redemption of humanity. This dissolution of society, as a particular class, is the proletariat."[18] Marx drew on Hegelian dialectics, but here the historical actor in the process of transformation is not the World Spirit but rather the emerging proletariat. In his critique of politics and society, Marx was replacing Hegel's abstract, idealist point of departure with one rooted in the social reality of the material world.

The *German and French Annals* quickly died for lack of funds, and personal and political differences caused Marx to break with Ruge—a recurring pattern throughout Marx's life. Soon, however, he established his enduring friendship with Engels, who arrived in Paris in 1844 via a very different path. The son of a Wuppertal textile manufacturer, Engels grew up in a conservative, pietistic, and industrious family that steered him into the world of commerce. In 1837, at age seventeen, he began his apprenticeship with an export firm in Bremen; in 1841, he performed his military service in Berlin; and a year later, the family sent him to its Manchester affiliate to learn the business. During those years, the erstwhile businessman read voraciously, and his explorations in literature, politics, and philosophy soon led him away from his conservative roots. He became a radical democrat and, like Marx, discovered Hegel.

Most important was his encounter in 1842 with Moses Hess (1812–1875). A colleague of Marx at the *Rhenish Gazette* and an early communist thinker, Hess strongly influenced the intellectual development of both men. In the mid-1830s, he had propounded a type of communism similar to that of Babeuf, but he later linked this approach with the ideas of the Young Hegelians. Hess believed that the abolition of private property was the only way to overcome the alienation and egotism of capitalist society. Acutely aware of the human costs of industrialization, he was also among the first to link the resulting "social question" to the Young Hegelian critique of religion and politics. History, Hess argued, was moving toward a revolutionary social upheaval in which Germany would provide the philosophical basis of communism, France its revolutionary experience, and England the popular explosion wrought by capitalism's advance. This was heady stuff for the young Engels. After corresponding with Hess and visiting him on his way to Manchester, he became a communist.

Engels was fascinated and horrified by the world he discovered in Manchester. Working days for the family firm, he spent much of his remaining time, often accompanied by his lover, a working-class Irish woman named Mary Burns, amassing the documentation for *The Condition of the Working Class in England*, a major work straddling the fields of political economy, urban history, and social history. Engels's gripping prose illustrated how industrialization transformed the landscape and impacted workers' lives. Describing Manchester's Old Town, for example, he wrote, "At the bottom flows, or rather stagnates, the Irk, a narrow, coal-black, foul-smelling stream, full of debris and refuse, which it deposits on the lower right bank. In dry weather, a long string of the most disgusting blackish green slime pools are left standing on this bank, from the depths of which bubbles of miasmatic gas constantly arise and give forth a stench unendurable even on the bridge forty or fifty feet above the surface of the stream." People nearby were housed in hundreds of "cattle sheds for human beings" amidst unspeakable conditions in which privies stood open and so filthy that "the inhabitants can pass into and out of the court only by passing through foul pools of stagnant urine and excrement." With workers crowded together in small, decrepit hovels in which pigs shared sties with children in the shadow of the factories and railways and just a short distance from the opulent dwellings of the rich, Manchester, "the first manufacturing city of the world," represented the contradictions of emerging industrial capitalism.[19]

As Hess had suggested, such economic and social contradictions gave rise to political conflict, and Engels paid close attention to the activities of Britain's Owenite, Chartist, and trade union movements. The emergence of these groups, he believed, marked workers' growing recognition of the need to organize to abolish competition and thus end the rule of property. In an 1843 essay published in Marx's *Annals*, he observed how, like Christianity, "competitive capitalism, through its systems of property, money, and exchange, involved an equally disfiguring process of alienation from the authentic human essence. Under capitalism, man was divorced from himself and became the slave of things."[20] Engels's work deeply impressed Marx, whose outlook was clearly moving in a similar direction, but Marx had not yet seriously studied political economy and did not have Engels's inside knowledge. Yet, over the course of the following year he, too, came to the conclusion that the solution to the problem of alienation was communism, which he defined as "the positive transcendence of private property, or human self-estrangement, and therefore as the real appropriation of the human essence by and for man."[21] Marx arrived at this point after years of academic study and experience as a journalist, while Engels did so through his observations and through his experience as a capitalist entrepreneur at the center of the system.

Marx and Engels had met once in 1842; two years later, however, they had a meeting of the minds. As Engels later recounted, "When I visited Marx in Paris in the summer of 1844, our complete agreement in all theoretical fields became evident and our joint work dates from that time."[22] According to Tristram Hunt, "They displayed markedly different but mutually supportive characteristics." Engels had a cheerier, more harmonious disposition. He was empirically oriented and could distance himself from his subject. Punctual, dapper, and physically robust, he could also hold his liquor. Marx was more intellectually self-absorbed and grew more easily indignant at the human suffering inflicted by capitalism. Unlike Engels, he was incapable of managing money, and his weaker constitution often suffered as a result of financial stress, overwork, and bad habits. The key to the success of their relationship was Engels's recognition of the enormous power of Marx's intellect and his willingness to sacrifice his own time, money, and intellectual projects to facilitate Marx's work. Over the next forty years, Engels helped Marx work out his ideas, supported his family financially, edited and promoted his publications, and, as we will see, played a key role in the development of Marxism after his friend's death.

Marx and Engels's collaboration consisted of two core components: first, a theoretical one in which they developed a conception of history (historical materialism) that allowed them to analyze the development of society from its origins to the present, and, second, a practical one in which they supported the proletariat's overthrow of capitalism and its replacement with socialism. We will deal first with the former, which the two men hammered out in a series of works completed before the Revo-

Figure 3.1.   From left: standing, Engels and Marx; sitting, Marx's daughters, Eleanor, Laura, and Jenny, mid-1860s. Courtesy of the AsD, Bonn.

lutions of 1848. The theoretical conclusions they drew in this period represented the fundamental basis of what later came to be called Marxism.

Between 1844 and 1848, Marx and Engels engaged in a process of "self-clarification." In works such as *The Holy Family* (1845), *The German Ideology* (unpublished until 1932), *The Poverty of Philosophy* (1847), and *The Communist Manifesto* (1848), they separated themselves from the idealism of their former Young Hegelian friends, criticized most other socialists, and worked out their own ideas. Thoroughly familiar with the works of socialist and communist thinkers such as Saint-Simon, Fourier, Owen, and Cabet, both men admired their attacks on "every principle of existing society," but they described their views as "utopian" because they neglected the importance of historically changing objective conditions, such as the industrial revolution, in the process of social change and ignored class struggle and the proletariat's role in overthrowing capitalism. The utopians conjured up "fantastic pictures of future society" that could be realized only when everyone became convinced of the new system's superiority. Eschewing political and especially revolutionary action, they hoped that a few small—and necessarily doomed—experiments would pave the way to the new world. In contrast, Marx and Engels intended "to make a science of socialism" by showing how the latter was rooted in the historical emergence of the proletariat, the only social class capable of seizing political power and wielding it to abolish the class system.

For Marx and Engels, the basic starting point for understanding a society is the economic framework within which it develops. The economic system is a "mode of production" in which men and women produce what they need to maintain themselves and their progeny. Each mode of production entails corresponding "relations of production," that is, the ways in which people work together. These relations differ in societies based on slavery, serfdom, or wage labor, and in each also exists a ruling class whose power rests on its control over the economic surplus. On this economic base arises a "superstructure" of ideas, legal forms, political institutions, and cultural attributes functional to that particular society. It also follows that the social consciousness of people born into society generally corresponds to its norms and axioms. As Marx put it, "It is not the consciousness of men that determines their being, but, on the contrary, their social being that determines their consciousness."[23]

Marx and Engels did not assert that the economy "determined" on a daily basis everything that occurred in people's lives. They knew that ideas and institutions, such as the church, shaped people's behavior in ways that often had little direct relation to economic matters. But they also held that the characteristics of the economic base and those of the ideological, political, and cultural superstructure were closely intertwined and reciprocally influenced one another. People could act to effect change, but the social, economic, and cultural framework in which they lived conditioned their actions. They could, indeed, make revolution, but social realities would always constrain their efforts.

Social revolutions tended to occur, Marx and Engels believed, when the social relations of production hindered the further development of the material forces of production in society. For example, under feudalism, new technical innovations and improved communications promoted the growth of commercial capitalism, but feudal property relations hindered further expansion. As emerging capitalism came into conflict with the feudal economic structure, ideological and political conflicts arose between the rising bourgeoisie and the old feudal elites. Once the latter had been overthrown, the new rulers were in a position to transform social relations, political institutions, and the dominant ideology in ways that conformed to the needs of the new mode of production.

Marx believed that, when examining the struggles that emerge from economic and social development, one could track the material changes of the system "with the precision of natural science," but one could not determine exactly how people would react to such transformations in the ideological sphere "in which men become conscious of this conflict and fight it out." He was confident, however, that just as feudalism had prepared the ground for the emergence of capitalism, the latter's development paved the way for the establishment of a new socialist order that would bring "the prehistory of humanity to a close" by eliminating the conditions that caused social antagonisms and thereby abolishing the class system as such.[24]

None of this could occur without political action. To that end, Marx and Engels were also deeply engaged in working-class politics. Paris in 1843 was home to approximately 100,000 foreign-born, German-speaking artisans, and many of them were active in conspiratorial, "communist" political organizations, such as the League of the Just, which had been founded in 1834 and had participated in Blanqui's failed insurrection of 1839. After fleeing to London, several of its leaders established the German Educational Society as a front for the League. In 1845, Marx and Engels met in London and then in Brussels with members of the League in an effort to build the Communist Correspondence Committee to coordinate international socialist agitation. At the same time, they criticized the most influential thinkers in the League. Foremost among them was the tailor Wilhelm Weitling (1808-1871), who espoused a brand of Babouvist communism rooted in a chiliastic Christian vision of violent revolution that would create heaven on earth. Marx and Engels rejected such religion-based millenarian radicalism and succeeded in marginalizing Weitling. They were less successful, however, in undermining the popularity of Proudhon, who was not a member of the League but whose ideas for creating small cooperative communities of craftsmen contradicted their view of historical change, capitalist competition, and the proletariat's revolutionary role.

Nevertheless, by 1847, Marx and Engels had gained a substantial following within the League. In June, its London congress renamed the organization the Communist League and determined to adopt a more open political profile. That fall, a second congress requested that the two men draw up "a complete theoretical and practical program," which became *The Communist Manifesto*, published in January 1848. This pamphlet provided a brief, powerfully written synopsis of their basic views. It eventually became one of the world's most widely read works.

The *Manifesto* addresses five general themes for understanding the emergence of contemporary society: historical materialism, class struggle, the nature of capitalism, the inevitability of socialism, and the road to socialism. We have already discussed historical materialism in abstract form, but in the pamphlet they apply it specifically to the development of capitalism from its origins under feudalism until the middle of the nineteenth century. Opening the text with the famous assertion, "The history of all hitherto existing society is the history of class struggles," Marx and Engels stress that conflict between social classes has been a feature of all societies since the advent of civilization and that in each of them ruling classes have appropriated the surpluses produced by subordinate groups. These antagonistic classes, such as freeman and slave, patrician and plebeian, lord and serf, and guild master and journeyman, developed their own, often conflicting, interests, and it was their striving to realize their aims that drove history forward.[25]

The most recent historical period, Marx and Engels held, was dominated by the bourgeoisie and was distinctive because it had simplified class antagonisms into essentially two hostile camps: the bourgeoisie and the proletariat. The "epoch of the bourgeoisie" is the epoch of capitalism (a term the authors do not actually use), which is a market or commodity-producing system that leaves "no other nexus between man and man than naked self-interest, than callous cash payment." Under capitalism, workers are mere commodities; they live by selling their ability to work to capitalists. The latter exploit workers' labor to earn profits, which they use to expand their capital.

Competition drives the imperative to expand and makes capitalism unique in its power to transform the world. It "cannot exist without constantly revolutionizing the instruments of production, and thereby the relations of production, and with them the whole relations of society." The need for new markets drives the bourgeoisie to "nestle everywhere, settle everywhere, establish connections everywhere." Using cheap commodity prices as the "heavy artillery with which it batters down all Chinese walls," the bourgeoisie forces foreign nations to capitulate to its needs and creates a global economy after its own image. As a result, "during its rule of scarce one hundred years, [it] has created more massive and more colossal productive forces than have all preceding generations together."

But this achievement was also beset by contradictions. Unlike all previous societies dominated by scarcity, bourgeois society faced repeated crises of "overproduction" in which "there is too much means of subsistence, too much industry, too much commerce." Capitalism produced great quantities of wealth, but its impoverished workers could not consume it all. This caused goods to remain unsold, prices and profits to plummet, enterprises to close, and workers to lose their jobs. Thus, the forces of production had advanced to the point where they were no longer compatible with the conditions of bourgeois society and the latter acted as fetter on them. Such crises could be overcome only temporarily through the destruction of means of production, that is, the closing down of firms, the expansion of the market, or some combination of the two.

The way out of this impasse was socialism. Marx and Engels argued that industrialization annihilated the craftsmen and undercut the middle classes while it simultaneously created a growing class of wage laborers whose existence was both the essential condition for the power of the bourgeoisie and a harbinger of its demise. Competition among workers was fundamental to the wage system, but, as capital concentrated workers in towns and large enterprises, it created the circumstances for them to become conscious of their condition, to organize unions, to end their mutual competition, and to challenge the ruling class for power. "What the bourgeoisie therefore produces," they confidently asserted, "are its own grave diggers. Its fall and the victory of the proletariat are equally inevitable."

If long-term communist aims were the abolition of private property and the erection of a new order based on cooperation rather than competition, the immediate aim was democracy. The *Manifesto* makes explicit that "the proletarian movement is the self-conscious independent movement of the immense majority in the interest of the great majority." Marx and Engels expected that, as workers gained experience in collective struggle, they would organize themselves as a class and form themselves into a political party. Their most pressing goal was the conquest of political power, "to raise the proletariat to the position of the ruling class, to establish democracy."

Marx and Engels viewed the state as an instrument of class rule. It followed that the proletariat in power would use its position to transform society. This meant "to wrest by degrees, all capital from the bourgeoisie, to centralize all instruments of production in the hands of the state, i.e., the proletariat as the ruling class; and to increase the total productive powers as rapidly as possible."

Carrying out such changes would require "despotic inroads" against private property and the norms of bourgeois society, and the authors certainly considered force a legitimate means to quash any resistance. But they also observe that specific measures would differ from one nation to another, and violence does not stand at the center of their analysis. They foresaw the proletarian state implementing policies that would eliminate the basis of class society and, therefore, its own reason for existence as an instrument of class power. In its place, they envisioned "an association, in which the free development of each is the condition for the free development of all."

The *Manifesto* was a polemic written to fire the imagination of workers and inspire them to action; it lacks the analytical depth of the authors' lengthier, more academic works. It also contains some interesting contradictions. In its opening paragraphs, Marx and Engels assert that class struggle ends "either in a revolutionary reconstitution of society at large or in the common ruin of the contending classes." Yet they later assert that the proletariat's victory is "inevitable." Such statements raise many questions regarding the teleological character of their views, but, couched in Marx's fiery prose, the central thrust of the work, that history was on the side of the proletariat, proved convincing to many workers. The overall analysis of capitalism has also held up well over time; in many ways, the authors' description of the rise of global capitalism is more applicable today than it was in 1847, when most people were still working in agriculture and industrialization was only in its infancy.

Closing the *Manifesto* with the clarion call, "Working men of all countries, unite!" Marx and Engels addressed an international audience, but they did not think that a proletarian revolution would occur everywhere at once. They expected workers' struggles to be fought out on the terrain of the national state, and they believed that a workers' revolution was most imminent in countries like Great Britain, where industrial development was most advanced and the labor movement best organized. They also sensed a bourgeois revolution approaching in Germany and believed it would act as a prelude to an immediately following proletarian revolution. They were right that revolution was immanent, but it began in France.

THE REVOLUTION OF 1848

On 25 February 1848, after almost eighteen years in power, King Louis Philippe ignominiously abandoned the throne. Like his predecessor Charles X, he fled the country after "three glorious days" of revolution in which students, middle-class people, and workers took to the barricades demanding reforms. Frustration had been widespread during the "hungry-forties," as the government's laissez-faire policies did little to alleviate depressed conditions. Agricultural crisis, skyrocketing food and fuel costs, and urban unemployment had caused widespread and frequent violence. In the wake of Louis Philippe's flight, the crowd proclaimed France to be a republic, and the Chamber of Deputies appointed a provisional government pending the election of a Constituent Assembly to write a new constitution. Under popular pressure, the new government, dominated by the propertied elite, agreed to add Louis Blanc to its ranks. It also immediately introduced universal manhood suffrage, banned slavery in the colonies, limited the workday to ten hours, and lifted restrictions on unions, political clubs, and other forms of association.

Social tensions still loomed large. With a small ostentatious Parisian elite living in close proximity to a large and increasingly destitute working class, the government found itself confronted with workers' demands for a "social republic." Many members opposed state intervention in the economy but made concessions to calm the streets. When Blanc called for the implementation of his plan for national workshops for the unemployed and the creation of a labor ministry, the government halfheartedly acquiesced. It placed Blanc at the head of a toothless "Luxembourg Commission" to study labor conditions and created national workshops, but these had little in common with his ideas and amounted to a program of out-relief for the unemployed. When enrollment rocketed from 21,000 to 94,000 in April, new taxes to cover the costs angered middle-class people and the peasantry, which resented and feared workers' demands. The April elections to the Constituent Assembly reflected this fear. Only 100 radical republicans and socialists won seats in the 900-member body in which conservative forces, including many monarchists, dominated. Counterrevolution was on the march.

Meanwhile, news of the February events precipitated revolutions across much of Europe. Uprisings, usually initiated by the middle classes and then strongly backed by the workers, engulfed Vienna, Milan, Prague, Berlin, and the major cities of all the German states. To save themselves, monarchs granted liberal constitutions abolishing the remnants of feudalism and introducing limited suffrage, freedom of the press, and trial by jury. The creation of parliamentary institutions in Prussia, Austria, and many other states, as well as the election of the Frankfurt parliament to write a constitution for the whole of Germany, including Austria, reflected the high tide of democratic and nationalist sentiments. These gains largely satisfied middle-class and student elements among the revolutionaries, but they did not satisfy the artisans, who were the majority of those taking part in bloody fighting in cities such as Berlin and Vienna. As in Paris, the artisans sought economic reforms to improve their condition and protect them from nascent industrial competition. They established clubs and workers' associations to promote their interests, and one organization, the Brotherhood of Workers, established a presence throughout the German lands. Led by Stefan Born (1824–1898), it had 15,000 members who called for universal manhood suffrage, the right to unionize, the establishment of producer and consumer cooperatives, and the introduction of pensions and sickness insurance.

Such demands, when combined with peasant protests against enclosure and challenges to the authority of rural elites, petrified the propertied middle classes. In the course of 1848 and 1849, as monarchs everywhere began rolling back revolutionary reforms, they faced the choice of either allying themselves with radical democratic and socialist workers or accepting compromise arrangements with the old landowning and government elites. Most chose the latter.

The counterrevolution won its first great victory in France. On 21 June, the Assembly closed the national workshops and urged the Parisian unemployed to either move to the provinces or join the army. Workers—mostly artisans from the building, metalworking, clothing, and furniture trades but also some industrial employees—responded by throwing up barricades in the central and eastern districts, but over 100,000 army, National Guard, and largely middle-class Mobile Guard troops moved to crush them. During four days of bloody fighting, General Cavaignac's forces killed or executed over 1,500 insurgents and arrested 12,000. Over 4,000 were later deported to distant colonies.

It would be inaccurate to claim that this conflict was simply a struggle of the workers against the propertied elite. There were, for example, various types of workers among Cavaignac's troops, just as some middle-class people allied themselves with the workers. Nevertheless, the general configuration of opposing forces was clear and the political trend for workers ominous. The government limited freedom of the press and assembly and closed down political clubs. General Cavaignac (1802–1857) became head of state until the November presidential election, when Napoleon's nephew, Louis Napoleon Bonaparte (1808–1873), became the candidate of those longing for "order" and won a sweeping electoral victory. When parliamentary elections in 1850 revealed growing support for radical democratic and socialist candidates, the Assembly narrowed the franchise to exclude many workers. Frustrated by constitutional limitations to his authority, Louis Napoleon launched a coup in December 1851, seized full control, and ruthlessly crushed a republican insurrection. Stocks soared after more than 90 percent of the voters approved of the coup in a plebiscite. After promulgating a new constitution giving him sweeping powers, Louis Napoleon proclaimed himself Napoleon III, Emperor of the French, on 2 December 1852. The revolution in France had come full circle.

The June Days heartened reactionary forces, which soon reasserted themselves across Europe. By December 1848, for example, Prussian King Frederick William IV (1795–1861) had dismissed his liberal cabinet, restored military control over Berlin, dissolved the new Prussian parliament, and crushed rebellions in the Rhineland and Silesia. His forces also supported other German princes who suppressed radical-democratic and socialist clubs and publications and rounded up dissidents. In the spring of 1849, the Prussians defeated a number of risings in their western and southwestern provinces, and the king subsequently dismissed a desperate offer from the hapless Frankfurt parliament to make him emperor of a united Germany. In Austria and Italy, the story was similar. Austria's military defeated Piedmont and retook Milan, smashed opposition in Prague, reasserted control over Vienna, and, with the help of the Russian army, crushed nationalist forces in Hungary. The King of Naples reconquered Sicily in May, and in July, ironically, French forces dispatched by the National Assembly helped the pope destroy the newly proclaimed Roman Republic.

The victory of the reaction was a massive defeat for radical democratic and socialist forces everywhere. Independent workers' political organizations were suppressed; many activists grew disillusioned and turned away from politics, and others fell to fighting among themselves. At least a decade would pass before the labor movement began to recover. It should be noted, however, that the conservative triumph did not return Europe to the status quo ante. Nationalism in Italy, Hungary, and Germany soon reemerged as a powerful force. And, while monarchs and traditional elites had salvaged much of their power, feudalism had been abolished, and in most states constitutions now limited royal power to some extent and gave parliamentary representation to the liberal bourgeoisie.

The latter then promoted economic policies that cleared the way for the advance of capitalism.

Meanwhile, thousands of nationalist, democratic, and socialist revolutionaries sought asylum outside of their homelands. Many, such as Marx and Engels, landed in London. With the outbreak of revolution, they had returned to Germany, where, among other things, Marx had edited a radical newspaper in Cologne and Engels had distinguished himself as an officer in the rebel army in Baden. With the revolution's defeat, both men escaped to London, where they joined a large exile community. Expecting a new revolutionary outbreak any day, they believed that their stay would be brief. Neither imagined that they would remain there for the rest of their lives.

FROM REPRESSION TO RENEWAL: FOUNDING THE INTERNATIONAL WORKING MEN'S ASSOCIATION

Marx and Engels arrived in London at the very moment when the radical British labor movement, especially its Chartist current, was collapsing and the country was about to enter into a long period of economic prosperity. For the next quarter of a century, British capitalism boomed, employment and living standards rose, and most skilled workers saw their collective interests best served by entering moderate, craft-oriented trade unions willing to cooperate with capital. New legislation in the 1860s and 1880s also extended the franchise to most male workers, who tended to look for representation to the Liberal Party until late in the century. Socialism as a political movement remained on the margins.

On the Continent, too, the economy expanded. Between 1850 and 1873, France and Austria-Hungary registered substantial industrial growth, but Germany, now entering its industrial revolution, set the pace with 4.8 percent yearly. The use of steam engines rose by 1,800 percent, production of coal quadrupled, and raw iron and steel output rose fourteenfold and fifty-four-fold, respectively. Alfred Krupp, one of Germany's arms manufacturers, employed sixty workers in 1836 and 16,000 in 1873. Workers' organizations were largely suppressed, but in the 1860s the situation began to improve. Although factory labor still remained the exception rather than the rule, the expansion of large-scale mining, metal, and chemical industries and the onset of mass production in the consumer goods sector fueled changes in the structure of the working class. Over time, these changes would lead socialists to rethink their goals as government repression eased and the movement reemerged as a force in European politics.

With no revolution in the offing and the Communist League effectively suppressed, Marx and Engels settled into British exile. Marx's growing family was impoverished. He worked as a journalist but had to rely on

Engels, who had assumed a post in the office of his family's firm in Manchester, for support. Engels's subsidies allowed Marx to return to his studies of capitalism, which he continued to the end of his life. After many delays due largely to chronic illness, financial problems, political distractions, and the sheer scope of the project, the final result of this work was the publication of *Capital*, the first volume of which appeared in 1867, with volumes 2 and 3, edited by Engels, appearing posthumously in 1885 and 1894, respectively.

Capital is an imposing work rich in irony and insight. Marx's purpose was to study what he called the "natural laws of capitalist production," and his laboratory was Britain, where the system was most developed. By including an investigation of the system's origins, he aimed to "lay bare the economic law of motion of modern society" in order to understand capitalism's emergence elsewhere and possibly "shorten or lessen the birth pangs." At the heart of the analysis was Marx's assertion that the origin of capitalist profit is to be found not in the process of exchange, where people trade equivalents, but in production. In bare outline, he argued that the production of commodities requires constant and variable capital. Constant capital consists of the necessary raw materials, machinery, and infrastructure; its value during production does not change. Variable capital, however, consisted of workers' labor power, the value of which could change. Workers sell their labor power to capitalists who employ them for a given amount of time to produce commodities for sale on the market. At a minimum, the value of a worker's labor power should be equivalent to what he and his family need to subsist. If this was $100 per day, a worker might produce its equivalent in four hours on the job. If, however, the employee worked for another four hours, then he would produce an additional $100. Marx calls this excess, which accrues to the capitalist, surplus value. From it owners derive capital for new investment or pure profit for consumption. Capitalists try to increase the surplus by extending the workday or by intensifying output. Workers try to gain a greater share of the surplus via higher wages. The constant struggle over the share of the surplus was at the core of capitalism's tendency to slip into crises of overproduction or, seen from another vantage point, underconsumption.

Marx aimed to illustrate how the extraction of surplus value (i.e., the exploitation of the worker) made capital accumulation possible. It was not a question of an individual capitalist's morality. Without exploitation, the system could not function. Yet Marx's powerful prose reveals that, despite his pretentions of scientific detachment, he found the system morally appalling. The means it used for raising productivity "distort the worker into a fragment of a man, they degrade him to the level of an appendage to a machine, they destroy the actual content of his labor by turning it into a torment; they alienate from him the intellectual potentialities of the labor process in the same proportion as science is incorporated in it as an independent power . . . they transform his lifetime into working time, and drag his wife and child beneath the wheels of the juggernaut of capital." As he had argued in the *Manifesto*, Marx insisted that "the accumulation of wealth at one pole is, therefore, at the same time the accumulation of misery . . . at the opposite pole."[26]

Despite this grim picture, Marx and Engels remained optimistic. Back in the early 1840s, they had criticized philosophers content with merely understanding the world. "The point," Marx had written, "was to change it."[27] They never wavered from that conviction, and when, after a decade of reaction, new possibilities for working-class politics emerged, they were ready. During the early 1860s, more liberal government policies in France and Germany (see chapter 3) led to a revival of workers' political activity. In 1862, worker delegations from a number of countries visited the London International Exposition, where they exchanged ideas and established longer-lasting contacts. In April 1864, during a meeting called in solidarity with the Polish struggle for independence against tsarism, English and French workers decided to create the International Working Men's Association. When the founders convened in St. Martin's Hall in London that September, Marx sat in the audience. By the evening's end, he was an elected member of the Association's General Council and, charged with drafting its statutes, soon became one of its most important leaders.

With the exception of Marx, all thirty-four members of the General Council were manual laborers, but otherwise they were a heterogeneous lot. English trade unionists constituted the largest group and were concerned mainly with strengthening collective bargaining, not revolution. The rest included English Owenite and Chartist remnants, French Proudhonists and Blanquists, and a mix of republicans and supporters of Italian and Polish independence. Marx understood that keeping this group united would require a deft hand. In his "Inaugural Address" outlining the International's program, he first sketched a history of the labor movement between 1848 and 1864 in which, despite the "unrivalled" development of industry, "the misery of the working masses has not diminished."[28] Toning down the language of revolution pervading the *Manifesto*, he then lauded workers' efforts to found producers' and consumers' cooperatives and praised the passage of the Ten Hours Bill, but he also made sure to conclude that piecemeal reforms alone could "never arrest the growth in geometrical progression of monopoly, to free the masses, nor even to perceptively lighten the burden of their miseries."

Instead, Marx asserted, cooperative labor "developed to national dimensions" and "fostered [by] national means" was required. Such a goal made the conquest of political power "the great duty of the working classes." Solidarity, the "bond of brotherhood" among them, was essential for success, and on that note Marx closed with the call, "Proletarians of all countries, Unite!"[29]

Over the course of the next eight years, the International's efforts to organize workers across Europe met with modest results. Dozens of unions and labor organizations in many countries, some with thousands of members, "affiliated," but the number of dues-paying individuals was probably not more than a few hundred. The Association made strenuous efforts to support striking workers, such as the London tailors in 1866 and the Parisian bronze workers the following year, by raising funds and campaigning against strikebreakers. These activities did not bring much real power but did enhance the organization's image as a defender of workers' interests and, of course, earned it the ire of the propertied classes. As we will see in the next chapter, factional infighting, in which Marx was often at the center, also weakened the organization. By 1872, just one year after being blamed, inaccurately, for the outbreak of revolution in Paris, the Association effectively dissolved.

Marx was a tough political infighter, but, as the "Inaugural Address" makes clear, he understood the need for tactical flexibility to weld together a diverse constituency. Although he looked ahead to a time when "the revival of the movement allows the old boldness of language," the address marked a shift in his thinking away from the conspiratorial approach of the Communist League and toward the idea of building a large, more open mass movement that could vie for political power on a parliamentary stage.[30] Such parties were just taking form as many European states, such as France and soon-to-be-united Germany and Italy, moved toward electoral systems allowing broader participation in politics. Marx and Engels understood the advantages and limitations of such systems from experience in Britain, and they supported making use of them as they emerged on the Continent. In the late 1860s, many workers still saw fighting on the barricades as an effective means of achieving revolution. That would change within a few decades.

DOCUMENT 3.1. LETTER FROM KARL MARX TO ARNOLD RUGE

This letter, sent by Marx to his coeditor at the Deutche-Französische Jahrbücher *in September 1843, reveals much about the young radical's evolving
ideas. Note especially the later author of the* Communist Manifesto's *remarks
on the limitations of communism in the resolution of human problems.*

Kreuznach, September 1843

I am glad that you have made up your mind and, ceasing to look back at
the past, are turning your thoughts ahead to a new enterprise. And so—
to Paris, to the old university of philosophy—*absit omen!* [May it not be an
ill omen] —and the new capital of the new world! What is necessary
comes to pass. I have no doubt, therefore, that it will be possible to
overcome all obstacles, the gravity of which I do not fail to recognise.

But whether the enterprise comes into being or not, in any case I shall
be in Paris by the end of this month, since the atmosphere here makes one
a serf, and in Germany I see no scope at all for free activity.

In Germany, everything is forcibly suppressed; a real anarchy of the
mind, the reign of stupidity itself, prevails there, and Zurich obeys orders
from Berlin. It therefore becomes increasingly obvious that a new rallying
point must be sought for truly thinking and independent minds. I am
convinced that our plan would answer a real need, and after all it must be
possible for real needs to be fulfilled in reality. Hence I have no doubt
about the enterprise, if it is undertaken seriously.

The internal difficulties seem to be almost greater than the external
obstacles. For although no doubt exists on the question of "Whence," all
the greater confusion prevails on the question of "Whither." Not only has
a state of general anarchy set in among the reformers, but everyone *will*
have to admit to himself that he has no exact idea what the future ought
to be. On the other hand, it is precisely the advantage of the new trend
that we do not dogmatically anticipate the world, but only want to find
the new world through criticism of the old one. Hitherto philosophers
have had the solution of all riddles lying in their writing-desks, and the
stupid, exoteric world had only to open its mouth for the roast pigeons of
absolute knowledge to fly into it. Now philosophy has become mundane,
and the most striking proof of this is that philosophical consciousness
itself has been drawn into the torment of the struggle, not only externally
but also internally. But, if constructing the future and settling everything
for all times are not our affair, it is all the more clear what we have to
accomplish at present: I am referring to *ruthless criticism* of all that exists,
ruthless both in the sense of not being afraid of the results it arrives at
and in the sense of being just as little afraid of conflict with the powers
that be.

Therefore I am not in favour of raising any dogmatic banner. On the
contrary, we must try to help the dogmatists to clarify their propositions
for themselves. Thus, communism, in particular, is a dogmatic abstrac-

tion; in which connection, however, I am not thinking of some imaginary and possible communism, but actually existing communism as taught by Cabet, Dézamy, Weitling, etc. This communism is itself only a special expression of the humanistic principle, an expression which is still infected by its antithesis—the private system. Hence the abolition of private property and communism are by no means identical, and it is not accidental but inevitable that communism has seen other socialist doctrines—such as those of Fourier, Proudhon, etc.—arising to confront it because it is itself only a special, one-sided realisation of the socialist principle.

And the whole socialist principle in its turn is only one aspect that concerns the reality of the true human being. But we have to pay just as much attention to the other aspect, to the theoretical existence of man, and therefore to make religion, science, etc., the object of our criticism. In addition, we want to influence our contemporaries, particularly our German contemporaries. The question arises: how are we to set about it? There are two kinds of facts, which are undeniable. In the first place religion, and next to it, politics, are the subjects which form the main interest of Germany today. We must take these, in whatever form they exist, as our point of departure, and not confront them with some ready-made system such as, for example, the *Voyage en Icarie*. [Etienne Cabet, *Voyage en Icarie. Roman philosophique et social.*]

Reason has always existed, but not always in a reasonable form. The critic can therefore start out from any form of theoretical and practical consciousness and from the forms peculiar to existing reality develop the true reality as its obligation and its final goal. As far as real life is concerned, it is precisely the political state—in all its *modern forms*—which, even where it is not yet consciously imbued with socialist demands, contains the demands of reason. And the political state does not stop there. Everywhere it assumes that reason has been realised. But precisely because of that it everywhere becomes involved in the contradiction between its ideal function and its real prerequisites.

From this conflict of the political state with itself, therefore, it is possible everywhere to develop the social truth. Just as *religion* is a register of the theoretical struggles of mankind, so the *political state* is a register of the practical struggles of mankind. Thus, the political state expresses, within the limits of its form *sub specie rei publicae*, [as a particular kind of state] all social struggles, needs and truths. Therefore, to take as the object of criticism a most specialised political question—such as the difference between a system based on social estate and one based on representation—is in no way below the *hauteur des principes*. [Level of principles] For this question only expresses in a *political* way the difference between rule by man and rule by private property. Therefore the critic not only can, but must deal with these political questions (which according to the extreme Socialists are altogether unworthy of attention). In analysing the superiority of the representative system over the social-estate system, the critic *in a practical way wins the interest* of a large party. By raising the representative system from its political form to the universal form and by bringing out the true significance underlying this system, the critic at the same time compels this party to go beyond its own confines, for its victory is at the same time its defeat.

Hence, nothing prevents us from making criticism of politics, participation in politics, and therefore *real* struggles, the starting point of our criticism, and from identifying our criticism with them. In that case we do not confront the world in a doctrinaire way with a new principle: Here is the truth, kneel down before it! We develop new principles for the world out of the world's own principles. We do not say to the world: Cease your struggles, they are foolish; we will give you the true slogan of struggle. We merely show the world what it is really fighting for, and consciousness is something that it *has to* acquire, even if it does not want to.

The reform of consciousness consists *only* in making the world aware of its own consciousness, in awakening it out of its dream about itself, in *explaining* to it the meaning of its own actions. Our whole object can only be—as is also the case in Feuerbach's criticism of religion—to give religious and philosophical questions the form corresponding to man who has become conscious of himself.

Hence, our motto must be: reform of consciousness not through dogmas, but by analysing the mystical consciousness that is unintelligible to itself, whether it manifests itself in a religious or a political form. It will then become evident that the world has long dreamed of possessing something of which it has only to be conscious in order to possess it in reality. It will become evident that it is not a question of drawing a great mental dividing line between past and future, but of *realising* the thoughts of the past. Lastly, it will become evident that mankind is not beginning a *new* work, but is consciously carrying into effect its old work.

In short, therefore, we can formulate the trend of our journal as being: self-clarification (critical philosophy) to be gained by the present time of its struggles and desires. This is a work for the world and for us. It can be only the work of united forces. It is a matter of a *confession*, and nothing more. In order to secure remission of its sins, mankind has only to declare them for what they actually are.

Source: *Marx Engels Collected Works, Vol. 3,* republished at http://www.marxists.org/archive/ marx/works/1843/letters/deutsch-fransosische-letters.htm. First published in *Deutsch-Französische Jahrbücher,* 1844.

DOCUMENT 3.2. KARL MARX TO PIERRE JOSEPH PROUDHON

In 1846 Marx, Engels, and others developed a network of like-minded political contacts in Britain, France, Belgium, and Germany. Among those they attempted to recruit to this Communist Correspondence Committee was Proudhon. Marx's letter and Proudhon's reply provide a clear sense of the two men's differing goals and temperaments. Within a short time, their differences would lead them into open conflict.

Brussels, 5 May 1846
My dear Proudhon,
I have frequently had it in mind to write to you since my departure from Paris, but circumstances beyond my control have hitherto prevented me from doing so. Please believe me when I say that my silence was attributable solely to a great deal of work, the troubles attendant upon a change of domicile, etc.

And now let us proceed in *medias res* [to the matter in hand]—jointly with two friends of mine, Frederick Engels and Philippe Gigot (both of whom are in Brussels), I have made arrangements with the German communists and socialists for a constant interchange of letters which will be devoted to discussing scientific questions, and to keeping an eye on popular writings, and the socialist propaganda that can be carried on in Germany by this means. The chief aim of our correspondence, however, will be to put the German socialists in touch with the French and English socialists; to keep foreigners constantly informed of the socialist movements that occur in Germany and to inform the Germans in Germany of the progress of socialism in France and England. In this way differences of opinion can be brought to light and an exchange of ideas and impartial criticism can take place. It will be a step made by the social movement in its *literary* manifestation to rid itself of the barriers of *nationality*. And when the moment for action comes, it will clearly be much to everyone's advantage to be acquainted with the state of affairs abroad as well as at home.

Our correspondence will embrace not only the communists in Germany, but also the German socialists in Paris and London. Our relations with England have already been established. So far as France is concerned, we all of us believe that we could find no better correspondent than yourself. As you know, the English and Germans have hitherto estimated you more highly than have your own compatriots.

So it is, you see, simply a question of establishing a regular correspondence and ensuring that it has the means to keep abreast of the social movement in the different countries, and to acquire a rich and varied interest, such as could never be achieved by the work of one single person. . . .

. . . I need hardly add that the correspondence as a whole will call for the utmost secrecy on your part; our friends in Germany must act with the greatest circumspection if they are not to compromise themselves.

Let us have an early reply and rest assured of the sincere friendship of Yours most sincerely,
Karl Marx

P.S. I must now denounce to you Mr. Grün of Paris. The man is nothing more than a literary swindler, a species of charlatan, who seeks to traffic in modern ideas. He tries to conceal his ignorance with pompous and arrogant phrases but all he does is make himself ridiculous with his *gibberish*. Moreover this man is *dangerous*. He *abuses* the connection he has built up, thanks to his impertinence, with authors of renown in order to create a pedestal for himself and compromise them in the eyes of the German public. In his book on French socialists [Grün, *Die soziale Beweg-ung in Frankreich und Belgien*], has the audacity to describe himself as tutor (*Privatdozent*, a German academic title) to Proudhon, claims to have revealed to him the important axioms of German science and *makes fun* of his writings. Beware of this parasite. Later on I may perhaps have something more to say about this individual.

Source: MECW Volume 38 p. 38; http://www.marxists.org/archive/marx/works/1846/letters/ 46_05_05.htm. Written: 5 May 1846. First published in *Die Gesellschaft*, Jg. IV, H. 9, Berlin, 1927.

DOCUMENT 3.3. PROUDHON'S REPLY TO MARX

Lyon, 17 May 1846
My dear Monsieur Marx,
I gladly agree to become one of the recipients of your correspondence, whose aims and organization seem to me most useful. Yet I cannot promise to write often or at great length: my varied occupations, combined with a natural idleness, do not favour such epistolary efforts. I must also take the liberty of making certain qualifications which are suggested by various passages of your letter.

First, although my ideas in the matter of organization and realization are at this moment more or less settled, at least as regards principles, I believe it is my duty, as it is the duty of all socialists, to maintain for some time yet the critical or dubitive form; in short, I make profession in public of an almost absolute economic anti-dogmatism.

Let us seek together, if you wish, the laws of society, the manner in which these laws are realized, the process by which we shall succeed in discovering them; but, for God's sake, after having demolished all the *a priori* dogmatisms, do not let us in our turn dream of indoctrinating the people; do not let us fall into the contradiction of your compatriot Martin Luther, who, having overthrown Catholic theology, at once set about, with excommunication and anathema, the foundation of a Protestant theology. For the last three centuries Germany has been mainly occupied in undoing Luther's shoddy work; do not let us leave humanity with a similar mess to clear up as a result of our efforts. I applaud with all my heart your thought of bringing all opinions to light; let us carry on a good and loyal polemic; let us give the world an example of learned and far-sighted tolerance, but let us not, merely because we are at the head of a movement, make ourselves the leaders of a new intolerance, let us not pose as the apostles of a new religion, even if it be the religion of logic, the religion of reason. Let us gather together and encourage all protests, let us brand all exclusiveness, all mysticism; let us never regard a question as exhausted, and when we have used our last argument, let us begin again, if need be, with eloquence and irony. On that condition, I will gladly enter your association. Otherwise—no!

I have also some observations to make on this phrase of your letter: *at the moment of action.* Perhaps you still retain the opinion that no reform is at present possible without a *coup de main*, without what was formerly called a revolution and is really nothing but a shock. That opinion, which I understand, which I excuse, and would willingly discuss, having myself shared it for a long time, my most recent studies have made me abandon completely. I believe we have no need of it in order to succeed; and that consequently we should not put forward *revolutionary action* as a means of social reform, because that pretended means would simply be an appeal to force, to arbitrariness, in brief, a contradiction. I myself put the problem in this way: *to bring about the return to society, by an economic combination, of the wealth which was withdrawn from society by another economic combination.* In other words, through Political Economy to turn the theory of Property against Property in such a way as to engender what you German socialists call *community* and what I will limit myself for the moment to calling *liberty* or *equality*. But I believe that I know the means of solving this problem with only a short delay; I would therefore prefer to burn Property by a slow fire, rather than give it new strength by making a St Bartholomew's night of the proprietors.
Your very devoted,
Pierre-Joseph Proudhon

Source: MECW Volume 38 p. 38; http://www.marxists.org/archive/marx/works/1846/letters/ 46_05_05.htm. Written: 5 May 1846. First published in *Die Gesellschaft*, Jg. IV, H. 9, Berlin, 1927.

DOCUMENT 3.4. THE ORGANIZATION OF LABOR (1840)

Louis Blanc

Appalled at the impact of industrialization and laissez-faire policies on workers and influenced by Saint-Simonian ideas for economic planning, Louis Blanc argued that the democratic state should take a hand in reorganizing the economy for workers' benefit. Although appointed the director of a government labor commission following the Revolution of 1848, conservative resistance undermined his plans.

The question should be put thus: Is competition a means of ASSURING work to the poor? To put a question of this kind means to solve it. What does competition mean to workingmen? It is the distribution of work to the highest bidder. A contractor needs a laborer: three apply. "How much do you ask for your work?" "Three francs, I have a wife and children." "Good, and you?" "Two and a half francs, I have no children, but a wife." "So much the better, and you?" "Two francs will do for me; I am single." "You shall have the work." With this the affair is settled, the bargain is closed. What will become now of the other two proletarians? They will starve, it is to be hoped. But what if they become thieves? Never mind, why have we our police? Or murderers? Well, for them we have the gallows. And the fortunate one of the three; even his victory is only temporary. Let a fourth laborer appear, strong enough to fast one out of every two days; the desire to cut down the wages will be exerted to its fullest extent. A new pariah, perhaps a new recruit for the galleys. . . .

Who would be blind enough not to see that under the reign of free competition the continuous decline of wages necessarily becomes a general law with no exception whatsoever? Has population limits which it may never overstep? Are we allowed to say to industry, which is subjected to the daily whims of individual egotism, to industry, which is an ocean full of wreckage: "Thus far shalt thou go and no farther." The population increases steadily; command the mothers of the poor to be sterile and blaspheme God who made them fruitful; for if you do not command it, the space will be too small for all strugglers. A machine is invented; demand it to be broken and fling an anathema against science! Because if you do not do it, one thousand workmen, whom the new machine displaces in the workshops, will knock at the door of the next one and will force down the wages of their fellow workers. A systematic lowering of wages resulting in the elimination of a certain number of laborers is the inevitable effect of free competition. . . .

The government ought to be considered as the supreme regulator of production and endowed for this duty with great power.

This task would consist of fighting competition and of finally overcoming it.

The government ought to float a loan with the proceeds of which it should erect *social workshops* in the most important branches of national industry.

As these establishments would demand considerable investments, the number of these workshops at the start ought to be carefully limited, still they would possess, by virtue of their organization—as we shall see later—an unlimited expansion.

The government, considered as the only founder of the workshops, must determine the statutes regulating them. This code, deliberated and voted for by the representatives of the people ought to have the power and force of a law.

All workmen who can give guarantee of morality shall be called to work in these social workshops up to the limit of the original capital gathered together for the purchase of tools. . . .

For the first years after the workshops are established, the government ought to regulate the scale of employment. After the first year it is no longer necessary, the laborers would then have time enough to truly estimate their respective work, and, all being equally interested as we will soon see, the success of the association would eventually depend on the elective principle. . . .

Every member of the social workshops would have the right to use, according to his discretion, the profits of his labor; but it would not be long before the evident economy and the incontestable excellence of this communal life would call forth other voluntary associations among the workmen according to their needs and pleasure.

Capitalists can also be taken into the association and would draw interest on their invested money, which would be guaranteed by the budget; but in the profits they would participate only if they were laborers at the same time.

If the social workshops were once established according to these principles, you could easily understand what the results would be. In every great industry, in machinery, for example, or the silk or cotton industry, or in printing establishments, the social workshops would be in competition with private industries. Would the fight be a long one? No, for the social workshops would have advantages over the others, the results of the cheaper communal life and through the organization by which all laborers, without exception, are interested in producing good and quick work. Would the fight be subversive? No, for the government would always endeavor to prevent the prices of the products of the social workshops from dropping to too low a level. If today an extremely rich man were to enter into a contest with another less wealthy, this unequal fight would be only disastrous, for the private man looks only to his personal interest, if he can sell twice as cheap as his competitors, he will do so, in order to ruin them and be master of the situation. But when the power itself steps into the place of a private individual, the question develops a different phase. . . .

From the common interest of all the laborers in the same workshop we infer the common interest of all workshops in the same industry. In order to complete the system, we must establish the solidarity of the various industries. Therefore, from the profit yielded by each industry, we must set aside a sum by means of which the State could give aid to every industry, which has suffered through extraordinary and unforeseen circumstances. Besides, in the system which we propose, crises would become rare. What causes them most frequently today? The veritable murderous contest between the interests, a contest from which no victor can come forth without leaving conquered ones on the field of battle; a combat, that like all wars, chains slaves to the chariot of the victor. In destroying competition we strangle at the same time the evils which it brings forth. No more victories and no more defeats! . . .

Is it necessary that I should continue to enumerate the advantages which the new system brings about? In the industrial world in which we live, all the discoveries of science are a calamity, first because the machines supplant the laborers who need work to live, and then, because they are also murderous weapons, furnished to industry which has the right and faculty to use them against all those who have not this right and power. What does *"new machines"* mean in the system of competition? It means monopoly; we have proven it. However, in the new system of association and solidarity there are no patents for inventors, no individual exploitation. The inventor will be recompensed by the State and his discovery is then placed at the service of all. What is today a means of extermination, becomes an instrument of universal progress; what today reduces the laborer to hunger, to despair and drives him to revolt, will serve only to render his task lighter and to produce a sufficient leisure to live a life of intelligence and happiness, in one word, that which has tolerated tyranny will aid in the triumph of fraternity.

Source: Louis T. Moore, J. M. Burnam, and H. G. Hartmann, eds., *University of Cincinnati Studies* (Cincinnati, 1911), Series II, Vol. 7, pp. 15–16, 51–56; republished at Internet History. *Sourcebook:* http://www.fordham.edu/halsall/mod/1840blanc.asp.

DOCUMENT 3.5. A PROGRAM FOR REVOLUTION: *THE COMMUNIST MANIFESTO* (1848)

Karl Marx and Friedrich Engels

Charged with writing a statement of principles for the newly founded Communist League, Marx and Engels used the opportunity to sum up the radical histor-

ical and political viewpoint that they had developed in the mid-1840s. Convinced that the "specter" of communist revolution was "haunting" Europe, they also equipped the work with the following brief synopsis of what steps a revolutionary movement should take to secure its power and transform society.

We have seen above, that the first step in the revolution by the working class is to raise the proletariat to the position of ruling class to win the battle of democracy.

The proletariat will use its political supremacy to wrest, by degree, all capital from the bourgeoisie, to centralise all instruments of production in the hands of the State, *i.e.*, of the proletariat organised as the ruling class; and to increase the total productive forces as rapidly as possible.

Of course, in the beginning, this cannot be effected except by means of despotic inroads on the rights of property, and on the conditions of bourgeois production; by means of measures, therefore, which appear economically insufficient and untenable, but which, in the course of the movement, outstrip themselves, necessitate further inroads upon the old social order, and are unavoidable as a means of entirely revolutionising the mode of production.

These measures will, of course, be different in different countries.

Nevertheless, in most advanced countries, the following will be pretty generally applicable.

1. Abolition of property in land and application of all rents of land to public purposes.
2. A heavy progressive or graduated income tax.
3. Abolition of all rights of inheritance.
4. Confiscation of the property of all emigrants and rebels.
5. Centralisation of credit in the hands of the state, by means of a national bank with State capital and an exclusive monopoly.
6. Centralisation of the means of communication and transport in the hands of the State.
7. Extension of factories and instruments of production owned by the State; the bringing into cultivation of waste-lands, and the improvement of the soil generally in accordance with a common plan.
8. Equal liability of all to work. Establishment of industrial armies, especially for agriculture.
9. Combination of agriculture with manufacturing industries; gradual abolition of all the distinction between town and country by a more equable distribution of the populace over the country.
10. Free education for all children in public schools. Abolition of children's factory labour in its present form. Combination of education with industrial production, &c, &c.

When, in the course of development, class distinctions have disappeared, and all production has been concentrated in the hands of a vast association of the whole nation, the public power will lose its political character. Political power, properly so called, is merely the organised power of one class for oppressing another. If the proletariat during its contest with the bourgeoisie is compelled, by the force of circumstances, to organise itself as a class, if, by means of a revolution, it makes itself the ruling class, and, as such, sweeps away by force the old conditions of production, then it will, along with these conditions, have swept away the conditions for the existence of class antagonisms and of classes generally, and will thereby have abolished its own supremacy as a class.

In place of the old bourgeois society, with its classes and class antagonisms, we shall have an association, in which the free development of each is the condition for the free development of all.

Source: Marx/Engels Selected Works, Vol. One, Progress Publishers, Moscow, 1969, pp. 98–137; http://www.marxists.org/archive/marx/works/1848/communist-manifesto/index.htm. Written in late 1847. First published in February 1848. Translated by Samuel Moore in cooperation with Frederick Engels, 1888. Transcription/Markup: Zodiac and Brian Baggins. Proofed and corrected against 1888 English Edition by Andy Blunden 2004.

———≈≈≈———

DOCUMENT 3.6. GENERAL RULES OF THE INTERNATIONAL WORKING MEN'S ASSOCIATION (1864)

Karl Marx

———≈≈≈———

Despite being hard at work on the completion of the first volume of Capital, *the revival of the Western European labor movement drew Marx back into political activity in the mid-1860s. Among the founders of the new International Working Men's Association, he was charged with formulating its rules, the preamble of which is provided below. Note its restrained language when compared with that of* The Communist Manifesto.

October 1864

Considering, that the emancipation of the working classes must be conquered by the working classes themselves, that the struggle for the emancipation of the working classes means not a struggle for class privileges and monopolies, but for equal rights and duties, and the abolition of all class rule;

That the economical subjection of the man of labor to the monopolizer of the means of labor—that is, the source of life—lies at the bottom of servitude in all its forms, of all social misery, mental degradation, and political dependence;

That the economical emancipation of the working classes is therefore the great end to which every political movement ought to be subordinate as a means;

That all efforts aiming at the great end hitherto failed from the want of solidarity between the manifold divisions of labor in each country, and from the absence of a fraternal bond of union between the working classes of different countries;

That the emancipation of labor is neither a local nor a national, but a social problem, embracing all countries in which modern society exists, and depending for its solution on the concurrence, practical and theoretical, of the most advanced countries;

That the present revival of the working classes in the most industrious countries of Europe, while it raises a new hope, gives solemn warning against a relapse into the old errors, and calls for the immediate combination of the still disconnected movements;

For these reasons—

The International Working Men's Association has been founded.

It declares:

That all societies and individuals adhering to it will acknowledge truth, justice, and morality as the basis of their conduct toward each other and toward all men, without regard to color, creed, or nationality;

That it acknowledges no rights without duties, no duties without rights;

And, in this spirit, the following Rules have been drawn up . . .

Source: MECW , vol. 20, September 1864–July 1868; http://www.marxists. org/history/international/iwma/documents/1864/rules.htm. Written between October 21 and 27, 1864. First published in *The Bee-Hive Newspaper*, November 12, 1864, and in the pamphlet Address and Provisional Rules of the Working Men's International Association . . . , London, November 1864.

—*စစစ*—

NOTES

1. Quoted in Dorothy Thompson, *The Chartists: Popular Politics in the Industrial Revolution* (New York: Pantheon, 1984), 25.

2. J. F. C. Harrison, *Quest for a New Moral World: Robert Owen and the Owenites in Britain and America* (New York: Charles Scribner's Sons, 1969), 200–201.

3. Harrison, *Quest*, 214.

4. A. L. Morton, *A People's History of England* (London: Lawrence and Wishart, 1979), 427.

5. G. D. H. Cole, *Socialist Thought: The Forerunners, 1789–1850* (New York: St. Martin's Press, 1965), 153–54; Paul Pickering, *Feargus O'Connor: A Political Life* (Monmouth: Merlin Press, 2008), 107.

6. John Merriman, *A History of Modern Europe: From the Renaissance to the Present* (New York: Norton, 2010), 585.

7. Paul A. Gagnon, *France since 1789* (New York: Harper and Row, 1972), 122.

8. Bernard H. Moss, *The Origins of the French Labor Movement, 1830–1914: The Socialism of Skilled Workers* (Berkeley: University of California Press, 1976), 32.

9. William H. Sewell Jr., "Property, Labor, and the Emergence of Socialism in France, 1789–1848," in *Consciousness and Class Experience in Nineteenth Century Europe*, ed. John M. Merriman (New York: Holmes and Meier Publishers, 1979), 55–56; Moss, *Origins*, 31–32.

10. Sewell, "Property," 58.

11. Moss, *Origins*, 34–35.

12. Quotations are from August Blanqui, "The Man Who Makes the Soup Should Get to Eat It," in *Socialist Thought: A Documentary History*, rev. ed., ed. Albert Fried and Ronald Sanders (New York: Columbia University Press, 1992), 193–99.

13. Quoted in Christopher H. Johnson, *Utopian Communism in France: Cabet and the Icarians, 1839–1851* (Ithaca, NY: Cornell University Press, 1974), 18–19.

14. James J. Sheehan, *German History 1770–1866* (Oxford: Oxford University Press, 1989), 566.

15. Karl Marx to Arnold Rugé, in Robert C. Tucker, ed., *The Marx-Engels Reader*, 2nd ed. (New York: Norton, 1972), 12–15.

16. Karl Marx, "On the Jewish Question," in Tucker, *The Marx-Engels Reader*, 31.

17. Marx, "On the Jewish Question," 36, 46.

18. Karl Marx, "Contribution to the Critique of Hegel's Philosophy of Right: Introduction," in Tucker, *The Marx-Engels Reader*, 60, 64.

19. Friedrich Engels, *The Condition of the Working Class in England* (Moscow: Progress Publisher, 1973), 89–92.

20. Quoted in Hunt, *Marx's General: The Revolutionary Life of Friedrich Engels* (New York: Metropolitan Books, 2009), 97.

21. Karl Marx, "Economic and Philosophical Manuscripts of 1844," in Tucker, *The Marx-Engels Reader*, 84.

22. *Marx/Engels Collected Works*, vol. 26 (New York: International Publishers, 1975–2004), 317.

23. Karl Marx, *A Contribution to the Critique of Political Economy*, edited and with an introduction by Maurice Dobb (New York: International Publishers, 1970), 21.

24. Marx, *Contribution*, 21–22.

25. All quotations in the following analysis are from Karl Marx and Friedrich Engels, *The Communist Manifesto* (New York: International Publishers, 1948).

26. Quoted in Francis Wheen, *Karl Marx: A Life* (New York: Norton, 2000), 301.

27. Karl Marx, "Theses on Feuerbach," in Tucker, *The Marx-Engels Reader*, 145.

28. Karl Marx, "Inaugural Address of the Working Men's International Association," in Tucker, *The Marx-Engels Reader*, 512.

29. Marx, "Inaugural Address," 518–19.

30. Karl Marx to Friedrich Engels, 4 November 1864, in *Marx/Engels Collected Works*, vol. 42, 11, http://www.marxists.org/archive/marx/works/1864/letters/64_11_04.htm.

FOUR

Socialism in the Era of Mass Politics, 1870–1914

"STORMING HEAVEN": THE PARIS COMMUNE

In 1848, German democrats failed in their efforts to create a unified Germany through revolution "from below." Two decades later, however, Prussian Chancellor Otto von Bismarck achieved that same goal, excluding Austria, via a revolution "from above." Culminating in a series of victorious wars against Denmark (1864), Austria (1866), and France (1870), his policy of "blood and iron" undercut liberal attempts to limit the power of the Prussian monarchy and, through skillful use of patriotic enthusiasm, economic and political enticements, force, and threats, succeeded in drawing the myriad German states into a united empire (Reich), federally constituted but dominated by Prussia, whose king now also became emperor, or Kaiser.

For France's Second Empire, Germany's birth, proclaimed at Versailles on 18 January 1871, meant death. For eighteen years, Louis Napoleon had ruled by promoting industrial growth, combining repression, and liberal concessions to play one class off against the other; engaging in colonial adventurism in Mexico; and fighting wars to expand France's borders at Austria's expense. By the late 1860s, however, economic difficulties, foreign policy failures, and halfhearted efforts to introduce liberal political reforms had made him increasingly unpopular among republicans, socialists, and even monarchists. In July 1870, Bismarck maneuvered Louis into war. In early September, Prussian forces smashed the French army at Sedan and captured the emperor. On 4 September, Parisian crowds responded by proclaiming a republic and establishing a Provisional Government, headed by General Jules Trochu (1815–1896).

As the Prussians advanced on Paris, government authority in the city weakened, and activists, including members of the International, established "vigilance committees," especially in the workers' districts. A flourishing radical press and myriad "Red" political clubs also sprang up. As tens of thousands of workers flooded into the National Guard and elected their own officers, that once-middle-class organization took on a pronounced working-class character. Observing this development from London, Marx noted, "Paris armed was the revolution armed."[1]

The revolutionary left aimed to mobilize Paris for a determined defense, while the propertied classes, fearful of the newly assertive workers, pressed for a rapid end to the war even on onerous terms. Sharing these fears, the conservative Provisional Government sought to deal with Bismarck. Tensions between these two groups intensified after the Prussian army surrounded Paris on 19 September. In late October, when the government's envoy, Adolphe Thiers (1797–1877), vainly pressed Bismarck for an armistice, an angry mob surrounded the Hotel de Ville, assailing the "traitors." As the siege dragged on, workers suffered most as the starving inhabitants ate dogs and rats to survive. After four months of inept efforts to organize military resistance, the French government accepted Bismarck's terms for an armistice on 28 January.

Many in Paris greeted the surrender angrily, but their fury increased when the government carried out elections for a new National Assembly eight days later, leaving the left no time to organize in the rural areas, where most voters lived and where the influence of the clergy and large landowners predominated. As a result, monarchists won over 400 of the 675 seats. This body then elected Thiers, a former monarchist and now a "moderate republican," to head the new government. It immediately further alienated Parisians by cutting off the pay of National Guard troops at a time of high unemployment and ending the wartime moratorium on debts. These actions favored the interests of the rich over those of the poor and intensified class tensions in Paris. As it became clear that the government intended to disarm the workers, many of the wealthier residents left the city.

On 18 March, Thiers ordered regular army troops to seize 200 cannon under the control of the National Guard on the heights of Montmartre. Surrounded by a large number of guardsmen and civilians, including women and children, who assailed them for their "shameful" act, the soldiers refused to fire into the crowd and allowed the arrest of their officers. Quickly grasping the extent of the crisis, Thiers ordered the army and government to withdraw to Versailles, twenty-five miles southwest of the capital. Meanwhile, the National Guard's elected "central committee" took control of the city. It then carried out citywide elections, based on universal manhood suffrage, to select a new governing council. Thus was born the new Paris Commune, arguably the world's first workers' government, dominated by Jacobins but also including strong contingents of Blanquists—though Blanqui himself had been arrested outside of Paris—and Proudhonists.

Communards were united by patriotism and anger at the surrender to the Prussians and at the rich who seemed to throw in their lot with Thiers. Taking advantage of the changing power relations in the city, many of the poor promenaded through neighborhoods from which they had previously been excluded and reveled in the destruction of symbols of despotic rule, such as the burning of the guillotine and the tearing down of the Vendôme Column, built by Napoleon I to commemorate his military triumphs. In the minds of its opponents, such acts reaffirmed the Commune as a threat to civilization, but to its supporters, they brought a sense of freedom and liberation.

In some ways, the Commune was different from any previous kind of government. It was expected to be a working body in which the elected representatives, rather than highly paid bureaucratic officials, implemented the laws they passed. In addition, members earned the same wages as average workers and were subject to immediate recall. At the same time, however, many of the Commune's political aims, such as freedom of the press, association, and assembly, along with separation of church and state and the abolition of the standing army, were fully in the Jacobin tradition. The Commune also intended to carry out ambitious social reforms. It banned night work in bakeries; introduced widows' pensions; mandated free, secular public education; and forbade employers from fining workers. Although it respected private property, the Commune allowed workers to take control of factories and shops abandoned by their owners, and it promoted the establishment of cooperative enterprises and trade unions. It also appointed Leo Frankel, a Hungarian socialist and friend of Marx, to head the new Commission of Labor and Exchange, which aimed to improve working conditions.

Although the Commune pursued social reforms, none challenged the capitalist order as such. They did not aim to socialize the means of production, eliminate private property, or directly carry out the redistribution of wealth. On the contrary, the Communards' acceptance of private property was so strong that they never availed themselves of the assets of the Bank of France standing stolidly in their midst. This outlook reflected the strong Jacobin and Proudhonist predilection for small property that prevailed among the Communards. As had long been true among French radicals, the latter outlook was rooted in the continued predominance of artisans in the working class, many of whom hoped to create a new world based on small property, mutual aid, and decentralized government authority. Although some members of the Commune were associated with the International, neither that organization nor Marx himself had significant influence on the Parisian events.

It is difficult to judge the Commune's effectiveness because it had little time and few resources to implement its plans. The Revolution failed to spread beyond Paris, and government forces besieged the city for nine weeks. As starvation set in, Thiers raised 130,000 troops consisting of provincial recruits and former prisoners released by the Prussians to crush the revolt. In mid-May, government forces defeated National Guard units in the suburbs and began bombarding Paris itself. On 21 May, they breached the city walls and precipitated a week of bloody street fighting. Government troops, often led by enraged Parisian émigrés, gave no quarter to the Communards who, furious in their turn, took and executed hostages. As they retreated across the city into the working-class neighborhoods, Communards set fire to the Tuilieries, the Louvre, the Palais Royal, and other buildings, while government shelling burned other parts of the city. On 27 May, 200 Communards made a last stand in the Père Lachaise Cemetery. When the fight ended, all 147 survivors were shot along the cemetery's back wall and buried in a mass grave. The "wall of the Communards" has since been a place of pilgrimage for radicals wishing to honor their sacrifice.

It is estimated that about 4,000 Communards and 1,000 government troops died during the fighting. These numbers pale, however, before the 20,000 to 30,000 men, women, and even children executed in mass shootings after the struggle had ended. About 40,000 suspected Communards were held in prison hulks for one year before being tried. The government deported 5,000 of them and meted out less draconian sentences to 5,000 others.

The defeat of the Commune was a crucial moment in the history of European socialism. The French labor movement was decimated, its organizations being banned and many of its leaders jailed or exiled. As Alistair Horne observed, by the time one tallied up the killings, banishments, and escaped exiles, "half the house painters, half the plumbers, the tile layers, the shoemakers and zinc workers had disappeared."[2] Thus, the Commune was the last great struggle on the barricades led by workers rooted in artisanal political traditions. By the time the movement recovered two decades later, it would consist to a much greater degree of wage laborers, and these would have a different political outlook.

The Commune also had great symbolic importance. For Marx, the Parisian workers had been "storming heaven" in their attempt not simply to take over the old bureaucratic-military apparatus "but to smash it" and create "the precondition for every real people's revolution on the continent."[3] In his ringing defense of the Communards, *The Civil War in France*, Marx pilloried the "civilization" of the bourgeoisie, whose "undisguised savagery and lawless revenge" contrasted with the heroic self-sacrifice of the men, women, and children who took to the barricades. "Working Men's Paris," Marx wrote, "with its Commune, will be forever celebrated as the glorious harbinger of a new society. Its martyrs are enshrined in the great heart of this working class."[4] Marx was right. The Commune became an inspiration for generations of later socialists, many of whom, like Lenin, would carefully study it as a classic example of what Marx and Engels called "the dictatorship of the proletariat."

The Commune's defeat also severely weakened the International. Its active Parisian branch was broken up, while in Britain Marx's passionate and very public statements alienated many of the moderate trade unionists, who had previously been a mainstay of the General Council. The organization was thus in poor shape to handle an intensifying internal rift between supporters of Marx and those of the anarchist Mikhail Bakunin (1814–1876) that, as we will see, soon brought about its demise.

Finally, the suppression of the French labor movement meant that the most important center of socialist activity now shifted to newly united Germany. That country, which had already witnessed the reemergence of the organized workers' movement in the 1860s, was now poised to enter into a period of explosive growth that transformed it into Europe's leading industrial power and created the context for the expansion of what many came to regard as socialism's model party.

THE RISE OF GERMAN SOCIALISM

At the time of Germany's unification in 1871, it was already the fourth most industrialized country in the world behind Britain, France, and the United States. By 1914, it had become Europe's strongest economy and trailed only the United States. Small-scale agricultural and craft producers remained important but proportionately shrinking elements of the overall economy as coal, iron, and steel production grew rapidly and Germany pioneered the expansion of the chemical and electrical industries. Agriculture's share of the total gross national product fell from 47 percent in 1850 to 23 percent in 1913, while industrial production increased its share of gross national product to 60 percent. During these decades, millions were on the move as farmers and rural workers left the countryside for the greater opportunities of Germany's burgeoning towns and cities and millions more moved abroad.

Industrialization transformed the social structure and the urban landscape of the country. For example, the number of mine workers increased from 209,000 in 1865 to 863,000 in 1913, employment in the metals industry rose from 109,000 in 1875 to 398,000 in 1913, and the number of construction workers tripled to 1.6 million between 1875 and 1913, while those working in the chemical sector quintupled to 290,000. Many of these new urban workers were unskilled, but others, whose skills were no longer competitive, came from the various crafts. As noted earlier, mechanization disrupted the labor processes previously done by hand and increased the pace and often the drudgery of work. It did not eliminate the need for skilled and semiskilled workers but did shift it into new areas. The needs of industry also fueled the growth of employment in the management and service sectors. The proportion of such "white-collar" employees (Angestellte)—who often saw their interests as separate from production workers (Arbeiter)—increased from 4.7 percent in 1882 to 10.7 percent in 1907.

Geographically, industrial growth was uneven and heavily concentrated in certain regions, such as the Ruhr Valley, Saxony, and Silesia, and in large cities, such as Berlin, Hamburg, Frankfurt am Main, and Leipzig. The growing economy supported a population that increased from 42 million in 1875 to 67 million in 1913. In 1871, only 4.8 percent of the people lived in cities of over 100,000 inhabitants, but by 1910 the total was over 21 percent. While many people also moved to small towns, in some regions large cities were practically conjured out of the ground. Between 1880 and 1910, for example, over 450,000 migrants, half of them Polish or Lithuanian speakers from the Reich's eastern provinces, moved to towns in the Ruhr area, such as Düsseldorf, Essen, and Bochum. Living conditions for workers in Germany's towns and cities varied greatly, but in many working-class districts, especially in the larger cities, they were very hard. Housing was expensive, and whole families were packed into one- and two-room apartments in enormous "rental barracks" (Mietskasernen) built quickly and cheaply with few amenities. Although Berlin was among the most overcrowded cities, there were many with similar conditions. In general, the situation improved somewhat over the next half a century even as the population rose, but it remained dire.

Industrial work was frequently dangerous and insecure. In a world without unemployment or accident insurance, losing one's job was a constant worry, and many families, even when all were employed, had few resources to fall back on. Living standards varied widely depending on region and skill level. In 1900, a skilled printer's 1,300-mark yearly wage was over two and a half times that of a textile worker and allowed for a substantially better living standard, but the typical worker's household barely subsisted on bread, potatoes, and gruel. Although real wages rose gradually between 1880 and 1913, the gulf between working-class families and other social groups was glaring. In 1896, the average yearly income in Prussia was 740 marks, but 1,600 individuals, including bankers, industrial owners, and large estate owners, brought in over 100,000 marks. As we will see, one response of German workers to these conditions was to build a socialist movement, but not all workers perceived their situation in the same way. Some craft workers, for example, saw industrialization as a threat, while others viewed it as an opportunity. Unskilled workers from the countryside, where living conditions were frequently much worse and work was largely seasonal, often saw the pay and regular hours of industrial work as an improvement, even when the workweek averaged seventy-two hours, as it did in 1871.

German industrial growth took place within the framework of a semi-autocratic state. Bismarck equipped the new nation with some attributes of a parliamentary government; its bicameral legislature included a lower house, or Reichstag, elected by universal manhood suffrage, and an upper house, or Bundesrat, consisting of representatives appointed by the states. Behind this democratic facade, however, stood a system designed to protect the power of the government's executive branch, headed by the Prussian king, who was also German Kaiser. The Bundesrat was an extremely conservative body. State governments, elected on the basis of restrictive property qualifications, appointed delegates charged with maintaining the status quo. Prussia's delegation, by far the largest, secured the interests of its ruling aristocracy, the Junkers, by blocking unwanted measures passed by the Reichstag. And, if any undesired legislation happened to slip through, the Kaiser's prime minister or chancellor could ignore it. Constitutionally, his government was responsible not to the parliament but to the Kaiser.

Bismarck initially believed that, given the right to vote, the masses would back the Crown. In case they did not, however, he designed his system to keep them in check. The ruling elites also buttressed their authority through the use of police power, censorship, and restrictions on the rights of assembly and political association, but the regime used these instruments sparingly enough to allow working-class politics to reemerge. The granting of suffrage to all males over the age of twenty-five in elections to the Reichstag created an important opening for mass participation in political life.

In the decade of repression after 1848, most workers retreated from direct political action and concentrated on building self-help organizations, such as producers' cooperatives, to promote their interests. Many also worked with middle-class liberal reformers, such as Hermann Schulze-Delitzsch (1808–1883), who believed that the promotion of production and savings bank cooperatives and self-funded social insurance schemes would help integrate craftsmen and small shopkeepers into an increasingly industrialized laissez-faire–oriented economy. Since many German liberals also favored universal manhood suffrage and the elimination of laws hindering the organization of unions, workers often saw liberals as allies against the authoritarian state.

German craftsmen saw workers' educational associations (WEAs), often founded and supported by middle-class reformers, as an essential means of achieving their hopes. These organizations advocated individual self-improvement through the cultivation of Bildung—lifelong education and learning—and personal thrift. As Stefan Berger has noted, they promoted a wide array of ideas and activities, a number of which were political. Some associations stressed cooperation and self-help, while others prioritized national unity and democratic reforms. WEAs provided workers with access to libraries and space for social activities, such as choral singing, theatrical performances, and gymnastics. They also created opportunities to learn the intricacies of democratic self-management.

Many middle-class liberals saw them as a means of harnessing the labor movement to their own project for reform, as their counterparts in Britain had done.

During the 1850s, the prospects for such an alliance seemed bright, but within a short time, the liberal-led coalition with labor faltered. Some workers chafed under middle-class tutelage and grew impatient with liberal adherence to laissez-faire economic strategies that ignored social reforms. Others resented high dues payments that effectively excluded workers from the newly formed National Association in 1863. Finally, the liberal split into a "National" wing supporting Bismarck's aggressive foreign policy and conservative domestic agenda and a "Progressive" wing seeking to increase the power of parliament and political and social reforms alienated many workers who began to construct new organizations of their own.

The latter development began in earnest during the early 1860s, when efforts were under way to construct a national federation of associations. A particularly important leader in this movement was Ferdinand Lassalle (1825–1864), a well-known lawyer and democratic radical based in Leipzig. In 1863, when a group of workers asked him for help establishing a new association, he responded by urging them to distance themselves from the liberal bourgeoisie, which had betrayed them in 1848, and to establish their own organizations. Viewing the bourgeoisie as the workers' main economic and political enemy, he called for the establishment of producer cooperatives that would enable workers to appropriate the full value of their labor. Through universal manhood suffrage, he fervently believed, workers could achieve political power within the framework of the existing German state. Lassalle did not believe that trade unions could improve workers' condition. The "iron law of wages," he thought, always drove their living standards toward subsistence. State power was the key to labor's advancement, a goal that could be achieved through parliamentary politics.

On 23 May 1863, 400 workers from eleven different cities gathered in Leipzig to found Germany's first social democratic party, the General German Workers Association (Allgemeine Deutscher Arbeiterverein [ADAV]). Aiming to "enlighten workers about their class situation" and to fight for universal manhood suffrage, it initially attracted many craftsmen, but it also recruited recent migrants from the countryside, who were unskilled and had had no experience in the traditionally craft-dominated labor movement. The adherence of the latter group was a substantial achievement on which German socialism would build.

Because Prussian law forbade the association of local political organizations, the ADAV was organized in a highly centralized fashion with power concentrated in the hands of its president, Lassalle, elected by the general membership. In part, this arrangement camouflaged the very real existence of party locals that came together to form the ADAV, but it also reflected Lassalle's predilections. An exceedingly dynamic and charismatic figure, Lassalle was intelligent and ambitious. Like Marx, he had abandoned Judaism for secular humanism and had imbibed at the well of Hegelianism and French socialism. A radical democrat, he had been imprisoned for his efforts in 1848 and in the decade that followed devoted much of his time to philosophical and political study.

Despite many commonalities, Lassalle and Marx had a tense relationship. In part, this was driven by Marx's jealous dislike for talented rivals, but it also stemmed from real theoretical and political differences. Like Lassalle, Marx believed that workers needed to organize political parties to win power, but he did not share the ADAV leader's Hegelian faith that the Junker-led Prussian state could be democratized and used to serve workers' interests. Marx held that a much more fundamental transformation of the state was necessary to introduce socialism and that eventually, after abolishing social classes, the state would disappear as an instrument of class rule. He criticized Lassalle's notion of the "iron law of wages," opposed his dismissal of trade unions, and completely rejected his view that in Prussia the bourgeoisie was the main enemy. On the contrary, as he had in 1848, Marx argued that, before confronting the bourgeoisie, the independent workers' movement should work with progressive middle-class democrats to oust the Junkers from power.

Although he professed to be Marx's admirer and certainly drew on his ideas in programmatic documents, such as *The Workers' Program* (1862), Lassalle shaped the ADAV as he saw fit. Unfortunately for him, his tenure at the helm was cut short in 1864, when a Romanian aristocrat shot him down in a duel over a woman. At that time, the party had only about 4,600 members, and it soon fractured over differing interpretations of the founder's legacy. Nevertheless, the core organization carried on for another decade and is important for several reasons. First, unlike other political parties in Germany, which were loosely organized institutions dependent on large contributions from wealthy supporters to operate during electoral cycles, the highly centralized and tightly structured ADAV depended on modest and regular dues payments from all members. Second, the president and the party executive committee maintained close contact with local organizations through official agents who were also responsible for supervising continual agitation and recruitment efforts. Third, local party organizations continued to cultivate many of the social and educational traditions of the WEAs. The cultural life of the party local played a key role in building a social democratic identity and a constituency loyal to a movement rather than a particular political leader.

Liberal advocates of an alliance with the workers reacted to the founding of the ADAV by quickly establishing a rival organization, the Federation of German Workers Associations (Verband Deutscher Arbeitervereine) in 1863. Within two years, however, internal discord grew over workers' support for strikes, trade union organization, social reform, and independence from the liberal parties. In 1868, the liberal minority withdrew from the organization. One year later, under the leadership of August Bebel (1840–1913) and Wilhelm Liebknecht (1826–1900), the majority met at Eisenach to establish the Social Democratic Workers Party (Sozialdemokratische Arbeiterpartei [SDAP]). Most members of this new party—often referred to as the "Eisenachers"—were skilled workers from southern German states.

Bebel's background was typical of many of his party comrades. Born near Cologne into the family of a noncommissioned officer in the Prussian army, Bebel experienced dire poverty after his father and stepfather died before he had turned eight years old. After attending an elementary school for poor children, in 1854 he apprenticed as a lathe operator and, after seven years of the journeyman's life, eventually settled down as an independent master in Leipzig in 1864. An autodidact, the young Bebel participated in Catholic and liberal-sponsored educational associations. In Leipzig, he joined the local liberal WEA and quickly rose into its leadership. A skilled, energetic organizer and a good speaker, he initially espoused moderate liberal sympathies and even argued that workers were too politically immature to vote. By 1865, however, his views began to shift in a more radical democratic direction as he deepened his knowledge of social issues and engaged in the political struggles of the day.

Meeting Wilhelm Liebknecht was a key moment in Bebel's political transformation. Liebknecht was born in Giessen in the state of Hesse into a middle-class family. While a philosophy student at the University of Marburg, his activity as a radical democrat resulted in his flight into Swiss exile, but the Revolution of 1848 soon brought him back to Germany. After participating in failed rebel military efforts in Baden, he escaped in 1850 to London, where he remained for twelve years. During his sojourn there, he befriended Marx and Engels and became a communist. When he returned to Germany after an amnesty in 1862, he functioned as an agent of "Marx's party" and actually joined the ADAV, where his efforts to weaken Lassalle's influence failed. Booted out of the ADAV and then expelled from Prussia for his political activities, he moved to Leipzig in 1865 and established a close relationship with Bebel. Under his influence, over the next few years Bebel developed a socialist orientation. Indeed, he gradually adopted a "Marxist" outlook that he worked to infuse into the German movement.

The Lassalleans and the Eisenachers had much in common, though several issues divided them. The Lassalleans accepted German unity imposed by Prussian power and had a positive attitude toward the Prussian state, which they believed could be democratized. They created a highly centralized structure to recruit members who would concentrate on the political struggle to win a parliamentary majority. The Eisenachers, on the other hand, feared antidemocratic Prussia's dominance in the process

Figure 4.1.   August Bebel (1892). Courtesy of the AsD, Bonn.

of unification. Moreover, they favored including Austria within a decentralized federal system. They were more critical of the state as an instrument of capitalist domination and explicitly called for the abolition of classes and the creation of a new "people's state." Unlike the ADAV, the SDAP supported trade unions as a means for workers to assert workplace rights. It built a less authoritarian party structure, with a leadership more responsible to rank-and-file members, and, finally, it was more receptive to the ideas of Marx and Engels and joined the International.

Despite these differences, pressure from members pushed the two parties to unify at a joint congress held in Gotha in 1875. Conditions in the country were decisive in this process. The creation of a German state under Prussian leadership had mooted divisions on the national question, and the onset of a major economic crisis in 1873 put concrete issues, such as employment and housing, rather than theoretical questions in the forefront of most members' minds. Finally, the government's intensifying harassment of both parties promoted their mutual understanding and rapprochement.

What were the principles uniting the new party? To Marx's chagrin, many of Lassalle's ideas, such as the "iron law of wages" and his notion that all nonproletarian parties constituted "one reactionary mass," found their way into its new program, but, next to the call for state-supported cooperatives in industry and agriculture, it also asserted that the liberation of the workers required the transformation of privately owned means of production into community property. Although the program recognized the workers' struggle as an international one, the party's focus was national, and its strategy adhered to legal, parliamentary means.

Few of the party's roughly 25,000 members were steeped in socialist theory. What drew most workers to the movement was the solidarity they felt in response to political and social oppression and the demands put forward to improve their daily lives: suffrage for all adults over twenty years of age, liberalism's classical palate of individual civil rights, the replacement of the professional with a people's army, separation of church and state, and free public education. The program also called for the replacement of indirect taxes with a progressive income tax, the right to organize unions, an end to child labor and to women's employment in dangerous jobs, a reduction of the working day, and laws to improve working and housing conditions and to allow the self-administration of mutual aid funds. Such demands brought the party steadily increasing support. In the elections of 1871, the ADAV and SDAP together won only 3.2 percent of the vote, but in 1874 their support climbed to 6.8 percent. In 1877, two years after the formation of the unified Social Democratic Party (SPD), it won the backing of 9.1 percent.

It also drew Bismarck's ire. The government's intolerance had already become especially marked following the outbreak of the Franco-Prussian War in 1870. When Bismarck called on the Reichstag to vote for war credits, the small ADAV and SDAP delegations split. The ADAV's Johann Baptist von Schweitzer (1833–1875), along with the SDAP's Friedrich Wilhelm Fritzsche (1825–1905), argued that the war was defensive in nature and voted in favor, while Bebel and Liebknecht abstained after publicly condemning the conflict as a "dynastic war" and calling for the end of aristocratic domination. When Prussia continued the war against the new French Republic, both workers' parties united in opposition despite the wave of nationalist fervor sweeping the country. Matters came to a head when they welcomed the revolt of the Commune and condemned the slaughter of the Communards. Standing before the Reichstag, Bebel boldly proclaimed that the events in Paris were merely a "preliminary skirmish." "In just a few years," he asserted, "the battle cry of the Commune: 'War on the palaces, peace for the cottages, death to privation and indolence' will be the battle cry of the whole European proletariat!"[5]

Such comments resulted in Bebel and Liebknecht's conviction for treason and allowed Bismarck to skillfully manipulate the already frightened nobility and middle classes for his own political ends. Searching for parliamentary majorities to legitimize his policies, he sought to unite disparate liberal and conservative interests by mobilizing them against supposed enemies of the state, such as the Catholic minority and the Social Democrats. Although the latter had never used violent means to achieve power, he exploited two attempts to assassinate the Kaiser to conjure up the image of a "red menace" aiming to foment violence and to destroy civilization. Aiming to halt social democracy's expansion, in 1878 he won a Reichstag majority to ban the party, its trade union allies, 175 newspapers and magazines, and 153 auxiliary organizations. Over the next twelve years, the state drove thousands of Social Democrats and their families into exile and imprisoned hundreds of others. Meanwhile, Bismarck attempted to win the loyalty of the working class by introducing laws providing basic health and accident insurance as well as system of disability and old-age pensions.

Despite this combination of repression and bribery, the government's policy failed. Indeed, it angered and alienated many workers who increasingly admired the tenacity of the persecuted socialists and were willing to vote for them. That remained a possibility because the antisocialist law permitted individuals to run for office as Social Democrats and to speak openly in the Reichstag. As a result of this loophole and the party's tenacious underground propaganda efforts—for example, it published its main newspaper, *Sozialdemokrat*, in Zurich and smuggled it into Germany—the SPD continued to field candidates and actually increase its support. After receiving only 312,000 votes in the Reichstag elections of 1881, in 1885 the party won 556,000 votes and regained its momentum. The leadership held successful congresses outside of Germany and improved clandestine operations. Two years later, 763,000 people marked their ballot for the Social Democrats, and following the expiration of the antisocialist law in 1890, they won 1,427,000 votes (19.7 percent). In a truly remarkable moment, the SPD emerged from illegality as Germany's largest party.

The changes experienced within the SPD during the years of underground work had far-reaching effects on the party's ideological outlook and approach to power once it returned to open political activity. Before examining these developments, however, we must take a look at the broader European context within which the German Social Democrats were operating.

THE COLLAPSE OF THE WORKINGMEN'S INTERNATIONAL

The 1870s were a difficult decade for Europe's socialists. In industrially advanced England, where Marx and Engels had high hopes for the emergence of a revolutionary proletariat, the labor movement remained focused largely on trade union organizing and political cooperation with the Liberal Party. The destruction of the Commune had shifted the locus of socialist activity from France to Germany, but Bismarck's repression seemed poised to halt social democracy's advance. In addition to these setbacks, the International also crumbled in the wake of political repression; the disaffection of key supporters, such as the British trade unionists; and, most decisively, internal conflicts between Marx's supporters and those of the anarchist leader Mikhail Bakunin.

Bakunin spent most of his adult life either actively engaged in revolution, conspiring to make revolution, or in prison. A controversial figure among his contemporaries and among historians, he was impressive physically, intellectually, and in terms of pure personal and political daring. Born into a conservative aristocratic Russian family, the six-foot-four-inch Mikhail became a commissioned officer but in 1835 abandoned his military career to study philosophy in Moscow. Drawn to Hegel, in 1840 he moved to Berlin, became involved with the Young Hegelians, and soon found himself enmeshed in radical politics. Over the next several years, he became well acquainted with Marx, Proudhon, Weitling, and many other revolutionaries. The tsarist regime noted his radical activity, especially his support for Polish nationalism, and in 1844 stripped him of his rights as a noble and ordered his arrest and exile to Siberia if he ever returned to Russia. A revolutionary leader in Dresden during the uprising of 1849, he was captured by the Prussians and eventually handed over to the Russians, who imprisoned him for eight years under brutal conditions in which he lost all his teeth. Amnestied and exiled to Siberia, he escaped to Japan in 1861 and circled the globe to return to Europe, where he leaped back into revolutionary politics.

The itinerant Bakunin lived by borrowing money or through the largesse of friends. A prolific but unsystematic writer, he left behind, as one of his editors put it, "a bewildering mass of fragments, articles, letters, speeches, essays, [and] pamphlets," which, though often convoluted and repetitive, also contained essential insights. Most fundamentally, Bakunin rejected virtually all forms of authority, including that of the patriarchal family, the church, the capitalist economy, and the state. For him, "order in society must result from the greatest possible realization of individual liberty, as well as of liberty on all levels of social organization."[6] Much more of a libertarian than Proudhon, Bakunin also realized that the latter's conception of a future society grounded in small-scale artisanal production had to make room for a model based on voluntary but larger-scale industrial associations. These would be organized in local communes linked through voluntary federation at the provincial, national, and international levels.

Bakunin's understanding of historical development and of the importance of class divisions was similar to Marx's. He, too, favored the abolition of private property, but he did not view the industrial proletariat as the key agent of progress and stressed that peasants and the very poorest people had as much if not more revolutionary potential. Like Proudhon, he rejected striving for political power via parliamentary or revolutionary means to transform society. Fully achieving human liberty, he argued, required the "radical dissolution of the centralized, aggressive, bureaucratic, authoritarian state."[7] Marx did not disagree with the goal of ultimately eliminating the state, which he conceived of as an instrument of class rule, and he certainly supported smashing its form under capitalism. But he was convinced that to create a socialist society, workers first had to win state power and wield it for themselves. This was the crux of the theoretical and political conflict between the two men.

Paradoxically, the libertarian Bakunin thought it necessary to create hierarchical, highly centralized, secret societies to raise the consciousness of the masses and ultimately to overthrow the state. In 1866, while living in Naples, he set up the International Brotherhood, which won few converts but did prepare a number of Bakunin's compatriots, such as Guiseppe Fanelli (1827–1877), for later "missionary" work. In 1868, Bakunin joined the Geneva branch of the International as well as the liberal International League for Peace and Freedom. When his efforts to radicalize the League failed, he set up a new organization called the Alliance of Social Democracy, which then applied to join the Workingmen's International en bloc. For Marx, this was a dangerous threat. His relations with Bakunin, stretching back twenty-five years, were a complicated mix of mutual admiration, petty jealousies, misunderstandings, and slanderous statements on both sides; neither man trusted the other. Now, having spent years fending off the Proudhon's followers in the International, Marx feared a new anarchist challenge, and Engels, equally suspicious, warned, "It is clear as daylight that the International cannot get involved in this fraud."[8] At their behest, the General Council denied the Alliance's application but agreed to admit its members as individuals. Bakunin acquiesced and dissolved the Alliance but continued cultivating support for his views among the International's branches in Spain, France, Italy, and Switzerland.

For the next three years, tensions simmered as Bakunin's and Marx's supporters avoided head-on conflict over issues of principle, but after the Paris Commune, the International could no longer sidestep the question of political power. At the Hague Congress of 1872, Marx defeated and expelled his rival by exploiting scandals in Bakunin's personal life and accusing him of operating a secret organization within the International. As Peter Marshall has noted, it is unclear whether the latter charge was true, but Bakunin certainly used his network of contacts to win the organization over to his own viewpoint. In the end, the struggle wrecked the International. Exhausted and unsure of their ability to match anarchist support, Marx and Engels decided to scuttle the organization by convincing the delegates to transfer its headquarters to New York, where it quietly expired in 1876.

Thus, Marx and Engels mustered enough support to prevent Bakunin from winning the upper hand in the International but ultimately at the cost of the organization's survival. Moreover, they could not prevent his brand of collectivism and federalism from spreading, and, as we will see, his success in many of the International's southern European outposts sowed the seeds for the later birth of the anarcho-syndicalist movement in those areas. Finally, the International's dissolution, along with the other setbacks encountered by socialists in Western Europe, helped induce Marx to reevaluate his earlier thinking on the prospects for revolution.

RUSSIA AND THE PROSPECTS FOR SOCIALISM

In the first edition of *Capital*, Marx had analyzed the laws of capitalist production as they had arisen in England in the belief that "the country that is more developed industrially only shows, to the less developed, the image of its own future."[9] During the 1870s, however, in light of new evidence, he altered that view. Indeed, in 1881, when Vera Zasulich (1849–1919), a leader of Russia's budding revolutionary movement, inquired whether it was possible for socialism to arise on the basis of existing rural communes or must Russia, as suggested in *Capital*, experience prolonged capitalist development before socialism could be feasible, Marx, after working up four drafts, replied in the affirmative. The "historical inevitability" of the process he analyzed in England, he wrote, applied only to Western Europe, where property relations were historically quite different from those in the East. In Russia, the commune (the *mir*) could function as "the fulcrum for social regeneration" if "the harmful influences assailing it on all sides" (e.g., the tax and administrative demands of the state as well as the growth of capitalist economic relations) could be eliminated.[10]

Marx did not arrive at this conclusion easily. Although historians frequently describe his last decade as one marked by chronic illness and exhaustion that hindered his completion of *Capital*'s second and third volumes, in many ways it was an enormously productive period during which Marx learned Russian, immersed himself in the study of Russian history and contemporary conditions, and ultimately compiled over 30,000 pages of notes on a variety of subjects. As Teodor Shanin has observed, Marx's interest in Russia grew out of several changes in the political and intellectual context in which he was operating: the first we have already mentioned as Marx evaluated the impact of the subsequent dissolution of the Commune and the International; the second was the major advance in the study of human prehistory that resulted from social scientists combining archaeological and ethnographical approaches in their work; while the third, which was linked to this focus on prehistory, was the growth in knowledge of rural noncapitalist societies as they were drawn into the expanding capitalist system. Marx followed these developments carefully and was particularly interested in capitalism's uneven global expansion. It is not surprising that Russia, the recent history of which stood in stark contrast with that of the West, drew his attention. Also important was the fact that, by the end of the 1870s, it was one of the few places in Europe where revolutionary movements were on the rise.

Russia in the late nineteenth century was Europe's last absolute monarchy. Facing no constitutional limits, the tsar ruled over a massive, Russian-dominated, multiethnic empire through a bureaucracy backed by the army and omnipresent police forces. The state forbade political parties and workers' associations and censorship expressly removed hundreds of subjects from public discussion. The landed nobility remained the country's most important social group. Numbering about 30,000 in 1861, it was closely intertwined with the bureaucracy, army, and the clergy. As late as 1897, at least 75 percent of the total population of 125 million consisted of largely poor and often illiterate peasants, and only 13 percent lived in towns (compared to 72 percent in Britain in 1891). Following Russia's defeat in the Crimean War, Tsar Alexander II (r. 1855–1881) abolished serfdom in 1861 and carried out a number of "great reforms" intended to modernize the country. These included the creation of a system of local representative assemblies (*zemstva*), changes to the judiciary, and the reorganization of municipal government. The reforms sped up capitalist development and expanded the middle classes, but most peasants benefited only marginally. Many remained tied to their rural communes, which regulated village life and were responsible for paying the large indemnity owed to the nobility for the land allotments that came with emancipation.

It was within this context of repression and limited reforms that many educated young Russians drew inspiration from the writings of intellectuals such as Alexander Herzen (1812–1870) and N. G. Chernyshevsky (1828–1889) for more radical change. Herzen was a socialist thinker who, after permanently moving to the West in 1847, became deeply disturbed by the individualism of capitalist society. He hoped that Russia could pursue an alternative path to modernization based on retention of the rural commune, traditionally controlled by village elders, who periodically redistributed land according the needs of families and the community as a whole, along with the artisanal cooperative workshop (*artel*). Once a revolution had swept away the tsarist order, these collectively run institutions, reconstituted along more rational and socialist lines, could underpin a new and more just society oriented around the community rather than the individual.

Chernyshevsky was a writer of less romantic bent than Herzen, and he had greater knowledge of Russian social conditions. Espousing a mix of utilitarian, positivist, and materialist views, he held that class struggle was an integral component of the historical process and that dislodging the dominant group from power required a violent revolution. Although more hesitant about the viability of the communes, he also believed that they could aid in the transition to socialism. His novel, *What Is to Be Done?* (1863), outlined a path to a socialist utopia that fired the imaginations of two generations of Russian revolutionaries. Its hero, Rakmetov, became the model of the driven, disciplined, ascetic revolutionary. Lenin read it five times as a youth and described it as "a work, which gives one a charge for a whole life."[11]

In the mid-1870s, thousands of Russian students followed Herzen's call to "go to the people" (*narod*) by moving to the countryside and living among them. These *narodniks*, or "populists," felt that they owed a debt to those whose labor had made their education possible. Idealizing the moral purity of the uncorrupted peasants, they wanted to learn from them and to show them the way to a better future. Many had purely practical aims and worked as teachers, scribes, doctors, veterinarians, nurses, and storekeepers. Others wanted to prepare the ground for a future revolution. Whatever their intentions, the peasants greeted these strangers with incredulity and suspicion. Instead of turning to revolution, they often summoned the police, who arrested hundreds of the young crusaders and soon brought their experiment to an end.

Many radicals then turned to a strategy of attacking the state directly. Land and Liberty, a revolutionary organization founded in 1876, split over the way forward. One group, the People's Will, demanded the creation of a constitutional order based on democratic and socialist principles. Its members believed that revolutionary terror, that is, the killing of top government officials, combined with mass propaganda, would educate the people for revolution. It achieved its greatest success in 1881 when, after several attempts, it assassinated Alexander II, but the severe repression that followed destroyed the organization and undercut many recently introduced reforms.

The other group, called the Black Partition, rejected terror but not revolution. It advocated raising people's consciousness through mass propaganda. Many of its members, such as Vera Zasulich and George Plekhanov (1856–1918), were a part of a growing number of Russian radicals attracted to Marx's ideas. *Capital* had appeared in Russia in 1872 after censors deemed it too difficult for most people to read or understand. It had sold well among intellectuals and was widely reviewed, and its arguments seemed increasingly applicable as capitalist development accelerated.

Plekhanov was a prolific and wide-ranging writer who broke with populism and became a follower of Marx in 1880. Known as the "father of Russian Marxism," it is a great irony that he also ignored Marx's own views on Russian developments. By the late 1870s, Marx had become convinced that, for noncapitalist societies, different roads to socialism were possible. Once capitalism began to establish itself, however, then its noncapitalist attributes had little chance of survival. In 1878, he believed that Russia could still escape that fate. If, however, it "continues along the path it has followed since 1861, it will lose the finest chance ever offered by history to a people and undergo all the fateful vicissitudes of the capitalist regime."[12] Marx sympathized with People's Will because he agreed with much of its program and respected its members' courage and willingness to act to transform Russia. He was less enamored of the Black Partition, whose members had taken refuge in Geneva and "were against all politico-revolutionary action."[13]

It was Plekhanov and his comrades, however, who survived the onslaught of tsarist repression and in 1883 founded the Emancipation of Labor Group, Russia's first social democratic organization. Plekhanov 's brand of "Marxism" put forward three main propositions that set it apart from the populist tradition. To arrive at socialism, Russia must have a liberal democratic political revolution; it must experience a prolonged phase of capitalist development; and the industrial proletariat, rather than the peasantry, must be the agent of society's revolutionary transformation. This theoretical model, which Marx believed was more applicable to Western Europe than to Russia at that time, ultimately became the dominant one among Russia's Social Democrats. As we will see, this schema would have a fateful influence on the future of Russian politics.

Marx and Engels had been enthusiastic about the prospects for revolution in Russia in the late 1870s. The tsarist government had dashed those hopes, and the decade following the destruction of People's Will was one of grim repression. In much of the rest of Europe, by contrast, the prospects for the socialist movement were improving as workers took advantage of new opportunities to found socialist parties that could vie for power. It is to this development that we now turn.

PARLIAMENTARY POLITICS AND THE GROWTH OF THE SOCIALIST MOVEMENT

The spread of parliamentary institutions in most of Europe during the last third of the nineteenth century opened the door to the creation of socialist political parties. Between 1871 and 1905, workers established over thirty political organizations describing themselves as "Socialist," "Social Democratic," or "Labor" parties. Prior to 1914, at least a dozen of these parties recruited dues-paying members in the tens and hundreds of thousands with the German Social Democrats leading the way with over a million in 1913. Socialist parties were particularly strong in the industrialized countries of central Europe and Scandinavia. On the eve of World War I, the Austrian Social Democratic Party had about 90,000 members, the Czech Social Democrats had a particularly impressive 243,000, and the Swedish and Norwegian Social Democratic parties peaked, respectively, at 133,000 and 53,000. Given the size of its national population, the membership of the French Section of the International (SFIO) of 93,000 in 1914 indicates more modest growth, as was true in Italy, where the Socialist Party reached 47,000 in 1901.

Growth in electoral support was equally strong. Between 1911 and 1914, thirteen socialist parties won at least 16 percent of the vote in parliamentary elections, and in several countries they emerged as by far the largest single party. For example, Social Democrats in Germany won 34 percent of the vote in 1912; in Finland, they garnered 43 percent in 1914, and even in relatively underdeveloped Bulgaria, they captured over 20 percent in 1913. These results demonstrated that socialism had emerged as a substantial force.

Another sign of the socialist movement's growing strength was the expansion of trade unionism. With the exception of Britain, where the unions ultimately created the Labor Party in 1900, in most places it was the parties that promoted union building. As unions established themselves, they formed broader labor federations with which the parties were allied. Three types of unions predominated. Craft unions were strongest in Britain, where they managed to broaden their base and absorb many skilled workers as industrialization unfolded. They also were a force on the Continent, but there they tended to rely on narrower constituencies and ultimately lost ground. Industrial unions, in contrast, organized all workers in a single industry regardless of skill level. These unions were strongest in Germany, where the Anti-Socialist Law hit craft unions hard. After its repeal, industrial unions expanded rapidly as organizers recruited metal- and woodworkers, construction workers, transport workers, textile workers, and miners. Within a decade, they outstripped the reconstituted but slower-growing craft unions. Finally, a third type of organization, known as a "general union," represented workers excluded from the crafts and not organized by industry. This form of union was also strongest in Britain, where industrial unions failed to catch on in the face of craft resistance.

Forms of union organizing varied across Europe, competition between the different types could be fierce, and the density of union representation was very uneven. How unionization unfolded depended on the extent and form of industrial development as well as local factors, such as the strength of the traditional crafts and their political outlook. In southern Europe, for example, craft traditions remained strong among organized production workers, while more centralized "industrial" models caught on among municipal, railway, and mine workers. There were few attempts to organize agricultural workers, but one exception was in northern Italy, where by 1913 the agricultural workers' union had 465,000 members, almost as many as were organized in industry.

Union membership far outstripped that of the socialist parties in part because workers saw them as more direct means of improving their living standards, but their rapid growth also reflected the growing concentration of large-scale industry and the development of vertically and horizontally integrated firms. Mass organizing followed. In Germany, for example, between 1890, when they were legalized, and 1913, unions gained 3.8 million members, of which 2.5 million belonged to the social democratic–oriented Alliance of Free Trade Unions. Seventy percent of the Alliance's workers were organized in seven industrial unions, the largest of which, the metalworkers, had 500,000 members. Other federations, such as the employer-friendly Hirsch Duncker unions and the Christian trade unions, were much smaller, with 106,000 and 342,000 members, respectively, in 1913. Between 1887 and 1913, British unions grew from 674,000 to over 4 million members, while their French counterparts increased from 139,000 to 900,000. In contrast, British Labor Party membership prior to 1914 peaked at fewer than 500,000, while the SFIO mustered fewer than 100,000.

The breadth and depth of socialism's expansion across Europe varied, depending on the histories and conditions of different locales. In Germany, the Anti-Socialist Law radicalized the movement, as moderation and legal methods seemed to count for little with the hostile Prussian state. The law deepened the gulf between social democracy and liberalism and intensified workers' sense of isolation in German politics and society. This development, within the broader context of advancing industrialization and its concomitant dislocations, increased the explanatory power of Marx's ideas. Popularized by Karl Kautsky (1854–1938) and Eduard Bernstein (1850–1932), Marxism became the dominant intellectual current within the movement, a development reflected in its increasingly "revolutionary" rhetoric.

Social Democrats such as August Bebel viewed the socialist future as a revolutionary alternative to bourgeois society, but they rejected taking radical action against the Prussian state. Indeed, they sought to restore the SPD's legal standing by adhering to a parliamentary approach and expelled party leaders, such as Johann Most (1846–1906), for intemperately attacking this strategy and using violent language in the press and in the Reichstag. When Most later moved toward anarchism, the SPD vigorously distanced itself from the latter in order to prevent the state from linking the party with violence. Paradoxically, the SPD emerged from illegality united around a rhetorically radical "Marxist" worldview and a parliamentary political strategy. As we will see, it was a formula that brought success but was also fraught with unsustainable tensions.

French socialism's very different evolution also reflected local conditions. Compared with Germany and Britain, industry grew slowly and remained oriented around small enterprises and luxury production. Craft traditions continued to exert strong influence, as did utopian socialist currents and the ideas of Proudhon, Blanqui, and Bakunin. As the labor movement recovered from the persecutions that followed the Commune, Marxism, championed by Jules Guesde (1845–1922) and Paul Lafargue (1842–1911)—the latter of whom had married Marx's daughter, Laura— established a foothold in the French Workers' Party, founded in 1882. Marx himself was unhappy about the doctrinaire way in which they interpreted his ideas, once telling Lafargue, "[if this is Marxism, then] I myself am not a Marxist."[14] Their stress on revolution conflicted with the reformism of the "possibilists" in the Federation of Socialist Workers led by Paul Brousse (1844–1912) and Benoît Malon (1841–1893). Such disputes plagued French socialists until 1905, when, led by the charismatic Jean Jaurès (1859–1914), they united to form the SFIO.

Anarchism also competed successfully with socialism in France. In addition to the ideas of Proudhon and Bakunin, during the late 1870s the teachings of Prince Peter Kropotkin (1842–1921) became influential. Kropotkin was a Russian nobleman, officer, and scientist who, appalled at tsarist tyranny, moved to the West, where his books, such as *The Conquest of Bread* (1892) and *Mutual Aid* (1901), made him anarchism's best-known figure after Bakunin's death. Eschewing Bakunin's idea of a secret revolutionary party and his violent inclinations, he shared his critique of the state. As Albert Lindemann asserts, Kropotikin's "communistic anarchism" was quite similar to Marx's vision of a postrevolutionary world in which the capitalist division of labor would be overcome and people could devote much more time to intellectual and aesthetic pursuits. His work on the role of cooperation as a means of survival in the animal and human worlds provided a powerful counterpoint to emerging social Darwinism.

After the repeal of laws prohibiting union organizing in 1884, anarchist workers drew eclectically from the teachings of these thinkers and incorporated them into the outlook of their new trade unions (*syndicats*). Rejecting participation in politics and piecemeal reforms, they pushed the General Confederation of Trade Unions (Conféderation général du Travail) to commit itself to class struggle and to the overthrow of capitalism by means of a general strike. Georges Sorel (1847–1922) was a major proponent of the latter idea. In his *Reflections on Violence* (1908) and in other writings, he rejected liberal democracy and parliamentarianism for a politics of action. Originally a monarchist, Sorel turned to Marxism in the early 1890s but soon sympathized with Edward Bernstein's challenge to historical materialism (see below) and orthodox economic determinism. Unlike Bernstein, however, he rejected reformist politics and held that the liberal democratic order, rife with corruption, had to be violently destroyed. The anarcho-syndicalist movement was the means of realizing that aim. By promoting the "myth of the general strike," he believed the movement would provide the image of a final reckoning with the bourgeoisie and thus inspire the workers to act.

In practice, the "anarcho-syndicalist" unions paid closer attention to the day-to-day needs of their constituents than to revolutionary action, but their antipolitical ideology and rhetorical focus on the general strike separated them from their socialist counterparts. Anarcho-syndicalism was strongest in France, southern Italy, and Spain, where large-scale industrialization was less pronounced. After peaking in the first decade of the new century, its strength in France faded in the wake of failed strikes, repression, and the rise of new leaders open to more reformist strategies as the country industrialized.

The creation of the British Labor Party (1900) occurred under circumstances very different from those on the Continent. Following the demise of Chartism, British workers built "new model" unions to defend their workplace interests, while in the political sphere they allied themselves with the Liberal Party. These unions organized skilled workers from related crafts into one organization. The Amalgamated Society of Engineers, for example, brought together steam engine and machine makers along with millwrights. Smaller and more exclusive than broader-based unions, their high dues rates allowed them to provide a range of services to members and to stand up to employers. The leaders of the most important London new model unions worked together on common issues while rejecting cooperation with larger, noncraft unions from the north. By the mid-1870s, however, they agreed to form a broadly based Trades Union Congress (TUC) to strengthen labor's voice in political matters. Some workers stood for office as independent "radicals," but no effort was made to form a workers' party.

During the 1880s, several socialist organizations, such as the Social Democratic Federation, led by the Marxist H. M. Hyndman (1842–1921), and the Socialist League, headed by William Morris (1834–1896), arose but attracted few followers. Another group, the Fabian Society, was a purposefully small organization of intellectuals and had a more lasting impact. The Fabians took their name from the Roman general Fabius Maximus, known as "the delayer" because he defeated Hannibal by conducting a war of attrition rather than meeting him head-on. The Fabians rejected class struggle and violent revolution as a means of establishing socialism. Instead, they advocated permeating capitalism with gradual socialist reforms at all levels of society. Their leading figures, such as Sidney (1849–1947) and Beatrice Webb (1858–1943), established outstanding academic reputations in history, economics, and other fields, and the organization attracted many prominent thinkers, such as playwright George Bernard Shaw (1856–1950), novelist H. G. Wells (1856–1950), and women's suffrage leader Emmeline Pankhurst (1858–1958). It later played an influential role in the Labor Party.

The great breakthrough in the reemergence of British socialism occurred in the wake of a worker upsurge beginning in the late 1880s. Large-scale unrest among the London unemployed, confrontations with the police, and a series of successful strikes attracted tens of thousands of recruits to new unions in a variety of industries. The Miners' Federation, for example, increased its membership from 36,000 in 1888 to 200,000 in 1893 by demanding such reforms as a minimum wage and the legal limitation of working hours. Believing that their movement needed its own political voice, some unionists and socialist leaders came together to found an Independent Labor Party in 1893. Led by Kier Hardie (1856–1915), the party was not Marxist, but its demands included the "the collective and communal ownership of the means of production, distribution, and exchange." The Independent Labor Party failed to elect any candidates in its early years, but the situation improved after it came together with the TUC, the Social Democratic Federation, and the Fabians in 1900 to form the Labor Representation Committee, a coalition that later became the Labor Party. For many years, this party was not as well organized as its continental counterparts, but it grew nevertheless. In 1901, the party had 469,000 members and five years later won twenty-nine seats in parliament. A formidable workers' party had emerged.

While Western Europe was home to a wide range of socialist mass parties by the turn of the century, in Eastern Europe, especially in Russia, socialism's progress was slower. In part, this was due to the nature of Russia's economic and social development. Although industrialization advanced rapidly, growth was uneven, and the country remained overwhelmingly agricultural: the growing urban proletariat was dwarfed by the peasantry, and Russia's emerging middle classes were economically and politically impotent when compared to their Western counterparts. Most decisive, though, for the slow development of the labor movement was the state's ruthless suppression of all political and trade union activity. Unlike workers in the West, who, despite continued oppression, could organize openly, Russian activists could operate only clandestinely.

Two groups dominated the socialist political landscape around 1900. Led by Victor Chernov (1873–1952), the Socialist Revolutionary Party (Socialist Revolutionaries) acted in the tradition of the populist People's Will and did not shy away from using terror against the tsarist state. It sought a democratic republic resting on broad local autonomy, self-determination for national minorities, social security for workers, and, most important, "socialized" agriculture controlled by peasant communes. The Socialist Revolutionaries did not oppose industrialization but aimed to halt Russia's march toward capitalism. Socialist industrial development would follow the development of socialist relations in the countryside, which they believed would go forward without need for compulsion among the peasants.

The Russian Social Democratic Labor Party (RSDLP), on the other hand, followed in the footsteps of Plekhanov, who had insisted that Russia would have to pass through a bourgeois-democratic revolution and a prolonged period of capitalist development before a proletarian revolution could establish socialism. Founded in 1898, the party soon divided into two hostile camps over the issue of how to pursue revolution in Russia. Vladimir Ilych Ulyanov (1870–1924), better known by the pseudonym Lenin, led the Bolshevik (majority) faction. Born in Simbirsk into the family of an ennobled school inspector, Lenin was intellectually gifted, energetic, and disciplined. After his brother, Alexander, was executed for conspiring to assassinate Tsar Alexander III in 1887, Lenin, too, became a devoted revolutionary. He completed a law degree in 1892, discovered Marxism, and joined the nascent social democratic movement. After meeting Plekhanov in Geneva in 1895, the police arrested him on his return home, and he spent three years in Siberian exile. Following his release, he went back to Western Europe, where, to paraphrase one comrade, he "thought and dreamt of nothing but revolution—twenty four hours a day."[15] From Geneva, Paris, and other Russian émigré centers, he spent most of the next seventeen years struggling to build a revolutionary party.

Lenin was enthusiastic about surging worker activism in Russia in the early years of the new century but was concerned about its future direction and how socialists should relate to it. In *What Is to Be Done?* (1902), he argued that Russian conditions made the building of a revolutionary mass party of politically conscious workers on the Western European model impossible. Agreeing with Karl Kautsky and other Western intellectuals that it was the party's task to help workers move beyond bread-and-butter "trade union consciousness" by educating them politically, he asserted that in Russia this could be done only by a party of disciplined, tightly organized, professional revolutionaries. Only this type of group could avoid the police and fend off ideas that undercut the élan and clarity of purpose that party activists required.

At the RSDLP's Second Congress in 1903, Lenin's viewpoint encountered stiff opposition from a faction led by Julius Martov (1873–1923), which wanted to build a more open, broadly based organization. This group understood the need for clandestine operations, and its draft statutes were almost identical to Lenin's, but it was leery of his stress on building a centralized hierarchy. This issue, along with other matters, such as who would control the Party's newspaper, *Iskra* (*The Spark*), fueled acrimonious debates. Lenin's opponents accused him of "Bonapartism" and Jacobinism, and he attacked them in turn for their "anarchism" and greater interest in talk than action. Although Martov's supporters outnumbered Lenin's, the latter carried the day after a number of his opponents walked out of the congress. Ironically, Lenin's supporters thereafter became known as the Bolshevik (majority) faction of the RSDLP, and their opponents became known as the Menshevik (minority) faction. The party never recovered from this split. Despite efforts to reestablish unity, each faction cultivated its own policies, newspapers, conferences, and organizing networks. Over the long term, especially in the revolutions of 1917, this development would have decisive ramifications.

THE SECOND INTERNATIONAL AND ITS CONSTITUENTS

Despite the important differences that characterized the growth of socialism in different countries across Europe, all of the major national parties identified themselves as part of one unified movement. This unity was embodied in the Second International, founded on 14 July 1889 in Paris. With the SPD as a prime mover, the opening congress attracted 391 delegates from twenty European countries to establish an organization linking the theoretical and practical aims of the member parties. Strongly influenced by Marxist theory, the International also paid attention to concrete issues such as the eight-hour workday, improved working conditions, the question of peace or war, replacing the standing army with a citizens' militia, universal suffrage, and using May Day demonstrations to promote workers' solidarity. Although it initially faced competition from reformist as well as anarchist rivals, the International soon eclipsed them. Reconvening roughly every three years in different European capitals, it maintained a secretariat in Brussels with the International Socialist Bureau to manage its affairs between congresses. Although some non-European parties also eventually joined (e.g., from Australia, Japan, and the United States), it remained primarily a European body.

The International's real power was symbolic. As historians such as Kevin Callahan have demonstrated, it promoted a powerful "demonstration culture," rooted in the activities of the national parties, linking them together, and building unity among them. The International skillfully used mass rallies, processions, marches, congresses, well-timed manifestos, rituals, symbols such as flags and banners, and the mass-circulation press to shape public discourse and react to international events, especially the threat of war. These activities, coordinated via the International Socialist Bureau, strengthened the bonds of the individual workers' parties, even when they were often divided on ideological or practical matters. The International had few means to pressure member parties to adhere to its decisions, but its prestige was substantial, and its meetings provided an important forum for debate. For millions of workers, it represented proof of their growing strength and buttressed their conviction that history was on their side: they were part of an international movement in which workers' solidarity would lead to victory.

Of course, for most adherents to socialism, the International was also a rather distant institution that had little to do with their decision to join the movement. Most people turned to socialism because its ideas helped them understand their own experiences and gave them hope for the future. Equally important was the fact that, in a society in which workers faced exclusion from the world of middle-class culture, socialist activists created a wide array of cultural institutions, including newspapers and publishing houses, workers' libraries and educational associations, and singing, theatrical, and even bicycling clubs. Such organizations did not always create a uniquely socialist culture; indeed, they often formed a bridge to middle-class culture for workers, but they were essential to the promotion of socialist politics and building solidarity among working people.

In order to win supporters and guide their political work, socialist parties put forward succinct, accessible programs. As noted earlier, the SPD approved its initial program at Gotha in 1875. In 1891, however, as the radicalized party emerged from illegality, it met in Erfurt to reformulate its message, which was now more thoroughly Marxist. Kautsky, the party's leading theorist, penned the opening section stressing how the concentration of industry and concomitant decline of small producers, the growth of monopoly, the expansion of the proletariat and its deepening poverty, and the intensification of class struggle amidst capitalism's worsening crises paved the way for the coming social and economic transformation. Although never openly calling for "socialist revolution," this section closely followed the narrative of *The Communist Manifesto*. The SPD's goal was a classless society in which all people, regardless of race or gender, enjoyed full equality.

The program's second part outlined a series of reforms that could be achieved within the existing system. Written by Eduard Bernstein, it jettisoned much of the earlier text's Lassallean language, but its concrete aims were similar and included universal suffrage; the full range of liberal civil rights; mandatory, free, and secular education; the replacement of the standing army with a people's militia; women's equality; separation of church and state; progressive income and steep inheritance taxes; and an array of measures to improve workplace safety, increase social security, and secure unions' rights. This combination of immediate aims and a radical vision of the future made the Erfurt Program an effective means of winning support. It did not, however, resolve the question of whether the party would pursue it goals via revolutionary or reformist means.

As the program of Europe's leading socialist party, Erfurt exerted much influence outside of Germany, but the programs of individual parties again reflected the diversity of views among socialists. When, for example, the Belgian Labor Party drew up its program in 1893, it contained several points setting it apart from Erfurt. The Belgians devoted more attention to the issue of workers' control over industry and were

Figure 4.2.   Coauthors of the Erfurt Program, Edward Bernstein (left) and Karl Kautsky (right), in 1910. Courtesy of the AsD, Bonn.

leery of concentrating too much power in the hands of the centralized state. They called for legislative councils representing different functions of society, including industry, commerce, agriculture, and education, and urged the dispersal of substantial powers to local communes in the spheres of transport, municipal and regional utilities, and health matters. Their insistence that the transformation of society along collectivist lines also required a moral transformation stressing altruism and solidarity reflected a concern not present in the Erfurt Program.

Social democracy's call for the universal emancipation of the oppressed attracted mainly workers but also supporters among the middle classes, oppressed minorities, and women. Europe's Jewish population provides an excellent example of one group drawn to the movement. By the late nineteenth century, Jews in most central and Western European societies had achieved full legal equality and were well represented in the middle-class professions, in industry, and in commerce. Still facing intense social and political discrimination, many turned to socialism as a means of winning full equality. Jews constituted about 5 percent of Germany's population, but according to Edward Bernstein, himself of Jewish origins, they constituted about 10 percent of the party in 1921. His colleague, Robert Michels, also estimated that between 20 and 30 percent of Jewish intellectuals were Social Democrats. In a movement lacking skilled people to staff its burgeoning organizations and press, educated Jews found many leadership opportunities. Popular figures such as Paul Singer (1844–1911), cochairman of the SPD; Victor Adler (1852–1918), the head the Austrian party; and Rosa Luxemburg (1871–1919), coleader of the party in Poland and Lithuania and later a dominant personality in Germany, are just a few examples of the success Jews enjoyed in central European social democracy. In Russia, where the Jewish population was much larger and anti-Semitism even more virulent, Jewish Social Democrats such as Julius Martov, Leon Trotsky (1879–1940), and Lev Kamenev (1883–1936) also played prominent roles.

If Jews joined social democracy in numbers sometimes well above their proportion of the overall population, the movement did far less well among women, though it was in the vanguard of those calling for women's equality. In 1882, the program of the French Workers' Party demanded women's full political and economic emancipation. In Germany, well before Erfurt, August Bebel's *Women under Socialism* (1878) was among the most widely read socialist tracts with fifty editions and fifteen translations by 1909. Bebel argued for women's suffrage, access to professional training, divorce, property rights, and sexual freedom. Most important, he recognized that women were economically dependent on men and that full equality would be chimeric unless they could achieve independence by working outside the home. Of course, ending women's exploitation at home and in the workplace was impossible under capitalism. It could occur only following the transformation of the existing state and social order, that is, the establishment of socialism.

The "women's question" was not a new one for socialists. The followers of Fourier and Saint-Simon had widely viewed the emancipation of women as an essential part of human liberation. But in a mass movement dominated by patriarchal male craft workers, the conservative social values of thinkers like Proudhon proved more popular than women's equality. There were occasional female voices, such as that of Flora Tristan (1803–1844) in France, for whom socialism and the liberation of women were inseparable, but most female advocates for women's rights approached the issue from a middle-class standpoint. These activists tended to focus on women's legal equality and gave relatively little attention to the very different problems facing poor women.

In the latter decades of the century, as the labor movement increasingly rested on the support of industrial workers and as Marxism became more influential, a new socialist feminist outlook emerged. This current drew heavily on Friedrich Engels's argument, developed in his *Origins of the Family, Private Property, and the State* (1884), that the locus of women's oppression lay in the family's relation to the mode of production, and it placed class struggle at the center of its analysis. To promote equality, socialist feminists supported political and legal equality for women along with a wide range of socioeconomic reforms, such as the provision of child care for working mothers, equal pay for equal work, and full access to education and birth control. They also held that capitalism's overthrow would have to precede women's complete emancipation; this prioritizing revolution rather than reform won wide though not universal acceptance among male and female Social Democrats.

Various factors, however, hindered the recruitment of women to social democracy. Women were almost universally denied the franchise; parties interested in winning elections had little incentive to seek their support, and in a number of countries, such as Germany, it was unlawful for women to attend political meetings or join a party. Women interested in social democracy often attempted to organize their own "educational" associations, but the police were assiduous in breaking them up, and those who dared attend local SPD meetings had to do so in disguise. Nevertheless, women in every country were engaged in the movement, and many, such as Madeleine Pelletier (1874–1939) in France, Anna Kulis-cioff (1857–1925) in Italy, Alexandra Kollantai (1872–1952) in Russia, and Klara Zetkin (1857–1933) in Germany, rose to prominence.

Zetkin joined the SPD during its underground struggle. At the International's founding congress in 1889, she delivered a speech, "The Liberation of Women," in which she demanded an end to all restrictions on women's employment, which she regarded as "the necessary condition for their social and political equality." She agreed fully with Bebel that "full emancipation" was possible only through socialism, and she knew that that struggle would be long and hard, in part due to the prejudices deeply embedded in society and in the party itself. Zetkin was a tireless agitator; she pushed successfully for the creation of a "women's department" with a seat on the party executive and helped create International Women's Day. She also edited the party newspaper, *Die Gleichheit* (*Equality*), targeting women. Along with other dedicated activists, she played a key role in attracting women to social democracy. After laws banning women's political activity were lifted in 1908, the number of female Social Democrats shot up from about 7,000 to 141,000, over 14 percent of the total membership, by 1914.

Few other socialist parties could match even this modest success. For example, following the unification of French socialism, women constituted only about 3 percent of the SFIO's membership, and in all socialist parties, very few women occupied top posts in the leadership. The situation in the trade unions was not much better. In Germany, where women made up over 20 percent of the industrial workforce in 1890, only 1.8 percent of women workers were unionized (increasing to 8.8 percent in 1913). In Britain, over half of the 275,000 unionized cotton workers were women in 1910, but no female activists qualified for leadership in either the Labor Party or the TUC. Such examples illustrate that social democra-

Figure 4.3.   Clara Zetkin in 1893. Courtesy of the AsD, Bonn.

cy often failed to recruit women into its organizations and that those who joined were underrepresented in its elected hierarchy.

One of the most important causes of the gulf between social democratic theory and practice was the attitudes of male socialists toward women. Many resented women's presence in the workplace and feared their competition in the job market. Some felt that, while women might enjoy the social side of movement life, with its festivals, parades, and music, they were not really interested in or able to grasp the realities of politics. Edmund Fischer, an SPD Reichstag delegate, expressed the widely held sentiment that women's "natural occupation" was "the care and upbringing of young children [and] the embellishment and stabilization of family life."[16] Thus, for many men, a woman's place remained in the home. Recruiting women to socialism was not a high priority; parties reserved few resources for the task.

Many strong supporters of women's equality were ambivalent about their aims. For example, French party leader Jules Guesde publicly proclaimed that "the place for woman is no longer more at home than anywhere else," and he welcomed talented women to the movement.[17] At the same time, however, he and his male colleagues blocked women's illegal—and therefore symbolic—efforts to stand as candidates for parliament. Concerned with winning seats, the leadership dismissed their candidacies. Women had to subordinate their interests to those of the men.

Finally, some female socialist feminists agreed with those men who felt that women's natural place was in the home. French activist Aline Valette (1850–1899), for example, attempted to reconcile socialism and feminism with a theory that she called "sexualism." This notion held that under capitalism, women faced exploitation and oppression not only in the economic and political spheres but also in their conjugal and maternal lives. Resting on rampant individualism and brute force, patriarchy allowed men to claim ownership over women's most important product: their children. A socialist revolution not only would eliminate capitalist exploitation and individualism but also recognize motherhood as the most important form of work. Supported by the community, women would be free to return to their "primary" maternal purpose. Such a viewpoint was congenial to many male French socialists who did not wish to associate social transformation with upheaval in their private lives. Guesde himself said that Valette was "the only woman who understood socialism."[18] Under his leadership, she rose to the position of secretary to the Executive Council of the French Workers Party, the highest post achieved by a socialist woman in France before 1914.

These factors, taken together, undercut the movement's ability to attract them and resulted, as Geoff Eley concludes, in a major lost opportunity. It was not the only one. Socialists also alienated many artisans and peasants who resisted slipping into the proletariat and feared socialism's vision of a collectivist future. It is important to note that Europe's socialist parties and their allied unions never won the direct adherence or electoral support of an absolute majority of workers in any country. Many workers simply rejected all or parts of social democratic ideology. In Germany, for example, Catholic workers tended to vote for the Catholic Center Party, which prioritized the needs of the Catholic community while also promoting its own allied trade unions. Other workers identified with liberal or nationalist parties, and a small number even looked to the so-called Christian-Social Workers' Party, a conservative, openly anti-Semitic formation headed by Adolf Stoecker (1835–1909), chaplain of the Kaiser's court. Thus, with many workers voting for nonsocialist parties, social democracy's failure to attract more women, peasants, and other nonproletarian supporters seriously limited its ability to win a majority.

During the two decades leading up to World War I, however, the movement's growth seemed irrepressible, and many in the ruling classes feared that the socialists would soon use the institutions of parliamentary democracy to challenge their power. This was especially true in Germany, where, in 1912, even a system rigged against urban voters could not prevent the SPD from winning 34 percent of the vote and 110 seats (one-quarter of the total) in the Reichstag. In light of such victories, many socialists sensed that they were marching with the tide of history; it was only a matter of time before absolute majorities gave them the power to carry out the transition to socialism. Most turned a blind eye to the cracks in social democracy's unified edifice.

REFORM OR REVOLUTION?

Following the establishment of the International, a series of conflicts simmered within European socialism. They were rooted, in part, in long-standing debates about social democracy's identity, but they also emerged as parties reacted to external events. Despite the acrimony that accompanied these disputes, none of them threatened immediately to split the movement.

As socialism enjoyed increasing electoral success in the 1890s, questions arose regarding the purposes of parliamentary politics. Most socialist leaders, especially in Germany, regarded themselves as revolutionaries and viewed parliament as a platform for movement building. They supported reforms but rejected close cooperation and coalitions with nonsocialist parties. Electioneering and parliamentary work aimed primarily to educate the masses and prepare them for the coming confrontation with their class enemies. Socialists should remain in "pure opposition" and avoid diluting their party's "proletarian character" by being drawn into the system. Some, such as Bebel, believed that capitalism's economic collapse, the great Kladderadatsch, would soon pave the way for socialism's ascension to power. Others, such as Rosa Luxemburg, were more willing to take active measures to promote the coming revolution, but there was broad agreement that, until that moment came, the movement should avoid adventurism and increase its strength.

A substantial minority, however, believed that social democracy should take advantage of its growing stature and, if opportune, join with liberals to promote reforms. In the early 1890s, Georg von Vollmar, an SPD leader in Bavaria, openly advocated gradualism and urged the party to endorse Germany's foreign policy and legislation in the Bavarian Assembly supporting private peasant farming. Under Kautsky's influence, the SPD rejected these ideas, but the dispute revealed a complex set of tensions, such as between the pragmatists and the purists and between local politicians aiming to attract a specific clientele and leaders at the center of the party concerned with different constituencies.

The conflict with von Vollmar had been primarily a German matter, but shortly thereafter, the "Millerand Affair" in France shocked the socialist world. Alexandre Millerand (1859–1943) was an independent socialist who, in 1899 entered a "Government of Republican Defense" headed by René Waldeck-Rousseau (1846–1904). He took this step because, like Jaurès and many other socialists, he was convinced that the republic was in danger following the conviction of Alfred Dreyfus, a Jewish officer framed as a spy by reactionary forces. When it became clear that General Gaston Gallifet (1830–1909), the "butcher of the Commune," would also be in the cabinet, radical socialists, such as the ex-Communard Édouard Vaillant (1840–1915) and Guesde, were incensed. In their eyes, the reforms that Millerand achieved, such as the ten-hour workday and the creation of labor councils, were unimportant. The fact that government forces also shot down striking workers in Chalon-sur-Saone revealed the bankruptcy of entering into a coalition with the bourgeoisie.

The acrimony over "ministerialism" unfolded over several years and can best be understood as part of a broader "revisionist" conflict within social democracy. Revisionism took its name from efforts made by Eduard Bernstein, one of the SPD's most revered intellectuals, to bring the movement's revolutionary theory into line with its reformist practice. In exile for many years in Britain, Bernstein had come under strong Fabian influence. In the mid-1890s, he published a series of essays, later brought together in a book titled *Evolutionary Socialism* (1899), in which he challenged many of Marx's fundamental premises. Bernstein considered himself Marx's pupil, but he was convinced that history had shown many of the master's prognostications to be flawed. He rejected the labor theory of value and pointed out that, contrary to Marx's expectations, workers' living standards were improving, not declining; economic crises were growing milder, not more severe; the peasants and the petite bourgeoisie were holding on, not disappearing; and, with the emergence of new middle-class groups, it was clear that society was not simply dividing into bourgeois and proletarian camps. Conflicts and oppression certainly continued, but Bernstein believed that socialism could be achieved through gradual reforms. History did not unfold dialectically, he asserted, in a process of periodic revolutions. It was an evolutionary process in which social democracy could achieve its aims using parliamentary means. To that end, it should abandon its revolutionary rhetoric and recognize itself as a reformist party prepared to reach out to nonproletarian groups and work with progressive liberals.

Taken individually, none of these theses would have caused much of a firestorm among Social Democrats. Many had been asserted before and were themselves subject to critique. (After all, what did happen to the peasants and the artisans?) The main issue was Bernstein's political conclusion, which unleashed widespread outrage. Bebel mobilized a powerful phalanx of "orthodox" Marxist critics to refute Bernstein's arguments, including the latter's longtime friend Kautsky and the dynamic newcomer Rosa Luxemburg. In *Reform or Revolution* (1900), she argued that, for social democracy, Bernstein's challenge was a question of "either/or." The socialist transformation was either "the consequence of the internal contradictions of the capitalist order" or, if he were correct, a utopian dream.[19] Most of the party leadership felt similarly and aligned itself against Bernstein. At the Dresden Party Congress of 1903, his views were rejected, and the orthodox conception of class struggle was reaffirmed.

One of the reasons that so many German socialists opposed Bernstein's approach was that it seemed to be clearly at odds with that country's political and social reality. Germany remained a semiautocratic state in which the Kaiser talked openly about shooting down his socialist opponents and the ruling classes obstinately denied workers full citizenship. Opportunities for collaboration with progressive liberals were few. In France, on the other hand, reformism among socialists was much stronger in part because the institutions of the republic provided them with greater opportunities for effective change. These different outlooks clashed at the International's Amsterdam Congress of 1904, where the charismatic Jaurès made an impassioned appeal for a reformist approach, only to encounter powerful German-led opposition. In the end, the delegates voted twenty-five to five with twelve abstentions to ban reformist alliances, and they reasserted the principle of class-based opposition.

Other issues, such as "imperialism," also divided Social Democrats. In the late nineteenth century, many observers used the term to describe the recent rapid expansion of the European powers (including the United States and Japan) into other regions of the world. In many areas, such as Africa and South Asia, the great powers forcibly established their direct "colonial" rule over foreign territories, while elsewhere, such as Latin America and China, they tended to exercise power indirectly using economic and diplomatic means. Keen to understand the degree to which imperialist expansion was rooted in the workings of capitalism, many leading socialists gave it close attention. Important works, such as Rudolf Hilferding's *Finance Capital* (1910) and Rosa Luxemburg's *Accumulation of Capital* (1913), focused on how imperialist expansion enabled the capitalist system to overcome its internal contradictions and extend its life while also linking colonialism to the intensifying arms race among the great powers. Although the International's Stuttgart Congress of 1907 condemned colonialism, which "by its very nature gives rise to servitude, forced labor, and the extermination of native peoples," a substantial minority of socialists viewed it in a more positive light.[20] When carried out justly, argued Bernstein and others, imperialism could bring jobs to the metropolitan countries and the benefits of economic development and "higher" Western culture to the colonies. This outlook revealed the depth of racial and nationalist prejudice that permeated even the international workers' movement. Such an attitude was also linked closely to strong nationalist sentiments, which, as we will see in the next chapter, played a decisive role in socialism's response to the coming of war in 1914.

In addition to imperialism, Social Democrats were also at odds over the use of the general, or "mass," strike as a political weapon. In contrast to strikes aiming to achieve limited economic gains, such as higher wages or better working conditions in one enterprise or economic sector, some socialists, like their anarcho-syndicalist rivals, believed that large-scale strikes involving workers across industrial lines could be the decisive instrument in a revolutionary confrontation with the bourgeoisie. Others, however, viewed such strikes as a means to achieve limited political reforms. In 1902 and 1903, Belgian and Swedish workers attempted to use large-scale strikes to extend the franchise, while Dutch workers struck in response to antistrike legislation. Each of these efforts failed in part due to the socialist leaders' unwillingness to pit unarmed workers against government troops. Interest in the general strike remained high, however, as workers in Germany agitated to end the three-class electoral system in Prussia, and when revolution exploded in Russia in 1905, workers there used them to force the tsar to grant a constitution.

Rosa Luxemburg had experienced the Russian events firsthand. When she returned to Germany in 1906, she argued for using the mass strike as a means of educating workers for revolution. Impatient with social democracy's stress on elections and organization building, she wanted to encourage workers to take action, learn from their mistakes, and gain confidence. In her view, struggle would build the movement, not cautious routine. However, many revisionists and trade union leaders, such as Karl Legien (1861–1920), opposed the general strike because they believed that it put their organizations at risk and would allow the party leadership to usurp control over union organizations. Meanwhile, a third "centrist" current emerged, supported by Bebel, Kautsky, and Rudolf Hilferding (1877–1941). Recognizing the general strike as a weapon in the class struggle, they argued that it should be used only in the final battle for socialism, when the bourgeoisie attempted to roll back the democratic rights that made peaceful advance possible. Such a position allowed the party to maintain its revolutionary posture without changing its parliamentary strategy.

At the SPD's Mannheim Congress in 1906, the trade unions won parity in decision making and thus effectively took the general strike off the table as a means of effecting change. But the issues raised during the debates did not disappear, and many of the divisions within the party became entrenched. Revisionism grew stronger among a new generation of party leaders moving into positions of authority and more concerned than ever about electioneering and organization building. Leaders of the

"Marxist Center," such as Bebel, Kautsky, and Hilferding, won majority support by holding high the party's radical identity but without challenging its reformist practice. Meanwhile, a party left wing emerged, led by Rosa Luxemburg and Karl Liebknecht (1871–1919), that aimed to push the movement's practice in a more radical direction.

Figure 4.4.   Rosa Luxemburg in 1890. Courtesy of the AsD, Bonn.

Similar though not identical divisions existed in many of Europe's socialist movements. It is important to recognize that, in some ways, their existence reflected the strength of social democracy's democratic culture. Although acrimonious, no one was expelled for his ideas, not even Bernstein, and there was no serious talk about precipitating a split. These people had devoted their lives to creating a movement that aimed to build a new world, and dividing it would have betrayed everything they had worked to achieve. On the eve of World War I, international socialism appeared to be strong and headed for victory. But it had not yet fully been put to the test.

DOCUMENT 4.1. SOCIALISM, UTOPIAN AND SCIENTIFIC (1877)

Friedrich Engels

This essay originally appeared as part of a series of articles responding to the criticism of rival socialist intellectual Eugen Dühring. Later compiled as a book titled Herr Dühring's Revolution in Science, *the last three chapters were later published as a separate pamphlet from which this excerpt is drawn.*

Active social forces work exactly like natural forces: blindly, forcibly, destructively, so long as we do not understand, and reckon with, them. But when once we understand them, when once we grasp their action, their direction, their effects, it depends only upon ourselves to subject them more and more to our own will, and by means of them to reach our own ends. And this holds quite especially of the mighty productive forces of today. As long as we obstinately refuse to understand the nature and the character of these social means of action—and this understanding goes against the grain of the capitalist mode of production and its defenders—so long these forces are at work in spite of us, in opposition to us, so long as they master us, as we have shown above in detail.

But when once their nature is understood, they can, in the hands of the producers working together, be transformed from master demons into willing servants. The difference is as that between the destructive force of electricity in the lightning of the storm, and electricity under command in the telegraph and the voltaic arc; the difference between a conflagration, and fire working in the service of man. With this recognition, at last, of the real nature of the productive forces of today, the social anarchy of production gives place to a social regulation of production upon a definite plan, according to the needs of the community and of each individual. Then the capitalist mode of appropriation, in which the product enslaves first the producer and then the appropriator, is replaced by the mode of appropriation of the products that is based upon the nature of the modern means of production; upon the one hand, direct social appropriation, as a means to the maintenance and extension of production—on the other, direct individual appropriation, as means of subsistence and of enjoyment.

While the capitalist mode of production more and more completely transforms the great majority of the population into proletarians, it creates the power, which, under penalty of its own destruction, is forced to accomplish this revolution. While it forces on more and more the transformation of the vast means of production, already socialized, into state property, it shows itself the way to accomplishing this revolution. *The proletariat seizes political power and turns the means of production into state property.*

But, in doing this, it abolishes itself as the proletariat. Abolishes all class distinctions and class antagonisms, abolishes also the state as state. Society thus far, based upon class antagonisms, had need of the state. That is, of an organization of the particular class which was *pro tempore* the exploiting class, an organization for the purpose of preventing any interference from without with the existing conditions of production, and therefore, especially for the purpose of forcibly keeping the exploited classes in the condition of oppression corresponding with the given mode of production (slavery, serfdom, wage-labor). The state was the official representative of society as a whole; the gathering of it together into a visible embodiment. But it was this only in so far as it was the state of that class which itself represented, for the time being, society as a whole: in ancient times, the state of slave owning citizens, in the Middle Ages, the feudal lords; in our own time, the bourgeoisie. When at last it becomes the real representative of the whole society, it renders itself unnecessary. As soon as there is no longer any social class to be held in subjection; as soon as class rule, and the individual struggle for existence based upon our present anarchy in production, with the collisions and excesses arising from these, are removed, nothing more remains to be repressed, and a special repressive force, a state, is no longer necessary. The first act by virtue of which the state really constitutes itself the representative of the whole of society—the taking possession of the means of production in the name of society—this is, at the same time, its last independent act as a state. State interference in social relations becomes, in one domain after another, superfluous, and then dies out of itself; the government of persons is replaced by the administration of things, and by the conduct of processes of production. The state is not "abolished." *It dies out.* This gives the measure of the value of the phrase "a free state," both its justifiable use at times by agitators, and as to its ultimate scientific insufficiency; and also of the demands of the so-called anarchists for the abolition of the state out of hand.

Since the historical appearance of the capitalist mode of production, the appropriation by society of all the means of production has often been dreamed of, more or less vaguely, by individuals, as well as by sects, as the ideal of the future. But it could become possible, could become a historical necessity, only when the actual conditions for its realization were there. Like every other social advance, it becomes practicable, not by men understanding that the existence of classes is in contradiction to justice, equality, etc., not by the mere willingness to abolish these classes, but by virtue of certain new economic conditions. The separation of society into an exploiting and an exploited class, was the necessary consequence of the deficient and restricted development of production in former times. So long as the total social labor only yields a produce which but slightly exceeds that barely necessary for the existence of all; so long therefore, as labor engages all or almost all the time of the great majority of the members of society—so long, of necessity, this society is divided into classes. Side by side with the great majority, exclusively bond slaves to labor, arises a class freed from directly productive labor, which looks after the general affairs of society: the direction of labor, state business, law science, art, etc. It is, therefore, the law of division of labor that lies at the basis of the division into classes. But this does not prevent this division into classes from being carried out by means of violence and robbery, trickery and fraud. It does not prevent the ruling class, once having the upper hand, from consolidating its power at the expense of the working class, from turning its social leadership into an intensified exploitation of the masses.

But if, upon this showing, division into classes has a certain historical justification, it has this only for a given period, only under given social conditions. It was based upon the insufficiency of production. It will be swept away by the complete development of modern productive forces. And in fact, the abolition of classes in society presupposes a degree of historical evolution at which the existence, not simply of this or that particular ruling class, but of any ruling class at all, become an obsolete anachronism. It presupposes, therefore, the development of production carried out to a degree at which appropriation of the means of production and of the products, and with this, of political domination, of the monopoly of culture, and of intellectual leadership by a particular class of society, has become not only superfluous but economically, politically, intellectually, a hindrance to development.

This point is now reached. Their political and intellectual bankruptcy is scarcely any longer a secret to the bourgeoisie themselves. Their economic bankruptcy occurs regularly every ten years. In every crisis, society is suffocated beneath the weight of its own productive forces and products, which it cannot use, and stands helpless, face to face with the absurd contradiction that the producers have nothing to consume, because consumers are wanting. The expansive force of the means of production bursts the bonds that the capitalist mode of production had imposed upon them. Their deliverance from these bonds is the one precondition for an unbroken, constantly accelerated development of the productive forces, and therewith for a practically unlimited increase of production itself. Nor is this all. The socialized appropriation of the means of production does away, not only with the present artificial restrictions upon production, but also with the positive waste and devastation of productive forces and products that are at the present time the inevitable concomitants of production, and that reach their height in the crises. Further, it sets free for the community at large a mass of means of production and of products, by doing away with the senseless extravagance of the ruling classes of today and their political representatives. The possibility of securing for every member of society, by means of socialized production, an existence not only fully sufficient materially, and becoming day by day more full, but an existence guaranteeing to all the free development and exercise of their physical and mental faculties—this possibility is now for the first time here, but *it is here.*

With the seizing of the means of production by society, production of commodities is done away with, and, simultaneously, the mastery of the product over the producer. Anarchy in social production is replaced by systematic, definite, organization. The struggle for individual existence disappears. Then, for the first time man, in a certain sense, is finally marked off from the rest of the animal kingdom, and emerges from mere animal conditions of existence into really human ones. The whole sphere of the conditions of life which environ man, and which have hitherto ruled man, now comes under the dominion and control of man, who for the first time becomes the real, conscious lord of Nature, because he has now become master of his own social organization. The laws of his own social action, hitherto standing face to face with an as laws of Nature foreign to, and dominating him, will then be used with full understanding, and so mastered by him. Man's own social organization, hitherto confronting him as a necessity imposed by Nature and history, now becomes the result of his own free action. The extraneous objective forces that have hitherto governed history pass under the control of man himself. Only from that time will man himself, more and more consciously, make his own history—only from that time will the social causes set in movement by him have, in the main and in a constantly growing measure, the results intended by him. It is the ascent of man from the kingdom of necessity to the kingdom of freedom.

Source: Marx/Engels Selected Works, Volume 3 (Moscow: Progress Publishers, 1970), http://www.marxists.org/archive/marx/works/1880/soc-utop/ch03.htm.

DOCUMENT 4.2. WOMEN IN THE FUTURE (1879)

August Bebel

Written during one of August Bebel's many sojourns in prison for his political activities, Women and Socialism *became a best-seller, appearing in over twenty languages and selling over 140,000 copies in Germany alone between 1879 and 1914. It remained one of socialism's most important statements on gender equality well into the twentieth century.*

The woman of the future society is socially and economically independent, she is no longer subjected to even a vestige of domination or exploitation, she is free and on a par with man and mistress of her destiny. Her education is the same as that enjoyed by men, with the exception of some modifications demanded by differences of sex and sexual functions. Living in natural conditions, she is able to develop and exercise her physical and mental powers and faculties according to her requirements. She chooses her occupation in such a field as corresponds with her wishes, inclinations and talents, and enjoys working conditions identical to those of men. Even if she is engaged in some trade for some hours she may spend another part of the day working as an educator, teacher or nurse, and devote a third part of the day to some art, or the study of some branch of science, and set aside yet another part of the day to some administrative function. She joins in studies and work, enjoys diversions and entertainment with other women or with men as she pleases and as occasion allows.

In choosing the object of her love, woman, like man, is free and unhampered. She woos or is wooed, and enters into a union from no considerations other than her own inclinations. This bond is a private agreement, arrived at without the intermediacy of a functionary—just as marriage was a private agreement till far into the Middle Ages. Socialism is creating nothing new here, it only restores at a higher stage of civilisation and under new social forms *what had prevailed universally before private property began to dominate society.*

Under the proviso that the satisfaction of his instincts inflicts no injury and disadvantage on others, the individual shall see to his own needs. *The gratification of the sexual instinct is as much a private concern as the satisfaction of any other natural instinct.* No one is accountable for it to others and no unsolicited judge has the right to interfere. What I shall eat, how I shall drink, sleep and dress, is my own affair, as is also my intercourse with a person of the opposite sex. Intelligence and culture, full independence of an individual—all qualities that will evolve naturally as a result of the education and the conditions pertaining in the future society—will guard everyone against committing acts that would be to his disadvantage. The men and women of the future society will possess a far higher degree of self-discipline and self-knowledge than those now living. The simple fact that all the stupid prudery and ridiculous affection of secrecy regarding the discussion of sexual matters will have vanished guarantees that intercourse between the sexes will be much more natural than it is today. If two persons who have entered into a union turn out to be incompatible, or are disappointed in or repulsed by each other, morality demands that this unnatural and therefore immoral bond be dissolved. Since the conditions that have up to now condemned a large number of women to either celibacy or the barter of their bodies will have vanished, men will no longer be able to maintain any superiority. On the other hand, the transformed social conditions will remove many of the inhibitions and inconveniences which affect married life today, often prevent it from unfolding, or even render it wholly impossible.

There is a growing awareness among wide circles of the inhibitions, contradictions and unnatural aspects of the position of the woman today, and this awareness finds graphic expression in social literature as well as in fiction, but often in a distorted form. That the present form of marriage is less and less compatible with its purpose no thinking person can deny. And hence it is no wonder that there are even people who consider freedom in the choice of love and in the dissolution of the bonds already sealed only natural, while they show no inclination to draw the necessary conclusions to the effect that the present social system should be changed. . . .

. . . Admittedly, freedom in choosing the object of love is impossible in bourgeois society—this all our preceding arguments have demonstrated—but place the whole community in social conditions similar to those enjoyed by the social and intellectual elite, and the whole community gains access to similar freedoms. . . .

. . . Bourgeois marriage is, we have proved this beyond contradiction, the consequence of bourgeois property relations. Closely bound up with private property and the right of succession, it is entered into for the purpose of begetting "legitimate" children as heirs. And under the pressure of the social conditions it is also forced upon those who have nothing to bequeath; it becomes a social law, whose violation the state punishes by sentencing men and women who live in adultery and who have separated to terms of imprisonment.

In socialist society there is nothing to be bequeathed, unless one regards domestic utensils and personal belongings as an inheritance; hence, the modern form of marriage becomes obsolete. The question of inheritance is thereby solved and socialism does not have to bother to abolish it. Once there is no private property, there can be no right of inheritance. Thus, woman is free and her children do not restrict her freedom, they can only multiply the joy she gleans from life. Nurses, teachers, women-friends, the rising female generation are at hand to assist the mother when she needs help.

It is possible that there will be men in the future who will say with Alexander von Humboldt: "I was not made to be the father of a family. Moreover, I consider marrying a sin and the begetting of children a crime." What of it? With others the power of natural instincts will see to it that equilibrium is maintained. We are worried neither by the hostility to marriage of a Humboldt nor by the pessimistic philosophy of a Schopenhauer, Mainländer or von Hartmann, who hold out for mankind the prospect of self-destruction in the "ideal state." In this respect we agree with F. Ratzel who has every justification for writing:

"Man must no longer look upon himself as an exception to the laws of Nature, but should at last begin to look for the regularities that underlie his own actions and thoughts, and strive to lead his life in accordance with natural laws. He will arrive at the point when co-existence with his fellows, that is, the family and the state, will be organized not according to the precepts stemming from long-forgotten centuries but in accordance with rational principles of the knowledge he has of Nature. Politics, morality, legal principles, which are still gleaned front all (possible sources, will be determined according to the laws of Nature alone. An existence worthy of the human, being that man has dreamed of for millennia will at last become reality."[1]

That day is approaching with rapid strides. Human society has, in the course of millennia, traversed all previous phases of development in order finally to arrive at the point where it started from, to communistic property and to full equality and fraternity, but no longer among congeners alone, but *among the whole human race.* Such is the great progress it makes. What bourgeois society strived for in vain and where it runs aground, and is bound to do so, is in establishing freedom, equality and fraternity for all people, a goal which socialism will achieve. Bourgeois society was able to evolve only the theory, but here, as in many other respects too, its practice was at odds with its theories. Socialism will combine theory and practice.

Yet, while man returns to the starting-point in his development, this is effected on an infinitely higher cultural level than the one from which he started. Primitive society had common property in the gens, in the clan, but only in the crudest form and at an extremely low level of development. The development that has since taken place has, on the one hand, done away with common property, apart from small and insignificant vestiges, has broken up the gens and finally atomized the whole of society, while at the same time during its various stages it has enormously increased the productive forces of society and the diversity of requirements, created nations and great states from among the gens and tribes, but simultaneously produced once more a state of affairs that stands in blatant contradiction to society's requirements. The task of the future is to resolve this contradiction by transforming property and the means of production back into collective property on the broadest possible basis.

Society takes back what was once its own and what it has created, but, in accordance with the newly created living conditions, it makes possible for all its members a standard of living on the highest cultural level, *that is, it grants to all what under more primitive conditions was the privilege of individuals or of individual classes.* To *woman,* too, is *restored* the *active* role she played in primitive society, not a dominating role, but the role of man's equal.

"The end of the development of the state resembles the beginning of human existence. The original equality finally returns. The maternal element opens and closes the cycle of everything human"—Bachofen wrote in his Matriarchy and Morgan said:

"Since the advent of civilisation, the outgrowth of property has been so immense, its forms so diversified, its uses so expanding and *its management so intelligent in the interests of its owners, that it has become, on the part of the people, an unmanageable power.* The human mind stands bewildered in the presence of its own creation. The time will come, nevertheless, when human intelligence will rise to the mastery over property, and define the relations of the state to the property it protects, as well as the obligations and the limits of the rights of its owners. *The interests of society are paramount to individual interests, and the two must be brought into just and harmonious relations.* A mere property career is not the final destiny of mankind, if progress is to be the law of the future, as it has been of the past. The time which has passed away since civilisation began is but a fragment of the past duration of man's existence; and but a fragment of the ages yet to come. *The dissolution of society bids fair to become the termination of a career, of which property is the end an aim; because such a career contains elements of self-destruction.*

"*Democracy in government, brotherhood in society, equality in rights and privileges, and universal education, foreshadow the next higher plane of society to which experience, intelligence and knowledge are steadily tending.*

"*It will be a revival, in a higher form, of the liberty, equality and fraternity of the ancient gentes.*" [2]

Thus, men representing diverse points of view arrive, on the basis of their scientific investigations, at identical conclusions. The complete emancipation of woman, and her equality with man, is the final goal of our cultural development, the achievement of which no power on earth can prevent. But it is possible only on the basis of a transformation, that abolishes all domination of man by man and hence also that of the worker by the capitalist. Only now will human development reach its peak. The "Golden Age" men have been dreaming of for millennia and for which they have yearned, will come at last. *An end will be put to class domination once and for all, and with it to Man's domination of woman.*

1. Quoted in Häckel's *Natürliche Schöpfungsgeschichte*, 4. Auflage.
2. Lewis H. Morgan, *Ancient History*, New York, 178, p. 552.

Source: This is an abridged version of the last part of a later German edition (probably 1910) of Bebel's 1879 book *Woman and Socialism*, published under this title in 1971 by Progress Publishers, Moscow. Original date written and translator unknown. Online version Marxists Internet Archive, 2004. Transcription by Ted Crawford. HTML by Mike B. Supplemental editing by Adam Buick.

—❧❧❧—

DOCUMENT 4.3. EVOLUTIONARY SOCIALISM (1899)

Edward Bernstein

*Edward Bernstein's attempt to revise some of Marx and Engels's basic theoreti-
cal conclusions caused a major uproar in the socialist movement. Bernstein's
assertions—and the sharp condemnation of his detractors—revealed that social
democracy's organizational and electoral successes also brought significant challenges to the future unity of the movement.*

Without a certain measure of democratic institutions or traditions, the
socialist doctrine of our day would not be possible at all. There might
well be a workers' movement, but no Social Democracy. The modern
socialist movement, as well as its theoretical expression, is in fact the
product of the influence exerted by conceptions of justice that came to
fruition in—and achieved general acceptance through—the great French
Revolution on the wage and work-time movement of industrial workers.
That movement would also exist without these conceptions, just as there
existed, without and prior to them, a popular communism derived from
early Christianity. But this popular communism was poorly defined and
half-mystical, and without the foundation of those legal institutions and
notions (which are, at least to a major extent, the necessary concomitants
of the capitalist development), the workers' movement would lack its
inner cohesion. And that is very much like the situation that exists today
in the Oriental countries. A working class that is without political rights
and has grown up in superstition and with inadequate schooling will no
doubt revolt from time to time and conspire on a small scale, but it will
never develop a socialist movement. It takes a certain breadth of perspective and a fairly developed consciousness of rights to turn a worker who
occasionally rebels into a socialist. That is why political rights and education hold a preeminent place within every socialist program of action. . . .

Does . . . Social Democracy, as the party of the working class and of
peace, have an interest in maintaining the nation's readiness to fight?
From a variety of perspectives it is tempting to answer this question in
the negative, especially if one starts with the statement in the *Communist
Manifesto*: "The proletarian has no fatherland." While this sentence might
apply to the workers of the 1840s, without rights and excluded from
public life, today, it has lost much of its validity, in spite of the enormous
increase in the intercourse among nations, and will lose even more, the
more the worker is transformed, under the influence of Social Democracy, from a proletarian into a citizen. The worker who has an equal right to
vote in the state, the municipality, and so on, and is thereby a co-owner of
the common good of the nation, whose children the community educates,
whose health it protects, whom it insures against injuries, will have a
fatherland without thereby ceasing to be a citizen of the world, just as the

nations are coming closer together without thereby ceasing to lead lives of their own. It might seem very convenient if all people were to speak only one language one day. But what a stimulus, what a source of intellectual enjoyment would be lost to future generations. The complete dissolution of nations is not a pleasant dream, and is not to be expected within the foreseeable future. But just as it is undesirable for any of the great civilized nations to lose its independence, it cannot be a matter of indifference to Social Democracy whether the German nation—which has, after all, contributed and contributes its proper share to the civilizing labor of the nations—is eclipsed in the council of nations.

Today, there is a lot of talk about the conquest of political power by Social Democracy, and it is at least not impossible, given the strength it has attained in Germany, that some political event in the near future will assign it a crucial role. But precisely under these circumstances, since neighboring countries are not so far advanced, Social Democracy—like the Independents of the English and the Jacobins of the French Revolution—would be compelled to be national to maintain power, that is, it would have to assert its ability to be the leading party, or class, by showing that it is capable of giving equal consideration to class interests and national interests. . . .

In principle, what has been said above has already indicated the perspective from which Social Democracy must take a position on questions of foreign policy under the current conditions. While the worker is not yet a full citizen, he is also no longer so bereft of rights that national interests can be a matter of indifference to him. And while Social Democracy is not yet in power, it does assume a position of power that imposes certain obligations on it. Its word carries considerable weight. Given the current composition of the army and the complete uncertainty about the moral effect of small-caliber firearms, the Reich government will think ten times before it hazards a war against the determined opposition of Social Democracy. Thus, even without the famous general strike, Social Democracy can speak a very weighty—if not decisive—word in favor of peace, and it will do so as often and as vigorously as is necessary and possible, in keeping with the time-honored motto of the International. Moreover, in accordance with its program, in cases where conflicts arise with other nations and direct resolution is not possible, it will advocate that these differences be settled through arbitration. But nothing commands it to support the renunciation of Germany's current or future interests, if, or because, English, French, or Russian chauvinists take offense at the relevant policies. Where we are not dealing with partiality or special interests of certain circles on the German side, which matter naught to the people's welfare or are actually deleterious to it, where important interests of the nation are, in fact, at stake, internationalism cannot be a reason for yielding weakly to the pretensions of foreign interests. . . .

Of greater importance than the question of pressing the demands that are already on the program is the question of adding to the program. In this regard, practice has put a series of issues on the agenda, some of which—when the program was created—seemed too far off in the future to be of any immediate concern to Social Democracy, some of which, however, were not sufficiently recognized for their full significance. They include the agrarian question, questions of municipal politics, the question of cooperatives, and various questions of industrial law. The great growth of Social Democracy in the eight years since the drafting of the Erfurt Program, its effects on domestic politics in Germany, as well as the experiences of other countries have made a more intense engagement with all these issues absolutely necessary, and, in the process, some of the views that were once held have been substantially revised.

As far as the agrarian question is concerned, even those who believe that the peasant economy is doomed have altered their views considerably as to the time it will take for this to occur. And while profound differences of opinion on this point have played a part in the more recent debates on the kind of agrarian policy that Social Democracy should endorse, in principle these debates have revolved around the question of whether—and if so, then up to what point—Social Democracy should lend support to the peasant as such, that is, as an independent entrepreneur, against capitalism. . . .

. . . In my mind, . . . the chief tasks of Social Democracy vis-à-vis the rural population can be divided into three groups, namely:

1. Opposition to all remaining remnants and pillars of land-holding feudalism and the struggle for democracy in municipality and district. That is, support for the abolition of entail, manorial holdings, hunting privileges, and so on. . . .

2. Protection and relief for the agricultural working classes. This includes worker protection in the narrower senses: abolition of the regulation for domestics, limitation on working time for the various categories of wage-workers, health policy, education, and such measures as would provide tax relief to the small farmer. . . .

3. Struggle against the absolutism of property and support for the cooperative system. This category includes demands such as "limitation on the rights of private ownership of the soil in order to promote: 1) separation, the abolition of the aggregation of land, 2) land cultivation, 3) the prevention of epidemics, . . . the reduction of excessive land rents through courts established for that purpose, . . . the construction of healthy and comfortable housing for workers by the municipalities, the facilitation of co-operative unions by legislation, . . . the right of municipalities to acquire land through purchase or expropriation and to lease it to workers and workers' cooperatives for low rent."

The last demand brings us to the question of cooperatives. . . . The issue today is no longer whether or not there should be cooperatives. They exist and will exist, whether Social Democracy likes it or not. To be sure, it could and can slow the spread of workers' cooperatives through the weight of its influence on the working class, but it would not be doing a service to itself or the working class. There is likewise little to recommend the rigid Manchester system, which is often held up within the party against the cooperative movement and justified with the explanation that no socialist cooperatives can exist within capitalist society. Instead, the important thing is to take a certain position and to be very clear about which cooperatives Social Democracy can recommend and morally support in accordance with its means, and which it cannot. . . .

. . . Where the economic and legal preconditions are in place, Social Democracy can allow the establishment of workers' consumer cooperatives for workers without any concerns, and it would do well to give them its full goodwill and to support them wherever possible. . . .

This, finally, brings us to Social Democracy's municipal policy. For a long time, it, too, was the stepchild of the socialist movement, or one of them. . . . What does Social Democracy demand for the local municipality, and what does it expect from it?

If a socialist municipal policy is to be possible, Social Democracy must demand for the municipalities, alongside the democratization of suffrage, an expansion of the right of expropriation, which is still very restricted in various German states. It must also demand that their administration, especially of the security police, be completely independent of the state. . . . Moreover, what has moved front and center, and for good reason, are demands pertaining to the development of municipal enterprises, public services, and the labor policies of the municipalities. As for the former, it will be necessary to raise the principled demand that all enterprises that concern the general needs of the members of the community and are monopolistic in character should be run by the municipality under its own control, and that the municipalities should, moreover, strive to constantly expand the range of services for their members. With respect to labor policies, we must demand that the municipalities, as employers of workers, whether on their own account or under contract, maintain, as the minimum condition, the wages and work hours accepted by the organizations of the workers in question, and that they guarantee these workers freedom of association. . . .

To be sure, Social Democracy is not entirely dependent on the franchise and parliamentary activity. It also has a large and rich area of work outside parliament. The socialist workers' movement would exist even if the parliaments remained closed to it. . . . But with its exclusion from the representative bodies, the German workers' movement would lose much of the internal cohesion that binds together its various parts today; it would take on a chaotic character; and in place of a calm and steady advance at a regular pace, there would be erratic forward movements, with the inevitable setbacks and weariness.

This kind of development cannot be in the interest of the working class, nor can it strike as desirable those enemies of Social Democracy who have realized that the current social order has not been created for all eternity, but is subject to the laws of change, and that a catastrophic development, with all its horrors and devastations, can be prevented only if legislation takes into account changes in the relationships of production and exchange and in the development of classes. And the number of those who understand this is growing steadily. Their influence would be much greater than it is today if Social Democracy could muster the courage to emancipate itself from a phraseology that is indeed obsolete and give the impression that it wants to be what it is in reality today: a democratic-socialist reform party.

I am not talking about renouncing the so-called right of revolution, this purely speculative right, which no constitution can enshrine and no law book in the world can prohibit, and which will exist for as long as the law of nature forces us to die if we renounce the right to breathe. This unwritten law is no more affected by the fact that one takes a stance on the ground of reform, than the right of self-defense is renounced by the fact that we create laws to regulate our personal and property disputes. . . .

As for the rest, I repeat that the more Social Democracy decides that it wants to appear to be what it is, the more its chances of carrying out political reforms will increase. Fear is certainly a major factor in politics, but one would be mistaken to believe that the incitement of fear could accomplish everything. It was not when the Chartist movement was at its most revolutionary that the English workers attained the right to vote, but when the revolutionary slogans had died down and they allied themselves with the radical bourgeoisie to fight for the attainment of reforms. And if someone counters that something similar is impossible in Germany, I would urge him to read up on what the liberal press was writing about labor union struggles and worker legislation only fifteen and twenty years ago, and how the representatives of these parties spoke and voted in the Reichstag when issues of that nature had to be decided. Perhaps he would then agree that the political reaction is by no means the most characteristic phenomenon in bourgeois Germany.

Source: Eduard Bernstein, *Die Voraussetzungen des Sozialismus und die Aufgaben der Sozialdemokratie* [*The Preconditions of Socialism and the Tasks of Social Democracy*] (Stuttgart, 1899). chap. 4, sec. D, 144 ff. German text reprinted in Ernst Schraepler, ed., *Quellen zur Geschichte der sozialen Frage in Deutschland. 1871 bis zur Gegenwart* [*Sources on the History of the Social Question in Germany. 1871 to the Present*], 3rd ed. (Göttingen and Zurich, 1996), 136–43. Republished in *German Historical Documents and Images: Wilhelmine Germany and the First World War*, ed. Roger Chickering and Steven Chase Gummer with Seth Rotramel, trans. Thomas Dunlap, http://germanhistorydocs.ghi-dc.org/sub_document.cfm?document_id=767.

—◈◈◈—

DOCUMENT 4.4. REFORM OR REVOLUTION (1900)

Rosa Luxemburg

Rosa Luxemburg delivered one of social democracy's most powerful responses to Bernstein's effort to revise the fundamentals of Marxism. In the excerpt that follows, Luxemburg expresses the views of many socialists who feared that acceptance of Bernstein's ideas threatened the essence of what it meant to be a socialist.

Foreword
The title of the present work may be surprising at first glance: social reform or revolution? Can Social Democracy possibly be against social reform? Or can it counter social revolution, the radical change of the existing order, which is its final goal, with social reform? Certainly not. In fact, the daily practical struggle for social reforms, for the amelioration of the condition of the working people within the framework of current conditions, and for democratic institutions, represents for Social Democracy the only way of leading the proletarian class warfare and working towards the end goal: the seizing of political power and the abolition of the wage system. For Social Democracy, there is an inseparable link between social reform and social revolution, in that the struggle for social reform is the *means*, but radical social change is the *goal*.

We find the counterposing of these two aspects of the workers' movement for the first time in the theory of *Ed. Bernstein*, as laid out in his essays "The Problems of Socialism" in *Neue Zeit* in 1896–97 and especially in his book *The Preconditions of Socialism and the Tasks of Social Democracy*. This entire theory essentially amounts to nothing other than the advice to give up radical social change, the final goal of Social Democracy, and instead to transform social reform from a means of class struggle into its goal. Bernstein himself formulated his views most aptly and most sharply when he wrote: "The final goal, whatever it may be, is nothing to me; the movement everything."

But since the final socialist goal is the only decisive aspect that distinguished the social democratic movement from bourgeois democracy and bourgeois radicalism, which transforms the entire workers' movement from a futile effort to repair the capitalist order into class warfare *against* this order, for the abolition of this order, the question "Social reform or revolution?" in the Bernsteinean sense poses for Social Democracy at the same time the question: "To be or not to be?" In the final analysis, the quarrel with Bernstein and his supporters is not about this or that method of the struggle, about this or that *tactic*, but about the very *existence* of the social democratic movement.

This realization is doubly important for the workers, because this is precisely about them and their influence in the movement, because it is their own lives that are being put at risk here. The opportunistic current in the party, whose theory has been formulated by Bernstein, is nothing other than an unconscious effort to secure the upper hand for the petty bourgeois elements that have joined the party, to reshape the practice and the goals of the party in their spirit. The question about social reform and revolution, about the final goal of the movement is, from a different perspective, the question *about the petty bourgeois or proletarian character of the workers' movement.*

Source: Rosa Luxemburg, "Sozialreform oder Revolution" ["Social Reform or Revolution?"], *Leipziger Volkszeitung* (1899). In Rosa Luxemburg, *Gesammelte Werke* [*Collected Works*], vol. 1, 1893–1905 (Berlin: Dietz, 1990), 369–71. Republished in *German History in Documents and Images: Wilhemine Germany and the First World War (1890–1918)*, ed. Roger Chickering and Steven Chase Gummer with Seth Rotramel, translated by Thomas Dunlap, http://germanhistorydocs.ghi-dc.org/sub_document.cfm?document_id=769.

DOCUMENT 4.5. WHAT IS TO BE DONE? (1902)

V. I. Lenin

Written to give direction to the nascent Russian Social Democratic Party, What Is to Be Done? *addressed issues arising in a very specific historical context and attracted little attention outside of Russian socialist circles when it appeared. However, after the split between the Bolsheviks and Mensheviks and especially following the former's victory in 1917, many observers, especially in the West, came to see it as one of communism's founding documents. The excerpt below is frequently regarded as one of the book's most important for understanding the ethos of Bolshevism.*

We are marching in a compact group along a precipitous and difficult path, firmly holding each other by the hand. We are surrounded on all sides by enemies, and we have to advance almost constantly under their fire. We have combined, by a freely adopted decision, for the purpose of fighting the enemy, and not of retreating into the neighboring marsh, the inhabitants of which, from the very outset, have reproached us with having separated ourselves into an exclusive group and with having chosen the path of struggle instead of the path of conciliation. And now some among us begin to cry out: Let us go into the marsh! And when we begin to shame them, they retort: What backward people you are! Are you not ashamed to deny us the liberty to invite you to take a better road! Oh, yes, gentlemen! You are free not only to invite us, but to go yourselves wherever you will, even into the marsh. In fact, we think that the marsh is your proper place, and we are prepared to render *you* every assistance to get there. Only let go of our hands, don't clutch at us and don't besmirch the grand word freedom, for we too are "free" to go where we please, free to fight not only against the marsh, but also against those who are turning towards the marsh! . . .

Without revolutionary theory there can be no revolutionary movement. . . . [F]or Russian Social-Democrats the importance of theory is enhanced by three other circumstances, which are often forgotten: first, by the fact that our Party is only in the process of formation, its features are only just becoming defined, and it has as yet far from settled accounts with the other trends of revolutionary thought that threaten to divert the movement from the correct path. . . .

We shall have occasion further on to deal with the political and organizational duties, which the task of emancipating the whole people from the yoke of autocracy imposes upon us. At this point, we wish to state only that *the role of the vanguard fighter can be fulfilled only by a party that is guided by the most advanced theory.* . . .

In the previous chapter we pointed out how universally absorbed the educated youth of Russia was in the theories of Marxism in the middle of the nineties. In the same period the strikes that followed the famous St. Petersburg industrial war of 1896 assumed a similar general character. Their spread over the whole of Russia clearly showed the depth of the newly awakening popular movement, and if we are to speak of the "spontaneous element" then, of course, it is this strike movement which, first and foremost, must be regarded as spontaneous. But there is spontaneity and spontaneity. Strikes occurred in Russia in the seventies and sixties (and even in the first half of the nineteenth century), and they were accompanies by the "spontaneous" destruction of machinery, etc. Compared with these "revolts," the strikes of the nineties might even be described as "conscious," to such an extent do they mark the progress, which the working-class movement made in that period. This shows that the "spontaneous element," in essence, represents nothing more nor less that consciousness in an *embryonic form*. Even the primitive revolts expressed the awakening of consciousness to a certain extent. The workers were losing their age-long faith in the permanence of the system which oppressed them and began . . . [ellipses in the original] I shall not say to understand, but to sense the necessity for collective resistance, definitely abandoning their slavish submission to the authorities. But this was, nevertheless, more in the nature of outbursts of desperation and vengeance than of *struggle.* . . . Taken by themselves, these strikes were simply trade union struggles, not yet Social Democratic struggles. They marked the awakening antagonisms between workers and employers; but the workers were not, and could not be conscious of the political and social system, i.e., theirs was not yet Social-Democratic consciousness. In this sense, the strikes of the nineties, despite the enormous progress they represented as compared with the "revolts," remained a purely sponta-neous movement.

We have said that there could not have been Social-Democratic con-sciousness among the workers. It would have to be brought to them from without. The history of all countries shows that the working class, exclu-sively by its own effort, is able to develop only trade-union conscious-ness, i.e., the conviction that it is necessary to combine in unions, fight the employers, and strive to compel the government to pass necessary labor legislation, etc. The theory of socialism, however, grew out of the philo-sophic, historical, and economic theories elaborated by educated repre-sentatives of the propertied classes, by intellectuals. . . .

Since their can be no talk of an independent ideology formulated by the working masses themselves in the process of their movement, the *only* choice is—either bourgeois or socialist ideology. There is no middle course (for mankind has not created a "third" ideology, and moreover, in a society torn by class antagonisms there can never be a non-class or an above-class ideology.) Hence, to belittle the socialist ideology in any way, to turn aside from it in the slightest degree, means to strengthen bour-geois ideology. . . .

The moral to be drawn from this is simple. If we begin with the solid foundation of a strong organization of revolutionaries, we can ensure the stability of the movement as a whole and carry out the aims of Social Democracy and of trade unions proper. . . .

I assert that it is are more difficult to unearth a dozen wise men than a hundred fools. . . . As I have stated repeatedly, by "wise men," in connec-tion with organization, I mean professional revolutionaries, irrespective of whether they have developed from among students or working men. I assert: (1) that no revolutionary movement can endure without a stable organization of leaders maintaining continuity; (2) that the broader the popular mass drawn spontaneously into the struggle, which forms the basis of the movement and participates in it, the more urgent the need for such an organization, and the more solid this organization must be (for it is much easier for all sorts of demagogues to side-track the more back-ward sections of the masses); (3) that such an organization must consist chiefly of people professionally engaged in revolutionary activity.

Source: V. I. Lenin, *Collected Works,* vol. 5 (Moscow: Progress Publishers, 1961), 355, 369–70, 374–75, 384, 460, 464. Translated by Joe Fineberg and George Hanna. Original transcription and markup by Tim Delaney (1999). Re-marked up and proofread by K. Goins (2008). Public domain, Lenin Internet Archive (1999).

—◈◈◈—

DOCUMENT 4.6. THE INTERNATIONALE (1871)

Eugène Pottier

Written by a French transport worker in the wake of the Paris Commune's crushing defeat, this song became the anthem of the international workers' movement and, after 1917, of the Soviet Union and the Communist International. Over the years, the original text has undergone frequent alterations in order to set it to music and to adapt it to changes in language and circumstances. The version below is an English translation from the French original.

The International
Arise ye workers from your slumbers
Arise ye prisoners of want
For reason in revolt now thunders
And at last ends the age of cant.
Away with all your superstitions
Servile masses arise, arise
We'll change henceforth the old tradition
And spurn the dust to win the prize.

Refrain:
So comrades, come rally
And the last fight let us face
The Internationale unites the human race.

No more deluded by reaction
On tyrants only we'll make war
The soldiers too will take strike action
They'll break ranks and fight no more
And if those cannibals keep trying
To sacrifice us to their pride
They soon shall hear the bullets flying
We'll shoot the generals on our own side.

No savior from on high delivers
No faith have we in prince or peer
Our own right hand the chains must shiver
Chains of hatred, greed and fear
E'er the thieves will out with their booty
And give to all a happier lot.
Each at the forge must do their duty
And we'll strike while the iron is hot.

Source: Marxists.org: http://www.marxists.org/history/ussr/sounds/lyrics/international.htm.
Lyrics by Eugène Pottier, Paris, June 1871. Music by Pierre Degeyter, 1888.

Figure 4.5.   May Day celebration. The textual halo around the sun calls for "Freedom, Equality, and Brotherhood!"—Germany, 1892. Courtesy of the AsD, Bonn.

Figure 4.6.   Published in 1911 by the Industrial Workers of the World, a radical American trade union organization, the "Pyramid of the Capitalist System" originally appeared in 1872 in the Berlin magazine *Kursbuch*, the "Pyramid of Exploitation." Courtesy of the AsD, Bonn.

Figure 4.7.   "Genocide: The Blessing of Militarism"—Germany, 1912. A poster urging people to vote for the "only party opposed to the arms race and war," the SPD. Courtesy of the AsD, Bonn.

NOTES

1. Karl Marx, *The Civil War in France* (Moscow: Progress Publishers, 1948), 33.

2. Alistair Horne, *The Fall of Paris* (New York: St. Martin's Press, 1965), 424.

3. Karl Marx to Ludwig Kugelmann, 12 April 1871, *Marx-Engels Selected Correspondence*, 3rd ed. (Moscow: Progress Publishers, 1975), 247.

4. Marx, *The Civil War in France*, 71, 78.

5. Quoted in Susanne Miller and Heinrich Potthoff, in *Kleine Geschichte der SPD: Darstellung und Dokumentation, 1848–1990*, 7th ed. (Bonn: Verlag J. H. W. Dietz Nachf., 1991), 47.

6. Mikhail Bakunin, "Revolutionary Catechism," in *Bakunin on Anarchy: Selected Works by the Activist-Founder of World Anarchism*, ed. Sam Dolgoff (New York: Alfred A. Knopf, 1972), 77.

7. Bakunin, "Revolutionary Catechism," 74.

8. Quoted in Trisram Hunt, *Marx's General: The Revolutionary Life of Friedrich Engels* (New York: Metropolitan, 2009), 253.

9. Karl Marx, *Capital: A Critical Analysis of Capitalist Production*, vol. 1, translated from the third German edition by Samuel Moore and Edward Aveling and edited by Frederick Engels (Moscow: Progress Publishers, reprint of the 1887 edition), 19.

10. Karl Marx to Vera Zasulich, 8 March 1881, in Teodor Shanin, *Late Marx and the Russian Road: Marx and "the Peripheries of Capitalism"* (New York: Monthly Review Press, 1983), 124.

11. Quoted in Helen Rappaport, *The Making of a Revolutionary Conspirator: Lenin in Exile* (New York: Basic Books, 2010), 14.

12. Quoted in Shanin, *Late Marx*, 58.

13. Karl Marx to Friedrich Adolph Sorge, 5 November 1880, in *Marx/Engels Collected Works*, vol. 46 (New York: International Publishers, 1975-2004), 42.

14. Friedrich Engels to Eduard Bernstein, 2–3 November 1882, in *Marx/Engels Collected Works*, vol. 46, 353.

15. Fedor Dan quoted in Rappaport, *Making of a Revolutionary Conspirator*, 204.

16. Quoted in Geoff Eley, *Forging Democracy: The History of the Left in Europe, 1850–2000* (Oxford: Oxford University Press, 2002), 100.

17. Quoted in Boxer, "Socialism Faces Feminism: The Failure of Synthesis in France, 1879–1914," in *Socialist Women*, ed. Marilyn J. Boxer and Jean H. Quataert (New York: Elsevier, 1978), 80

18. Quoted in Boxer, "Socialism Faces Feminism," 87.

19. Rosa Luxemburg, "Reform or Revolution," in *Selected Political Writings*, ed. Dick Howard (New York: Monthly Review Press, 1971), 59–60.

20. Julius Braunthal, *Geschichte der Internationale, Bd. 1* (Bonn: J. H. W. Dietz, 1978), 325–26.

FIVE

The Birth of Communism and the Transformation of Socialism, 1914–1945

The outbreak of World War I destroyed the International and precipitated thirty years of upheaval that transformed Europe's political landscape and fundamentally changed what it meant to be a socialist. The war opened the way for the Russian Revolutions of 1917, the emergence of communism, and the permanent division of the labor movement into competing social democratic and communist currents. It also laid the groundwork for counterrevolution and the rise of fascism. By 1940, internecine warfare between Social Democrats and communists and their simultaneous struggle against the forces of conservatism and fascism led to the destruction of organized social democracy in most of Europe. It was able to reemerge only following the victory of the Allied powers, including the Soviet Union, over the fascist states in 1945. By that time, what it meant to be a "socialist" had changed in ways virtually unimaginable to those who had matured in the movement prior to 1914.

WORLD WAR I AND THE COLLAPSE OF THE SECOND INTERNATIONAL

During the first week of August 1914, most of Europe's socialist parties faced the most difficult choice since their founding: should they support their respective states in the slide toward war, or should they, in accordance with the International's principles, "do everything possible" to prevent its outbreak?[1] Party leaders in the belligerent countries agonized but ultimately decided to support their respective governments: first in Germany and then in France, Austria-Hungary, Britain, and Belgium, they turned away from internationalism and voted to grant war credits to their respective governments. Only Serbian and Russian socialists (both Mensheviks and Bolsheviks) said "no." The impact was profound. The International effectively collapsed, and its leading force, the German Social Democratic Party (SPD), lost its credibility. Europe's ruling classes had expected resistance, but their concern proved unwarranted as workers' parties patriotically rallied around their respective flags. To a minority of socialists, however, the decision was a "betrayal" and marked a split in the labor movement. From exile in Galicia, Lenin summed up such feelings most pointedly. On 5 August, after learning of the German decision to support the war, he remarked, "From today I cease to be a social democrat and have become a communist."[2] For some like him, it was now imperative for socialists to distance themselves from the "chauvinists" supporting war and to build a movement committed to revolutionary action.

War had long been a major concern of the International. For many socialists, capitalism and war were inextricably intertwined. Despite a generation of European peace, intense competition among the colonial powers, an arms race on land and sea, the Russo-Japanese War of 1905, and the establishment of the Triple Alliance (Germany, Austria-Hungary, and Italy) and its rival the Triple Entente (France, England, and Russia) made conflict seem inevitable. Some socialists, such as Hilferding and Lenin, believed that war could be a catalyst for proletarian revolution. Paradoxically, however, many of them also were fervent opponents of war and hoped that workers could hinder its outbreak. To that end, the International's Stuttgart Congress of 1907 had unanimously supported a resolution—written by a subcommittee that included Bebel, Jaurès, and Luxemburg, among others—calling on socialists to resist war by all possible means. Failing that, it bound them to fight with all their power to end the war and overthrow capitalism.

Despite this bold language, it was not clear exactly how the member parties should take action. Heated debates regarding the efficacy of agitation, mass demonstrations, and the general strike resulted in no concrete commitments. Socialists proudly organized protests and strikes when aggressive state actions, such as Germany's effort to displace France in Morocco in 1910 and Italy's seizure of Libya in 1911, threatened war, but their effect was hard to discern. From mid-October to the end of November 1912, following the outbreak of war in the Balkans, the International promoted mass protests across Europe and brought the full weight of its organizational machinery to bear in an effort to prevent the intervention of the great powers. This campaign culminated in an extraordinary congress and mass demonstration in Basel, Switzerland, attended by over 550 delegates and tens of thousands of demonstrators. Although little of substance resulted from the gathering, there was much inspired rhetoric, which fueled growing confidence. As the optimistic Jaurès asserted to a friend, "Don't worry, the Socialists will do their duty. Four million German socialists will rise like one man and execute the Kaiser if he wants to start a war."[3]

But when war descended on Europe the following year, most socialists were unprepared to do their duty. It was Jaurès who, on 31 July 1914, was shot down by a nationalist fanatic, while Kaiser Wilhelm II remained unscathed. The International Socialist Bureau in Brussels attempted once again to mobilize demonstrations against the impending war. It tried to move its planned congress from Vienna to Paris and vainly called for international arbitration. All eyes were on Germany in late July, as tens of thousands of workers demonstrated for peace in Berlin, Dresden, Leipzig, and elsewhere, but by the first week of August, events and prowar sentiment overtook the socialists. As recent studies have shown, Europe's workers did not share the enthusiasm for war so widespread among the

Figure 5.1.   Jean Jaurès in 1913. Courtesy of the AsD, Bonn.

middle classes. Impressed by the growing chauvinism in the streets, however, and fearful of opposing what the government called a "defensive" war against Russian aggression, the German socialist leaders, like their counterparts almost everywhere, capitulated.

A variety of factors shaped this decision. Many German party and trade union leaders, for example, feared the state's ability to crush their organizations and wipe out the accomplishments of the past twenty years. Most of the new generation of social democratic leaders were used to working within the system and had risen through the movement's institutions as administrators, journalists, organizers, and parliamentarians. They regarded ideas such as a general strike, especially one that crossed national borders, as impractical and dangerous. To challenge the state head-on seemed foolhardy.

Patriotic and nationalist sentiments were also important. Most socialist leaders believed that nations had the right to self-defense and had never really accepted Marx and Engels's assertion in *The Communist Manifesto* that workers had no country. This was especially true among the French, for whom patriotism was a strong element of their revolutionary tradition. For leaders like Jaurés, there was no contradiction between the respect and cooperation embodied in socialist internationalism and a commitment to defend the republic against reactionary internal or external enemies. Most German socialists also harbored strong patriotic feelings despite their second-class status under the monarchy. Many were proud of the nation's achievements and longed for equality in a democratized Germany. They, too, were willing to defend their country against attack and to prove their worth as citizens. Moreover, just as French socialists had not forgotten the humiliation of 1870 and regarded Germany's monarchy as a threat to French civilization, German socialists, echoing Marx and Engels's own views, felt that it was their duty to fight against Russia, Europe's most reactionary power.

For many revisionists, such as the German parliamentarian Edward David (1863–1930) and party cochair Friedrich Ebert (1871–1925), the war presented a great opportunity. In return for socialist sacrifices at the front, they expected sweeping changes that would eliminate the three-class electoral system in Prussia, introduce wide-ranging social reforms, and grant the trade unions collective bargaining rights and a greater say in economic decision making. Others reveled in the freedom to promote national rather than international aims. Such sentiments had been percolating among certain revisionists for some time. Joseph Bloch (1871–1936), veteran editor of the revisionist *Sozialistische Monatshefte* (*Socialist Monthly*), had long supported protectionist trade policies and German imperial expansion. Now the war gave full flower to such views as right-wing socialists such as David, Albert Südekum (1871–1944), and Max Cohen-Reuss (1876–1963) increasingly emphasized "national" rather than social democracy. Germany's attack on neutral Belgium, its invasion of France, and an extensive list of annexationist war aims did not alter these leaders' support for the government.

Meanwhile, French and English socialists were no less patriotic. In August, the French Section of the International (SFIO) entered a broad coalition government to save the republic, and the British Labor Party followed suit early in 1915. Given Austrian and German military aggression, it was relatively easy for them to stand for the defense of democracy against Prussian tyranny, though their alliance with tsarist Russia tarnished such claims. In February 1915, Belgian, French, and British socialists (along with Russian Socialist Revolutionaries [SRs]) convened in London to condemn their former comrades in the opposing camp, to call for the liberation of Belgium and the self-determination of occupied lands, and to equate Germany's defeat with the victory of freedom and democracy. For their part, the Germans, Austrians, and Hungarians met in Vienna two months later and, while silent about the occupation of Alsace, Belgium, and Serbia, also supported self-determination and stressed the right of all countries to defend their independence.

Meditation efforts by socialist parties in neutral countries fell on deaf ears. Prompted by the American Socialist Party, a call went out to members of the International to send representatives to Copenhagen in January 1915. Socialists in the belligerent states refused to participate, and only delegates from Scandinavia, Holland, and the Jewish Bund appeared. Aside from issuing resolutions appealing to all the warring parties to return to their prewar principles, the conference accomplished nothing.

In the face of the continued bloodletting, however, the Italian Socialist Party (PSI), the Swiss, and others made new attempts to pull together forces opposed to the war. The Italian occupation of Libya in 1911 had radicalized the PSI. In an unusual move for any prewar socialist party, it expelled its proimperialist right wing and embarked on a path of confrontation with the state. Perceiving the aggressive nature of the Austrian and German war effort, the PSI resisted Italy's entrance into the war. In May 1915, when the government decided to abandon the Triple Alliance and, in return for territorial spoils, to fight with the Entente, the PSI mobilized opposition in the streets. Although this effort failed and the party retreated to a "neutral" stance toward the government's policy, it also continued to seek out international allies against the war. It took the lead in organizing an antiwar conference in Zimmerwald, Switzerland, in September 1915.

By that time, opposition to the war was growing. Although no major divisions emerged among the socialist parties within the Entente, in Germany matters were very different. Following the outbreak of war, the SPD had joined the government sponsored Burgfrieden, or "civil peace," that, in the name of national unity, set aside class struggle. Unity eroded, however, as casualty lists lengthened and it became clear that the government's claim to be fighting a "defensive" war was fraudulent. In August 1914, despite the opposition of fourteen members, the SPD's 110 Reichstag delegates had bowed to party discipline and voted unanimously for war credits. One year later, one-third defied the party and voted "no." Despite the majority's anger, left-wing activists such as Liebknecht, supported by the imprisoned Luxemburg, began systematic agitation against the war. In June 1915, over 1,000 party and union officials petitioned the SPD executive committee, criticizing the "imperialist" war and calling for a new policy. They were joined by leaders of the party center, such as Kautsky, and Cochair Hugo Haase (1863–1919), and even some revisionists, such as Bernstein, who criticized government repression and the Burgfrieden. Stopping short of outright opposition to the war, they called for a negotiated peace without annexations.

Division also plagued the thirty-eight "official" delegates of dissident groups who assembled at Zimmerwald. Stemming from Russia (Bolsheviks, Menshevik Internationalists, and the left-wing of the SRs), Germany, Bulgaria, Italy, Switzerland, Romania, France, Sweden, and Holland, most of the participants aimed to restore the unity of the International and to call for a peace rejecting annexations and war indemnities and resting on the principle of national self-determination. For Lenin and a small group of supporters, however, such demands did not go far enough. Arguing that socialists should transform the imperialist war into a civil war against capitalism and for socialism, Lenin insisted that revolutionaries must separate themselves from the treacherous opportunists on the socialist right wing and from the vacillating "social pacifists" of the center, such as Kautsky and Haase, who focused on ending the war rather than making revolution. It was time, he asserted, to found a new revolutionary "Third International."

Lenin's grounded his position in his *Imperialism: The Highest Stage of Capitalism (1916)*. Having read the work of leading theorists such as Hilferding, Luxemburg, J. A. Hobson (1858–1940), and Nicolai Bukharin (1888–1938), Lenin agreed with Hilferding that, during the most recent phase of capitalist development, the process of concentration and centralization had resulted in the merging of bank and industrial capital into "finance capital," which sought investment opportunities around the world and pushed governments to secure markets and sources of raw materials by acquiring colonies and spheres of influence, if necessary by force. But Hilferding thought that imperialist rivalries increased the *likelihood* of war among the capitalist powers (and, therefore, also the possibility of proletarian revolution); Lenin believed that war was *inevitable*. Consequently, World War I was not the result of one side or the other being "right" or "wrong" in 1914 but rather the result of contradictions within capitalism. Moreover, Lenin held that, by extracting massive profits from around the world, capital was able to placate a section of the working class and its leadership with higher wages and better living conditions.

The creation of a "labor aristocracy" fueled the rise of reformism in the workers' movement and explained the attitude of the socialist leadership in 1914.

Only seven of the Zimmerwald delegates supported Lenin's viewpoint. The majority opted for a manifesto, written by Leon Trotsky, condemning the war and the Burgfrieden and calling on workers to demand a negotiated peace without annexations or indemnities. Such demands made no headway, however, as the war continued, social conditions in the belligerent states declined, and political tensions rose. All the warring states found it necessary to combine the rhetoric of unity and patriotism with a sharp curtailment of civil freedoms, suppression of opposition, and the strict regimentation of labor. Governments drafted millions of workers for the front, and millions more, including many unskilled rural migrants and women, flowed into booming war industries. Needed by the state and the military, organized labor's influence grew, but many workers, whether skilled members of the prewar unions or unskilled, inexperienced new arrivals, did not perceive this enhanced power as an advantage. In many countries, anger over massive casualties and frustration with falling real wages, shortages (especially of food), and increasing labor burdens fueled a growing militancy that union leaders found difficult to control.

As discontent intensified, strike activity rose. In France, for example, the number of strikes increased from 341 in 1916 (41,000 workers) to 696 in 1917 (294,000). In Germany, the escalation was especially sharp. Few strikes occurred in 1914, but by 1916 there were massive actions, such as the 300,000-strong Berlin metalworkers' strike in April. In January 1918, as many as 4 million German, Austrian, and Hungarian workers struck in protest against economic hardships and, increasingly, against the war.

Against this background, a second antiwar conference convened in Kienthal, Switzerland, in April 1916. The forty-six delegates at this meeting represented essentially the same groups that had participated at Zimmerwald, but they now struck a more radical tone. Indeed, while still rejecting Lenin's standpoint, they sharply criticized the majority socialists' support for the war and the International's passivity. Lenin won only a few more backers at Kienthal, but it seemed that attitudes were shifting. This trend continued as the war dragged on.

THE RUSSIA REVOLUTIONS OF 1917

The year 1917 was decisive for the socialist movement. In January, the SPD leadership expelled the antiwar opposition, thus consummating a split that had long been in the making. By April, the dissidents had regrouped to form the Independent Social Democratic Party of Germany (USPD). The party contained some antiwar revisionists, such as Bernstein; a larger and rather variegated "centrist" group, including Kautsky, Hilferding, and Haase; and a small radical left, organized in the Spartacus League, led by Liebknecht and Luxemburg. This division of Europe's leading socialist party was the first of many soon to follow. They would be precipitated by events in Russia, where the collapse of tsardom opened the way for the victory of Bolshevism and Lenin's political program.

Among the great powers, Russia was the most unprepared for war in 1914. The process of casting aside the remnants of feudalism was incomplete, and although the country's industrial base had grown, it remained poor and agricultural with a massive and largely illiterate peasantry, an underdeveloped transportation infrastructure, and a government dominated by the inept Tsar Nicholas II, his wife Alexandra, and bizarre characters in the royal entourage, such as the "holy man," Rasputin. The decade prior to 1914 had been turbulent. Failure to respond to the social and political needs of the people, defeat in the Russo-Japanese War, and repression—culminating in the shooting down of hundreds of peaceful protesters in St. Petersburg on 9 January 1905 (Bloody Sunday)—had unleashed a popular revolution that almost toppled the regime. Only the tsar's reluctant granting of a constitution, including an elected parliament (the Duma), along with harsh repression, prevented collapse, but it did not resolve Russia's problems. Nicholas chafed under the new system, scaled back its democratic elements, and asserted his autocratic prerogatives. Unrest continued, manifested most clearly by the SRs' unremitting terror campaign against government officials, the alienation of even the propertied classes from the crown, and growing worker militancy.

War brought even greater social polarization. By late 1916, German and Austrian armies stood deep in Russian territory, millions of soldiers had been killed or wounded, there were serious shortages of military and civilian goods, and the black market and speculation fueled rampant corruption. Unwilling to cooperate with the liberal-dominated Duma and a failure on the battlefield, Nicholas lost support. Tensions escalated as the masses, rather than the propertied, bore the brunt of the sacrifices. Petrograd experienced numerous strikes and bread riots in January and February; at one point, 30,000 workers in the giant Putilov munitions plant—Europe's largest factory—downed tools. Matters came to a head on 23 February 1917, International Women's Day, when women in Petrograd (formerly St. Petersburg) launched protests against high bread prices that suddenly turned into a general strike involving 200,000 workers—half the city's industrial workforce—within twenty-four hours. Underground socialist activists had planned a day of leafleting and public events, but protesters' anger transformed these limited actions into a movement against the war and the government. The police lost control of the unrest. Ordered to fire on the crowds, local army and naval units mutinied and joined the insurgents. With Petrograd in the hands of armed rebels, Nicholas hoped to mobilize frontline soldiers to march on the city, but his generals demurred. Isolated and in despair, he abdicated on 2 March.

It was now unclear where power would lie as two centers of political authority emerged. On 27 February, workers and soldiers created the Petrograd Soviet of Workers' and Soldiers' Deputies. Soviets were councils of representatives—subject to immediate recall—elected by workers in their enterprises and soldiers in their units; later they spread to the countryside. A form of grassroots democracy, this revolutionary innovation had first appeared in Petrograd during the Revolution of 1905. Initially dominated by the Mensheviks and SRs, the revived Petrograd Soviet sent emissaries to other cities, and the movement grew quickly. It did not, however, demand full political power. During the first week of March, when the bourgeois parties of the Duma created a provisional government under the liberal Prince Lvov, the soviet acquiesced. Rather than take power, it aimed to keep a sharp eye on the policies of the new government and to make sure that they conformed to workers and soldiers' interests. Over time, its executive committee added representatives from around the country and in June convened an All-Russian Congress of Soviets in Petrograd. Thus, soviet power became a national force.

It quickly became clear that the Petrograd Soviet and the Provisional Government were operating at cross-purposes. When, for example, the latter tried to reestablish the authority of military officers over their units, the soldiers in the ranks, who often mistrusted their tsarist superiors, resisted. In response to this sentiment, on 1 March the Petrograd Soviet issued "Order No. 1," which asserted that soldiers did not have to obey any command not approved by the soviet. Since the soldiers were armed and the government was not, it soon became clear where the real power lay.

The Provisional Government consisted of representatives of Russia's business and landed elite. Most of them, such as Pavel Miliukov (1859–1943), leader of the Constitutional Democrats (Kadets), had wanted a reformed monarchy and feared popular revolution. Now that the latter was on them, they implemented wide-ranging but still limited liberal reforms. They introduced a full range of civil liberties, the right to strike, and the democratization of local governance but deferred any far-reaching social reforms, especially regarding the distribution of land, until a constituent assembly had approved a new constitution. Lvov's government also insisted on meeting the tsarist regime's commitment to the Allies and continuing the war.

The Petrograd Soviet, by contrast, stood under the influence of the socialist parties. They saw the government's reforms as steps toward more far-reaching social changes, although, as we will see, they often disagreed about their character and the speed of their implementation. They were also divided, between and among themselves, about the war.

Some Mensheviks and SRs saw it as a necessary defensive struggle. Others, such as the Menshevik Internationalists, the left-wing SRs, and the Bolsheviks opposed it altogether. While all the factions joined in the fight against the monarchy, they drifted apart once the dust had cleared and the struggle to shape the new order had begun.

As Ronald Suny has argued, the upheavals of 1917 were actually a series of overlapping revolutions. These included the February rebellion of workers and soldiers that overthrew the monarchy and established two centers of authority in the country. Within this system of "dual power," the lower classes tended to look to the soviets to represent their interests, while the middle classes, the landlords, the officer corps, the bureaucracy, and the educated identified with the Provisional Government. From March to October, the forces supporting the latter attempted to carry out a liberal revolution but were stymied by a renewed wave of worker unrest that resulted in the victory of "soviet power" under Bolshevik leadership. Meanwhile, a massive peasant revolt destroyed the nobles' power in the countryside and redistributed land in favor of smallholders. Finally, revolts among the non-Russian peoples shattered the unity of the former empire and led to the founding of new states in Poland, Ukraine, Georgia, and elsewhere.

After the tsar's fall, thousands of exiles returned to this revolutionary maelstrom. Among them were many socialists back from Siberia, Western Europe, and, even, as in Trotsky's case, New York. All of them were eager to work for revolution but none more so than Lenin. Isolated in Switzerland at the Revolution's outbreak, he and a few supporters used the German government's desire to stir up trouble in Russia to arrange transportation back to his homeland. After traveling through Germany in a sealed train, Lenin arrived in Petrograd, via Sweden and Finland, on 3 April. Greeted at the station by a large crowd of well-wishers from across the socialist spectrum, he immediately gave a series of speeches—one from the back of an armored car—calling for the overthrow of capitalism and the transfer of power from the Provisional Government to the soviets. "The people needs peace; the people needs bread, the people needs land," he asserted, "[The Provisional Government] gives you war, hunger and no bread. [It] leaves the landlords on the land. . . . We must fight for the social revolution; fight to the end, to the complete victory of the proletariat. Long live the world social revolution!"[4] His audience was stunned. Almost all Mensheviks and Bolsheviks had accepted Plekhanov's idea that a bourgeois democratic revolution and a prolonged period of capitalist development had to precede a proletarian revolution in Russia. Now, only five weeks after the overthrow of the tsar, Lenin was telescoping the bourgeois-democratic phase of this process immediately into the proletarian one.

Lenin's standpoint derived from his understanding of the situation in Russia and wartime Europe. In his view, the Russian proletariat, not the weak bourgeoisie, had toppled the old regime. With the economy in chaos, the war grinding on, and class struggle intensifying, he now adopted a position similar to the concept of "permanent revolution" developed much earlier by Trotsky. The workers, Lenin now believed, should not give up the power they had achieved in the soviets but should press ahead, in alliance with the poor peasants, to crush the bourgeoisie and overturn capitalism. This was the class war he had urged socialists to lead at Zimmerwald and Kienthal. It would start in Russia but succeed only if it sparked revolution across Europe. The war, fueling social tensions everywhere, made that a real possibility. Like all other Marxists, Lenin did not believe that socialism could be built in isolation even in the most developed countries. It was all the more unlikely to succeed in backward Russia if the revolution failed to spread.

The day after his arrival, Lenin presented his "April Theses" to the party's Central Committee. These amounted to a program calling for the transfer of political power to the soviets, Russia's immediate withdrawal from the war, land to the peasants, and the creation of a new revolutionary international. A political masterstroke, the program enabled the Bolsheviks to differentiate themselves from all other groups. It was unambiguously against an unpopular war, and its call for land to the peasants co-opted the main plank of the SRs' political platform. By demanding all power to the soviets, the Bolsheviks proclaimed their faith in the workers' ability to master Russia's problems. Finally, by presenting the Russian Revolution as part of a larger international movement, they inspired hope and the will to act among growing numbers of supporters.

It is important to recognize that, prior to taking power, the Bolshevik Party was not a dictatorship. Organized according to the principles of "democratic centralism," the party expected members to adhere to the decisions of higher bodies, such as the party congress and the Central Committee it elected, but it allowed for substantial internal debate. Lenin's theses initially encountered widespread opposition. For example, Lev Kamenev and Joseph Stalin (1878–1953), editors of the party's newspaper, *Pravda (Truth)*, had taken a conciliatory line toward the Provisional Government in March. Now the paper openly criticized his views, and the Central Committee voted thirteen to five to reject them. Lenin refused to capitulate and after a few weeks of relentless effort managed to win a majority. He even persuaded some non-Bolshevik revolutionaries. Trotsky, who had long hovered between the factions and had criticized Bolshevik centralism, joined the party and immediately became a key figure.

Events soon unfolded to the Bolsheviks' advantage. As noted above, initially most workers were not interested in directly governing Russia, and the Petrograd Soviet's wary toleration of the Provisional Government reflected that view. Instead, workers wanted to gain more control over their lives. They organized new unions and elected factory committees to represent their interests, get rid of hated foremen, and maintain production. They did not expropriate the capitalists but aimed to establish "workers' control" over management. In March, they won substantial pay raises and a reduction in daily working hours from ten to eight. Soon, however, inflation wiped out the wage gains, and industrialists tenaciously resisted new increases. Between March and October, prices doubled, food and other commodities became scarce, and unemployment increased as many plants closed due to raw material shortages or because owners, reacting to worker militancy or unable to make profits, shut them down. In response, factory committees often stepped in to keep enterprises open and maintain employment.

On the land, too, tensions ran high. Peasants expected the Provisional Government to redistribute land from the big landlords to those who tilled it. When the state procrastinated, they took the initiative and in May began attacking manor houses and seizing land. In keeping with rural traditions, the leadership of the village communes generally oversaw the land reallocation process. Individual land seizures were more the exception than the rule.

The unrest in the countryside also had important implications for the army, as millions of peasant soldiers chafed at the continuation of the war. Like their brethren back in the villages, most saw the revolution as a means to achieve peace and land. As it became clear that the Provisional Government intended to continue the war, morale fell, insubordination increased, and the number of desertions rose. As the wave of land seizures gained steam in the late spring and summer, it became increasingly difficult to hold the army together.

With the exception of Alexander Kerensky (1881–1970), a well-known lawyer and secret SR who served as minister of justice, no socialist parties initially were willing to join the Provisional Government, but this attitude changed as the latter lurched from one crisis to the next. In March, for example, Foreign Minister Miliukov resigned in the face of mass protests against his policy of fulfilling Russia's military commitment to the Entente and achieving Russian control of Constantinople and the Dardanelles. Concerned about a conservative coup, the Petrograd Soviet allowed the Mensheviks and SRs to join a coalition with the liberals in early May.

Although the socialists were a minority in the new government, their sharing of responsibility for the country's welfare played into the hands of the Bolsheviks, who remained firmly in the opposition. For example, in mid-June, the new war minister, Kerensky, backed by the coalition, launched an offensive that was simply beyond the army's strength. The resulting fiasco led to a major German advance, fueled mass desertions, strained the economy to the breaking point, and allowed the Bolsheviks to exploit the resulting social and political crises. In Petrograd, the central locus of revolutionary action, the party's membership increased from

2,000 in early March to 40,000 in July; nationwide, it rose from 25,000 to 240,000. With Petrograd's workers concentrated in large industrial plants, Bolshevik worker-agitators were well placed to criticize the government. In the army and navy, too, and especially among troops in the Petrograd garrison and the nearby Kronstadt naval base, their antiwar message won many adherents.

The growing popularity of the Bolsheviks' political demands soon became evident on Petrograd's streets. On 18 June, a giant rally of 400,000 people called for soviet power and an end to the war. By early July, the government seemed poised to collapse. Between 3 and 5 July, huge demonstrations of workers, soldiers, and sailors brought half a million people into the streets. Bolshevik activists initially urged insurrection, but the party leaders soon realized that they were unprepared and retreated. When the crowds arrived at their headquarters, Lenin told them to exercise restraint, and when they marched to the Tauride Palace, where the Petrograd Soviet met, its leaders ignored their demand to take power. Soon the Provisional Government restored order with the arrival of fresh troops.

The "July Days" were a disaster for the Bolsheviks. The party appeared to be indecisive, and Lenin, accused in the press of being a German agent, lost credibility. The government blamed the Bolsheviks for the disorder and arrested a number of their leaders, including Trotsky. Many went into hiding, and Lenin, disguised as a workman, escaped over the border into Finland. For a moment, it appeared that the Bolsheviks' prospects were wrecked and that the Provisional Government would survive.

But Bolshevik fortunes quickly revived. In late July, Kerensky became prime minister of a fractious coalition in which the socialists felt the leftward pull of radicalized workers and the liberals felt the rightward pull of conservative elites. Kerensky's efforts to round up the Bolsheviks and restore order in the military inspired little confidence among elite groups anxious to reassert their authority. In late August, the reactionary commander in chief of the army, General Lavr Kornilov (1870–1918), decided to save the country by marching on Petrograd and establishing a military regime. Popular among religious and business leaders, Kornilov apparently thought that he had Kerensky's support, but he had miscalculated. The prime minister mobilized the city's defenses by granting a general amnesty and arming 13,000 "Red Guards" from the factories. Emerging from prison and the underground, the Bolsheviks energetically helped prepare Petrograd's defense. As Kornilov's troops approached, however, railway workers blocked their advance, and metalworkers from the capital convinced them that their mission was unnecessary. As a result, they surrendered before any major engagement had occurred.

Kerensky had survived, but the balance of forces in Petrograd had fundamentally changed. With the Germans advancing, the army leadership discredited, the economy in free fall, and social tension between the poor and the rich peaking, the public increasingly blamed all the parties of the coalition, including the moderate socialists. The Bolsheviks' popularity, however, soared. Over the summer, their support in the municipal Dumas of Petrograd, Moscow, and other cities had steadily increased. On 31 August, for the first time, they won a majority in the Petrograd Soviet. A week later, they repeated this feat in Moscow. Russia's workers were growing more radical as the divided government failed to address their needs.

From Finland, Lenin bombarded the Central Committee with letters urging it to prepare for an immediate insurrection. Once again, however, many Bolshevik leaders vacillated, fearing to take unnecessary risks when the momentum was going their way. Lenin returned to Russia in early October but, fearing arrest, remained in hiding. On 10 October, after a heated debate in the Central Committee, a ten-to-two majority voted in favor of insurrection. The two dissenters, Kamenev and Zinoviev, were so concerned about workers' opposition to a violent seizure of power and the slim chances of the revolution's spread that they published a letter of protest. Having tipped the Bolsheviks' hand, the letter forced the party to act.

It was well placed to take the initiative. With Trotsky now the chairman of the Petrograd Soviet, the Bolsheviks controlled its Military Revolutionary Committee (MRC), which had been set up to mobilize armed workers against counterrevolution. This body was closely connected with other military forces in the city, including the Red Guards, now 23,000 strong. The MRC played a central role in convincing other military forces to either join the revolution or remain neutral. Trotsky, a magnificent orator, also brought key units, such as the garrison at the Peter and Paul Fortress, over to the Bolsheviks' side. Headquartered in the Smolny Institute (which also housed the soviet), the Bolshevik leaders, at Trotsky's urging, timed the uprising to begin on 24 October, one day prior to the opening of the Second All-Union Congress of Soviets. Although Kerensky had ordered the party leaders arrested, MRC troops quickly occupied the telegraph offices, railway and power stations, and key government buildings. Armed units controlled the streets and surrounded the Winter Palace, where the Provisional Government was in session.

Outnumbered by about ten to one, Kerensky's troops resisted feebly. On 25 October, under the guns of the cruiser *Aurora* and encircled by superior forces, the Women's Battalion of Death defending the Winter Palace surrendered, and Red Guards arrested the government. Kerensky had escaped earlier in an American embassy car, but his efforts to rally loyal troops floundered. Although the insurrection was virtually bloodless in Petrograd, in Moscow the fighting lasted a week and cost over 1,000 casualties. In other cities, such as Kiev, and in many rural areas, it took Soviet forces much longer to assert their authority, but in Petrograd and Moscow, the issue was not long in doubt.

When the Second Congress of Soviets convened on 25 October, the Bolsheviks aimed to use it to legitimize their actions. Of the 670 delegates, 300 were Bolsheviks, but together with the left-wing SRs, they controlled a majority. Since fourteen of the twenty-two members on the presidium were Bolsheviks, including Lenin, Trotsky, Kamenev, and Zinoviev (now back in the party's good graces), they dominated the tumultuous proceedings. Initially, the Congress voted to form an all-socialist coalition government, but after furiously criticizing the Bolsheviks' actions, the Mensheviks and right-wing SRs walked out. The radical majority then voted to transfer power to the soviets. Shortly thereafter, Lenin appeared to issue a Decree on Peace, calling for an immediate armistice, and a Decree on Land, nationalizing agricultural lands and charging local peasant soviets with implementation. They passed with virtually no opposition.

The Congress then created a new government, the Council of People's Commissars (Sovnarkom). When the left-wing SRs, desiring a broader socialist coalition, refused to join with them, the Bolsheviks opted to go it alone. Lenin assumed the chairmanship. Trotsky became minister of foreign affairs; Stalin, nationalities; Alexander Schliapnikov (1885–1937), labor; Anatoly Lunacharsky (1875–1933), education; and Aleksei Rykov (1881–1938), interior. Although nominally subordinate to the Executive Committee of the All Russian Council of Soviets, the Sovnarkom, guided by the Bolshevik Party, became the decisive body. The Bolsheviks had seized power; it remained to be seen how they would use it.

REVOLUTIONARY CHANGE AND THE COMING OF CIVIL WAR

The Bolsheviks won control of the state because their leaders, Lenin in particular, were prepared to fill the power vacuum that had developed as Russia's elites lost legitimacy, class war intensified, and the country's institutions crumbled. Well organized and disciplined compared to their rivals, they grasped what the people wanted and promised to meet their needs. By the fall, they enjoyed genuine popularity in Russia's main cities and, riding this wave of support, skillfully acquired the means to challenge the Provisional Government directly and decisively. Unlike their comrades in the West, the Bolsheviks were willing to act.

They had few blueprints, however, to guide them in the construction of a new society. No socialists had ever controlled a national government before. Aside from a list of transitional steps stressing the role of the state in *The Communist Manifesto*, Marx's pamphlet on the Paris Commune, and a few other scattered writings, Marx and Engels had mainly analyzed capitalist development and tried to avoid setting up "utopian" models for the future. They provided few clues about what socialism might look like. Socialism's programmatic documents, such as the *Erfurt Program*, also focused on the movement's goals under capitalism and were of little help in guiding a revolutionary transition. As we have noted, in the nineteenth century, many socialists stressed the importance of cooperatives, but with the rise of large-scale commercial and industrial corporations, thinkers such as Kautsky and Hilferding stressed the role of the democratic state in taking over and managing the highly concentrated core sectors of the economy. This approach to "socialization" did not exclude cooperatives or even small-scale private property, but it remained unclear how the different parts of the economy would function as a whole. Generally, socialists looked forward to a world in which meeting human needs through planned, cooperative production replaced competitive individualism and profit making as social priorities. They envisioned a society in which material and political equality, democracy, and the rights of the individual were axiomatic, thus making it possible for every person to freely and fully develop his or her personality. How to achieve such goals through the development of specific policies was anybody's guess, especially in underdeveloped Russia.

Lenin had some ideas. While in Finland, he had sketched out a vision for the transition to communism, drawing on the most radical and utopian elements of Marxism. Published in November 1917 as *State and Revolution*, his pamphlet argued that the coercive nature of the capitalist state necessitated its violent overthrow by armed workers. Like previous ruling classes, once in power, the workers would then implement what Marx called "the dictatorship of the proletariat," using the state (i.e., the soviets) to suppress their opponents, but they would simultaneously destroy the basis of class society and political oppression by abolishing capitalism, creating a planned economy (which Lenin likened to running the post office), and establishing a system of self-administration based on mass participation in all aspects of governance. The transition to communism would occur in two phases: the lower, or socialist, phase would still bear the scars of the old system as capitalism was dismantled and the new order arose. During that period, wage labor, the state, and therefore politics would still exist, but society would be much more democratic and egalitarian. As productivity increased and people mastered the self-administration of social production, society would enter into a higher, or communist, phase of development in which material want and the division of labor would disappear and political coercion—even in its democratic form—would no longer be necessary. The state, as Engels put it, would "wither away" and be supplanted by simple administration.

The pragmatic Lenin certainly viewed such goals as belonging to the distant future. But *State and Revolution* was a polemic asserting that violent insurrection and state coercion were necessary to secure workers' power. It provided a clear sense of the radical ideals driving Lenin and his comrades. The Bolsheviks wanted power in 1917 not for its own sake; they meant to fundamentally change the world and were prepared to take ruthless action to achieve their aims.

Once formed, the Sovnarkom attempted to make good on the Bolsheviks' promises to the Russian people while also implementing reforms in keeping with traditional socialist aims. Soon, however, they also found themselves taking actions that undermined those very goals. Ultimately, these contradictory developments, shaped by Russia's economic and political circumstances, civil war, foreign intervention, and the changing nature of the Bolshevik Party, resulted in the construction of a new order bearing little resemblance to the one described in *State and Revolution*.

Following the Congress of Soviets, the Sovnarkom quickly introduced "workers' control" into all factories with more than five employees, took over the state bank, nationalized the private banks, annulled Russia's foreign debt, and assumed control over foreign trade. Many of these economic actions took place on an ad hoc basis in reaction to popular pressure and the need to respond to rapidly changing conditions. The overall trend was toward the centralization of economic power in the state's hands.

Figure 5.2. Lenin in his study reading *Pravda*, early 1920s. Courtesy of the AsD, Bonn.

In the social sphere, the government abolished all civil and social ranks and privileges that had favored the nobility and the rich. It declared the equality of all ethnic groups and religions, proclaimed women's equality, and implemented measures eliminating child "illegitimacy," easing divorce, secularizing marriage, legalizing abortion, and improving women's status in the workplace. Although the rather Victorian and overwhelmingly male Bolshevik leaders eschewed radical ideas regarding the abolition of the family and "free love," they created a special department to address women's issues and appointed the socialist feminist Alexandra Kollantai (1872–1952) as people's commissar for social welfare. As Europe's first female government minister, she put the creation of communal nurseries and clinics for children on the political agenda.

To consolidate the revolution's authority, the Sovnarkom merged municipal and regional governments into the soviets, abolished the old judicial system, and set up new revolutionary tribunals in which trained judges sat with lay representatives to dispense justice. It separated church and state and asserted its control over the often hostile bureaucracy by forbidding strikes and fixing salaries. In the army, it did away with all signs of rank and institutionalized soldier's election of their officers.

These changes illustrated the Bolsheviks' commitment to the egalitarian and democratic transformation of Russian life, but it soon became clear that they were unwilling to promote such aims if their power were threatened. In mid-November 1917, Russians elected a Constituent Assembly to write a new constitution. Although the Bolsheviks won in the main cities, they did poorly in the countryside and emerged with only 25 percent of the total vote. The SRs, having won 40 percent, were in a position to control the Assembly when it convened on 18 January. In response, after one day of deliberations, the Bolsheviks deployed Red Guards to close it down. As justification, Lenin claimed that the electoral lists, drawn up before the October revolution and the split of the SRs, were invalid, but such claims were disingenuous. In reality, the Bolsheviks saw it as a necessary action of the proletarian dictatorship, which, anticipating world revolution at any moment, it was their duty to maintain.

Lenin had opposed creating an all-socialist coalition in October, but the sobering results of the Constituent Assembly elections convinced him of the need to broaden the government's political base by working with the Left SRs. The latter now agreed to enter the cabinet with responsibility for the agricultural, justice, and postal ministries. In early December, the coalition established the All-Russian Extraordinary Commission for Struggle Against Counterrevolution, Sabotage, and Speculation (the Cheka), which initially focused on halting the disorder and looting that had followed the seizure of power but soon functioned as a security force ruthlessly combating perceived enemies of the regime.

The elimination of political pluralism did not occur overnight. Initially, the government banned only the bourgeois parties and their press. Other groups remained active in the soviets. Within a short time, however, the forces of the old order began to reorganize and arm themselves. Disaffection spread, even among other socialist parties, as the Sovnarkom implemented its policies. A key catalyst in the move toward civil war was the Bolshevik decision to sign the treaty of Brest-Litovsk with Germany in March 1918. Unable to halt Germany's military advance and determined to secure the revolution even if it meant losing Ukraine, the Baltic States, and Poland, Lenin overcame fierce opposition from within his own party and from the Left SRs, who then abandoned the coalition.

Thereafter, the slide toward civil war was swift. During the spring, conflicts with the Mensheviks and Left SRs intensified. In June, the latter openly declared their opposition to the government, launching a coup attempt in July and a wave of assassinations that claimed the lives of hundreds of Bolshevik officials. In August, Lenin himself was seriously wounded, prompting the Bolsheviks to unleash a terror campaign in which hundreds were executed.

Meanwhile, counterrevolutionary "White" armies, led by former tsarist officers and buttressed by British, French, American, and Japanese forces, organized in Russia's south, in Siberia, and even close to Petrograd. Different nationalist movements in Georgia, Ukraine, and many other regions also attempted to assert their independence. Thus, by the end of the summer of 1918, Russia was in the midst of a complex and brutal civil war in which the Bolsheviks held a relatively small territory surrounding Moscow (now the capital) and Petrograd.

The Bolsheviks responded to these challenges by mobilizing for all-out war. Under Trotsky's leadership, they raised a new "Red" Army of 5 million soldiers drawn from the urban working class and the peasantry. Using former tsarist officers under the political supervision of Bolshevik commissars, Trotsky reinstituted tough discipline and ultimately defeated all of the revolution's military enemies. The key to the Bolsheviks' victory was their ability to hold onto peasant support. Although the peasants were suspicious of their ideas about modernizing agriculture via large-scale industrial farming and resented their efforts to turn poor peasants against their better-off neighbors, the Bolsheviks had sanctioned the breaking of landlord power and the redistribution of land that followed. Since the Whites promised little more than a return to the old order, many peasants supported or at least tolerated the Reds.

To maintain the army, the Bolsheviks centralized state control over the economy. Workers' control gave way to "one-man management," military discipline on the job, and the concentration of production almost solely on military goods. Widespread shortages fueled hyperinflation, and people relied on rationing, barter, and the black market to survive. Reds and Whites forcibly seized grain when necessary for the troops or to

Figure 5.3.   Trotsky Addressing Red Guards. Bain Collection. Library of Congress.

feed the cities. Later referred to as "War Communism," optimistic radicals such as Bukharin believed that these developments cleared the way for the communist future. The reality was very different. While the policy ensured military victory, it consumed the substance of the economy and alienated the people.

By 1920, the Bolsheviks had defeated the Whites and reestablished their control over most of the former empire. Although in theory they supported the right to national self-determination, in practice they used all means, including military force, to place local Bolsheviks in control of "autonomous" governments established in the non-Russian territories. They were largely successful but suffered some defeats. In 1920, for example, the Red Army drove a French-supported Polish invasion back to the gates of Warsaw, but the Poles rallied and ultimately forced Moscow to sign a treaty ceding substantial territory to Poland. Finland, Lithuania, Latvia, and Estonia also secured their independence.

The Bolsheviks were victorious for several reasons. They were united and disciplined, while their enemies failed to coalesce around a single leadership or program. They controlled most industrial areas of the country and effectively used their interior lines of communication and transport. They had superior military and civilian leadership. Willing to use terror, the Bolsheviks knew how to fire the élan of their followers and win mass support. Ironically, they skillfully used nationalism to win over many who resented foreign intervention on behalf of the Whites.

The civil war fundamentally changed Russia's political landscape: the Bolsheviks, now calling themselves the Communist Party, banned all opposition and created a one-party state. The soviets, once vibrant centers of grassroots political life, were now the instruments of a transformed ruling party. From a small underground group headed by Marxist intellectuals, it had become a mass organization of hundreds of thousands, many of whom had sacrificed at the front and served as "cadre" in the military and governmental administration. At all levels, the party had been infused with a military ethos reflected in its uniforms and rhetoric, its concern with discipline, and its focus on action rather than debate. Democratic centralism now meant that decision making and political appointments flowed from the top down and that the space for internal discussion narrowed.

Lenin and the Bolshevik leaders knew that their victory was tenuous. By 1921, the revolution in the west had stalled, while in Russia unrest and misery stalked the land. They had seized power in the name of the proletariat in an overwhelmingly peasant society. Most of the proletariat had abandoned the cities as industrial production fell to 13 percent of the level of 1914 and food supplies disappeared. In the countryside, suffering villagers could not feed the millions of urban refugees, and famine struck wide areas, fueling rebellion. Most tellingly, in March, as the Tenth Party Congress assembled in Petrograd, sailors at the Kronstadt naval base, once a bastion of Bolshevik support, revolted and demanded soviet power without Communists. The Red Army crushed the uprising, and the party intensified internal discipline. Concerns about the subordination of the unions to the party's will and about the decline of internal democracy met with harsh criticism, and Lenin won a "temporary" ban on factions. In addition, it became clear to Lenin that only major concessions to the peasants could end the food crisis and create a basis for economic recovery. As we will see, the introduction of this new economic policy (NEP) would effectively restore Russia's economy and stabilize the dictatorship.

REVOLUTION AND COUNTERREVOLUTION IN THE WEST

In hindsight, it is easy to regard Lenin's expectation of international socialist revolution in 1917 as profoundly mistaken. In the end, the socialist revolution in the west did not take root, and revolutionary Russia remained isolated and surrounded by enemies. However it turned out, Lenin's wager on the coming upheaval was anything but far fetched. Europe did, indeed, stand on the brink of international revolution in which socialists seemed poised to take and hold power. As it had in Russia, the war drove other European nations to the brink of collapse.

Societies became more polarized, and political institutions strained to maintain order while the fighting continued. As we have seen, working-class unrest, manifested in large-scale and frequent strikes, had grown. In the armies, too, there was rising anger. In 1917, tens of thousands of soldiers in the French, Italian, and British armies mutinied or rebelled, and only draconian punishments, including executions and selective concessions, restored discipline. Meanwhile, morale in Germany and Austria-Hungary also declined. In July 1918, after the failure of its last major offensive in France, the German army retreated in the face of superior Allied forces, while on the home front material deprivation intensified and demonstrations against the war became more frequent.

In September, the tottering Austro-Hungarian Empire collapsed as myriad ethnic groups rebelled and established separate states. The German High Command decided that it would be better for a democratic government rather than the country's military leaders to negotiate with the Allies and take the blame for the defeat. In October, under a new chancellor, Prince Max von Baden (1867–1929), the Reichstag passed laws making cabinet ministers responsible to it rather than the Kaiser. At Prince Max's invitation, the SPD, the parliament's largest party, entered the government for the first time. Thus, through a "revolution from above," Germany became a parliamentary democracy.

But the revolution from below was not long in coming. As the new government negotiated with the Allies, the German Admiralty decided to save its honor by sending the fleet to fight the British one last time. The fleet's sailors, however, mutinied. On 4 November, they disarmed the garrison in Kiel, set up a sailors' council, and seized control of the city. Their action sparked a nationwide movement as workers and soldiers took control of towns and cities across the land. On 7 November in Munich, USPD leader Kurt Eisner (1867–1919) proclaimed Bavaria to be a socialist republic. Two days later, as tens of thousands of armed workers and soldiers demonstrated on the streets of Berlin, Karl Liebknecht proclaimed the "socialist republic" from the balcony of the imperial palace. Not far away, however, SPD leader Philippe Scheidemann (1865–1939) proclaimed a "republic" from the balcony of the Reichstag building. Meanwhile, after announcing the Kaiser's abdication, Prince Max handed power over to SPD leader Friedrich Ebert. Ebert then invited the USPD to form a coalition government. On 10 November, 1,500 delegates of the Berlin Workers' and Soldiers' Council approved of this Council of People's Commissars.

Thus, over the course of several weeks, two of Europe's most important empires had collapsed, precipitating the political transformation of central and Eastern Europe. Their demise effectively annulled the Treaty of Brest-Litovsk and paved the way for the emergence of new states, almost all of them parliamentary democracies, and new revolutionary movements. Inspired by the Russian Revolution, many workers in the east and west hoped for fundamental change. Most remained loyal to the old socialist parties, but a substantial minority now joined newly founded communist parties to compete for power.

In March 1919, the communist movement in the west received a boost with the creation of the Third International (the Comintern) in Moscow. Dominated by the Bolsheviks, it put "democratic centralism" into practice on a world scale. According to the "Twenty One Conditions" adopted for admission at its Second Congress in 1920, all member parties had to expel reformists, transform their organizations along Bolshevik lines, and submit to the Comintern's decisions. As a result, supporters of the radical left (usually in the minority) frequently quit the socialist parties to form communist parties. This tactic, pursued by Lenin since 1914, effectively made the rupture of the world socialist movement permanent.

From 1918 until 1920, much of Europe was wracked by turmoil, which in some countries, such as Germany and Italy, continued for several years. During this period, the revolutionary wave crested, but capitalism hung on everywhere. It survived by combining the use of force with the adroit cooptation of parts of the labor movement into the system, a process that succeeded because many socialists regarded it as the most promising way forward. Thus, as Charles Maier has argued, Europe's bourgeoisie was able to "recast" its hegemony while leaving the labor movement with modest and largely ephemeral gains. Local conditions shaped this process as it unfolded in each state. It is beyond the scope of this work to examine it everywhere in detail. Instead, we will identify general trends and key exceptions that explain socialism's trajectory during the interwar period.

Between 1918 and 1921, European socialism essentially split into three separate currents that paralleled the internal divisions of the decade prior to 1914. The largest of these consisted of the old social democratic parties (e.g., the SPD, the SFIO, and the Labor Party) and their trade union allies. These formations had participated in wartime governments and, with the war over, now wished to continue operating within the parliamentary framework. All claimed to desire socialism but were now committed to a reformist approach. They criticized the Bolshevik Revolution, especially its use of terror, and opposed its spread. A second, revolutionary current had regarded opposition to the war as an opportunity to oppose capitalism itself. Most of its members joined the communist movement, while a third group, epitomized by the USPD, took a more "centrist" position. Its myriad adherents supported parliamentary democracy, the socialization of industry, the purging of monarchists from the bureaucracy and the courts, and a place for workers' councils in the new order, but they split about the Bolshevik Revolution, the issue of working in coalition governments, and the strategy going forward.

It was in Germany where the results of this threefold division were most profound. When Ebert, a man who hated revolution "like sin," formed the Council of People's Commissars with the USPD, he had no intention of pursuing radical socialist aims.[5] He wanted to negotiate peace, maintain order, restore civilian production, and carry out elections to a National Assembly to write a new constitution. The SPD implemented some political changes, such as granting equality to women and abolishing the three-class electoral system in Prussia, but, desiring an end to the brutal Allied blockade and fearing invasion and civil war, it resisted more far-reaching changes demanded by the USPD. The latter's radical left wing, organized as the Spartacus League and led by Luxemburg and Liebknecht, wanted a revolution based on the workers' councils. Ebert, thinking of recent Russian events, had no intention of going the way of Kerensky. On the day he took power, he cut a deal with the army's deputy chief of staff, General Wilhelm Groener (1867–1939), to accept military aid in putting down revolutionary unrest. The SPD had thus formed a pact with its former archenemy, the High Command.

A few days later, the socialist unions and the leaders of German industry reached an accord in which the latter recognized workers' right to collective bargaining, dropped their support for company unions, and conceded the eight-hour workday. In return, the unions agreed to accept the existing system of property. From the capitalists' point of view, this arrangement undercut the radicals and secured their continued authority, while the unions were pleased to achieve long-sought-after but not revolutionary goals.

Ebert and his comrades in the party and unions overestimated the danger posed by the workers' and soldiers' councils. Indeed, while a small minority wanted them to serve as the fulcrum of a future socialist republic, when the first Congress of Workers' and Soldiers' Deputies met in Berlin in mid-December, two-thirds of the 500 delegates belonged to the SPD. The Congress voted to socialize industries that were "ripe" for it, to disarm counterrevolutionary forces, and to create a people's militia, but it also supported elections to the National Assembly in January. For half a century, German socialists had argued for parliamentary democracy as a key step toward socialism, and most politicized workers in 1918 held to that goal.

The SPD responded to the Congress's call by moving ahead with elections but stalling on other pressing matters. This policy put it on a collision course with the USPD. In December, when Ebert used troops to quell unrest in Berlin without consultation, the USPD quit the coalition, leaving its rival in full control. Meanwhile, the Spartacus League, frustrated with the indecisive Independents, broke away to form the German Communist Party (KPD) on 31 December. On 5 January, the tiny KPD, together with other radicals, rashly attempted to head off the elections to the National Assembly with an uprising in Berlin. The SPD crushed the rebels using radical anticommunist volunteer units, known as Freikorps. They also captured and brutally murdered Luxemburg and Liebknecht.

Such actions deepened the breech between the SPD and many of its erstwhile comrades on the radical left. Over the next six months, the SPD, using the army and the Freikorps, repeatedly smashed left-wing uprisings in the industrial Ruhr Valley, Bavaria, and elsewhere. In January 1919, the SPD won the most votes to the National Assembly with 37.9 percent, but with the USPD winning only 7.6 percent, the socialist parties lacked a majority to shape the new constitution. Instead, the SPD formed a government with the Catholic Center and the liberal Democratic parties. Together, this "Weimar Coalition" (taking its name from the city in which the Assembly met) forged a constitution that was one of the most democratic in the world, introducing proportional representation, individual civil rights, a range of welfare benefits, and even a limited role for employee councils in German enterprises, but it was not socialist. By securing the rights of property and leaving the German economic and social hierarchy intact, it limited the revolution to the political sphere and allowed the nation's reactionary elites, who chafed at the changes and largely hated the republic, to carry on to fight another day.

Indeed, within a year, the right launched a direct attack against the SPD-led government. Blaming the democrats and socialists for losing the war and, in June 1919, signing the humiliating Treaty of Versailles, in March 1920 conservative politician Wolfgang Kapp, backed by Freikorps troops, seized power in Berlin. When the army refused to move against the rebels, the government fled the capital but called a general strike that won the support of all coalition parties, the USPD, the KPD (after some vacillation), the socialist and Christian unions, and even many conservative state employees. Within days, the economy ground to a halt, and the Putsch collapsed. For a moment, the victory appeared to clear the way for a workers' government, including the SPD, the USPD, and trade union representatives, but this proposal foundered on constitutional objections to the unions' role and friction between the socialist parties. Meanwhile, the SPD again sent the army to crush an uprising of radical workers in the Ruhr. Thus, the socialist left missed a major chance to rebuild unity and implement more thorough reforms of the economy, army, and bureaucracy.

The parliamentary elections of June 1920 illustrated the volatility of the socialist electorate. The USPD more than doubled its support from the year before, while that of the SPD slipped by almost half. Many workers clearly were dissatisfied with the latter's leadership and moved leftward. The USPD, however, was unable to take advantage of its growth. In October, two-thirds of its 900,000 members quit to join the KPD, which became a mass party. Germany now had three substantial socialist parties, and although the rump USPD merged with the SPD in 1922, the rivalry between the Social Democrats and the communists continued. With the left fractured and the antirepublican right regaining momentum, the German revolution was in retreat. The Social Democrats and

their moderate bourgeois allies—whose share of the vote declined steadily—found themselves in a constant defensive struggle against the
counterrevolutionary right and the procommunist left.

In Italy, too, the socialists split under quite different circumstances. In
1918, the antiwar PSI had emerged from the conflict radicalized and united behind a "maximum program" demanding the immediate "institution
of the socialist republic and the dictatorship of the proletariat." Led by
Giacinto Serrati (1874–1926), the maximalists rejected coalition politics
and for the next two "red years" contested elections and supported labor
struggles using the rhetoric of revolution. Party and union membership
surged among urban workers and even among peasants in large areas of
the north. In 1920, with the socialists dominating local and regional elections across northern Italy, large-scale strike activity increasing, and
peasant unrest rising, many among Italy's bourgeoisie expected revolution at any moment.

In reality, however, the PSI was unprepared for revolution. In August
and September, when a lockout of Milanese engineers led 500,000 workers in the metal and other industries to occupy their factories, the PSI
leaders debated whether to transform this movement into a revolutionary one. In the end, they passed the buck to the trade union leaders, who,
in turn, put the matter to their constituents. The latter voted against insurrection. With the socialist leadership paralyzed, the forces of order
regained the initiative. Italy's elites did not hesitate to use the armed
street gangs (*squadristi*) of the growing fascist movement, led by the ex-
socialist turned radical nationalist Benito Mussolini. Soon the socialists
found themselves permanently on the defensive.

As Geoff Eley has argued, the PSI failed because its maximalist leaders
believed in the "automatic Marxism" of the Second International, which
emphasized revolution as the result of "objective" historical development
rather than concrete political action. Turning Marx on his head, Serrati
observed, "We, as Marxists, interpret history; we do not make it."[6] Not
all Italian leaders concurred, of course. Both reformists and Bolshevik
sympathizers demanded action, albeit of a very different kind, and the
PSI soon tore itself apart over the issue. At its January 1921 congress,
however, the pro-Bolshevik minority, headed by Amadeo Bordiga
(1889–1970) and Antonio Gramsci (1891–1937), quit the PSI and formed
the Italian Communist Party. The following year, the maximalists expelled the reformers after the latter advocated forming coalitions with
antifascist groups. After the reformists founded the United Socialist Party, Italy, like Germany, had three rival socialist formations. As they dith-
ered, the fascists acted. Backed by radical nationalists, Italy's propertied
elites, and liberals fearful of the left, in October 1922 Mussolini became
prime minister. After changing the electoral law to favor the Fascist Party, the latter swept the elections of 1924. In 1926, Mussolini banned all

opposition and imprisoned many communist and socialist leaders, including Gramsci. Their defeat was complete.

Unlike Germany and Italy, where the revolutionary tide was powerful, in France and England the situations were very different. In France, there was much working-class unrest after the war, though it never a seriously challenged the state, which was dominated by a coalition of centrist and right-wing parties. The SFIO returned to the opposition but was unable to avoid a split at its Tours Congress of 1920. After a majority quit to form the Communist Party (PCF), the SFIO reverted to its prewar strategy of principled opposition. Over the next decade, it competed successfully with the communists to win back old supporters and recruit new ones, but it did not seek to govern.

In England, by contrast, the Labor Party did not split, and it sought opportunities to govern. Although a British Communist Party formed, it remained a negligible force. Marxism had never struck strong roots in the British labor movement, which maintained close ties to liberalism well into the twentieth century. The war brought the fledgling Labor Party to center stage, as it entered the government and won broad public support. Although Fabian gradualism was its dominant influence, by war's end Labor had moved sharply leftward and attracted workers seeking social justice. Between 1917 and 1920, party membership exploded from 2.5 million to 4.4 million, while that of the trade unions reached 6.5 million. As was the case in all the belligerent states, the British government had played a decisive role in managing the production and distribution of goods through planning, rationing, and coordination of the labor market. This experience convinced many union and party leaders that state power was necessary to ameliorate particular injustices and to build a new society. Unlike the SFIO, Labor was prepared to participate in governance, even without full control.

The first major opportunity presented itself in 1923. After years of postwar economic crises in which the Conservative government had worked to drive down wages to restore British competitiveness, Labor overtook the Liberals to become the second-largest party. Because the Conservatives did not have enough seats to rule alone, Labor leader Ramsey Macdonald (1866–1937) formed a government with Liberal support. It sought to improve workers' housing, increase educational opportunities, and promote employment, while its foreign policy promoted the Dawes Plan, which facilitated Germany's payment of war reparations and helped stabilize its finances. Negotiations to recognize the Soviet Union brought Labor into conflict with the Liberals and forced new elections. Although the Conservatives won, Labor gained over a million votes and reconfigured British politics.

Just as postwar changes in the socialist movements in France and England provide a study in contrasts, so too did the revolutionary wave in the former Austro-Hungarian Empire break in different directions. In

Hungary, for example, in late October 1918, Count Michael Karolyi (1875–1955) led a coalition of nationalists and Social Democrats aiming to introduce social reforms, convene a constituent assembly, and fend off Czech, Romanian, and Yugoslav territorial claims. A land reform program that Karolyi initiated by redistributing his own 50,000-acre estate quickly angered the landed elites, while discontent rose in the face of economic problems caused by reconversion to peacetime production, shortages of raw materials and consumption goods, and rising unemployment. As the trade unions became increasingly involved in economic affairs, interest in establishing workers' control grew, and in late December workers formed councils and organized formations of Red Guards. Amidst rising social tensions, the Treaty of Triannon, ceding three-quarters of Hungary's territory to its neighbors, dealt a mortal blow to Karolyi's cabinet, and he resigned in March 1919.

A new and more radical government then emerged whose dominant figure was Bela Kun (1886–1937), a communist journalist. Proclaiming Hungary a Soviet republic, it nationalized banks, insurance companies, and large industries and undertook the collectivization of agriculture. A Hungarian Red Army invaded Slovakia to spread the revolution, but the regime had overreached. Broad opposition grew as inflation skyrocketed and shortages worsened, while Britain and France, aiming to roll back the revolution, supported a Romanian invasion and a counterrevolutionary government based in Szeged. Faced with mounting internal opposition and invasion, Kun's government imposed a "Red Terror," but without hoped-for military aid from the Bolsheviks, it collapsed as Romanian troops entered Budapest on 31 July. After an interlude of "White Terror," Hungary's resurgent elites created a conservative, pseudoparliamentary regime led by a former Habsburg admiral, Miklos Horthy (1868–1957).

While the postwar Hungary spiraled out of control, Austria's socialists skillfully preserved party unity and worked to maintain order rather than promote social revolution. Under the leadership of Karl Renner (1870–1950) and Otto Bauer (1881–1938), two leading theorists of the Austro-Marxist school, they initially hoped to facilitate Austria's union with Germany. After the Allies blocked that effort, they aimed to secure the national borders and create a democratic republic. Believing that the socialization of the economy could succeed only if carried out in the context of broader international transformation, they reined in radicals calling for the expropriation of industry and a republic based on workers' councils. This caution resembled that of their German counterparts, though they adopted a more radical political rhetoric and, at least initially, a more effective strategy for governance. The Austrian Social Democratic Party (SPÖ) created a liberal democratic constitution and carried out meaningful democratic reforms of the officer corps, the courts, and the police. This combination of radical discourse and democratic reforms allowed the

SPÖ to isolate the small Austrian Communist Party and create a stable but capitalist polity.

In 1920, the party withdrew from the government and reverted to its prewar strategy of principled opposition. Over the next decade, it built one of European socialism's most formidable organizations, providing over 500,000 members with a dense network of political, social, and cultural institutions that created a social democratic world within the wider capitalist one. Regularly winning 40 percent of the national vote, the SPÖ dominated Viennese elections with about 60 percent. On this basis, "Red Vienna" became a model of municipal socialism with progressive taxation funding large-scale, high-quality housing projects for workers, such as the Karl Marx Hof; major investments in social and health services for working-class families; and subsidized kindergartens, recreational, and cultural opportunities. Despite this success, however, the SPÖ was unable to achieve comparable gains on the national level, where it remained out of power. As we will see, this would have far-reaching implications as conditions in Austria changed.

In sum, by the early 1920s it was clear that bourgeois Europe had survived the challenge of radical socialist revolution. Much had changed since 1914. The Russian, German, and Austro-Hungarian empires were gone, and almost all of Europe now enjoyed parliamentary rule in which formerly excluded social democratic parties often participated. Moreover, the once-united socialist movement had fractured into competing currents, a condition reflected in the existence of rival international organizations: the Moscow-controlled Comintern and, after 1923, its revived social democratic counterpart, the Labor and Socialist International, dominated by the SPD. For the Bolsheviks the failure of the revolution to spread meant that the great gamble had failed, at least temporarily, and Lenin and his comrades now had to rethink the future.

NEP RUSSIA AND THE COMING OF STALIN'S REVOLUTION

Marx, Engels, and most other socialist thinkers expected the construction of socialism to build on the historical achievements of capitalism, especially its highly productive industry and agriculture. In 1921, such a project was impossible in isolated, war-torn Russia with its cities virtually empty, its industry in ruins, and the countryside verging on renewed rebellion. Lenin recognized that, in order to hold power and fight another day, the Bolsheviks had to revive the agricultural economy by placating the peasantry. Only then could they restore industry and rebuild the urban proletariat—the core of their political base. To that end, the NEP, introduced in March 1921, created a mixed economy that maintained state control over the "commanding heights" of large-scale industry, transport, and foreign trade but restored market relations in agriculture and small industry. Peasants paid a tax to the state (first in kind, later in cash), but were free to sell any surpluses privately, to employ wage labor, and to sell their grain to middlemen (so-called NEPmen). Thus, in a country in which peasants constituted 80 percent of the population, for most people the NEP marked the restoration of capitalism.

In general, the new policy succeeded. After famine in 1921, within three years grain production returned to the level of 1913, while industrial output recovered more slowly, reaching 88 percent of its prewar peak in 1927. With grain supplies up, the urban population recovered, and a sense of normalcy returned as people more easily carried on with their daily lives. Yet serious problems persisted. Dissatisfied with the high cost and low quality of industrial goods, peasants often withheld grain from the market, either for their own consumption or until prices rose. Such behavior was in their interest, but it hindered the state's ability to supply the towns with food and to sell grain surpluses for much-needed foreign exchange. Many Bolshevik activists also resented the NEP. After the sacrifices of the civil war, it seemed incongruous for the proletarian dictatorship to allow "exploiters" such as NEPmen and richer peasants, called kulaks, to prosper, while unemployment for workers, fueled largely by rural-to-urban migration that outstripped industrial growth, remained relatively high and wages low. They longed for renewed movement toward socialism.

Although the Bolsheviks had relaxed state controls over the economy, they had no intention of easing their grip on power. Rival political parties remained suppressed, and in 1922 Lenin supported the arrest and deportation of hundreds of "enemy" intellectuals. To "break" the power of the Orthodox Church, he urged the seizure of its wealth and the arrest and even the execution of "a very large number" of its local leaders, and he did nothing to empty the 107 labor camps established during the Red Terror to incarcerate "class enemies." After the civil war, the Cheka, rechristened as the GPU, continued to root out opposition.

Yet, despite the one-party dictatorship, the NEP period emerged as one of relative cultural freedom and creativity. The Bolsheviks recognized that they needed both technically skilled and more broadly educated specialists, and after 1922 they adopted a "soft line on culture," which meant that censors generally tolerated works of literature, art, and film not judged "counterrevolutionary." Heated debates unfolded about the content and role of literature and art in creating a revolutionary society, and intellectuals often clustered around competing journals. The Futurist magazine *Left*, edited by Vladimir Maiakovskii, demanded that artists and writers exhibit clear revolutionary commitment, while *Red Virgin Soil*, edited by Aleksandr Voronskii, tended to attract less fully committed "fellow travelers," who believed that art and literature should be pursued to discover truth and beauty rather any specifically utilitarian purpose. In this atmosphere, space existed for diverse views expressed in a variety of forms, including modernist abstraction and proletarian realism. The latter was particularly prevalent in novels such as Dimitrii Furmanov's *Chapaev* (1923) and Fedor Gladkov's *Cement* (1926), focusing on the civil war and socialist construction, respectively.

The NEP stabilized the revolutionary regime, but controversial issues repeatedly rent the Bolshevik leadership. Debates ensued over the structure of the Soviet state, the growth of the party and state bureaucracies, the prospect of building socialism in one country, and the status of the NEP. After 1922, when Lenin suffered the first of a series of strokes that finally killed him two years later, the question of whether any one person would assume his dominant place in the leadership overshadowed everything.

After the civil war, the Bolsheviks struggled to construct a polity that would unify the country's various national republics (e.g., Russia, Ukraine, Georgia, and several others) into one federal state. Local communist parties dominated them all, but relations among them were not clear. Stalin, commissar of nationalities and recently appointed party general secretary, wanted a highly centralized system under Moscow's control, but Lenin thought that long-term unity would be better served by granting substantial autonomy. By the fall of 1922, relations between Stalin and Lenin had soured over this issue. Conflict intensified when, during Lenin's first serious illness, Stalin's emissaries used rough methods, including physical intimidation, to force Georgia's communists to accept his plans. Lenin certainly was no pacifist against noncommunists, but such behavior toward comrades infuriated him, as did Stalin's rudeness to his wife, Nedezhda Krupskaya (1869–1939).

In December, Lenin dictated what came to be called his "Testament," in which he analyzed the qualities of the Bolshevik leaders. None were given unequivocal praise, but he had particularly harsh words for Stalin, whom he described as "too rude" to use his power as party general secretary with sufficient caution and suggested his removal from that post. Incapacitated shortly thereafter, Lenin was unable to prevent Stalin from pushing through his scheme for the Union of Soviet Socialist Republics (USSR), in which the Kremlin held decisive authority.

In the early 1920s, Stalin was not as well known to the public as Trotsky, the popular head of the Red Army, or Zinoviev, Petrograd party chief and president of the Comintern. Lacking the rhetorical and theoretical brilliance of many of his colleagues, he was a skilled administrator who took on many unexciting but important tasks in the party organization. Born in 1879 in Gori, Georgia, Josif Jughashvili was the son of an impoverished cobbler. He attended a seminary but became a Marxist, joined the Bolsheviks in 1903, and accepted a variety of assignments in the underground. Like so many other Bolsheviks, he spent years in Siberian exile. Lenin thought highly of him and in 1913 assigned him to write the party's most important work on the nationalities question. After returning to Petrograd in 1917, he edited *Pravda*, became commissar for Nationalities, and carried out important though secondary assignments during the civil war. In 1919, he joined the Politburo (the Central Committee's top policymaking body) and headed the Orgburo (which mobilized the resources needed to carry out Politburo decisions). These posts—and his appointment to the unheralded but important position of general secretary in 1922—gave him decisive influence. As a dispenser of patronage, he built a network of supporters against future political opponents.

Hotheaded, tough, and vengeful, Stalin also was a skillful infighter. Often posing as a voice of moderation, he effectively built alliances within the Politburo to isolate and defeat rivals. For example, after Lenin's death, fearing Trotsky as a potential party leader, Zinoviev and Kamenev convinced the Central Committee to retain Stalin as general secretary, and the group also decided to suppress Lenin's Testament, in which none had fared well. Stalin then took the initiative to assert himself as the interpreter of Lenin's legacy and, in decisive struggles, mobilized his organizational support network to undercut opponents' appeals to the party rank and file.

As Lenin lay dying, the future lines of internal conflict were emerging. Broadly speaking, on one side stood the "left opposition," whose chief spokesman was Trotsky. This group criticized the decline of free discussion within the party, the growth of the increasingly intertwined party and state bureaucracies, and the top-down appointment of leading officials. Against them stood the bulk of the leadership, led by Stalin, Zinoviev, and Kamenev, which stressed the need for unity and accused the left of factionalism. In the fall of 1923, the Central Committee reprimanded Trotsky, who many resented for having joined the party only on the eve of the revolution. Stalin clearly recognized him as his key political enemy. The two had had sharp disputes during the civil war, and Trotsky, a worldly intellectual of Jewish background, regarded Stalin as a mediocrity. Stalin, in turn, despised Trotsky's intellectualism, Jewish heritage, and popularity. He quickly pushed Trotsky onto the defensive. For example, when Lenin died, Trotsky was recuperating from illness in the south. Stalin, in charge of the funeral, tricked him into missing the ceremonies by giving him the wrong date. In the subsequent struggles to claim Lenin's mantle, such "errors" on Trotsky's part worked against him.

Meanwhile, Stalin expanded his political base. In early 1924, as the party's "Lenin Enrollment" recruited 240,000 worker members and increased its size by 50 percent, Stalin undertook a series of lectures at Moscow's Sverdlov University titled the "Foundations of Leninism." With Petrograd now renamed Leningrad and the great man's body mummified and enshrined in a mausoleum on Red Square, the party was creating a cult of "Leninism," in which Stalin aimed to become high priest. Stalin succeeded against his rivals by skillfully manipulating policy discussions to raise questions about their fidelity to Lenin's teachings and ultimately to Bolshevism.

The most important disputes revolved around the future of the NEP. All the Bolsheviks agreed that Russia needed to build up its industrial base and modernize agriculture in order to defend the revolution from its enemies and raise the living standard, but how to do this was unclear. There were also sharp disagreements about whether Russia could build socialism without international revolution. These issues were closely intertwined. After Lenin's death, Trotsky had argued that it would not be possible to build a socialist economy in Russia unless the proletariat took power in Europe's most important countries. This view implied a sober assessment of what could be accomplished at home, but it also pointed toward a more aggressive role for the Comintern in promoting world revolution. Stalin and Bukharin, on the other hand, asserted that while the final victory depended on the aid of the international proletariat, building socialism in one country was possible. Arguing, falsely, that Lenin had also held this view, they won the broad support of party members eager to move ahead regardless of events abroad. Moreover, with international revolution no longer imperative, it followed that the Comintern would now serve primarily the national interests of the USSR.

From 1921 to 1927, a majority supported the strategy put forward by Bukharin, the party's leading economic theorist. Backed by Stalin, he argued that a propeasant policy would facilitate the gradual development of socialism. He favored setting up cooperative farms as models to which peasant communities might aspire but opposed coerced collectivization. A prosperous peasantry, purchasing products of Soviet industry, would generate capital that the state could then invest in modern plant and equipment—the key to socialist construction. By the mid-1920s, this approach had revived the economy, but the process had been slow and restored largely only industrial capacity sidelined during the civil war. Not desiring to break up the "worker–peasant alliance" achieved under the NEP, Bukharin resisted squeezing the peasantry in order to more rapidly accumulate the surpluses needed for investment.

Trotsky, the economist Evgenii Preobrazhenskii (1886–1937), and the left were less hesitant. They argued that rapid industrialization could move ahead via increased state planning and the transfer of more wealth from the peasants to the industrial sector by raising the prices peasants paid for industrial goods. This process of "primitive socialist accumulation" could be enhanced through the introduction of large-scale, state-run, collective farms. Bukharin's and Trotsky's differences were more of emphasis than of kind, but the Opposition's assertions, along with its critique of the party's "bureaucratic degeneration," raised the ire of the majority. At successive party conclaves, pro-Stalin majorities levied increasingly harsh criticisms of all dissident views.

Indeed, Stalin and his allies began systematically driving opposition-ists from posts at all levels. At the top, Trotsky lost his position as head of the Red Army in 1925, and though he remained in the Politburo, his star was clearly in eclipse. Zinoviev and Kamenev, suddenly fearing Stalin's ascendency, joined Trotsky in the "United Opposition in 1926. Attempt-ing to build support among the party rank and file, they met increasing repression. Stalin brought sycophantic new supporters, men like Viaches-lav Molotov (1890–1986), Kliment Voroshilov (1881–1969), and Mikhail Kalinin (1875–1946), into the Politburo. After the United Opposition pub-lished an official platform in September 1927, the Central Committee expelled Trotsky and Zinoviev. One month later, when the United Oppo-sition organized demonstrations commemorating the tenth anniversary of the October Revolution, the police intervened. By year's end, Trotsky, Zinoviev, and Kamenev were expelled from the party. Although the lat-ter two recanted, Trotsky refused to capitulate and, in January 1928, was exiled to Alma Ata in Kazakhstan. In 1929, he was deported to Turkey with his wife and son, eventually migrating to Mexico, where a Stalinist agent murdered him in 1940.

The defeat of the left opposition took place just as the NEP entered into serious crisis. With agricultural prices low and industrial goods in short supply, peasants reduced grain deliveries or switched to more prof-itable products. Rather than make concessions, the government initially adopted a program similar to the left's and decided to accelerate industri-al growth by squeezing the peasants, especially the kulaks, if necessary by seizing grain. In December 1927, the Fifteenth Party Congress called for a "socialist offensive" to industrialize the country through the crea-tion of a Five Year Plan of economic development. Bukharin still thought that the basic parameters of the NEP could be maintained, but Stalin thought otherwise. As the food shortages worsened early in 1928, he called for extraordinary measures against grain hoarders and speculators and attacked the kulaks in particular for precipitating the crisis. Stalin then moved to collectivize agriculture. In effect, he adopted a radicalized version of the left's program and now accused Bukharin and supporters of the NEP of a "right deviation." Bukharin attempted to hinder this return to War Communism, but it was too late. By 1930, Stalin was strong enough to remove him and his allies from the Politburo.

The defeat of the "right" gave Stalin virtually complete control of a governing system based on the party and state bureaucracy. He and his supporters now embarked on a gigantic program of forced draft industri-alization and agricultural collectivization that would, at enormous cost in lives and treasure, transform the Soviet Union into an industrial power within a decade. At the same time, this "revolution from above" created a new kind of civilization that appropriated the language of socialism but in fact had little to do with that project. Indeed, the regime effectively destroyed the capitalist order based on private property and the market,

Figure 5.4.   Stalin (center) on his fiftieth birthday in 1929. With him, from left to right, are Politburo members Ordzhonikidze (candidate member), Voroshilov, Kuibyshev, Kalinin, Kaganovitch (candidate), and Kirov (candidate). Courtesy of the AsD, Bonn.

but the new one it created, resting on state ownership and centrally planned bureaucratic management, had nothing in common with the socialist goals of individual freedom, social justice and equality, and workers' power. Stalin established a brutal tyranny underpinned by a massive bureaucracy in which one's position in the party-state hierarchy (the Nomenklatura) brought power and privilege. The higher a person's rank, the greater his authority and access to "collective" wealth owned by the state. Neither capitalist nor socialist, this "bureaucratic collectivist" society, to borrow Hal Draper's term, was something completely new. It was sui generis.[7]

Planning had long been important to the Soviet economy. State management of large-scale industry and an extensive electrification program begun in 1921 involved centralized management, but the "Great Turn" initiated with the first Five Year Plan (1928–1932) involved planning of an entirely different order. Now all economic investment and resource distribution fell within the purview of a massive central planning agency (Gosplan), the goals of which derived from political decision making rather than market imperatives. To build an economy capable of arming itself with modern weapons, Stalin's government focused on the expansion of heavy industrial "investment goods," such as plant, machinery, and raw materials, rather than consumer goods. Between 1928 and 1932, the proportion of investment in the means of production rose from 32.8 to

53.3 percent. In 1950, it reached over 68 percent. Conversely, consumer goods' production got short shrift.

To finance industrialization, the state planned to use agricultural surpluses generated through production on modernized collective farms. Theoretically, peasants joined these enterprises on a "voluntary" basis, but in reality the party apparatus used mass coercion to achieve compliance. Resistance was fierce; peasants often burned their outbuildings and crops and slaughtered their animals rather than turn them over to the state. The government blamed opposition on the kulaks and deported millions to Siberia, where many died in the open or in the expanding system of forced labor (the GULAG). Those left behind worked either on *sovkhozy*, state farms where they worked for wages, or in *kolkhozy*, farms that rented state land and delivered goods on contract. The Bolsheviks hoped that, supported by investments in machinery, such collectives, like American industrial farms, would rapidly increase productivity. The actual result, however, was otherwise. The system alienated and infuriated the peasants, and the chaos and actual lack of state support disrupted grain output. From 1929 to 1933, the number of horses declined from 36 million to 15 million and cattle from 67 million to 34 million. Famine was widespread, and the government's political priorities exacerbated the crisis. In Ukraine, the country's "breadbasket," draconian grain procurement broke the back of perceived peasant resistance by precipitating genocide as 4 million to 5 million people starved to death in 1932–1933. While the state did manage to feed the cities, the standard of living for urban workers declined by 50 percent by 1934.

Ignoring early setbacks, the Bolsheviks did not relent, and by 1936, 93 percent of peasants worked on collective farms. They also forged ahead with their industrial program. Despite enormous waste and inefficiency due to inexperience, poor planning, and the loss of many skilled managers and technicians at the height of the purges (see below), there is no question that in the sectors of heavy industry (iron and steel), energy production (oil and electricity), chemicals, and farm machinery, the system achieved substantial successes. While the West wallowed in the Great Depression, the Soviet economy grew at a rate of 27 percent a year between 1929 and 1934. Whole "socialist" cities, such as Magnitogorsk, the "Soviet Pittsburgh" in the Ural Mountains, were conjured up out of the ground. Inhabitants of these new cities were sometimes driven there by force or desperation, while others were inspired by idealism and the possibility of a better life.

Forcing such sacrifices on the population required draconian police repression. Space for political debate, even within the party, was eliminated and dissidence crushed. In place of the relative cultural openness of the NEP period, the state now imposed an ultraconformist "socialist realism." The state harnessed expression to its goals, paid the salaries of writers and artists, and rigorously censored them. While roughly 10,000 people were executed in 1921, the last year of civil war, the number rose to 20,000 in 1930 and increased exponentially by 1938 (see below). In order to find scapegoats for economic failures and to intimidate the dissatisfied, beginning in 1928 the government staged a number of show trials against "bourgeois specialists," such as mining engineers, planners, and trade officials, accusing them of espionage on behalf of foreign governments, "wrecking," and economic sabotage. Finally, the People's Commissariat for Internal Affairs (NKVD; formerly the GPU) arrested many ordinary and frequently innocent people for all kinds of supposed economic and political crimes. NKVD records show that during the 1930s, it had custody of 3,593,000 people with 1,360,000 sent to forced-labor camps, often in isolated parts of the country, where under brutal conditions they extracted natural resources, built infrastructure (such as the White Sea Canal), and established settlements. Thus, mass terror served economic as well as political purposes.

Although the regime relied heavily on its iron fist, it also won the support of millions who agreed with its explicit aim of building the economy as a basis for a strong state and a brighter future. Millions also benefited from the social mobility that the new system (and the purges) made possible. The government vastly expanded opportunities for education and training for workers and their children, and 9 million peasants were absorbed into the urban–industrial economy during the first Five Year Plan alone. Soviet policy toward workers was inconsistent. In the late 1920s, workers received privileged advancement in training opportunities, and wage and benefit policies promoted equality. After 1931, however, access to higher-skilled jobs depended on merit, and the government restored one-man factory management (earlier used in the civil war) and wider wage differentials to raise productivity. With labor in short supply, however, it was difficult to prevent workers from resisting discipline by changing jobs. In general, living conditions, especially access to consumer goods and housing, remained hard, but many workers hoped that the sacrifices of the present would build a better future.

The position of women also shifted after the Great Turn. The first decade of the revolution had brought women equality before the law, easier access to divorce and abortion, and improvement in their workplace status, but the patriarchal Bolshevik leaders did not prioritize feminist aims to equalize work and family responsibilities, and most Russians, especially the peasants, resisted such notions and were disconcerted by the social changes occurring around them. Under Stalin, the party reversed course. Desperate for labor, it encouraged millions of women to enter the labor force after 1929, but it also made divorce more difficult, outlawed most abortions, promoted larger families, and basically returned to the Victorian family model. Day-care facilities were expanded, but women were expected to also manage the household. Thus, the double burden became the norm for many Soviet women, some of whom rose into new positions of responsibility but also encountered difficulty entering the highest echelons of the political and economic hierarchy.

Paradoxically, the more Stalin's personal power grew, the more insecure he became. By the early 1930s, he was the object of a full-blown personality cult that deified his person and made him infallible, but he feared popular rivals, such as the leader of the Leningrad party organization Sergei Kirov (1886–1934). His assassination in 1934, probably on Stalin's order, touched off waves of mass arrests, political purges, and highly choreographed show trials of supposed terrorists, spies, and saboteurs in the pay of Trotsky, the German Gestapo, or other groups. Organized by NKVD chief Genrikh Iagoda (1891–1938) and, after his own arrest and execution, Nikolai Ezhov (1895–1940), they resulted in the liquidation, usually following a farcical "confession," of almost all the remaining "Old Bolshevik" leaders, including Bukharin, Zinoviev, and Kamenev. By 1938, the process of purging, arresting, and executing "enemies" had engulfed all levels of the party and state, including the army officer corps, and society at large. Much of the initiative came from above, but persecutions on the local level also gave many people the chance to settle scores for all sorts of reasons. According to the NKVD archives, in 1937–1938 the authorities executed 681,682 people.

It is difficult to identify any single cause of the "Great Terror." Stalin's paranoia was certainly a key factor, but, as Grigor Suny has noted, it is important to also consider the wider context of Soviet politics in which Stalin and his confederates saw a world sharply divided into friends and enemies. The struggle to build a new order justified all measures to root out opponents, and in a society transfused with social tensions, fear, and resentment, the government unleashed a hunt in which people struck out at the privileged and intellectuals as well as those considered to be different. Anyone could be denounced, and many acted to protect themselves, to gain status, or to get revenge. By 1939, even high-ranking Bolsheviks, such as Andrei Vyshinsky (1883–1954), the government's chief prosecutor, expressed concern about excessive numbers of communists subjected to arrest and expulsion. Stalin brought in Lavrentii Beria (1899–1953) to replace Ezhov, who was shot the following year. Beria, himself a brutal figure, drastically reduced arrests, improved conditions in the camps, and released some prisoners, including thousands of military officers who returned to duty. When the Eighteenth Party Congress met in March 1939, it was clear that the intense search for internal enemies had run its course.

By the end of the 1930s, Stalin's position was unassailable, and he ruled unchallenged until his death in 1953. The Great Terror had ravaged the society from top to bottom, but he stood at the apex of a state apparatus that was loyal and disciplined. Moreover, despite the carnage, the "revolution from above" had transformed the country into a major industrial power. There is no legitimate justification for the coercive and bloody means used to modernize the country, but Stalin thought otherwise and acted accordingly. In 1931, he asserted that Russia had "fallen behind the advanced countries by fifty to one hundred years. We must close that gap in ten years. Either we do this or we'll be crushed."[8] To meet this goal, his regime attempted to condense a brutal process of modernization that had unfolded over centuries in the West into the space of a decade. It was not entirely successful, but when the Germans invaded Russia ten years later, it was the USSR's industrial capacity, built at terrible cost, that made it possible to defeat them.

PARLIAMENTARY SOCIALISM: RECOVERY AND CRISIS

Social democracy's great challenge during the interwar period was to win state power via elections as a means to introduce socialist reforms. As the revolutionary movements ebbed in the postwar years, the socialist parties recovered from their schism with the communists. Although the interparty competition was fierce, each tended to recruit from different segments of the population. In France, for example, the SFIO attracted primarily skilled workers and white-collar employees, such as teachers, while the PCF struck roots among unskilled industrial workers. Although a majority of socialists quit to join the PCF in 1920, by 1932, SFIO membership had returned to its earlier peak of 120,000, while the PCF retained only 30,000. In the elections of that year, the socialists won over 2 million votes and 132 seats in parliament compared to the communists' 800,000 votes and only eleven seats.

In most of Europe, the situation was similar. German social democracy, for example, once again had over a million members by the late 1920s. It recruited primarily skilled industrial workers (60 percent) and white-collar employees (14 percent), while the remainder came from other middle-class groups. In the elections of 1928, Germany's largest party, the SPD, won 7.8 million votes (29.8 percent for 153 seats), its strongest showing since 1919. Communist membership, on the other hand, slipped from around 450,000 in 1921 to 130,000 in 1928. Over 80 percent were workers, the bulk of them unskilled. In 1928, the KPD won only 2.7 million votes (10.6 percent for fifty-three seats).

The communists' relative decline during the 1920s was rooted in the flawed politics of the Comintern. In Germany, for example, Comintern directives to the KPD to seize power in March 1921 and October 1923 were disastrous. These efforts were crushed, and tens of thousands abandoned the party either to rejoin the SPD or to withdraw from politics. More important over the long term were the processes of Bolshevization and Stalinization, which transformed the new parties along democratic centralist lines and repeatedly replaced their leadership in accordance with the changing political winds in Moscow. An extreme version of this process occurred in the Czechoslovak Communist Party, where, between 1928 and 1930, purges reduced the membership from 150,000 to 25,000. As the party changed into a top-down, disciplined organization obedient to Stalin, it detached itself from its working-class base, and most former members returned to social democracy.

The apparent stabilization of parliamentary systems in most countries and communism's decline gave social democratic leaders new confidence by the mid-1920s. This feeling was buttressed by the health of their cultural organizations, which, in Austria and Germany, for example, reached their high-water mark. Run by tens of thousands of activists and attracting hundreds of thousands of workers, social democratic associations of all types, ranging from singing and sports clubs to cooperative, trade union, "freethinker," professional, and prorepublican paramilitary organizations, flourished and were a point of pride for party leaders. For many, this finely woven "community of solidarity" represented the nucleus of the future socialist society that would evolve within the framework of the democratic republic.

A leading spokesman of this point of view was Rudolf Hilferding, whose theory of "organized capitalism" underpinned German socialism's parliamentary strategy. Hilferding argued that capitalism had entered into a new phase of development in which the expansion and further concentration of capital, the formation of cartels and trusts, and the increasing power of finance capital were bringing the era of capitalist competition to a close. In place of anarchic, competitive, crisis-prone capitalism, a new system was emerging, characterized by economic regulation and planned production. If left undisturbed, this process would create a hierarchical social order in which the economy was indeed "organized" but under capitalist control. In the wake of the war, state regulation had grown increasingly important. The socialist party's task was to use the recently democratized state, which Hilferding saw as a neutral instrument, to gradually assume control over the economy for the public's benefit.

Concomitant with this political aim, the socialist unions demanded "economic democracy." Promoted by Fritz Napthali (1888–1961) and others, this idea identified reforms to enhance workers' economic power. These included, for example, the expansion of collective bargaining rights, the right of workers to comanage their workplaces (codetermination), trade union participation in the regulation of cartels and trusts, public ownership of key industries, and equal union representation in public organizations concerned with economic policy. Hilferding, Naphtali, and most of their colleagues did not assert that the class struggle had ended. They believed, however, that it could be channeled through the system's democratic institutions (e.g., parties operating within parliament). By building a stronger party and more potent unions, they aimed to transform capitalism from within.

Achieving such goals in Germany or elsewhere faced serious obstacles. Divisions among the Social Democrats about the efficacy of coalition politics and, after 1929, how to grapple with the capitalism's economic collapse paralyzed the socialists and undercut their ability to meet the challenges of reviving communist and fascist movements, which, battening on the mass suffering caused by the crisis, aimed to destroy the parliamentary order.

Despite their support for the parliamentary system, most socialist parties after 1918 remained wedded to their prewar reticence to cooperate with bourgeois parties of any stripe. As a result, the French, Italian, and, after 1920, the Austrian parties refrained from governing at the national level. The German socialists participated in several coalitions through 1924 to manage crises stemming from the French occupation of the Ruhr Valley in 1923, accelerating hyperinflation, and serious communist and right-wing threats to the republic. Once these crises had passed, however, the party's slipping electoral support convinced it to withdraw into the opposition for the next four years. During that time, no cabinet governed on the basis of a clear majority, fueling the sense of instability that plagued Weimar. Although the SPD achieved some important reforms, such as the introduction of unemployment insurance and state-supervised arbitration in labor disputes, it was difficult for socialist parties outside of government to facilitate change.

Achieving an absolute majority required them to rethink their self-identification as proletarian parties engaged in class struggle. As long as they stuck to a vision of a secular, urban, and industrial future in which the working class remained supreme, it remained difficult to attract religious people, small businessmen, white-collar employees, rural workers, and peasants. The workers' parties also tended to be overwhelmingly male. In France, where women could not vote and it was difficult for them to engage in public affairs, only 3 percent of the SFIO membership was female in 1932, while for the PCF the number was around 1 percent. In Germany, where women could vote, the parties did better. Between 1919 and 1930, the SPD increased the proportion of its female membership from 15 to 23 percent, and it had the largest number of female delegates in the Reichstag. In 1929, women constituted about 16 percent of the KPD. But in a society in which most women remained attached to conservative ideals and voted for religious and nationalist parties, the workers' parties were sailing into the wind. Moreover, their male-oriented cultures, their view of women's issues as of secondary importance when compared to class, their slowness to promote women to responsible posts in the party and unions, and their hypocritical support for prioritizing male employment in economic crises hindered their ability to attract women.

Most social democratic leaders continued to adhere to the prewar principles of Erfurt. Eventually, they believed, capitalist development would shift what Otto Bauer called "the balance of class forces" from the bourgeoisie to the proletariat, thus bringing them to power. Yet, as was true before 1914, a number of revisionists challenged this view. In Italy, for example, following Italian socialism's collapse in the face of fascism, Carlo Rosselli (1899–1937) developed a withering critique of the PSI's deterministic Marxism, which he asserted had nothing to do with the realities of life. He called instead for a "liberal socialism" that made room for the will to act and stressed justice, liberty, and the collective good as principles to inspire people. As Sheri Berman notes, he aimed to detach the ideals of freedom embodied in liberalism from "free market" economics and to reconnect them to the socialists' call for economic justice. But he also wished to strip Marxism from socialism and thereby replace class struggle and internationalism with an emphasis on the collective whole and the legitimacy of patriotism.

Belgian intellectual Hendrik de Man (1885–1953) echoed Rosselli's sentiments. His widely read book _The Psychology of Socialism_ (1926) and a series of subsequent works advocated a non-Marxist approach to the socialist future. De Man shared many of Bernstein's prewar criticisms of Marxism but unlike Bernstein argued that reason is not central to most people's worldview and behavior. Indeed, he emphasized the importance of irrational, emotional sentiments and pointed out that the deeply embedded nationalism exhibited during the war proved to be a more powerful motivator than class consciousness. Rejecting notions of capitalism's collapse, he believed that building on the system's strengths, socialists could construct a society of freedom, equal rights, equal opportunity, and solidarity. De Man suggested that socialists strive for broad, cross-class support by appealing to people's emotions and proposing concrete changes that could be achieved immediately rather than in the distant future. As we will see, to that end, he put forward his _Plan du Travail_, widely heralded among socialists in the 1930s.

Rosselli and de Man's ideas on human motives and their desire for action had much in common with the views of Georges Sorel, who, as we have seen above, hoped to inspire the workers to revolution by propagating the myth of the general strike. By 1910, Sorel was disappointed in the revolutionary potential of the proletariat and looked to nationalism as a means of building a multiclass mass movement against liberal democracy. Drifting into the orbit of radical nationalist and anti-Semitic groups, such as the Action Française, he became a prophet to activists of the far right, such as Mussolini, but his ideas, especially his use of myth and nationalism to mobilize the masses, struck a chord among radicals across the political spectrum. Revisionist socialists, such as de Man, aimed to enhance liberal democracy, but they, too, were willing to use myths, such as nationalism, to build cross-class alliances to achieve political aims serving the broad community. Like orthodox Marxists, they saw the state as an instrument of change, but their concerns were more immediate.

The revisionist arguments of Rosselli, de Man, and others won little backing among party leaders in the 1920s. Yet it was at that very moment when activists on the far right, often calling themselves "fascists" and "National Socialists," used similar approaches to build broad cross-class alliances that aimed to destroy Europe's parliamentary order. By the early 1930s, as the Great Depression undercut the legitimacy of democracy and liberal capitalism, many of social democracy's orthodox leaders understood the gravity of the situation, but they failed to effectively meet the fascist challenge.

Fascism was one of several authoritarian responses to the severe political and economic dislocations caused by the war, repeated economic crises, capitalist modernization, rapid cultural change, and the rise of the socialist and communist left. Many elements of its often-vague ideology had already emerged in the nineteenth century but were then synthesized in locally unique ways in the twentieth. In general, fascism drew its support disproportionately from the propertied classes, small and large, rural and urban, which had lost faith in parliamentary democracy's ability to protect their interests. In some places, however, such as in Germany, they also made inroads among workers, particularly the unemployed. Led by dynamic, charismatic figures such as Mussolini in Italy and Adolf Hitler (1889–1945) in Germany, fascism's great achievement was to pull together disparate and often conflicting social groups into unified "people's parties" willing and able to seize power.

Fascists viewed parliamentary government as corrupt, weak, and unable to overcome the class divisions proliferating under liberal capitalism. They favored the establishment of authoritarian regimes dominated by strong leaders who would reorganize society along corporatist lines and unify the country around the achievement of a nation's "historic destiny." Despising democracy, they vehemently opposed democrats, socialists, communists, and trade unionists and sought to eliminate any group perceived as a threat to the nation. In many places, they targeted Jews, Gypsies, and other ethnic minorities as aliens to be purged from the body politic. Such sentiment assumed a murderously virulent form in German "national socialist" (Nazi) ideology, which, unlike Italian fascism, defined membership in the community using racial criteria. Attacking Marxist socialism and plutocratic capitalism, fascist rhetoric was populist and promised to protect the interests of all those doing "honest" work. It also glorified militarism and called for imperialist expansion. Attractive to many demobilized soldiers traumatized and angered by the results of 1918, the movement came to embody the continuation of war in a new guise.

After taking power in the early 1920s, Mussolini's movement became a model for others. For example, a key weapon in the Italian fascist arsenal was the use of demobilized soldiers as paramilitary street fighters who attacked rivals while simultaneously posing as forces of order. Taking his cue from Mussolini's black-shirted *squadristi*, Hitler equipped his notorious "storm troopers" in brown. More important, Hitler also learned from Mussolini's use of parliamentary means to take power and destroy democracy. In 1923, after failing to overthrow the government through an armed Putsch, Hitler adopted a strategy combining the use of terror and constitutional means to carry him to the chancellorship in 1933.

National Socialism came to power in Germany because most Germans, including the nation's elites, opposed the Republic. They associated the latter with Germany's defeat in 1918 and with the humiliating Versailles Treaty, which stripped the country of its colonies, one-sixth of its territory, and its navy, air force, and the bulk of its army while requiring it to pay enormous reparations, to accept a lengthy French occupation of the Rhineland, and to assume sole responsibility for the war. Faith in the system slipped further when the French occupied the industrial Ruhr Valley in January 1923. Severe inflation then accelerated into hyperinflation: between 1919 and late 1923, the mark's value fell from 9 to the dollar to 4.2 trillion to the dollar. Before the government could restore order the following year, many middle-class families had lost all their savings, while a tiny elite had amassed large fortunes. During these years, the Weimar Republic had withstood several communist and right-wing efforts to overthrow it, but even after returning to relative prosperity in 1924, it stood on shaky ground.

The Depression undercut much of Weimar's remaining support and opened the door to Nazism. Labeling socialists and liberals as "November criminals" for betraying the fatherland in 1918 and blaming democrats, Marxists, Jews, and plutocrats for Germany's weakness, the Nazis used the economic crisis to attack the republic's institutions and culture. They promised a new empire, a "Third Reich," in which a strong state would establish a healthy national community (Volksgemeinschaft) based on membership in the Aryan race. They called for the restoration of Germany's military power, for state action to put people to work, and for the elimination of modernist trends in aesthetics, which they described as "cultural Bolshevism." Making clear their intention to crush the workers' parties and the unions, they reassured big capitalists while also swearing to protect the interests of small artisans and peasants. Nazi propaganda was often vague and contradictory, but it skillfully targeted its audiences and used modern techniques and innovative symbols. Polling only 2.8 percent in the elections of 1928, two years later they won 18 percent and, in July 1932, they became Germany's largest party with over 37 percent of the vote. The KPD grew stronger as well. Drawing heavily on unemployed industrial workers, its support increased steadily to over 14 percent. Thus, the two antirepublican parties could paralyze the parliament.

When the Depression struck, SPD leader Hermann Müller (1876–1931) headed a coalition government with several liberal parties. As unemployment skyrocketed and state income plummeted, its deficit grew. In March 1930, the cabinet collapsed after squabbling over new taxes to fund the unemployment insurance program. For the next three years, repeated elections saw the extremist parties grow stronger at the liberal parties' expense as the crisis deepened and their middle-class supporters turned to the Nazis. Meanwhile, the liberals also moved rightward, leaving the SPD, which maintained its electoral support of 20 to 25 percent, isolated. Since no cabinet could govern on the basis of a parliamentary majority, Germany's reactionary president, von Hindenburg, appointed an antirepublican conservative Catholic, Heinrich Brüning (1885–1970), as chancellor. Brüning governed by emergency decree and pursued a draconian austerity program. Fearing that new elections could bring the Nazis to power, the socialists "tolerated" this "hunger chancellor" from 1930 to 1932. As unemployment rose to almost 40 percent and the state slashed support for impoverished workers, the SPD's policy confused and demoralized many supporters and drove new voters, especially the young and unemployed, into the arms of the communists and the Nazis.

The depression and the political crisis it generated caught the socialists unprepared. They had expected to introduce progressive reforms in the context of capitalist economic growth using parliamentary majorities garnered within a stable polity. Now, with the economic debacle fully upon them, they responded with austerity, balanced budgets, and low taxes on capital, that is, economic solutions supported by conservative economists and big business. Hilferding, like most other orthodox Marxists of his day, understood capitalist development, but as finance minister in Müller's cabinet, he had no ready alternative to supply-side orthodoxy. Even after almost two years of disaster under Brüning, he resisted innovative trade union proposals for deficit spending to finance public works and stimulate the economy. Fearing renewed inflation, he convinced the SPD's cochairman, Otto Wels (1873–1939), and a majority of his colleagues in the party leadership to oppose the plan.

Hilferding accurately recognized that the Nazis attracted broad cross-class support due to the crisis and that, once in power, they would destroy the republic. By tolerating Brüning, he and his colleagues in the leadership hoped to prevent Hitler from taking power before an economic turnaround took the wind out of the Nazis' sails. They saw few other options. Writing to Kautsky, Hilferding lamented that worst of all "is that we can't say anything concrete to the people about how and with what means we would end the crisis."[9] Of course, he did make policy recommendations, but his calls for free trade, the use of French and American gold reserves to restore international credit, and more state regulation of banking and industry were vague and required parliamentary majorities beyond social democracy's reach.

KPD policy also undermined the republic. In 1928, the Comintern reversed the strategy pursued during the NEP of cooperating with some noncommunist movements. Following the radicalization of Soviet politics, the Comintern asserted that capitalism was entering into a new crisis that opened the way for a "third period" of revolutionary advance. Calling for a struggle of "class against class," it now labeled Social Democrats as "social fascists," who were the main enemy. This shift had catastrophic effects across Europe, for it deepened the hostility between the workers' parties just as the radical right revived. In Germany, cooperation against the Nazis became impossible as the KPD, led by Ernst Thälmann (1886–1944), viewed the SPD and the Nazi Party as "twins." Hoping to pave the way for a communist revolution, it worked to bring down the republic.

Like the Nazis and the communists, the SPD also had a large paramilitary force, the Reichsbanner, at its disposal, and in late 1931, that force, the unions, and the social democratic sports associations coalesced into an "Iron Front" to defend the republic. Yet, although the SPD leaders often repeated that they would use "all means" to defend democracy, they were not actually prepared to do so. In July 1932, for example, when Brüning's replacement, the arch-reactionary Franz von Papen (1879–1969), illegally deposed the SPD-led coalition in Prussia, social democracy's leaders elected to go to court rather than fight. Aware that mass unemployment had weakened the unions and fearful that the Iron Front was no match for the army, they recoiled from confronting the state.

Following the November elections, the Nazi Party was the largest party in the Reichstag with 33 percent of the vote and 197 seats. Together with other right-wing parties, the Nazis could lead a majority-based coalition if Hindenburg listened to the antirepublican conservatives in his circle and appointed Hitler as chancellor. With the voters having elected an antidemocratic majority to the Reichstag and Hitler's appointment in the offing, the SPD leaders faced a classic example of what Peter Gay has called the dilemma of democratic socialism: should they act to overthrow such a government if it came to power via constitutional means? Fearing civil war, after Hitler's appointment on 30 January 1933, they chose to "wait and see" if he broke with the constitution before calling for action. Thus, they sealed their own destruction. Hitler swiftly used parliamentary power, manipulation of the law, and terror to destroy his enemies and the constitutional order. Thousands of communists and socialists were arrested, driven underground, or put into exile.

The German Social Democrats had failed to react effectively to Germany's economic crisis, they had underestimated the political opposition to which it gave rise, and they overestimated the degree to which the republic's institutions supported the democratic order. They paid a heavy price for such errors, but they were not cowards. Many had been in the thick of dangerous events during the revolution of 1918, in the tumultuous years that followed, and again in the face of Nazi violence. By the late 1920s, however, like their counterparts all over Europe, many had grown staid. They were part of a long-serving oligarchy that had grown used to comfortable bureaucratic and parliamentary routine. Elected and reelected, sometimes for decades, the top leaders rarely encountered serious challenge from within and over time grew less receptive to new ideas or innovative approaches. Beyond these failings, however, it was the Social Democrats' basic human decency that made them unwilling to unleash a bloody civil war that they feared they could not win. It made them hesitate for too long and gave their much more ruthless opponents the decisive advantage.

The German socialists were not alone. In Austria, France, the Low Countries, and Spain, reaction was on the march, aiming to roll back parliamentary democracy and destroy the left. In Austria, Hitler's victory split the fascists into a pro-Nazi movement and a much larger conservative Catholic one backed by the Christian Social Party. The latter dominated politics on the national level and was allied with fascist paramilitary Home Guard organizations and big business. In March 1933, Engelbert Dollfuss (1892–1934), the Christian Social Party leader, decided to fend off the Nazis and undercut the Social Democrats in a single stroke by shutting down parliament and ruling by decree. He soon dissolved the prorepublican paramilitary force, the Schutzbund; cut off financial support for Vienna's socialist municipal government; pressured socialist workers to join his new party, the Patriotic Front; and announced plans to establish a Christian, corporate, and federal state.

As in Germany, SPÖ leaders Karl Renner and Otto Bauer hesitated. Throughout the 1920s, the party had complemented its cautious political actions with radical rhetoric as a means of maintaining unity. As tensions rose, however, it became clear that, despite their formidable organization and the sizable Schutzbund, the leadership had little stomach for a fight. Even after Dollfuss had eliminated parliament, the SPÖ leaders still hoped to come to an arrangement. They vacillated between resistance and accommodation, thus paralyzing and demoralizing the party and leaving the initiative to Dollfuss. On 12 February, a police raid on the SPÖ headquarters in Linz precipitated a firefight that sparked civil war. Party leaders in Vienna called a general strike, but poor preparation and low morale weakened the response. For four days, however, the outnumbered and outgunned Schutzbund defended Vienna's working-class districts, but the army overwhelmed them, killing hundreds. Another of Europe's great socialist movements had gone down to defeat as the government rounded up its leaders, executed eleven of them, and drove the rest into exile or underground. Unlike their German comrades, however, the Austrian workers' willingness to fight inspired others across Europe to stand against the surging right.

In February 1934, it seemed that the French Republic would be the next to fall. Feeding on ultra-Catholicism, xenophobic objections to France's growing immigrant population, opposition to democracy, the depressed economy, and a major financial scandal, the growing radical right, led by groups such as the fascist Cross of Fire, aimed to topple the weak Radical government of Eduard Daladier (1884–1970). On 6 February, a huge rightist demonstration in Paris rioted and tried to seize the Chamber of Deputies, but troops dispersed them. Three days later, millions of French men and women marched in support of the republic. These included workers summoned to a general strike by the CGT, the largest union confederation, as well as members of the SFIO and the PCF. Despite having only days before attacked the SFIO as "social fascist," communist rank and file now marched with socialists amid shouts of "unity." This show of support broke the right's momentum. It also demonstrated the workers' fervent hope for a unified struggle to defend the republic.

The communist parties had long hoped to split their socialist rivals by attacking their leaders at the top and encouraging communist-controlled "unity" from below, but in 1934 Stalin's fear of German rearmament led the Comintern to reconsider its "class against class" line. By the summer of 1935, it was calling for cooperation with socialists and liberals to defend bourgeois democracy. Speaking in Moscow at the Comintern's Seventh Congress, Bulgarian communist leader Georgi Dimitrov (1882–1949) asserted that fascism was the "open terrorist dictatorship" of finance capital, which aimed "to destroy the democratic liberties of the toilers, to distort and curtail the rights of parliament, and to intensify the repression of the revolutionary movement."[10] To defeat it required a "united front" of all democratic forces. Ultimately, noncommunist workers would recognize the errors of the Social Democrats and liberals and move toward a revolutionary standpoint. Until then, it was imperative to cooperate against the fascist threat.

In France, this shift opened the way for the PCF, the SFIO, and the Radicals to form an alliance or "Popular Front" in the elections of May 1936. Campaigning on a joint platform calling for tax reform, a shorter workweek, increased unemployment benefits, support for the League of Nations, disarmament, and dissolution of the fascist organizations, the Popular Front won a clear majority of 59 percent, and the SFIO emerged as France's largest party. Its leader, Leon Blum (1872–1950), an intellectual of widely recognized integrity, became prime minister of a coalition with the Radicals. The PCF refused to join the cabinet but agreed to support it in parliament. The selection of Blum, a Jew, infuriated the anti-Semitic right, but his ability to manage the SFIO's conflicting factions made him a clear choice. Blum knew that, as the coalition's leading party, the SFIO could "exercise power" to make real change, but it could not operate as it if had "conquered power" and governed alone. Thus, he was prepared to compromise.

France's workers, however, had other ideas. Even before Blum took office in early June, strikes and factory occupations involving over 2 million workers swept the country. Workers' demands were not always clear, but hope for sweeping change was in the air. While the SFIO radicals shouted, "Everything is possible," the British ambassador compared Blum's situation to that of Kerensky. But it did not go as far as that. Meeting with incensed but petrified business representatives at his office in the Hotel Matignon, Blum hammered out a set of accords marking the most thoroughgoing economic reforms in French history. Aside from nationalizing the arms industries and imposing more state oversight on the National Bank, the "Matignon Agreements" recognized workers' collective bargaining rights and conceded large pay increases, the forty-hour workweek, and two-week vacations. Strikes and tensions continued for several weeks, but these agreements were the high-water mark of the government's social achievements. Fearing a breakup of the coalition, the PCF leaders, such as Maurice Thorez (1900–1964), urged the workers to return to the bench, and their paper, *L'Humanité*, answered the radicals with the headline "Everything is not possible!"

Blum followed up this success by banning fascist organizations that had participated in the 6 February events, but he was less decisive in the

Figure 5.5.   Leon Blum (1928). Courtesy of the AsD, Bonn.

foreign policy arena. Despite France's overwhelming military superiority, he was unwilling to risk armed conflict to reverse the Hitler government's illegal remilitarization of the Rhineland, which had occurred in March. Worse, when the Spanish military, led by General Francisco Franco (1892–1975), rebelled against Spain's own Popular Front government in July 1936, he failed to win legislative support to intervene on the loyalist side. Repelled by the idea of going to war and aware that a large part of French society loathed the social revolution occurring under the auspices of the Spanish government (see below), Blum vacillated. When conservative Britain announced its opposition to intervention, he promoted a nonintervention pact that was ultimately signed by Germany, Italy, England, France, and Russia. While the democracies fulfilled the pact, the fascist states sent troops and war material to support Franco, and the Soviets backed Madrid.

Domestically, too, Blum's government ran into problems. The economy faltered as entrepreneurs and bankers resisted implementing the agreements with labor, reduced investment, and moved capital out of the country, while workers' higher wages and reduced workweek cut into profits. By early 1937, Blum had to devalue the franc, declare a "pause" in his reform program, and cut back on social expenditures to balance the budget. Under fire from the left and the right, Blum resigned in July after the Senate rejected a bill giving him enhanced financial powers. The coalition staggered along for another nine months, but the Popular Front had run out of steam. Conservative forces soon rolled back many of its gains.

As in France, the Popular Front in Spain also appeared to mark a major political breakthrough. Except for industrial enclaves in Catalonia and the Basque provinces, Spain in the 1920s was a semifeudal, regionally divided, impoverished, and overwhelmingly agricultural country controlled by the landed nobility, the Catholic Church, and the army. From 1923 until 1930, General Miguel Primo de Rivera dominated politics, sidelining the parliament (the Cortes) and the hapless king, Alfonso XIII. Following de Rivera's fall, a strong antimonarchist majority in municipal elections prompted Alfonso's departure and the establishment of a republic in 1931. Supported by the Socialist Party (PSOE), the republican Manuel Azaña (1880–1940) formed a coalition that introduced separation of church and state, new taxes on the rich, a minimum wage, and land reforms. These changes infuriated the old elites but left the workers and peasants dissatisfied. With strikes and land seizures widespread, social tensions rose, and the elites grew increasingly hostile to the republic. Their sentiments were echoed on the left by Spain's large anarchist movement, which opposed the state in principle.

Azaña fell in September 1933 to be replaced by a right-wing coalition that reversed his reforms. When a new party (CEDA), backed by the big landowners and industrialists, monarchists, admirers of fascism, and the

Catholic hierarchy, entered the government in October 1934, long-simmering violence exploded in rebellion. Leftists in Madrid, Catalonian autonomists, and miners in Asturias rose up and established soviets, but only in the mining region of Asturias, where communists, socialists, and anarchists stood together, was resistance effective. It took Franco's army two weeks to crush them. The reign of terror that followed presaged the slaughter that soon engulfed the country.

The right-wing coalition had defeated the rebels and imprisoned 30,000 of them, but it could not solve Spain's deepening political and economic crises and soon fell apart. In preparation for new elections in February 1936, the PSOE, the small communist party PCE, the liberal Radical Party, and even some anarchists formed the Popular Front, which emerged with a slim popular majority but, due to the nature of Spain's electoral rules, won a sweeping parliamentary majority. The new government, initially headed by a succession of liberal prime ministers, was not itself revolutionary, but the victory buoyed the confidence of the workers who joined the anarcho-syndicalist CNT unions and the Socialist UGT unions in droves. As had occurred in France, strikes and demonstrations spread across the country, and the leader of the PSOE left wing, the "Spanish Lenin" Largo Caballero (1869–1946), declared, "The revolution we want could only be achieved by violence." The right responded to such statements with violence that the left reciprocated. By June, 269 people had died, and almost 1,300 had been wounded in street fighting, with 380 buildings, including many churches, damaged or gutted along with dozens of newspaper offices. In March, the government banned the Falange, Spain's small fascist movement, but the army leadership was well along in its plans to overthrow the republic.

In July, Franco's army revolted and, aided by German and Italian air transport, soon seized much of northwestern and southwestern Spain. The government in Madrid responded with confusion, initially attempting to treat with the rebels, while the latter acted decisively to occupy the cities. The workers' response saved the republic. The UGT and CNT unions called a general strike, and wherever possible, workers' organizations seized weapons and moved against the rebels. In many places, it was too late, but in others, the workers, together with the prorepublican Civil Guard, maintained control. They also got help from the thousands of foreign volunteers who poured into the country and fought with great distinction in "international brigades," such as those that successfully defended Madrid in November 1936.

Meanwhile, wherever triumphant, the nationalist forces slaughtered loyalists by the thousands, while large swaths of republican-held territory, such as Catalonia and Andalusia, experienced a social revolution in which workers seized factories and peasants expropriated large estates. Cooperative enterprises and collective farms proliferated, and workers' committees took control over entire regions, unleashing widespread ter-

ror against the upper classes and the clergy. Some cities, such as an-
archist-controlled Barcelona, wonderfully described in George Orwell's
Homage to Catalonia, became enclaves of radical social equality where
workers' coveralls replaced the trappings of the middle class, people
ceased using the formal "you," and tipping was no longer tolerated.
These developments frightened the bourgeoisie and threatened to destroy the tottering Popular Front. In response, the socialists and communists reined in the revolution they had once touted. Ironically, it was the
PCE that most fervently pursued this strategy. It grew sixfold in the wake
of the revolution, but it also became thoroughly Bolshevized and intoler-
ant of its socialist and anarchist rivals. Although it did not enter the
coalition headed by Caballero in September 1936, its influence grew in
tandem with the government's dependence on military advisers and material aid from the USSR.

Backed by German and Italian troops and airpower, Franco's armies
made steady progress against the republican forces, which lacked training and weapons. Although in many ways their élan compensated for
such deficiencies, the republicans' main problems were political. The
government's effort to roll back the social revolution precipitated a virtu-
al civil war within the civil war. The communists withheld weapons from
anarchist and socialist units and persecuted opponents, such as the dissident Workers' Party for Marxist Unification. In May 1937, the government used massive force to assert its authority over anarchist-dominated
Barcelona. Such self-defeating actions weakened the war effort and demoralized its supporters.

Wracked by internal strife and abandoned by the French and the British, the republic gradually succumbed to Franco's military juggernaut.
The fall of Barcelona in January 1939 ended the military conflict while
simultaneously precipitating the slaughter of 150,000 loyalists.

ALTERNATIVE SOCIALIST STRATEGIES: BELGIUM AND SWEDEN

The Popular Fronts in France, Spain, and elsewhere were efforts to meet
the right-wing challenge that arose in the midst of depression. Initially
successful, they failed to master the economic crisis and were weakened
by internal contradictions. Their defeats and the simultaneous expansion
of German power in central Europe caused Stalin to rethink his diplomatic strategy. Before turning to that discussion, however, it is important that
we look at two other efforts to deal with the economic and political crises:
one in Belgium and the other in Sweden. Their experience would be of
particular importance to the later history of socialism in the West.

As noted earlier, during the 1920s, de Man had sharply criticized both
orthodox Marxism and Bernstein's rationalist reformism. In the wake of
Nazism's victory, he promoted his *Plan of Labor*, usually called the *Plan de*

Man, to capture workers' imagination through the achievement of concrete, transformative changes that would move society toward socialism. In 1933, the Belgian Workers' Party (POB) adopted his ideas into its program and promoted the *Plan* in an innovative campaign that included all forms of media, theater, song, study courses, retreats, mass meetings, and even teams of bicycle agitators. De Man called for a dynamic mixed economy in which the government nationalized large-scale monopolistic industries, introduced generalized economic regulation, and provided substantial support for small-scale private enterprise. Framing these actions would be broad planning encompassing the entire economy. Democratized institutions would oversee investment, trade, social spending, training, and more. By giving real support to small businesses, de Man aimed to allay the fears of the middle classes and win their support.

The *Plan* energized the POB and slogans such as "The Plan; All of the Plan, Nothing but the Plan" gave it a distinct profile as conservative governments failed to lift Belgium out of the crisis. Matters came to a head in 1935 as party and union leaders debated whether to directly confront the state with a general strike in the wake of new social spending cuts. Like their Italian counterparts in 1920, the Belgian unionists put the matter to a vote, and it lost by around 581,000 to 481,000. The POB drew back from the brink and, with de Man's support, soon entered into a coalition with the Christian Democrats. The *Plan* was effectively dead.

The POB retreated because, like most of its sister parties elsewhere, it was not prepared to precipitate a violent confrontation. As Geoff Eley has noted, "When tested, social democrats—and except rarely, Communists too, could never take the insurrectionary plunge."[11] What was different about this case, however, was the POB's effort to develop an innovative campaign for a concrete plan of action that would build broad support well beyond the working class. In addition, while the *Plan* called for some nationalization of industry, even more essential was its emphasis on *control* through democratic planning.

The latter was especially important in Sweden. We will discuss the "Swedish model" at length in the next chapter; here it suffices to note that, unlike socialist parties all over Europe, Swedish Social Democracy (SAP) embraced the democratic revisionist approach to politics wholeheartedly and used it successfully to fend off the right and build a long-lasting majority coalition. Founded in 1889, the SAP initially followed the German party's programmatic lead, but the circumstances of its development were much different. Class conflict was rife in Sweden, but the state did not ban the party, and the country was more homogeneous, more literate, and less preoccupied with foreign policy concerns. Under the leadership of Hjalmar Branting (1860–1925), in the early 1890s the Swedish party formed alliances with liberals to win the franchise for male workers, thus gaining real political influence. Over time, the party came to regard democratization as a goal in itself rather than as a means to an end, and it energetically pursued political and social reforms within bourgeois society.

The SAP entered government for the first time in 1917. Although Sweden was not a belligerent, it joined a liberal-led coalition to manage economic problems caused by the war and to promote democratic reforms. In 1920, the party passed a new program stressing planning and state financing to promote collective production rather than the expropriation of private property and on this reformist basis was prepared to participate regularly in parliamentary governance. Sweden was under conservative rule when the Depression hit, but in 1932 the SAP struck a bargain with the Farmers' Party and assumed power. Using the ideas of economist Gunnar Myrdal (1898–1987), under the leadership of Per Albin Hansson (1885–1946), the farmer–labor coalition used debt-financed public expenditure to compensate for the lack of private investment and stimulate the economy. Although the banks initially resisted, the effort worked: by 1937, unemployment had fallen from 150,000 to 10,000, and the government easily retired the debt.

The SAP's approach, like the *Plan de Man*, aimed to promote economic policies that broadened the party's social reach and achieved goals that benefited the whole society. Less traditionally socialist because it eschewed nationalizing large-scale industry, it nevertheless showed that the state could still play a large role in shaping economic outcomes. For the Swedes, like the Belgians, control was more important than ownership in the transformative process. As we will see, after 1945 this outlook would have a major impact on Western socialism.

THE HITLER-STALIN PACT AND THE COMING OF WORLD WAR II

The SAP's success in meeting the crisis was a sideshow in the 1930s. Mainstream social democracy remained wedded to orthodoxy, while the communist movement functioned largely as an arm of Stalin's foreign policy. By the late 1930s, it was clear that the Popular Front strategy had run aground as a means of reversing fascism's momentum. Franco's triumph and, even more ominously, Germany's bloodless seizure of Austria, approved by England and France, in March 1938, of the Sudetenland in October, and of the rest of Czechoslovakia the following year set off alarm bells in the Kremlin as Stalin considered his options.

Even before the Comintern's turn to the Popular Front, the USSR had edged toward more cooperation with the West. As early as November 1933, Stalin sent Foreign Minister Maxim Litvinov (1876–1951) to Washington to negotiate American recognition of the Soviet Union. Embracing collective security, in 1934 the USSR joined the League of Nations and shortly thereafter signed peace and friendship treaties with France and Czechoslovakia. The agreement with the latter obliged the Soviets to send aid in the event of an unprovoked attack (presumably by Germany), but unless Poland or Romania allowed Soviet troops to cross their territories—a highly unlikely possibility—it had little meaning. With no provisions for military cooperation, the French Treaty was also toothless, but these agreements illustrated the USSR's effort to move closer to the Versailles powers intent on reining in Germany and Italy.

Between 1935 and 1939, the USSR sought collective security with the West, but Stalin kept his options open via back-channel communication with the Nazis. He made few distinctions among the capitalist powers and feared that the democracies might, in the end, unite with Germany against the Soviet Union. At the same time, he knew that Nazi plans for expansion, which Hitler often reiterated, lay in the Soviet Union. Stalin's policy, therefore, aimed to prevent the formation of such a bloc and to keep the USSR out of a war among the imperialist powers. By the end of 1938, however, it seemed that pursuing collective security with the Western democracies was no longer viable. Appalled at the purges and distrustful of the Soviets, the Western powers kept them at a distance while accommodating Hitler's efforts to revise the Versailles settlement and absorb Austria and much of Czechoslovakia into the German Reich. It appeared to Stalin that the West aimed to steer Germany into war with the Soviet Union.

As tensions between Germany and Poland increased in the spring and summer of 1939, Stalin undertook negotiations with the British and, secretly, with the Germans. On 23 August, he met with the German foreign minister, Joachim von Ribbentrop (1893–1946), and suggested an accommodation ending their mutual hostility and dividing Eastern Europe between them. By midnight, the two powers had signed a ten-year pact of nonaggression and cooperation that also contained secret protocols allotting Finland, Estonia, Latvia, eastern Poland, and Bessarabia to the Soviet Union and western Poland and Lithuania to the Germans. This arrangement, Stalin believed, not only would allow the USSR to reclaim territory lost after 1918 but also would buy time and space to prepare for a future war with Germany. Stalin could not know, of course, how quickly that conflict would be on him.

The Nazi-Soviet Pact sent shock waves around the world. Communist parties did not know how to respond, and most tried to defend the pact while still opposing fascism. Following the outbreak of the war on 1 September, however, Moscow clarified the party line: communists were to agitate against the "imperialist" war, cease attacking Nazi Germany, and support the partition of Poland. This conflation of the fascist powers and the bourgeois democracies and new German–Soviet cooperation confused party members and threw their organizations into disarray. The French Communist Party, for example, had grown tenfold in the 1930s, reaching a membership of 350,00 in 1939, and was the only substantial communist party on the Continent that could still function legally. After the pact, however, membership collapsed, and the party achieved pariah status as an instrument of a foreign power. Soon the government banned it and drove its remnants underground.

Stalin's deal with Hitler was only the last in a series of betrayals of the many dedicated revolutionaries who served international communism. Not only were foreign communists continually subject to the caprice of the Bolshevik leader, but at the height of the purges thousands of Comintern officials and communists exiled in Russia became ensnared in their murderous net. In some cases, such as that of the Polish Communist Party, so many militants were annihilated that it had to be dissolved. The penultimate symbol of the world turned upside down occurred when, in February 1940, the Soviets turned 500 mostly communist German exiles over to the Gestapo for internment in Nazi camps.

Despite the Comintern's efforts to enforce its new line, reality soon led many communist parties to defy its policy. In Germany and Italy, the ruthlessly persecuted communist underground continued to resist, and as fascist armies overran Europe, all the parties in Greece, Yugoslavia, Bulgaria, France, and elsewhere went into active opposition. Matters were not always clear, however. In France, PCF leader Jacques Duclos (1896–1975) initially attempted to negotiate the legalization of the PCF and the publication of *L'Humanité* with the Nazi occupiers, but the party soon shifted into active resistance by distributing literature, supporting strikes, and stockpiling weapons.

The contradictory situation ended only on 22 June 1941, when Nazi Germany invaded the Soviet Union. Despite clear warnings, the attack caught the Soviets completely by surprise, and the poor leadership of Stalin—who apparently had a nervous breakdown in the first days of the assault—and some of his generals further undermined military resistance. Vast areas came under German control; millions of Soviet soldiers were killed, wounded, or captured; the Soviets lost massive numbers of tanks and planes; and the Nazis were soon poised to seize Leningrad and Moscow. But the Soviets held on. Declaring the struggle to be a "Great Patriotic War" in defense of the motherland, the regime used patriotism to mobilize the population against the invaders. Although some citizens welcomed the Germans, especially in Ukraine, the murderous exploitation of the conquered territories by the Nazis soon made clear that liberation was not on the agenda. Tens of thousands answered Stalin's call for partisan warfare against the invaders, and millions endured great hardships at the front or in production at home to carry on the war.

In December 1941, the Red Army halted the Germans in a great battle for Moscow. Although the Nazis resumed the offensive the following year, they suffered devastating defeats at Stalingrad in the winter of 1942–1943 and at Kursk in July 1943. By then, the productivity of Soviet industry began to tell as factories turned out far more tanks and planes than the Germans anticipated. While much that had been built in European Russia was destroyed by the invaders and by Soviet forces practicing a scorched-earth policy, the Soviets also managed to dismantle many factories and transport them to the east for reassembly out of bombing range. Hunger was widespread, civilian goods were scarce, and people suffered enormous deprivation, but the centrally planned economy functioned effectively in wartime. Together with substantial U.S. aid (such as boots and trucks), Soviet industry enabled the army to absorb massive losses and still drive the Germans back.

Meanwhile, for Europe's communists, the Nazi invasion transformed their situation overnight as Stalin declared the war to be a "united front of the peoples standing for freedom and against enslavement."[12] With the USSR now part of a broad alliance including Britain and the United States, communists across Europe were thrust into the vanguard of the antifascist opposition. In many occupied territories, they took the lead organizing partisan units, intelligence operations, sabotage, and political alliances. In France, for example, they joined the Committee for Free France headed by the conservative patriot Charles de Gaulle (1890–1970). In Italy, they came together with socialists, Catholics, liberals, and others to form the Committee of National Liberation in September 1943 and the following year entered an antifascist coalition government. Conditions were very different in Eastern Europe, where it proved difficult to build broad alliances. In Yugoslavia, for example, Josip Broz Tito (1892–1980) ignored the authority of a royalist government in exile and led communist partisans in a brutal resistance war against the Germans while also fighting against a rival movement on the extreme right. In Greece, the communist partisans also had royalist rivals to their right, but there, unlike in Yugoslavia, the British actively aided the latter and hindered unified action. Although a new Polish Workers' Party emerged in Poland in 1942, it remained isolated from the broader resistance and ultimately came to depend on the power of the Red Army as it advanced through the country.

Despite these conditions in the East, for many in the West the broad coalitions that defeated fascism opened the way for a new beginning in 1945. Isolated during the period of the Hitler-Stalin Pact, the wartime experience had returned communism to the center of democratic politics and won it respect and mass support. The Soviet Union, too, now enjoyed enhanced prestige. It was the Red Army that bore the brunt of the fighting against Germany and was largely responsible for the Allied victory that made it possible for socialists across Europe to emerge from the underground and rebuild. Much had changed since the halcyon days of the pre-1914 era. Chastened, socialists had to rethink their old assumptions about progress and creating alternatives to capitalism. But they were also hopeful of a new beginning and determined to reconstruct a society that would make a resurgence of fascism impossible. It is to that story that we now turn.

DOCUMENT 5.1. STATE AND REVOLUTION (1917)

V. I. Lenin

Written while Lenin was hiding in Finland during the late summer of 1917 (but not published until after the Bolshevik seizure of power), this work provides one of the clearest statements of Lenin's understanding of the coming revolution and its long-term goals.

The Presentation of the Question by Marx in 1852

... It is often said and written that the main point in Marx's theory is the class struggle. But this is wrong. And this wrong notion very often results in an opportunist distortion of Marxism and its falsification in a spirit acceptable to the bourgeoisie. For the theory of the class struggle was created not by Marx, but by the bourgeoisie before Marx, and, generally speaking, it is acceptable to the bourgeoisie. Those who recognize only the class struggle are not yet Marxists; they may be found to be still within the bounds of bourgeois thinking and bourgeois politics. To confine Marxism to the theory of the class struggle means curtailing Marxism, distorting it, reducing it to something acceptable to the bourgeoisie. Only he is a Marxist who extends the recognition of the class struggle to the recognition of the dictatorship of the proletariat. That is what constitutes the most profound distinction between the Marxist and the ordinary petty (as well as big) bourgeois. This is the touchstone on which the real understanding and recognition of Marxism should be tested. And it is not surprising that when the history of Europe brought the working class face to face with this question as a practical issue, not only all the opportunists and reformists, but all the Kautskyites (people who vacillate between reformism and Marxism) proved to be miserable philistines and petty-bourgeois democrats repudiating the dictatorship of the proletariat. Kautsky's pamphlet, The Dictatorship of the Proletariat, published in August 1918, i.e., long after the first edition of the present book, is a perfect example of petty-bourgeois distortion of Marxism and base renunciation of it in deeds, while hypocritically recognizing it in words (see my pamphlet, The Proletarian Revolution and the Renegade Kautsky, Petrograd and Moscow, 1918).

Opportunism today, as represented by its principal spokesman, the ex-Marxist Karl Kautsky, fits in completely with Marx's characterization of the bourgeois position quoted above, for this opportunism limits recognition of the class struggle to the sphere of bourgeois relations. (Within this sphere, within its framework, not a single educated liberal will refuse to recognize the class struggle "in principle"!) Opportunism does not extend recognition of the class struggle to the cardinal point, to the period of transition from capitalism to communism, of the overthrow and the complete abolition of the bourgeoisie. In reality, this period inevitably is a period of an unprecedently violent class struggle in unprecedentedly acute forms, and, consequently, during this period the state must inevitably be a state that is democratic in a new way (for the proletariat and the propertyless in general) and dictatorial in a new way (against the bourgeoisie).

Further. The essence of Marx's theory of the state has been mastered only by those who realize that the dictatorship of a single class is necessary not only for every class society in general, not only for the proletariat which has overthrown the bourgeoisie, but also for the entire historical period which separates capitalism from "classless society," from communism. Bourgeois states are most varied in form, but their essence is the same: all these states, whatever their form, in the final analysis are inevitably the dictatorship of the bourgeoisie. The transition from capitalism to communism is certainly bound to yield a tremendous abundance and variety of political forms, but the essence will inevitably be the same: the dictatorship of the proletariat. . . .

The Transition from Capitalism to Communism

. . . Democracy for an insignificant minority, democracy for the rich — that is the democracy of capitalist society. If we look more closely into the machinery of capitalist democracy, we see everywhere, in the "petty" — supposedly petty — details of the suffrage (residential qualifications, exclusion of women, etc.), in the technique of the representative institutions, in the actual obstacles to the right of assembly (public buildings are not for "paupers"!), in the purely capitalist organization of the daily press, etc., etc., — we see restriction after restriction upon democracy. These restrictions, exceptions, exclusions, obstacles for the poor seem slight, especially in the eyes of one who has never known want himself and has never been in close contact with the oppressed classes in their mass life (and nine out of 10, if not 99 out of 100, bourgeois publicists and politicians come under this category); but in their sum total these restrictions exclude and squeeze out the poor from politics, from active participation in democracy.

Marx grasped this essence of capitalist democracy splendidly when, in analyzing the experience of the Commune, he said that the oppressed are allowed once every few years to decide which particular representatives of the oppressing class shall represent and repress them in parliament!

But from this capitalist democracy — that is inevitably narrow and stealthily pushes aside the poor, and is therefore hypocritical and false through and through — forward development does not proceed simply, directly and smoothly, towards "greater and greater democracy," as the

liberal professors and petty-bourgeois opportunists would have us believe. No, forward development, i.e., development towards communism,
proceeds through the dictatorship of the proletariat, and cannot do otherwise, for the resistance of the capitalist exploiters cannot be broken by
anyone else or in any other way.

And the dictatorship of the proletariat, i.e., the organization of the
vanguard of the oppressed as the ruling class for the purpose of suppressing the oppressors, cannot result merely in an expansion of democracy. Simultaneously with an immense expansion of democracy, which
for the first time becomes democracy for the poor, democracy for the
people, and not democracy for the money-bags, the dictatorship of the
proletariat imposes a series of restrictions on the freedom of the oppressors, the exploiters, the capitalists. We must suppress them in order to
free humanity from wage slavery, their resistance must be crushed by
force; it is clear that there is no freedom and no democracy where there is
suppression and where there is violence.

Engels expressed this splendidly in his letter to Bebel when he said, as
the reader will remember, that "the proletariat needs the state, not in the
interests of freedom but in order to hold down its adversaries, and as
soon as it becomes possible to speak of freedom the state as such ceases to
exist."

Democracy for the vast majority of the people, and suppression by
force, i.e., exclusion from democracy, of the exploiters and oppressors of
the people—this is the change democracy undergoes during the transition from capitalism to communism.

Only in communist society, when the resistance of the capitalists have
disappeared, when there are no classes (i.e., when there is no distinction
between the members of society as regards their relation to the social
means of production), only then "the state . . . ceases to exist," and "it
becomes possible to speak of freedom." Only then will a truly complete
democracy become possible and be realized, a democracy without any
exceptions whatever. And only then will democracy begin to wither
away, owing to the simple fact that, freed from capitalist slavery, from
the untold horrors, savagery, absurdities, and infamies of capitalist exploitation, people will gradually become accustomed to observing the
elementary rules of social intercourse that have been known for centuries
and repeated for thousands of years in all copy-book maxims. They will
become accustomed to observing them without force, without coercion,
without subordination, without the special apparatus for coercion called
the state.

The expression "the state withers away" is very well chosen, for it
indicates both the gradual and the spontaneous nature of the process.
Only habit can, and undoubtedly will, have such an effect; for we see
around us on millions of occasions how readily people become accustomed to observing the necessary rules of social intercourse when there is

no exploitation, when there is nothing that arouses indignation, evokes protest and revolt, and creates the need for suppression.

And so in capitalist society we have a democracy that is curtailed, wretched, false, a democracy only for the rich, for the minority. The dictatorship of the proletariat, the period of transition to communism, will for the first time create democracy for the people, for the majority, along with the necessary suppression of the exploiters, of the minority. Communism alone is capable of providing really complete democracy, and the more complete it is, the sooner it will become unnecessary and wither away of its own accord.

In other words, under capitalism we have the state in the proper sense of the word, that is, a special machine for the suppression of one class by another, and, what is more, of the majority by the minority. Naturally, to be successful, such an undertaking as the systematic suppression of the exploited majority by the exploiting minority calls for the utmost ferocity and savagery in the matter of suppressing, it calls for seas of blood, through which mankind is actually wading its way in slavery, serfdom and wage labor.

Furthermore, during the transition from capitalism to communism suppression is still necessary, but it is now the suppression of the exploiting minority by the exploited majority. A special apparatus, a special machine for suppression, the "state," is still necessary, but this is now a transitional state. It is no longer a state in the proper sense of the word; for the suppression of the minority of exploiters by the majority of the wage slaves of yesterday is comparatively so easy, simple and natural a task that it will entail far less bloodshed than the suppression of the risings of slaves, serfs or wage-laborers, and it will cost mankind far less. And it is compatible with the extension of democracy to such an overwhelming majority of the population that the need for a special machine of suppression will begin to disappear. Naturally, the exploiters are unable to suppress the people without a highly complex machine for performing this task, but the people can suppress the exploiters even with a very simple "machine," almost without a "machine," without a special apparatus, by the simple organization of the armed people (such as the Soviets of Workers' and Soldiers' Deputies, we would remark, running ahead).

Lastly, only communism makes the state absolutely unnecessary, for there is nobody to be suppressed—"nobody" in the sense of a class, of a systematic struggle against a definite section of the population. We are not utopians, and do not in the least deny the possibility and inevitability of excesses on the part of individual persons , or the need to stop such excesses. In the first place, however, no special machine, no special apparatus of suppression, is needed for this: this will be done by the armed people themselves, as simply and as readily as any crowd of civilized people, even in modern society, interferes to put a stop to a scuffle or to prevent a woman from being assaulted. And, secondly, we know that the fundamental social cause of excesses, which consist in the violation of the rules of social intercourse, is the exploitation of the people, their want and their poverty. With the removal of this chief cause, excesses will inevitably begin to "wither away." We do not know how quickly and in what succession, but we do know they will wither away. With their withering away the state will also wither away.

Without building utopias, Marx defined more fully what can be defined now regarding this future, namely, the differences between the lower and higher phases (levels, stages) of communist society. . . .

The Higher Phase of Communist Society

. . . The state will be able to wither away completely when society adopts the rule: "From each according to his ability, to each according to his needs," i.e., when people have become so accustomed to observing the fundamental rules of social intercourse and when their labor has become so productive that they will voluntarily work according to their ability. "The narrow horizon of bourgeois law," which compels one to calculate with the heartlessness of a Shylock whether one has not worked half an hour more than anybody else—this narrow horizon will then be left behind. There will then be no need for society, in distributing the products, to regulate the quantity to be received by each; each will take freely "according to his needs."

From the bourgeois point of view, it is easy to declare that such a social order is "sheer utopia" and to sneer at the socialists for promising everyone the right to receive from society, without any control over the labor of the individual citizen, any quantity of truffles, cars, pianos, etc. Even to this day, most bourgeois "savants" confine themselves to sneering in this way, thereby betraying both their ignorance and their selfish defence of capitalism.

Ignorance—for it has never entered the head of any socialist to "promise" that the higher phase of the development of communism will arrive; as for the greatest socialists' forecast that it will arrive, it presupposes not the present ordinary run of people, who, like the seminary students in Pomyalovsky's stories, are capable of damaging the stocks of public wealth "just for fun," and of demanding the impossible.

Until the "higher" phase of communism arrives, the socialists demand the strictest control by society and by the state over the measure of labor and the measure of consumption; but this control must start with the expropriation of the capitalists, with the establishment of workers' control over the capitalists, and must be exercised not by a state of bureaucrats, but by a state of armed workers. . . .

. . . But the scientific distinction between socialism and communism is clear. What is usually called socialism was termed by Marx the "first," or lower, phase of communist society. Insofar as the means of production becomes common property, the word "communism" is also applicable here, providing we do not forget that this is not complete communism. The great significance of Marx's explanations is that here, too, he consistently applies materialist dialectics, the theory of development, and regards communism as something which develops out of capitalism. Instead of scholastically invented, "concocted" definitions and fruitless disputes over words (What is socialism? What is communism?), Marx gives an analysis of what might be called the stages of the economic maturity of communism.

In its first phase, or first stage, communism cannot as yet be fully mature economically and entirely free from traditions or vestiges of capitalism. Hence the interesting phenomenon that communism in its first phase retains "the narrow horizon of bourgeois law." Of course, bourgeois law in regard to the distribution of consumer goods inevitably presupposes the existence of the bourgeois state, for law is nothing without an apparatus capable of enforcing the observance of the rules of law.

It follows that under communism there remains for a time not only bourgeois law, but even the bourgeois state, without the bourgeoisie!

This may sound like a paradox or simply a dialectical conundrum of which Marxism is often accused by people who have not taken the slightest trouble to study its extraordinarily profound content.

But in fact, remnants of the old, surviving in the new, confront us in life at every step, both in nature and in society. And Marx did not arbitrarily insert a scrap of "bourgeois" law into communism, but indicated what is economically and politically inevitable in a society emerging out of the womb of capitalism.

Democracy means equality. The great significance of the proletariat's struggle for equality and of equality as a slogan will be clear if we correctly interpret it as meaning the abolition of classes. But democracy means only formal equality. And as soon as equality is achieved for all members of society in relation to ownership of the means of production, that is, equality of labor and wages, humanity will inevitably be confronted with the question of advancing further from formal equality to actual equality, i.e., to the operation of the rule "from each according to his ability, to each according to his needs." By what stages, by means of what practical measures humanity will proceed to this supreme aim we do not and cannot know. But it is important to realize how infinitely mendacious is the ordinary bourgeois conception of socialism as something lifeless, rigid, fixed once and for all, whereas in reality only socialism will be the beginning of a rapid, genuine, truly mass forward movement, embracing first the majority and then the whole of the population, in all spheres of public and private life.

Democracy is of enormous importance to the working class in its struggle against the capitalists for its emancipation. But democracy is by no means a boundary not to be overstepped; it is only one of the stages on the road from feudalism to capitalism, and from capitalism to communism.

Democracy is a form of the state, it represents, on the one hand, the organized, systematic use of force against persons; but, on the other hand, it signifies the formal recognition of equality of citizens, the equal right of all to determine the structure of, and to administer, the state. This, in turn, results in the fact that, at a certain stage in the development of democracy, it first welds together the class that wages a revolutionary struggle against capitalism—the proletariat, and enables it to crush, smash to atoms, wipe off the face of the earth the bourgeois, even the republican-bourgeois, state machine, the standing army, the police and the bureaucracy and to substitute for them a more democratic state machine, but a state machine nevertheless, in the shape of armed workers who proceed to form a militia involving the entire population.

Here "quantity turns into quality": such a degree of democracy implies overstepping the boundaries of bourgeois society and beginning its socialist reorganization. If really all take part in the administration of the state, capitalism cannot retain its hold. The development of capitalism, in turn, creates the preconditions that enable really "all" to take part in the administration of the state. Some of these preconditions are: universal literacy, which has already been achieved in a number of the most advanced capitalist countries, then the "training and disciplining" of millions of workers by the huge, complex, socialized apparatus of the postal service, railways, big factories, large-scale commerce, banking, etc., etc.

Given these economic preconditions, it is quite possible, after the overthrow of the capitalists and the bureaucrats, to proceed immediately, overnight, to replace them in the control over production and distribution, in the work of keeping account of labor and products, by the armed workers, by the whole of the armed population. (The question of control and accounting should not be confused with the question of the scientifically trained staff of engineers, agronomists, and so on. These gentlemen are working today in obedience to the wishes of the capitalists and will work even better tomorrow in obedience to the wishes of the armed workers.)

Accounting and control—that is mainly what is needed for the "smooth working," for the proper functioning, of the first phase of communist society. All citizens are transformed into hired employees of the state, which consists of the armed workers. All citizens become employees and workers of a single countrywide state "syndicate." All that is required is that they should work equally, do their proper share of work, and get equal pay; the accounting and control necessary for this have been simplified by capitalism to the utmost and reduced to the extraordinarily simple operations—which any literate person can perform—of supervising and recording, knowledge of the four rules of arithmetic, and issuing appropriate receipts.

When the majority of the people begin independently and everywhere to keep such accounts and exercise such control over the capitalists (now converted into employees) and over the intellectual gentry who preserve their capitalist habits, this control will really become universal, general, and popular; and there will be no getting away from it, there will be nowhere to go."

The whole of society will have become a single office and a single factory, with equality of labor and pay.

But this "factory" discipline, which the proletariat, after defeating the capitalists, after overthrowing the exploiters, will extend to the whole of society, is by no means our ideal, or our ultimate goal. It is only a necessary step for thoroughly cleansing society of all the infamies and abominations of capitalist exploitation, and for further progress.

From the moment all members of society, or at least the vast majority, have learned to administer the state themselves, have taken this work into their own hands, have organized control over the insignificant capitalist minority, over the gentry who wish to preserve their capitalist habits and over the workers who have been thoroughly corrupted by capitalism—from this moment the need for government of any kind begins to disappear altogether. The more complete the democracy, the nearer the moment when it becomes unnecessary. The more democratic the "state" which consists of the armed workers, and which is "no longer a state in the proper sense of the word," the more rapidly every form of state begins to wither away.

For when all have learned to administer and actually to independently administer social production, independently keep accounts and exercise control over the parasites, the sons of the wealthy, the swindlers and other "guardians of capitalist traditions," the escape from this popular accounting and control will inevitably become so incredibly difficult, such a rare exception, and will probably be accompanied by such swift and severe punishment (for the armed workers are practical men and not sentimental intellectuals, and they scarcely allow anyone to trifle with them), that the necessity of observing the simple, fundamental rules of the community will very soon become a habit .

Then the door will be thrown wide open for the transition from the first phase of communist society to its higher phase, and with it to the complete withering away of the state.

Source: Lenin, *Collected Works*, Volume 25 (4th English Edition, Progress Publishers, Moscow), 381–492. First published in 1918. Transcription/markup: Zodiac and Brian Baggins. Online version, Lenin Internet Archive (marxists.org) 1993, 1999: http://www.marxists.org/archive/lenin/works/1917/staterev.

DOCUMENT 5.2. THE TRANSFORMATION OF POLITICS (1922)

Rudolf Hilferding

By 1922, it was clear to most German socialists that the revolution of 1918 had fallen short of their earlier hopes for a socialist transformation. Nevertheless, many, such as Rudolf Hilferding, believed that the establishment of a parliamentary republic created a framework for further progress. Unlike Lenin, he ascribed great value to parliamentary democracy and its potential to facilitate reform. The excerpt below illustrates the importance he placed on compromise within the political process.

The most essential thing we have achieved as a result of the collapse [of 1918] is political self-determination, the autonomy of the German people, the parliamentary system. What does that mean? Might it not presage disaster given the political parties' unpreparedness, a condition and heavy burden transmitted to us from the recent past? The answer depends upon the development of the German party system. For the party now really must become political, the molder of the political will and, as such, a necessary and indispensable element of the state. Politically considered, the state is nothing other than the conscious regulation of social relations, and is therefore identical with the government in all its functions; the parties, however, are the actual or potential bearers [of state power]. Modern constitutional institutions must make possible the formation of a coherent governmental will (*Staatswillen*) to which, as a consequence of social power relations, all the classes of modern society subordinate themselves. This process can unfold only through the formation and struggle of political parties. It is politically senseless to want to anticipate the respective results of social struggles through artificial means. Any representation by social station; any decision-making power by economic groups is an impossibility in modern society. It presumes that some all-wise lawgiver knows from the beginning the measure of each group's social power, which in fact only can be ascertained in political struggles of social groups that have transformed themselves into political parties....

It is not the replacement of political parties that is necessary, but their transformation. The parliamentary system brings this about. It forces the parties to [adapt] to political reality and to give up doctrinaire attitudes. This does not entail the repudiation of great, radical, transformative final goals. But mere propaganda and simple professions of faith no longer suffice. It becomes necessary to show the practical way [forward], to place the next step—the task that has to be carried out immediately—in the foreground, and to conquer a majority alone or with allies in order as the ruling party to implement the demands put forward when in the opposition. This also impacts the behavior of the opposition. It must reckon with being summoned at any time to execute its program and must therefore limit its demands to what is immediately doable. Moreover, in a developed democracy, because the respective social and political power relations are clear, the use of extra-parliamentary means is limited.

Such tendencies must fight hard in the new Germany in order to achieve a breakthrough, but they are slowly advancing. The internal process of development experienced by Social Democracy, the strongest party, is significant. The party most alienated from the old state has now consciously become the champion of the Republic and adopted an attitude toward political problems permeated by a strong sense of responsibility. The position of the [Catholic] Center party is rather singular. Born in the Kulturkampf, it united all strata of modern society linked together by a non-political, religious bond. The Center's leaders were constantly forced to deal with the results of the various forces and currents represented in the party, a kind of political schooling denied to the other parties. The religious bond also gave it greater freedom of movement and adaptability. After successfully withstanding the Kulturkampf, the Center was the party best able to pursue politics rather then theology. This extraordinary adaptability also made it one of the ruling parties of the new era. But what had previously been its strength is now becoming its weakness. The religious bond makes it an eternal minority and separates its members—for non-political reasons—from society. It becomes problematic. If dropped, the Center would become the decisive bourgeois party [and] party building would rapidly move ahead. For the parliamentary system [and] the compulsion to govern drive the concentration of political forces and the movement toward a two-party system. The inherited political groups resist [this development], but it is underway. The dividing lines among the parties are growing thinner and coalitions and working groups are forming. . . . At the same time there is new ferment in the old parties. In all bourgeois parties the antagonism is growing between the right wing, which traditionally holds fast to its narrow interests, and the left, which clearly senses, if it doesn't fully recognize, the need for a change in political attitude toward the state.

And that is what is significant and hopeful.

Source: Rudolf Hilferding, "Wandel in der Politik," *Die Frankfurter Zeitung*, 31 December 1922 (second morning edition). Translated by William Smaldone.

DOCUMENT 5.3. STALIN'S REVOLUTION (1929)

J. V. Stalin

Having eliminated Trotsky and the leftist opposition, by the late 1920s Stalin was prepared to turn against Bukharin and his former allies on the Communist Party's "right." This selection outlines the arguments that Stalin marshaled to delegitimize any remaining opposition to his authority and to pave the way for his policies calling for collectivization of the farms and rapid industrialization.

What is the theoretical basis for the blindness and bewilderment of Bukharin's group?

I think that the theoretical basis for this blindness and bewilderment is Bukharin's incorrect, non-Marxian approach to the question of the class struggle in our country. I have in mind Bukharin's non-Marxian theory that the kulaks will grow into socialism, his failure to understand the mechanism of the class struggle under the dictatorship of the proletariat. . . .

Hitherto, we Marxist-Leninists thought that between the capitalists of town and country, on the one hand, and the working class, on the other, there is an *irreconcilable* antagonism of interest. This is exactly what the Marxian theory of the class struggle rests on. But now, according to Bukharin's theory that the capitalists will *peacefully grow* into socialism, all this is turned topsy-turvy; the irreconcilable antagonism of class interests between the exploiters and the exploited disappears, the exploiters grow into socialism. . . .

Either one thing or the other; either there is an irreconcilable antagonism of interests between the capitalist class and the class of the workers who have assumed power and have organized their dictatorship, or there is no such antagonism of interests, in which case only one thing remains: to proclaim the harmony of class interests. . . .

What can there be in common between Bukharin's theory that the kulaks will grow into socialism and Lenin's theory of the dictatorship as a fierce class struggle? Obviously, there is not, nor can there be, anything in common between them.

Bukharin thinks that under the dictatorship of the proletariat the class struggle must *subside* and *pass away* so that the abolition of classes may be brought about. Lenin, on the contrary, teaches us that classes can be abolished only by means of a stubborn class struggle, which under the dictatorship of the proletariat becomes *ever fiercer* than it was before the dictatorship of the proletariat. . . .

. . . In addition to the ordinary taxes, direct and indirect, which the peasantry is paying to the estate, it also pays a certain supertax in the form of an overcharge on consumer goods, and in the form of low prices received for agricultural produce. . . .

... We also call it "the scissors," "drainage" of resources from agriculture into industry for the purpose of speeding up industrial development.

Is his "drainage" really necessary? Everybody agrees that it is, as a temporary measure, if we really wish to maintain a speedy rate of industrial development. Indeed, we must at all cost maintain a rapid growth of our industry, for this growth is necessary not solely for our industrial production, but primarily for our agriculture, for our peasantry, which at the present time needs most of all tractors, agricultural machinery and fertilizers.

Can we abolish this supertax at the present time? Unfortunately, we cannot. We must abolish it at the first opportune moment, in the coming years. But we cannot abolish it right now.

Now, as you see, this supertax obtained by means of "the scissors" is in fact "something like a tribute." Not a tribute, but "something like a tribute." It is "something like a tribute" which we are paying for our backwardness. We need this supertax to stimulate the development of our industry and to do away with our backwardness. ...

... It was no accident that Bukharin and his friends took exception to the word "tribute" and began to speak of military-feudal exploitation of the peasants. Their outcry about military-feudal exploitation was undoubtedly an expression of their extreme discontent with the Party policy toward the kulaks, which is being applied by our organizations. Discontent with the Leninist policy of the Party in its leadership of the peasantry, discontent with our grain-purchasing policy, with our policy of developing collective and state farms to the utmost, and lastly, the desire to "unfetter" the market and to establish complete freedom of private trade—there you have the underlying reason for Bukharin's screams about military-feudal exploitation of the peasantry.

In the whole history of our party I cannot recall another single instance of the Party being accused of carrying on a policy of military-feudal exploitation. This anti-Party weapon was not borrowed from a Marxian arsenal. From where, then, was it borrowed? From the arsenal of Milyukov, the leader of the Constitutional Democrats . . . .

... We have two different plans of economic policy.

The Party's Plan:

1. We are re-equipping industry (reconstruction)
2. We are beginning seriously to re-equip agriculture (reconstruction)
3. For this we must expand the development of collective farms and state farms, employ on a mass scale the contract system and machine-and-tractor stations as means of establishing a bond between industry and agriculture in the sphere of production.

4. As for the present grain-purchasing difficulties, we must admit the necessity for temporary emergency measures that are bolstered up by the popular support of the middle and poor-peasant masses, as one of the means of breaking the resistance of the kulaks and of obtaining from them the maximum grain surplus necessary to be able to dispense with imported grain and to save foreign currency to the development of industry.

5. Individual poor-and-middle peasant farming plays, and will continue to play, a predominant part in supplying the country with food and raw materials; but alone it is no longer adequate—the development of individual poor-and-middle peasant farming must therefore be *supplemented* by the development of collective farms and state farms, by the contract system applied on a mass scale, by accelerating the development of machine-and-tractor stations, in order to facilitate the squeezing out of the capitalist elements from agriculture and the gradual transfer of the individual peasant farms to large-scale collective farming, to collective labor.

6. But in order to achieve all this, it is necessary first of all to accelerate the development of industry, of metallurgy, chemicals, machine building, of tractor works, agricultural-machinery works, etc. Failing this it will be impossible to solve the grain problem, just as it will be impossible to reconstruct agriculture.

Conclusion: *The key to the reconstruction of agriculture is the speedy rate of development of our industry.*

Bukharin's Plan:

1. "Normalize" the market; permit the free play of prices on the market and a rise in the price of grain, undeterred by the fact that this may lead to a rise in the price of manufactured goods, raw materials, and bread.

2. The utmost development of individual peasant farming accompanied by a certain reduction of the rate of development of collective farms and state farms (Bukharin's theses of July and his speech at the July plenum).

3. Grain purchasing on the spontaneity principle, precluding under all circumstances even the partial application of emergency measures against the kulaks, even though such measures are supported by the middle- and poor-peasant masses.

4. In the event of a shortage of grain, to import about 100,000,000 rubles worth of grain.

5. And if there is not enough foreign currency to pay for imports of grain and equipment for industry, to reduce imports of equipment and, consequently, the rate of development of our industry—oth-

erwise our agriculture will simply "mark time," or will even "directly decline."

Conclusion: *The key to the reconstruction of agriculture is the development of individual peasant farming.*

This is how it works out, comrades.

Bukharin's plan is a plan to *reduce* the rate of development of industry and to *undermine* the new forms of the [worker-peasant] bond.

Such are our divergencies. . . .

. . . The fight against the Right deviation is one of the most important duties of our Party. If we, in our own ranks, in our own Party, in the political General Staff of the proletariat, which is directing the movement and is leading the proletariat forward—if we in this General Staff should tolerate the free existence and the free functioning of the Right deviationists, who are trying to demobilize the Party, to demoralize the working class, to adapt our policy to the tastes of the "Soviet" bourgeoisie, and thus yield to the difficulties of our socialist construction—if we should tolerate all this, what would it mean? Would it not mean that we want to send the revolution downhill, demoralize our socialist construction, flee from difficulties, surrender our positions to the capitalist elements?

Does Bukharin's group understand that to refuse to fight the Right deviation is to betray the working class, to betray the revolution?

Does Bukharin's group understand that unless we overcome the Right deviation and the conciliationist tendency it will be impossible to overcome the difficulties facing us, and that unless we overcome these difficulties it will be impossible to achieve decisive success in socialist construction?

Compared with this, what is the value of this pitiful talk about the "civil execution" of three members of the Political Bureau?

No, comrades, the Bukharinites will not frighten the Party with liberal chatter about "civil execution." The Party demands that they should wage a determined struggle against the Right deviation and the conciliationist tendency side by side with all the members of the Central Committee of our Party. It demands this of the Bukharin group in order to help to mobilize the working class, to break down the resistance of the class enemies and to make sure that the difficulties of our socialist construction will be overcome.

Either the Bukharinites will fulfill this demand of the Party, in which case the Party will welcome them, or they will not, in which case they will have only themselves to blame.

Source: Stalin, "The Right Deviation in the CPSU(B)" (Speech to the Central Committee, April, 1929; *Problems of Leninism*, 309–13, 326–27, 331, 336–37, 371–72. Reprinted in: Robert V. Daniels, ed., *A Documentary History of Communism in Russia, from Lenin to Gorbachev* (Hanover, NH: University Press of New England, 1993), 170–73.

Figure 5.6. "Workers of the World Unite!" A poster by Alexander Apsit commemorating the Russian Revolution, Russia, 1918. Courtesy of IISH, Amsterdam.

Figure 5.7.   "Women! Equal Rights Means Equal Duties. Vote Social Democratic!" Germany, 1919. Courtesy of the AsD, Bonn.

Figure 5.8.   A summons to participate in the "First International Week of Workers' Children" organized by the Communist Youth International, Germany, 1921. Design by Gandermann. Courtesy of the IISH, Amsterdam.

Figure 5.9.   "Against Papen, Hitler, Thälmann." A German social democratic electoral poster exhorting voters to reject monarchism, Nazism, and communism. 1932. Courtesy of the AsD, Bonn.

Figure 5.10. Stalin, 1938. The text reads, "Long Live the Marx-Engels-Lenin National Holiday [May Day] That Will Live on Forever!" (Translation courtesy of Edward J. Lazzerini.) Design by E. M. Mirzoev, Azerbaijan Courtesy of the IISH, Amsterdam.

NOTES

1. "The Stuttgart Resolution," in James Joll, *The Second International, 1889–1914* (New York: Harper & Row, 1966), 198.

2. Quoted in Helen Rappaport, *Conspirator: Lenin in Exile* (New York: Basic Books, 2010), 246.

3. Joll, *The Second International*, 157.

4. Quoted in Edmund Wilson, *To the Finland Station* (New York: Farrar, Strauss & Giroux, 1972), 549.

5. Quoted in Werner Maser, *Friedrich Ebert: Der erste deutscher Reichspräsident* (Munich: Droemer Knaur, 1987), 176.

6. Quoted in Geoff Eley, *Forging Democracy: The History of the Left in Europe, 1850–2000* (New York: Oxford University Press, 2002), 172.

7. On the concept of bureaucratic collectivism, see, for example, Hal Draper, "The Neo-Stalinist Type: Notes on a New Political Ideology," *The New International* 14, no 1 (January 1948): 24–26.

8. Quoted in Robert Service, *Stalin: A Biography* (Cambridge, MA: Harvard University Press, 2004), 273.

9. Quoted in William Smaldone, *Rudolf Hilferding: The Tragedy of a German Social Democrat* (Dekalb: Northern Illinois University Press, 1998), 166.

10. Georgi Dimitrov, "The Working Class against Fascism," in *Marxists in the Face of Fascism*, ed. David Beetham (Totowa, NJ: Barnes & Noble, 1984), 179–86.

11. Eley, *Forging Democracy*, 241.

12. Eley, *Forging Democracy*, 282.

SIX

Socialism and Communism during the Cold War, 1945–1991

In April 1933, Nazi Propaganda Minister Joseph Goebbels boldly asserted that, with the victory of National Socialism, "The year 1789 is hereby eradicated from history."[1] Twelve years later, however, it was the liberal, social democratic, and communist "children" of 1789 who won the day. Indeed, it was they who now had the opportunity to rebuild European society in accordance with the Revolution's ideals of democratic freedom, human rights, and equality. They were ultimately unable to achieve this lofty goal. Liberalism, socialism, and communism all have their ideological roots in the Enlightenment, but, as we have seen, the meanings that their adherents ascribed to such concepts as "freedom" and "equality" were often radically different. These differences had fueled intense struggles between liberals and socialists prior to 1914 and among liberals, socialists, and communists after the Bolshevik Revolution of 1917. Nazi aggression had forced an alliance of necessity, but the war had not resolved their differences. After their joint victory, conflicts soon reemerged over the place of democracy in society, the role of the state in economic affairs, and the relationship of individual rights to the needs of the broader community. Tensions were particularly acute between the liberal and social democratic West and the communist East. The resulting "Cold War" framed international relations on a global scale for the next four decades.

THE DIVISION OF EUROPE

Although very real differences divided the Western powers and the Soviets, in 1945 many believed that long-term cooperation was possible.

223

During the spring, American, British, and Soviet forces cooperated in the conquest and occupation of Germany, and in a meeting at Potsdam in July, Stalin, American President Harry Truman (1884–1972), and, after Winston Churchill's defeat in the British elections, Labor Prime Minister Clement Attlee (1883–1967) worked out agreements regarding the expulsion of over 12 million Germans from Eastern Europe and the administrative division of Germany and Berlin. All saw the need to "democratize," "demilitarize," and "decartelize" Germany; to treat that country as a single economic unit; and to allow the Soviets to extract reparations from their own as well as the western zones of occupation. Although many issues were left open, including the meaning of "democratization," it was expected that future negotiations would lay the groundwork for a peace treaty formalizing a new postwar settlement.

In the West, communist parties emerged from the war with greatly strengthened popular support. They gained prestige from the Red Army's eastern victories and from their leadership in antifascist resistance coalitions with socialists and democrats. Stalin had dissolved the Comintern in 1943 as a gesture to the Allies, and at war's end communists in France, Italy, Belgium, and elsewhere were part of a body politic anxious to punish collaborators, restore national unity, and carry out democratic and social reforms. In the first postwar national elections, after winning 26 and 19 percent of the vote, respectively, French and Italian communists entered broad coalition governments with socialists and Christian Democrats. They now committed themselves to parliamentary politics and broadly shared republican programs emphasizing planned economic modernization, comprehensive social security, and moral reform of the state and society.

In the East, where conditions were completely different, the main issue was the extent to which the Soviets would impose their control. Compared to the West, the region had been utterly devastated. Most of its great cities, such as Leningrad, Königsberg, Warsaw, and Budapest, had been laid to waste; Soviet and German scorched-earth policies had destroyed much of the area's industry and agriculture; tens of millions of civilians had been set in motion as refugees, deportees, settlers, and forced laborers; and tens of millions more were dead. Of Poland's 30 million people in 1939, 6 million had perished, including 3 million Jews. Over 28 million Soviet soldiers and civilians died in the war, most of European Russia lay in ruins, and famine loomed. The Red Army had extracted brutal revenge on its march to Germany, and its actions deepened hostility to the Union of Soviet Socialist Republics (USSR) in much of the region. With the exception of Yugoslavia, where Josip Broz Tito's communist partisans liberated the country without direct Soviet aid, its postwar omnipresence guaranteed Soviet authority.

Having borne German invasion twice in a quarter of a century, the USSR had no intention of tolerating unfriendly regimes in Eastern Europe. During the war, despite talk of democratic elections, Stalin had made this view quite clear to the Allies, and at a meeting in October 1944, Churchill had conceded Soviet dominance, excepting Greece. Operating on the basis of this arrangement, the extent of direct Soviet intervention in the region depended on circumstances, but Stalin assumed the USSR's hegemony. As in the West, Eastern Europe's communist parties participated in coalition governments, but here they retained decisive power. In places where their candidates had virtually no chance of winning, such as Poland, elections were rigged, but in cases where they were popular, as in Czechoslovakia, they were largely free. To broaden their support, communist parties spoke the language of gradualism and of different "national" roads to socialism.

This moment of apparent communist cooperation in the West and relative flexibility in the East did not last long. Although Stalin was not planning a war of aggression with the West, he was insecure and suspicious of Western motives. The USSR's land army remained Europe's largest, but expecting a renewed capitalist crisis and a possible falling out among the imperial powers, he aimed to secure Soviet interests in Eastern Europe at all costs. In the West, too, Truman and Attlee were highly suspicious of Soviet intentions and aimed to protect their own interests in territories under their control. Tensions increased as the occupying powers clashed over Germany's future and as the West, erroneously, held Stalin responsible for Tito's support of a communist insurgency against the British-backed Greek monarchy. Meanwhile, as communist parties in Vietnam, Malaysia, Indonesia, and elsewhere fought against European efforts to reassert their colonial authority, civil war exploded in China between communist and nationalist forces.

Germany was a microcosm and focal point of the systemic conflict as the occupying powers, despite earlier pledges of joint management, reshaped their respective zones in their own image. Fearful that Europe's moribund economy would fuel support for communism, the Western powers concluded that renewed prosperity required Germany's rapid economic recovery as an industrial and capitalist state. For their part, the Soviets expropriated substantial industries in their zone, introduced major elements of centralized planning, and demanded large-scale reparations from their own and the other allied zones. As the Western Allies integrated their zones economically, they also encouraged the revival of political parties, including the Social Democratic, Communist, and Christian Democratic parties, among others, and the election of local and regional governments. The Soviets did the same in their zone, but when it became clear that the German Communist Party (KPD) could not match the popular support of the German Social Democratic Party (SPD), they forced the two parties to merge in April 1946. Although each nominally had equal representation in the leadership of the new Socialist Unity Party (SED), veteran communists such as Walter Ulbricht (1893–1973)

and Wilhelm Pieck (1876–1960) were in control. Propped up by the Soviets, the SED dominated politics in their zone. Thus, the Western and
Soviet zones were moving in different economic and political directions.

In March 1946, Winston Churchill famously declared that "an iron
curtain had descended across Europe," but matters came to a head the
following year. In January, rigged elections secured communist control in
Poland, while in March, in response to British appeals, the United States
moved to support Greece and Turkey against perceived Soviet aggression and announced the Truman Doctrine pledging "to support free people . . . resisting attempted subjugation by armed minorities or outside
pressures." In May 1947, the French, Italian, and Belgian coalition
governments expelled their communist partners, and the following
month, the United States announced the introduction of the Marshall
Plan to provide economic aid for Europe. Although the Americans extended the offer to the eastern European states, including the USSR, it
required the latter to open its economy in ways incompatible with the
Soviet system, and Stalin, always suspicious, rejected it and pressured his
Eastern allies to do the same.

As tensions increased, Stalin tightened his control over Europe's communist movement, especially in the East. In September 1947, he summoned the Eastern parties, as well as the French and the Italians, to a
conference in Poland to establish the Communist Information Bureau
(Cominform). Ostensibly, the aim of the new organization was to "coordinate" the parties' work, but its real purpose was to discipline them. It
jettisoned the idea of different "national roads" to socialism, touted the
Soviet model as the only legitimate one, and sharply criticized the French
and Italians for their openness to coalition politics and to the Marshall
Plan. As Stalin's representative, Andrei Zdanov (1896–1948), put it, the
world was now divided into "two camps," one imperialist and antidemocratic led by the United States, the other anti-imperialist and democratic
led by the USSR. Soviet interests overrode local ones.

The costs of the drive to conformity were quickly illustrated in Czechoslovakia. The Czechs and Slovaks had greeted the arrival of the Red
Army, and many saw the USSR as a protector against threatening neighbors. Genuinely popular, the KSC's membership rose from 50,000 in 1945
to over 1.3 million in 1948. In the free elections of May 1946, it won 38
percent of the vote and thereafter led a coalition government with cooperative partners. Its leader, Klement Gottwald (1896–1953), was confident
of the party's continued growth. The government had already introduced
state ownership and centralized planning on a substantial scale, and it
seemed that the KSC, via parliamentary means, aimed to lead the country
on its own independent path to communism. Nevertheless, under intense
Soviet pressure, in February 1948 the KSC stunned the world by seizing
complete power. To the West, this ruthless action was a mark of Soviet

aggression. To Stalin, more concerned about his own power, it was a necessary step to bring the USSR's satellite into line.

He was particularly irked by developments in Yugoslavia. Under Tito's leadership, the Yugoslav Communists had quickly moved to Bolshevize the country. They rode roughshod over the opposition, modeled their new constitution on the USSR's, and forcibly collectivized agriculture. Relations with the Soviets were excellent for a time, and at the Cominform's first meeting, Stalin had used Yugoslav leaders Edvard Kardelj (1910–1979) and Milovan Djilas (1911–1995) to whip the Western parties into line. He soon grew angry, however, over Tito's support for a Balkan federation that would include Yugoslavia, Albania, Bulgaria, and parts of Greece, his backing of Greece's communist insurgents, and his insistence on Italian territorial concessions in a dispute over Trieste.

Stalin perceived Tito's self-confidence and popularity as an affront to his authority and an obstacle to his policy against the West. Tensions resulted in an open break in February 1948 when Stalin condemned the Balkan project and broke off trade negotiations. Shortly thereafter, the USSR withdrew its military and civilian advisers, and in June the Cominform expelled Yugoslavia for pursuing a "nationalist" foreign policy. Unable to remove Tito through internal machinations, Stalin sought to isolate his government. Tito held firm and, deftly using Yugoslavia's strategic location to advantage, turned to the West for the aid and trade that prevented the collapse of Yugoslavia's economy.

"Titoism" now became a criminal offense on par with "Trotskyism." The Cominform launched a campaign to root out supposed Titoist counterrevolutionaries, spies, and fascists everywhere. Longtime communist leaders fell victim to a new wave of purges. The lucky ones, such as Polish party chief Vladislav Gomulka (1905–1982), were imprisoned, but many others, such as Koçi Xoxe (1917–1949) in Albania, Lásló Rajk (1909–1949) in Hungary, and Trajco Kostov (1897–1949) in Bulgaria, were executed. Mass purges and show trials returned. Under Mátyás Rákosi (1892–1971), Hungarian communists executed 2,000 of their comrades, imprisoned 150,000, and expelled 350,000 from the party. The penultimate show trial took place in Czechoslovakia in 1952. Under massive Soviet pressure, after initial persecutions of nonparty individuals and low-ranking communists, a number of leading figures were arrested, tried, and executed, including the party's general secretary, Rudolf Slansky (1901–1952). Of the fourteen leaders in the dock at the latter's trial, the fact that eleven were of Jewish origin revealed the strength of resurgent anti-Semitism emanating from the Kremlin.

The tightening of Soviet control also meant the annihilation of civil society throughout Eastern Europe. The remnants of press freedom disappeared, and universities, professional associations, sports and social clubs, and churches all lost their remaining autonomy, as did the civil service and army. As was true in the USSR, the party and state grew increasingly intertwined, with the latter losing its independent existence. These policies had nothing to do with the ideals of socialism. On the contrary, they were rooted in Stalin's own murderous megalomania and paranoia and with the logic of bureaucratic collectivism.

In Stalin's view, that hypercentralist model had proved itself during the war. Many Soviet citizens had hoped that, after years of sacrifice, the regime might alter its postwar policy by easing state controls, breaking up collective farms, and granting more freedom. But Stalin continued the economic policies of the 1930s with most investment concentrated in heavy industry (especially the military sector). Millions of people, especially repatriated prisoners of war and residents of the newly annexed Baltic States and former territories of eastern Poland (whose loyalty Stalin viewed as suspect), were deported to slave labor camps. The government reasserted tight controls over the collective farms and squeezed the peasantry relentlessly for grain and taxes. As a result, millions left the countryside for the towns, where opportunities, however modest, were better.

As the Soviets consolidated their political hold on Eastern Europe, they also imposed their economic system. Soon the economies of all of the "People's Democracies" were characterized by nationalized industry, collectivized agriculture, and multiyear economic plans coordinated, at least in theory, with those of their allies and the USSR. The implications of these changes were enormous. Economic and social relations throughout the region were transformed as most owners of private property, large and small, lost their wealth, status, and power, while state investment in new industry and the creation of massive planning and management institutions created new opportunities, particularly for those from the lower classes, to move into a variety of blue- and white-collar jobs. As was true in the USSR, these beneficiaries, especially in the upper ranks of the bureaucracy, had a stake in this new world and formed the social basis of the party-state. As we will see, however, the effort to impose homogeneity across the Soviet-controlled "East bloc" did not last. While the basic structure would endure, within a short time considerable variations also emerged.

Stalin was able to secure his grip over most of Eastern Europe, but he had less success in Germany. Initially convinced that its workers eventually would decide for socialism and close relations with the Soviet camp, he aimed to create a unified but disarmed and neutral Germany. In June 1948, however, the Western powers announced their intention of founding a West German state (the Federal Republic of Germany) and moved ahead with a currency reform in their respective zones. The Soviets responded with their own currency reform and, hoping to forestall West German independence, blockaded land transport to West Berlin. After the Allies successfully supplied the city by air for almost a year, Stalin backed down. In May 1949, the West German Parliamentary Council accepted a temporary constitution, or "Basic Law," to guide a new federal republic until Germany could be reunited. Once again forced to improvise, Stalin formally proclaimed an East German state (the German Democratic Republic or GDR) on 7 October.

Thus, by the end of 1949, Europe's political and economic divisions had hardened. Soon, most of the West's leading states, including a rearmed West Germany, joined a military and political alliance, the North Atlantic Treaty Organization (NATO), led by the United States. In response, the Soviet Union organized its satellites, including a rearmed East Germany, into the Warsaw Pact. Concomitantly, the Organization for European Economic Cooperation in the West and the Council for Mutual Economic Assistance in the East promoted the economic integration of each system's member states. Europe's Cold War order was in place.

POSTWAR SOCIAL DEMOCRACY

During the period of fascist domination, most of Europe's socialist parties, unions, and other allied organizations, like their communist counterparts, were outlawed with many leaders imprisoned or driven underground or into exile. While some socialist leaders resisted, sometimes paying with their lives, most of them, like millions of former party members, simply kept their heads down and waited for better days. Splits were common among the disparate exile and underground groups as they argued over the reasons for their failure and how to move forward. Only later, as the tide of war turned, did their active resistance increase.

Socialists throughout Western Europe were part of the broad antifascist coalition that emerged during the war, but they remained suspicious of the communists, who had labeled them "social fascists" and defended the Hitler-Stalin Pact. Some German socialists, such as Fritz Erler (1913–1967), thought that wartime cooperation might lead to later unity, a sentiment widely shared among the rank and file of both groups. Not all agreed. London-based SPD leaders such as Hans Vogel (1881–1945) and Erich Ollenhauer (1901–1963) strongly opposed collaboration with the communists, a view shared by future party leaders, such as Kurt Schumacher (1895–1952) and Willy Brandt (1913–1992). Leaders of the French Section of the Workers' International (SFIO) shared these sentiments while also recognizing the communists' contributions to the resistance. Many agreed with Leon Blum's conclusion that cooperation was both "necessary and impossible."[2]

Yet Europe's socialists emerged from the war with great expectations for the future. As Donald Sassoon has noted, "If the war had shattered anything, it was the already damaged belief that capitalism, if left to its own devices, would be able to generate the 'good society.'"[3] Many believed that unbridled capitalism had led to the Great Depression; it was now widely assumed that the democratic state, which the socialists fully embraced, would have to take the economy in hand. With fascism crushed and liberal economics discredited, socialists believed that their moment had come at last. As we will see, their moment had, indeed, arrived, but it did not unfold as many expected, for success required them to rethink their identity and goals in fundamental ways.

After the war, Western Europe's socialists were willing to govern. They formed part of ruling coalitions across the region, generally sharing power with newly formed "Christian Democratic" people's parties to their right and communist parties to their left. In the immediate postwar years, all three of these groups espoused similar aims: eliminating collaborators, restoring parliamentary governance, enhancing social security, and pursuing economic modernization managed by the democratic state. The center-right Christian Democrats also supported the latter goal. In its Ahlen Program of 1947, for example, Germany's Christian Democratic Union (CDU) declared that "the period of unencumbered rule by private capitalism is over."[4]

Such goals were not by themselves "socialist," but socialists regarded them as necessary steps toward the new society that would be achieved gradually via democratic means. In response to the electoral imperative, after 1945 socialists gradually jettisoned the tenets of orthodox Marxism, such as the centrality of class struggle, state ownership of the means of production, central planning, and internationalism, and replaced them with an emphasis on building cross-class support for reforms based on Keynesian approaches to economic management carried out within the framework of the nation-state. There was some general agreement among the parties on long-term goals, but their practical approaches were diverse. Socialism, declared the newly reconstituted Socialist International in 1951, "aims to liberate the [world's] peoples from dependence on a minority which owns or controls the means of production." It seeks "to put economic power in the hands of the people as a whole, and to create a community in which free men work together as equals."[5] But the International also explicitly eschewed any uniformity of approach and recognized that a wide range of perspectives, such as Marxist, Christian humanist, and others, drew people to the movement. This attitude reflected reality as socialists in different countries responded to widely varying local circumstances.

The centrality of national factors in determining postwar social democratic trajectories is illustrated by the parties' different policies across the West in the immediate postwar years. Ironically, it was in Great Britain, where radical Marxism was weakest, that Labor, after winning a landslide victory in 1945, carried out reforms that were the most sweeping. During the war, Labor leaders had gained experience from participation in a coalition cabinet with the Tories. Having successfully managed shared wartime sacrifice, they were confident that the state could also create social justice in peacetime. On coming to power, Atlee's government undertook the nationalization of key industries (with full compensation to former owners), including transport; coal, iron, and steel; electrical and gas utilities; and the Bank of England, and put into place a series of welfare measures with socialized medicine as the centerpiece. These were substantial reforms and improved the quality of life for many Britons.

Labor won the election because most British voters wanted a fairer society and associated the party with reform. Although some Laborites saw the changes as the beginnings of socialism, most people regarded them as practical means of maintaining full employment and opening access to basic public goods, such as education and health care. Indeed, capitalism continued to flourish in Britain, and deeply embedded class divisions remained. The British civil service effectively carried out the nationalization process, and some industries, especially utilities, were well run, but the economic and social system survived intact. There was no planning for a national economy, management of state-owned enterprises remained top down and bureaucratic, and there were no efforts to empower workers. The Labor government did nothing to reform the structure of the monarchy or to pare the privileges of Britain's upper classes, whose inherited wealth remained essentially untouched.

While the British placed nationalization of industry at the core of their reforms, Scandinavian socialists, also in power after 1945, continued down the path the Swedes had pioneered in the interwar years. The Norwegian Labor Party took control over transport, communications, and the central bank but left industry virtually unscathed. Sweden, meanwhile, entered the postwar era in the strongest position. Having avoided war, its intact industries were well placed to take advantage of demand generated by Europe's reconstruction. With unemployment low and real wages rising, the Swedish Workers' Party felt less pressure to expand the state sector even after the communists achieved 11 percent of the vote in the local elections of 1946. After proposals for expanded public ownership encountered opposition from the right, the party dropped the issue. Instead, it used a range of other means, such as state fiscal and social policies, planning, and cooperation between labor and business sectors, to simultaneously promote growth and redistribute the results of production. Over time, the Swedish Workers' Party was able to use its legislative powers to rein in the sovereignty of capital and create a generous welfare state that encouraged broad social equality and upward mobility for workers. Eventually, Sweden became the model social democratic state.

Socialists elsewhere in Europe did not dominate the political scene to the same extent as in Britain and Scandinavia, but movement toward a mixed economy and the welfare state occurred virtually everywhere. In France, for example, the SFIO emerged from the war as part of a governing coalition that included the French Communist Party (PCF) and the Catholic Popular Republican Movement. In the fall 1945 elections, each party had campaigned for political and social reforms and received about a quarter of the total vote. Despite internal tensions concerning the new constitution, the coalition passed key elements of the wartime program put forward by the National Council of the Resistance. It nationalized the coal, gas, and electricity companies as well as the most important banks and insurance firms; created the basis of the French social security system; and established a planning commission to work out a four-year strategy to modernize industry.

From the start, however, the SFIO found itself trapped between its use of radical rhetoric reminiscent of the interwar years and its reformist practice as a participant in a series of shaky coalitions that governed France until the Fourth Republic's collapse in 1958. In 1946, a left majority chose Guy Mollet (1905–1975) to lead the party. He initially attempted to outflank the larger PCF from the left but after the onset of the Cold War pushed the party toward the center in tune with increasingly prevalent anticommunism. Unlike the more proletarian PCF, the SFIO's support among industrial workers was small, and the party's constituency rested on small farmers along with teachers, postal workers, and low-level civil servants. Rather than build on this heterogeneous base to create a cross-class people's party, however, Mollet and his supporters insisted on using the language of class struggle to attract workers, whom they saw as the agents of socialist revolution. This approach alienated many non–working-class backers and stood in stark contrast to the party's reformist domestic policies, which strengthened the welfare state and an imperialist foreign policy seeking to preserve French power in Indochina, Algeria, and elsewhere. As a result of this confusion, despite its prominence in government, the SFIO's membership slipped from 350,000 to 100,000, and its electoral support fell from 24 to 12 percent between 1945 and 1960. When the Fourth Republic gave way to the Fifth based on a powerful presidency, the party drifted into obscurity.

While the SFIO sought to differentiate itself from the PCF and remained engaged in national governance after the latter's expulsion from the cabinet in 1947, its sister party in Italy, the Italian Socialist Party (PSI), cleaved to the communists and shared their exclusion from national power. Postwar Italy, too, was initially dominated by a coalition consisting of the Communist, Socialist, and Christian Democratic (DC) parties. Under Palmiero Togliatti (1893–1964), the Italian Communist Party (PCI) aimed to promote national unity and democratic reform while remaining loyal to the USSR. Building on Gramsci's theoretical legacy stressing the fight for power as a long-term "war of movement" among contending social and ideological forces, Togliatti aimed to build the PCI into a counterhegemonic force in Italian society. This approach meant reaching out to peasants, the middle classes, intellectuals, partisans, and women by creating organizations, such as cooperatives and peasant leagues or the Union of Italian Women, as a means of developing their desire and capacity for radical change. It bore fruit. Between 1943 and 1945, the PCI grew from 5,000 to 1,750,000 members and won 19 percent in the elections of 1946. It was particularly strong in the northern industrial regions, where it eventually dominated local government.

Led by the radical socialist Pietro Nenni (1891–1980), the PSI rejected Leninism but maintained its Marxist commitment to revolutionary class struggle. After winning 20 percent of the vote in 1946, it cooperated closely with the PCI, and the two parties formed the Popular Democratic Front against the DC two years later. Such cooperation alienated reformist segments of the party, which then broke away to form the Italian Workers' Socialist Party, headed by Giuseppe Saragat (1898–1988), and weakened the PSI's electoral strength. Amidst mounting Cold War tensions and backed by the United States and the Catholic Church, in 1948 Alcide de Gaspari's DC won 48 percent to the combined 31 percent of the Communist and Socialist parties. For more than a decade, the PSI remained marginalized and out of government. The small Italian Workers' Socialist Party, however, joined Gaspari's cabinet, which adopted a free market–oriented policy but, nevertheless, assigned the state a major role managing the economy. For example, it controlled large holding companies, established earlier by the corporatist fascist regime, including steel, shipbuilding, auto, and energy producers. It also carried out land reform, especially in the underdeveloped south. Although Italy remained socially and politically polarized, the mixed economy laid the groundwork for the economic boom of the 1950s and the expansion of the welfare state.

Like their Italian counterparts, West Germany's socialists also retained their allegiance to the theoretical tenets of Marxist orthodoxy, but unlike the PSI, they did not face strong competition from the communists. In the wake of the Red Army's brutal conquest of the east, characterized by mass rape, widespread pillage, and the death, deportation, and imprisonment of vast numbers of soldiers and civilians, the KPD faced an uphill battle for popular support. Soviet occupation policies in the east and the SED's increasing intolerance of noncommunist rivals also undermined communism's reputation in the west and marginalized the KPD. Thus, without a major rival to its left, the SPD was in a strong position to assert itself against the large and heterogeneous Christian Democratic "people's party" that emerged after the war along with several smaller liberal and more conservative parties.

In Kurt Schumacher, the SPD also had a fiery and dedicated leader. After fighting in World War I, he joined the SPD in 1918 and eventually won a seat in the Reichstag, where his assertion that Nazism was an "appeal to the inner swine in man" earned him their unremitting hatred.[6] After ten years in Nazi camps, he emerged physically broken but politically determined. Schumacher successfully warded off efforts to merge the SPD and the KPD in western Germany and quickly rebuilt member-ship to 600,000. The resurrected SPD, however, was much different than its prewar predecessor. Although it maintained close relations with the revived but now more independent German trade unions, much of its vast infrastructure of social, political, and cultural organizations, along with its 200 newspapers, was gone. Thus, in the postwar world, social democracy became more than ever a vehicle for electoral politics rather an "alternative culture" for workers. The SPD was not alone in experienc-ing such changes, but in most other countries, where fascist authority had been less thorough, they occurred more gradually.

After 1945, the SPD called for the nationalization of mines, heavy industries, power, transport, insurance, and banking and stressed the planned management of the economy. Such demands were at least partly acceptable to the CDU before 1948, but the American occupiers effective-ly blocked them. By the time West Germany emerged as a state, the Cold War and the CDU's turn to economic liberalism had altered the situation completely. Now the SPD could implement its vision, which also in-cluded the enhancement of workers' rights and the creation of a thor-oughgoing welfare state, only by winning parliamentary elections.

And therein lay the problem. Between 1949 and 1966, the CDU domi-nated West German politics. Led by Konrad Adenauer (1876–1967), in each electoral cycle the Christian Democrats broadened their support among all social groups until in 1957 the party won an absolute majority. Economics Minister Ludwig Erhard (1897–1977) introduced the "social market economy," which combined a generally liberal approach with "discriminatory intervention" that allowed the state to establish national investment priorities, such as in Volkswagen, while also promoting com-petition, such as by breaking up cartels. Aware of competitive capital-ism's tendency to promote social polarization and insecurity, CDU governments also laid the groundwork for an extensive social safety net to meet the needs of a vast array of groups, including the millions of postwar Germans who were refugees, unemployed, ill housed, and underinsured. Using this approach, the CDU presided over the onset of Germany's "economic miracle," its rearmament, its entry into the West-ern Alliance, and its integration into the European Coal and Steel Com-munity in 1951 and the subsequent European Economic Community (EEC) in 1957.

In the context of West Germany's rising prosperity and the CDU's general success in achieving sovereignty and integration into Western Europe, the SPD's resistance to virtually all of Adenauer's major policies led to the party's isolation. Its anticapitalist and class struggle rhetoric and insistence that Western integration consolidate Germany's division did little to win new supporters among a population that was increasing-ly anticommunist, benefited from improving economic circumstances, and was concerned more with day-to-day matters of reconstruction (and forgetting the recent past) than with national unity. The SPD won some regional elections and, with their trade union allies, pushed through the workers' right of "codetermination" in the coal and steel industries, but as long as the party retained its traditional Marxist outlook, it attracted only about a third of the national electorate.

Thus, in the decade after 1945, even Western European countries following "liberal" economic principles implemented policies that included substantial state management and measures to improve social security. To some extent, these policies drew on the legacy of fascist "corporatism," in which the state, via its control over the institutions of civil society, including those representing the interests of capital and labor, used its political power to set and implement economic and societal goals, but they also drew on the Swedish interwar experience and the ideas of reform socialists, such as Hendrik de Man. Now, in the postwar framework of parliamentary democracy, corporatism reemerged as governments brought together representatives of labor and capital to achieve politically determined social aims, such as the creation of the welfare state. As we will see, these developments caused many European socialists to conclude that their earlier concepts of change were no longer applicable in postwar society. In response, they would adapt their approach to take advantage of the possibilities within the postwar order while also conforming to its limits.

KHRUSHCHEV AND THE CRITIQUE OF STALINISM

On 5 March 1953, Stalin died suddenly. Always murderous toward perceived enemies, there had been signs of an impending purge. In the fall of 1952, the Kremlin's six Jewish doctors (along with a few non-Jewish colleagues) were arrested, ostensibly for murdering Zhdanov in 1948. Rumors flew of plans for a new round of show trials and of the deportation of all Soviet Jews, now labeled "rootless cosmopolitans," to Siberia. Meanwhile, many of Stalin's closest henchmen, such as Molotov and Anastas Mikoyan (1895–1978), lived in growing fear of their increasingly unpredictable boss, who in October 1952 rebuked them in front of the Central Committee for alleged softness in the struggle against world capitalism and excluded them from meetings of his inner circle. Thus, Stalin's death came as a godsend to the members of his court, who immediately began maneuvering for power.

Although many in the USSR and elsewhere certainly welcomed Stalin's demise, for most Soviet citizens and communists around the world, it came as a shock and evinced heartfelt sadness. Hundreds of thousands rushed to Moscow to pay their respects to the person whom they associated with the revolutionary transformation of the country and with victory against Nazism. Many had experienced great suffering under Stalin's rule but, generally unaware of the scale of his crimes, saw him as a great leader. A great void had now opened up in the country.

The three most important figures were Beria, chief of the state security apparatus; Georgy Malenkov (1902–1988), who headed the government; and Nikita Khrushchev (1894–1971), leader of the party secretariat. All three were tough, brutal insiders who had served Stalin loyally, had benefited from the system, and aimed to preserve it. At the same time, however, they all recognized the necessity for reforms. Stalin's insistence on prioritizing heavy industry and the military had impoverished the society and fueled widespread discontent. The government crushed open dissent but, beginning as early as March 1953, also instituted a "New Course" in domestic policy that eased repression and shifted economic policy to better meet the people's needs. Ironically, it was Beria, one of Stalin's most sycophantic courtiers, who began many of the changes later associated with the process of "de-Stalinization." He ended wasteful projects, such as the building of a gigantic Volga-Baltic canal, and urged the release of most labor camp prisoners. The government proclaimed the first amnesty only weeks after Stalin's death.

Although the leadership publicly stressed "collective" decision making, Khrushchev, Malenkov, and others feared Beria's power and conspired to eliminate him. Arrested in the Kremlin during a late June meeting of the top leaders, Beria was tried in secret for "criminal, anti-party, and anti-state activities" and executed in December. Meanwhile, the regime continued its new policies. Between 1953 and 1956, it released over 5 million prisoners from the GULAG, reduced taxes on the peasants by 50 percent, and tightened supervision of the security services. Focusing on agricultural development, Khrushchev implemented a plan to open up millions of acres of "virgin land" in the Volga region, Kazakhstan, and parts of Siberia. Initially, this project substantially increased grain output and raised his political stature. By 1956, he had enough political allies in the Central Committee and the Politburo (now called the Presidium) to assert his authority and marginalize his rivals.

The decisive moment came in February 1956 at the Twentieth Party Congress, where, in a "secret speech" circulated only among the party elite, Khrushchev set the communist movement on the path away from Stalinism. Elaborating a litany of Stalin's monstrous crimes against party members, he described his errors in preparing for the Nazi invasion, attacked his "violations of socialist legality," and condemned the "cult of personality" that surrounded him. Accusing his former chief of "ignoring the norms of party life" and "trampling upon Leninist principles of collective party leadership," Khrushchev took the focus off his many enablers (such as himself and the rest of the top leaders) and made it difficult for Stalin's acolytes to muster support against him. Khrushchev rehabilitated a number of Stalin's victims though not Trotsky, Bukharin, or any other of the other Old Bolshevik leaders murdered in the purges. He also did not criticize collectivization or forced industrialization, which still stood as examples of Soviet achievements. A convinced communist, Khrushchev wanted to show that Stalin, not the Leninist system, was responsible for the USSR's problems, to isolate his political opponents, and to create a space for new policy initiatives.

Of course, the secret speech could not be kept secret, and it landed like a bombshell in the communist and noncommunist worlds. The broad context was very important. In the West, Khrushchev's revelations confused many communists who, despite much evidence to the contrary, had looked to the USSR as a beacon of hope for a better world. The Twentieth Congress upended such illusions and led many to leave the movement. Others felt a sense of relief; to them, it cleared the air and laid the groundwork for renewal. It was in the east, of course, where the impact was most profound. For three years, the Soviets had been encouraging the satellite states to adopt the "New Course." The reforms came too late to prevent an uprising in East Germany, where tensions exploded into open rebellion on 17 June 1953. Intent on rapidly "building socialism," the SED's decision to raise workers' output norms sparked strikes and political demonstrations that only Red Army tanks could quell. Not wishing to base their power solely on military might, however, the Soviets continued to urge the adoption of new economic priorities, collective leadership, and an end to show trials and terror throughout the East bloc. Symbolizing this more flexible attitude, in 1955 Khrushchev dissolved the Cominform and began mending fences with Tito.

In the wake of the Twentieth Congress, changes in the east occurred unevenly. In Czechoslovakia, for example, the Stalinist regime resisted the New Course and blocked reforms for over a decade. In Poland, however, matters were very different. Following Stalin's death, the party had slowed collectivization, eased police repression and censorship, and released leading "national communists," such as Gomulka, from house arrest. Political conflict soon erupted as intellectuals called for an end to censorship, national communists demanded freedom from Soviet control, and Stalinists attempted to hold the line. At the grassroots level, factory workers began forming "workers' councils" and raised concrete demands of their own. In late June 1956, Internal Security forces crushed a two-day worker uprising for "bread and freedom" in Poznan. To diffuse the crisis, in October the Polish United Workers' Party (PUWP) removed the defense minister, Soviet Marshal Konstanty Rokossowski (1896–1968), and brought Gomulka back to power. Although the Soviets threatened armed intervention, Gomulka successfully convinced Khrushchev that the situation was under control. He forswore collectivization, eased state controls over cultural matters, and came to an arrangement with the Catholic hierarchy. But, crucially, he preserved single-party rule, central planning, and adherence to the Soviet alliance.

While Gomulka was able to persuade Khrushchev that changes in Poland did not threaten Soviet interests, events in Hungary represented the most serious threat to the bureaucratic collectivist order. In July 1953, reform-oriented communist Imre Nagy (1896–1958) replaced the notorious Stalinist Rákosi as premier. Nagy, who earlier had been imprisoned for opposing forced collectivization and the execution of Rajk, advocated closing forced labor camps, allowing peasants to leave the collectives, and reorienting investment priorities away from heavy industry. Rákosi and his supporters hindered Nagy's efforts and in 1955 convinced the Soviet leadership that he was unreliable. The Soviets restored Rákosi to power in March, but his support was weak, and unrest at the grassroots among intellectuals, students, Catholics, and workers accelerated after Khrushchev's revelations. Public calls multiplied for the rehabilitation of purge victims and the punishment of those responsible, for press freedom, and for Nagy's return. Rákosi's lack of support and his history as one of Stalin's anti-Tito inquisitors led the Soviets, now trying to win Tito back into the fold, to cut him loose. In July, another Stalinist, Ernö Gerö (1898–1980), replaced him.

Gerö was unable to halt the collapse of the government's legitimacy. On 6 October, the public reburial of the rehabilitated Rajk provided an opportunity for speakers to condemn the "lawlessness, arbitrariness, and moral decay" of the Stalinist regime, and soon the Hungarian Writers' Union, the Central Council of Trade Unions, the Petöfi Circle (an important student club), and the independent League of Hungarian Students were demanding reforms. On 22 October, students at the Technical University in Budapest issued a manifesto demanding economic reforms, free speech, democracy, the return of Nagy to power, the prosecution of Rákosi and his henchmen for their crimes, and the withdrawal of Red Army units from Hungary. The next day, student demonstrations in Budapest spiraled out of control after Gerö denounced the meeting in a public broadcast. Locally based Soviet troops entered the city and attacked the crowds. The next morning, after an all-night meeting, the Hungarian Central Committee named Nagy prime minister.

Nagy declared martial law while also attempting to negotiate with the demonstrators, but turmoil continued and soon became revolutionary. New student organizations and a network of workers' councils sprang up along with radicalized "national committees," though the goals of these rebels were not unified. Many workers, for example, aimed to replace the tyrannical "communist" system with a new, authentically socialist one, and they drove the party and trade union bosses out of their workplaces. Other rebels aimed for restoration of bourgeois democracy along Western lines, while there were also elements of the extreme right in the streets. By late October, Nagy had publicly acknowledged the legitimacy of many of the people's demands and promised the abolition of the secret police as well as the withdrawal of Soviet forces from Budapest, but that was not enough to halt the unrest. On 30 October, crowds attacked the Communist Party headquarters in the capital and killed twenty-four of its defenders.

To halt the unrest and fend off Soviet intervention, Nagy then decided on a bold gamble. After proclaiming the restoration of a multiparty democracy in the country, he announced Hungary's plans to withdraw from the Warsaw Pact. The Soviet government responded swiftly. In order to avoid the appearance of weakness in the eyes of Western "imperialists," it ordered Red Army units in Romania and Ukraine to invade Hungary. Budapest fell after three days of fighting on 7 November, and all other major cities quickly succumbed. Although sporadic armed resistance continued for a month, the revolution had been crushed. After seeking asylum in the Yugoslav embassy, Nagy eventually fell victim to Soviet subterfuge and was arrested, tried, and executed. The Soviets replaced him with a colleague, János Kádár, who dominated the country for the next thirty years.

Although many Hungarians hoped for Western assistance against the Soviets, the United States and its NATO allies were unwilling to launch a European war to liberate Eastern Europe. Indeed, at the very moment of the Soviet invasion, France, Britain, and Israel were attacking Egypt in a failed attempt to seize control of the Suez Canal. Despite the rhetoric of Radio Free Europe, Hungary was of little importance to them.

It was, of course, of great importance to Khrushchev and his colleagues. Their fear of the spread of radical movements to other satellites made them turn against Nagy, whose policies initially seemed to promise restored order. All the bureaucratic collectivist regimes were particularly worried about worker unrest. Dissent among intellectuals was relatively easy to corral, but mass unrest by workers in a "workers' state" was the greatest of all possible challenges to their claims of legitimacy. It was not surprising, then, that Kádár and the Soviets especially targeted Hungary's working class in reasserting authority. In a population of 9 million, 2,000 people were killed, 15,000 imprisoned, and 200,000 driven into exile. Damage was greatest in working-class districts, where resistance was heaviest, and all independent worker organizations were abolished. Even the miserable remnant of the Hungarian Communist Party, which many workers had abandoned during the struggle, was thoroughly purged.

For Khrushchev, the events in Poland and Hungary caused considerable difficulties back at home, as did his plans for partially decentralizing economic decision making and reorganizing industrial production. In mid-1957, Malenkov, Molotov, and Lazar Kaganovich (1893–1991) attempted to organize a majority in the Presidium to unseat Khrushchev, but using his leverage as head of the party to advantage, he turned the tables on them by mobilizing a majority in the Central Committee. This group ousted all his "antiparty" opponents from the top leadership. As a sign of how things had changed since Stalin's death, none of the defeated was executed. Instead, Khrushchev packed them off to distant, unimportant posts. Khrushchev's assumption of the post of prime minister as well as that of party chief marked his ascendency in Soviet politics, but his authority was limited. He was the leading figure in the post-Stalin oligarchy, and his colleagues in the Presidium and Central Committee expected decisions to rest on consultation and consensus.

Khrushchev's career embodied the type of upward social mobility possible in revolutionary Russia. The son of a coal miner, he grew up in the Donets area of Ukraine and worked as a shepherd, a factory hand, and a miner. With the outbreak of the Bolshevik Revolution he joined the Red Guards, became a communist, and quickly used the educational and career opportunities that came his way to move up the political ladder. Trained as an engineer and a friend of Stalin's second wife, by 1934 he was a member of the Central Committee and soon afterward became the party's first secretary in Ukraine. For two decades, he served Stalin faithfully but also became aware of many of the problems plaguing the system. A true believer in communism's egalitarian goals, once in power he worked frantically to overcome its shortcomings.

Militarily and economically, the USSR was always much weaker than the United States and its allies, and Khrushchev, like all Soviet leaders until Gorbachev, aimed to reverse that situation. Overestimating the USSR's capacity, he believed that it was possible to simultaneously build up the military and raise the standard of living. Khrushchev directed resources into the Soviet space program, which stunned the world with the launching of *Sputnik* in October 1957, and into the creation of a long-range nuclear missile program to counter America's enormous advantage in air and naval power and its much larger stockpile of atomic weapons. But breaking with Stalin's assumptions, he thought that a powerful military would secure "peaceful coexistence" with the capitalist world in which nonlethal competition between the two systems would reveal socialism's superiority. At a time when Western colonial empires were dissolving, Khrushchev believed that many of the newly independent states would view socialism as a viable model.

Khrushchev promised his people a rapid transformation in their living standard. Indeed, in 1957 he prophesied that the USSR would surpass the United States in the production of milk, meat, and butter within four years, and at the party's Twenty-Second Congress held in 1961, he predicted that, within twenty years, productivity would rise so prodigiously that the dictatorship of the proletariat would give way to the realm of communist abundance and equality for all Soviet citizens. Such aims required action. In addition to putting large new areas under the plow, he raised the level of investment in agriculture substantially, gave the collective farmers more autonomy, and integrated them into the social security system for the first time. Initially, such policies seemed to bring success. Agricultural production increased 51 percent between 1953 and 1958, both improving supplies and earning Khrushchev substantial political capital.

In industry, Khrushchev also improved workers' living standards by raising wages, repealing harsh labor laws, reducing the workweek from forty-eight to forty-one hours between 1956 and 1960, and doubling the rate of housing construction during roughly the same period. Most important, to improve the output and quality of industrial production, he attempted to reform Stalin's rigid, hypercentralized, top-down planning system by transferring some decision-making authority from the national and union republic levels to over 100 regional economic councils. Such changes, which included the elimination of a number of bureaucratic agencies, shook the planning apparatus to the core. Old central planners fumed at their loss of status, while Khrushchev won new supporters in the new institutions. In the early 1960s, after these changes failed to adequately resolve the problems of supply and low quality that plagued the system, economists such as Evsei Liberman (1897–1981) began discussing reforms giving enterprises more autonomy, using market mechanisms to determine prices, and using profits as a measure of success. These ideas also influenced economic thinking in East Germany and Hungary, where reformers pondered mechanisms to improve the system's performance.

During the 1950s, the Soviet model appeared to hold great promise. Annual gross national product increased at a rate of 7.1 percent, more than twice as fast of that of the United States. But with an economic base much smaller than that of its capitalist rival, it proved impossible for the USSR to substantially close the gap in living standards. Moreover, between 1958 and 1964, the growth rate slowed to 5.3 percent, a trend that would continue as policymakers failed to shift priorities from extensive growth (basic "heavy" industry) to intensive growth (in newly emerging industrial sectors characterized by rapid technical innovation). Khrushchev recognized that the Stalinist model needed reforms to achieve his lofty aims, but the plethora of changes he introduced did not alter the fundamental problems of a system dominated by top-down planning mechanisms. These could successfully carry out certain focused, national projects, such as the development of the space program or new weapons, but were ineffective in meeting the overall needs of an increasingly complex, modernizing society.

These economic discussions were a part of the overall revival of intellectual life that followed Stalin's death. Taking its name from the title of Ilia Ehrenburg's 1954 novel *The Thaw*, this period saw writers, artists, and filmmakers reemerge from the straitjacket of socialist realism as practiced under Stalin to take on formerly taboo subjects, such as corruption within the party, generational conflicts, and, with the publication of Solzhenitsyn's *One Day in the Life of Ivan Denisovich* (1962), even the injustice and brutality of life in the GULAG. Censorship, however, remained a fact of life, and it was often inconsistent and arbitrary. While many previously banned authors, such as Isaac Babel and Michael Bulgakov, circulated once again, the regime banned works such as Boris Pasternak's *Dr. Zhivago* (published in the West in 1957). Khrushchev certainly did not believe in relinquishing the party's control over cultural life. The opening that he permitted, however, gave hope to many Soviet intellectuals that it was possible to move toward greater freedom and the realization of humanistic socialism's goals.

Bringing day-to-day terror to an end for average citizens as well as members of the bureaucratic elite and achieving initial economic success in agriculture brought Khrushchev substantial political support through the late 1950s. Soon, however, domestic and foreign policy setbacks began to undermine his position. For example, the initial bumper crops achieved in the virgin lands quickly evaporated in the wake of giant dust storms caused by drought, the use of techniques ill suited to the soils of the region, and the lack of irrigation. Even when decent crops could be harvested, inadequate storage and transportation infrastructure plagued the system. In addition, Khrushchev's efforts to expand and consolidate the state farm sector at the expense of cooperative farms; to radically expand maize production even when it was incompatible with local conditions; to rein in peasants' long-tolerated use of small, highly productive private plots (the fruits of which could be privately marketed); and to unrealistically increase the output of milk and meat often led to poor results. In 1963, bad weather and mismanagement forced the USSR again to import large amounts of grain.

Khrushchev's tinkering with the planning and administrative system led to confusion, disorganization, and dismay. In 1962, for example, state and party organs were divided into "industrial" and "agricultural" sections at all levels, throwing the officials concerned into disarray. To some party leaders, these reforms, along with Khrushchev's proposals for term limits for officials, threatened to undermine the party's authority and their own power and privileges. They tried to block many proposed changes or dragged their feet implementing new policy decisions. Khrushchev's support in the hierarchy began to ebb.

In the realm of foreign policy, too, Khrushchev's record was mixed at best. His aim of pursuing peaceful coexistence contained the promise of better relations with the West, but it undermined the Soviet alliance with China. The Chinese chafed at Soviet tutelage, rejected de-Stalinization, called for a more aggressive policy against imperialism in the developing world, and fumed at Khrushchev's hesitancy to help them construct atomic weapons. By 1960, the split was complete, and the two hostile communist states now competed for influence around the world.

In the West, Khrushchev's impulsiveness and led to inconsistent and risky policies. For example, hoping to prevent West Germany's rearmament and to end the mass migration of disgruntled East Germans through the portal still open to West Berlin, in 1958 he demanded that the

Allied powers sign a peace treaty with Germany within six months and that Berlin be declared a free city. Khrushchev visited the United States in 1959, but the dialogue over Berlin, arms control, and other issues collapsed after the Soviets shot down an American U-2 spy plane and the Eisenhower administration refused to apologize. In the end, despite Khrushchev's threats, West Germany rearmed, and Berlin remained divided. In August 1961, Khrushchev allowed the East Germans to build a wall separating East Berlin from West Berlin. Rather than symbolizing the GDR's control over the situation, this act marked the regime's desperation to halt the flight of its young, best-educated, and most skilled citizens.

Khrushchev gambled again in 1962 when he attempted to redress the USSR's strategic inferiority to the United States by placing missiles in Cuba. At that time, the United States had eight times the number of nuclear warheads than the Soviets, and its arsenal of was infinitely superior to that of the Soviets. The victorious Cuban Revolution in 1959 had led to increasingly cooperative relations between Fidel Castro's new government and the USSR. After a U.S.-backed invasion at the Bay of Pigs in April 1961 failed to dislodge Castro, the Cubans welcomed Khrushchev's suggestion that the Soviets place nuclear missiles in Cuba. The American discovery of these missiles in October led the Kennedy administration to threaten war if they were not removed; Khrushchev was not willing to push the issue that far. In return for American promises not to invade Cuba and to remove its missiles from Turkey, he backed down. Although the world had been spared a nuclear catastrophe, many Soviet leaders viewed Khrushchev's defeat as a great humiliation.

Khrushchev's foreign policy blunders and his domestic efforts to shake up the system fueled the opposition of conservative forces in the party. Between 1962 and 1964, they resisted new reforms and further de-Stalinization efforts. While Khrushchev spent much of his time traveling outside of Moscow, leading members of the Presidium, such as Leonid Brezhnev (1906–1982) and Nikolai Podgornyi (1903–1983), supported by the KGB leadership, plotted his removal. By October 1964, they were ready. Interrupting Khrushchev's vacation on the Black Sea, they summoned him back to Moscow, where for two days the Presidium and Central Committee berated him for "sowing disorganization in industry and agriculture," foreign adventurism, "rudeness," "conceit," and the pursuit of his own personality cult, among other things.[7] Recognizing his isolation, he capitulated and "requested" to step down due to ill health. Brezhnev replaced him as party first secretary, and Alexsei Kosygin (1904–1980) became prime minister. This change marked the victory of conservative leaders who, after rising through the ranks, resented policies that threatened their security and power.

Khrushchev had done much to ensure that Soviet bureaucrats could die in their beds rather than with a bullet in the back of the head or in a forced labor camp. At the same time, however, his efforts to overcome many defects of the Stalinist order turned many of those same bureaucrats against him. A product of the system, Khrushchev was alert to many of its weaknesses and tried to reform them but stopped short of a thoroughgoing transformation. His fate reflected the changes he had brought to Soviet society. Permitted a pension, a car and driver, and comfortable accommodations, he was not free to move about, publish, or participate in public life. Stripped of his position in the party hierarchy, he became, like the rest of his fellow citizens, a prisoner in his own country.

THE TRANSFORMATION OF SOCIAL DEMOCRACY

As we have noted, after 1945 most socialist and nonsocialist Western leaders agreed that, in order to prevent a return to the conditions that had paved the way for fascism and war, the state should regulate economic activity and promote policies facilitating greater social security. In addition, the consolidation of communist power in the East and the growth of communist parties in the West made such compromises all the more acceptable to Western Europe's political and economic elites. By the late 1950s, it was clear that the latter's efforts to reinvigorate capitalism had succeeded. Indeed, the system had entered a period of unprecedented stability and growth characterized by full employment, rising wages, and an expanding system of social security that benefited workers as well as the middle and upper classes. With revolution clearly not in the offing and their constituencies limited largely to workers, most European socialists concluded that, in order to win power and facilitate more thoroughgoing social change, they had to build "people's parties" with a broader base of cross-class support. Such a strategy required them to eschew their emphases on class struggle and the goal of overthrowing capitalism. Instead, they called for the creation of a generous welfare state and the rigorous regulation of the economy with the goal of promoting social solidarity and overcoming class antagonisms. Thus, half a century after he had initially put forward his "revision" of Marx, Bernstein's perspective became dominant among European socialists.

An excellent example of this transformation was that of the German Social Democratic Party. After the Christian Democrats won an absolute majority in 1957, one young SPD leader, Erhard Eppler (b. 1926), expressed the views of many others when he told the senior leadership that the problem was strategic rather than tactical. As long as the party focused primarily on the needs of industrial workers, he argued, it would be unable to become a broad-based, nonideological, left-of-center people's party capable of winning power. This position soon won the day. At its 1959 congress at Bad-Godesberg, the SPD jettisoned much of its Marxist heritage and adopted a more broadly conceived ideological frame-work. According to its new program, "democratic socialism" rested on the fundamental values of freedom, justice, and solidarity. "Rooted in Christian ethics, in humanism, and in classical philosophy, [it] had no intention of proclaiming absolute truths, but strove to create a way of life based on these principles." Socialism was not an end state. Rather, it consisted "of the long term task of fighting for freedom and justice, pre-serving them, and testing itself through them."[8]

After Godesberg, the SPD accepted West Germany's rearmament, par-ticipation in NATO, and its membership in the Common Market. Most important, it now adhered to the "social market" economy. The state, the program asserted, should "restrict itself mainly to indirect methods of influencing the economy." It should support "as much competition as possible" and "as much planning as necessary." These changes eliminat-ed the SPD's traditional rhetorical opposition to the system and made the party a more attractive choice for a wider range of voters. In 1960, over 55 percent of new party members were blue-collar workers and 21 percent white-collar employees, but by 1972, blue-collar workers made up only 27 percent of new recruits, while employees and students made up 34 and 16 percent, respectively. The face of the party became more middle class and also much younger. In 1960, about 55 percent of new members were under forty years old; twelve years later, it was 75 percent.

Led by the charismatic mayor of West Berlin, Willi Brandt, the SPD's electoral performance also improved. In 1966, in the wake of West Ger-many's first post-1949 recession and its attendant fears of a neofascist revival, the party entered the national government for the first time as junior partner in a "grand coalition" with the CDU. With the SPD's Karl Schiller in control of the Economics Ministry, the coalition convinced the trade unions and employers to cooperate on wages and other issues as the state used Keynesian strategies to pull the country out of its economic doldrums. The success of this "concerted action" and Foreign Minister Brandt's initiatives opening new channels of communication to Eastern Europe (so-called Ostpolitik) paved the way for the party's first clear electoral victory in 1969. With over 42 percent of the vote, Brandt was able to form a coalition government with the small liberal Free Democrat-ic Party.

At that time, Germany already had one of Europe's most elaborate welfare states. A new pension system established in 1957 allowed living standards for older citizens to rise, increasingly generous unemployment and health insurance programs were established, and the state provided those unable to work with a guaranteed minimum of support. These programs, along with rising wages, growing disposable income, and de-creasing working hours, made West Germany's living standard among the highest in Europe, trailing only the Scandinavian countries. Once in office, Brandt and, after 1974, his successor, Helmut Schmidt, enhanced

Figure 6.1.   Willi Brandt (center) and Leonid Brezhnev (left) in Bonn, 1973. Courtesy of the AsD and Sven Simon Fotoagentur.

the welfare state by improving the material and legal status of workers, women, and tenants, but gains were limited due to opposition from the Free Democratic Party and, as we will discuss below, declining economic circumstances. Among their most important achievements, however, was a revised Works Councils law in 1971 giving workers in most enterprises the right to be consulted on personnel matters. In addition, in 1976 the government passed new legislation granting workers in corporations with more than 2,000 employees the right to substantial representation on the firm's supervisory board. These laws did not fully undercut employers' power, but they substantially democratized economic life and strengthened cooperation between labor and capital.

Although Germany's welfare state was impressive, it rested on the overall growth of the postwar economy; the SPD did not significantly alter the country's uneven distribution of wealth. Pockets of poverty persisted, especially among the unemployed, the unskilled, immigrants, and the elderly, while a small part of the population grew very rich. In 1970, for example, only 1.7 percent of the population controlled over 35 percent of the private wealth, while workers' families, constituting one-third of the population, owned only 17 percent. This ratio did not improve much in subsequent years, nor did the distribution of national income. In 1980, the top 20 percent of the population earned over 43 percent, while the bottom 20 percent earned only 7 percent. The SPD-led coalition passed significant legislation, but it did not substantively challenge the country's established patterns of capital accumulation.

As Tony Judt has noted, it was the Scandinavian countries that came closest to achieving the social democratic ideal. They had dropped their proletarian orientation long ago and, by striving to build broad coalitions among workers, farmers, and elements of the middle class, had integrated a growing portion of the whole nation into the social democratic project. Holding power for long periods, the Danish, Norwegian, Finnish, and Swedish socialists focused on redistributing capitalist profits for public purposes rather than on the nationalization of industry. As a result, they created educational, welfare, medical, insurance, retirement, and leisure services that set the standard for the world, and they did so without diminishing their countries' global competitiveness. In the 1970s, Sweden and Finland were among the world's four richest countries (along with the United States and Switzerland) when measured by purchasing power per head of population.

Success depended on more than simply taxing profits. The Swedish state, for example, used a variety of tools—including planning, the manipulation of investment funds, fiscal policy, and cooperation among government, unions, and employers associations—to promote industrial growth and social harmony. The sophisticated Rehn-Meidner system of centralized wage bargaining set wages in different sectors of the economy depending on their profitability as a means of improving income equality and pushing weaker firms to become more productive. Ultimately, the government aimed to keep unemployment as low as possible in order to decommodify the labor market and reduce the financial costs of unemployment on the state. In general, this system worked well, and despite some relatively difficult years, the Swedish economy rode out the economic downturns of the late twentieth century quite well, though, of course, class antagonisms in Scandinavia did not disappear.

Contrary to Marx's expectations, during the postwar era, the outlook of Europe's bourgeoisie became increasingly international—exemplified by capital's support for the EEC—while the social democratic project was largely national in scope and character. Austria provides a good example of this specificity. Like its Scandinavian counterparts, Austria had been a small, rural, and poor country, but after 1945 it developed into a prosperous social democratic welfare state. Fearing a return to the fratricidal politics of the 1930s, the Austrian Social Democratic Party and the conservative People's Party created a system of "proportionality" through which they essentially divided government posts between themselves and ran the country jointly until the mid-1960s. Thereafter, a strong ethos of consensus building characterized the society, in which interests groups, like labor and small business, were organized into "chambers" with which government often consulted. Austria had a sizable state sector after 1945, but it, too, managed its economy mainly via regulation rather than nationalization. Under Social Democratic leaders such as Bruno Kreisky (1911–1990), by the 1970s the country had a welfare state rivaling that of the Scandinavian countries.

The state's role in steering the economy and providing social benefits reached its peak in the late 1960s and early 1970s regardless of whether social democracy was at the helm. The Italian state, for example, dominated by Christian Democracy (after 1963 in alliance with the increasingly reformist PSI), invested in a variety of industries, such as transportation, banking and energy, housing construction, and food production, at all levels and in all regions. Patronage jobs won the party votes but also provided resources in cash and services to those in need, such as the country' millions of landless peasants. In France, too, Gaullist governments continued the French tradition of using the state to guide national investment priorities. Although these were not governments that gave priority to the workers' interests, they did assume that the state had a major role to play in shaping economic and social life. American and European political and economic elites tolerated this pattern of development because it left capitalism intact and provided an attractive alternative to the communist model in the east.

The social democratic approach to taming capitalism and providing broadly shared social security was the twentieth century's closest approximation of the ideas put forward by Paine and Condorcet two centuries earlier. Modern capitalism had changed much since their day, and the world of small independent producers had given way to one of large-scale, "Fordist" production and highly concentrated corporate ownership, but the core features of the system, private property and the market, remained intact, as did the goals of ordinary people seeking freedom to shape their own lives and social security. Social democracy aimed to help people achieve those goals by harnessing capitalism's ability to create great wealth and directing it toward public ends. During the great postwar economic boom, the system worked quite well. As we will see, however, many people, some initially sympathetic toward social democracy, also became highly critical of the top-down nature of its domestic policies, of its foreign policy (which was often tied to that of the United States), and of its neglect of issues such as gender equality and the environment. Even more important, weaknesses in the system became evident when capitalism entered into a renewed crisis calling many of the recently achieved gains into question.

THE FAILURE OF REFORM IN EASTERN EUROPE

Following Khrushchev's fall, the new Soviet leadership around Leonid Brezhnev slowed down the process of de-Stalinization. During Brezhnev's sixteen-year tenure, the USSR settled into a long period of economic stagnation and political stability. Initially acceptable growth rates of over 5 percent gradually slowed to near zero, and it became increasingly difficult to meet the rising material expectations of a population growing steadily more urban, educated, and aware of the wider world. The system provided most people with low-cost housing, cheap basic food and mass transportation, basic health care, and schooling, but the quality of many goods and services was low and often in short supply. Brezhnev, like Khrushchev, came from a working-class family and had moved steadily up the bureaucratic ladder through hard work and astute use of political connections. Unlike his former chief, however, he scorned reforms and insisted that people simply needed to work better to improve the system's performance.

During the late 1960s, some members of the party leadership, such as Kosygin, hoped to implement some of Liberman's proposed reforms measuring enterprise performance based on sales and profits and using material incentives to boost productivity. Efforts to implement such changes did not get very far, however, because they could not be combined with central planning and the government's insistence on fixing prices. By the early 1970s, Kosygin's efforts had been defeated. A majority of party leaders hoped, instead, to reinvigorate the system using new technology and trade with the West.

While the Soviets tinkered, other reform efforts also went forward in Eastern Europe. They went furthest in Yugoslavia, where Tito straddled the line between East and West. In 1950, his government scuttled the Soviet "command economy" model and introduced a decentralized system of workers' self-management through locally elected councils. These bodies could appoint and dismiss enterprise directors and determine annual plan targets, bonuses, and working conditions.

Simultaneously, political authority in Yugoslavia became increasingly concentrated in the state's constituent, ethnically based republics and on the local level rather than in Belgrade. Tito's powerful personality, federal institutions, and the Communist Party organization linked the republics together, but the leadership was very conscious of the country's ethnic and regional tensions. Aiming to balance regional interests, in 1952 the party renamed itself the League of Communists and detached itself from the local government hierarchy. At the national level, it created the Federal Chamber, the Chamber of Republics and Provinces, and a nine-person presidency elected every five years.

The Yugoslav system functioned fairly well through the early 1970s. Tito maneuvered skillfully to gain access to aid, credit, and trading opportunities with the West and to restore economic links with the East. As in the USSR, industrial growth in this still largely agricultural country tended to be extensive rather than intensive, but the annual growth rates of over 11 percent between 1953 and 1961 were impressive. Industry absorbed most of the workers leaving the land for the towns, real wages rose modestly, trade with the West expanded, and the range of goods and services available in Yugoslavia was generally much greater than that of neighboring East bloc countries. A variety of problems, however, plagued the system. Productivity growth lagged behind that of Western economies and reduced Yugoslavia's competitiveness. Lack of trained managers, a tendency to pay out bonuses rather than reinvest in modern equipment, a price mechanism distorted by government intervention and enterprise collusion, a corrupt banking system, and uneven investment among the various regions weakened economic performance and fueled tensions among the republics.

For many years, Tito used the party's monopoly on power and his own political skills to rein in nationalist forces straining to undermine the federal state and liberals who aimed to push economic reforms too far. By the late 1970s, however, matters began to change. Rapidly rising energy prices following the Arab oil embargo of 1973 exacerbated the country's already serious balance of payments deficit and forced it to export more of its increasingly uncompetitive goods abroad to pay its debts. By the early 1980s, Yugoslavia's 22 million people owed about $20 billion to foreign creditors, workers' real income was falling, and unemployment was over 13 percent. As in many indebted developing countries, labor power became its chief export, and over a million Yugoslavs moved abroad. When Tito died in 1980, it was increasingly apparent that Yugoslavia's decentralized political system was failing to manage the crisis. As we will see, nationalist forces quickly filled the vacuum.

While Yugoslavia undertook its reforms outside of the constraints of the Soviet bloc, Hungary's leaders approached change with 1956 on their minds. Under Janos Kádár, the Communist Party brutally reasserted its authority, recollectivized agriculture, and demonstrated its loyalty to the USSR. In the early 1960s, however, the regime relaxed its repression and undertook efforts to win the tolerance, if not the support, of peasants, workers, Catholics, and intellectuals. Political prisoners were released, censorship and travel restrictions were eased, and the government signed an accord with the Catholic Church. Although the collective farms remained in place, the state gave them broad commercial and managerial autonomy while encouraging peasants to open private sideline businesses and making substantial investments in rural services. These policies had positive effects; agricultural output boomed, and food and wine exports to Western markets led the way in earning needed hard currency to purchase imports.

Unlike most other East bloc countries, the government encouraged the gradual expansion of the service and handicraft sectors, which functioned largely on a private basis. In 1968, it introduced the New Economic Mechanism for the industrial economy, ending the centralized allocation of production targets and resources. Five-year indicative planning replaced the use of rigid, detailed annual plans, and profit became the measure of enterprise success. In this "market-oriented" system, the state had to reform the price system in order for firms to compete effectively. Enterprises were also expected to rely primarily on bank credit rather than direct state support for new investment capital.

These reforms were not fully implemented and often caused new problems. For example, bureaucratic resistance led to the reimposition of centralized planning for fifty of the country's largest enterprises in 1973, the price reform remained incomplete, and the expansion of the untaxed and private "second economy" led many workers to take on additional "unofficial" jobs. Large income differentials resulted as those without second jobs were left behind. Rapidly rising incomes and slow productivity growth fueled inflation, and falling real wages left many facing poverty.

Hungary existed between two worlds. Most of its trade was with the Soviet bloc, but it joined the General Agreement on Tariffs and Trade in 1973 and the International Monetary Fund and the World Bank in 1982. To compete in the world market, Hungarian firms imported technology that they financed by borrowing from Western creditors. Such loans could be paid off with export earnings, but only if productivity outpaced rising debt. As we will see, by the early 1980s, it was clear that Hungary's "market socialism" was not up to the task. The partially liberalized economy appeared to improve many aspects of life, and a broad array of services and products were available for those who could afford them. But Hungary's limited ability to pay for imported consumer and producer goods ultimately fueled a crisis that brought the system to its knees.

While Hungary sought reform via market mechanisms, East Germany, the East bloc's most important frontline state in the Cold War, adopted a different approach. Following the workers' uprising of 1953, Walter Ulbricht had tenaciously hung on to power, resisted de-Stalinization, and effectively run the country into the ground. The GDR's economy had suffered grievously after 1945 as the Soviets shipped a large proportion of its industry and transportation infrastructure back to the USSR. During the 1950s, reconstruction moved ahead, but efforts to rapidly "build socialism" following the Soviet model and the political repression of dissenters, religious people, and citizens of middle-class background overtaxed the country's limited resources and alienated much of the population. By 1961, over 3 million people, including many skilled workers, dispossessed farmers, newly educated youth, and the politically

disaffected, abandoned the "workers' and peasants' state" for the economic opportunities and political freedom of booming West Germany.

The Berlin Wall gave the GDR's leaders breathing space. Cherishing
the notion that the correct economic strategies would enable the East to
outshine the West and eventually make reunification possible under socialist auspices, Ulbricht reversed his earlier opposition to reforms. In the
wake of the Liberman discussion, he adopted many ideas from reform-
minded SED economists, such as Fritz Behrens (1909-1980) and Arne
Benary (1929-1971). In 1963, the SED announced the introduction of the
New System of Economic Planning and Management (NES), which, as
Jeffrey Kopstein has noted, aimed primarily to "improv[e] enterprise performance without introducing a full-blown capital or labor market" and
focused on "upgrading the quality and qualifications of leading economic personnel without sacrificing a commitment to socialist values."[9]

In practice, the reform intended to use the Central State Planning
Commission to forecast the economy's long-term needs and goals while
continuing to oversee overall resource allocation. Meanwhile, authority
devolved to lower-level officials who coordinated the activities of related
firms as well as to the directors of individual enterprises. With profits
now viewed as the main criterion of success, firms would have to make
salable goods, and surpluses could be reinvested to promote innovation
in line with the findings of marketing research and technological needs.
Determining costs accurately required price reform, and the state gave
the training of new, highly skilled managerial personnel high priority.

There is no question that the economy experienced a significant up-
turn in the 1960s. East Germany developed the highest standard of living
in the Soviet bloc, whose citizens flocked to East Berlin to buy goods
unavailable at home. At no time, however, did the economy begin to
catch up with its sister republic in the West, bottlenecks and shortages
continued to hamstring production, and the extent to which the reforms
underpinned the improvements is unclear. Opposition to Ulbricht's policy emerged quickly from several quarters. It proved difficult to change
the planning and pricing systems in the time frame desired by the impatient leadership, many planners chafed at the new decision-making hierarchy, and some in the party leadership resented the new emphasis
placed on technical competence. Not wishing to give up large-scale pet
projects that they believed would push the country forward, many leaders demanded special resource allocations that skewed the overall economic plan. Finally, the USSR's own economic priorities and the Brezhnev leadership's growing antipathy to reforms hindered the implementation of the NES. Raw material exports to East Germany slowed, and the
Soviets supported SED conservatives. By the late 1960s, recentralization
was under way, and, following the Warsaw Pact's intervention in Czechoslovakia (see below), the reformers were in full retreat. In 1971, Brezh-

nev backed the effort of Ulbricht's former protégé Erich Honecker (1912–1994) to oust his boss and end the reforms.

The reforms discussed above aimed to improve the performance of the centrally planned, state-owned economies. Communist leaders viewed them as a means of securing, not overturning, the political order. In Czechoslovakia, however, reformers saw economic and political reform as intertwined. Their efforts to move the system in a more open, pluralist direction challenged the Soviet model and ultimately resulted in the Warsaw Pact's invasion of the country in August 1968.

De-Stalinization had moved slowly in Czechoslovakia. Although some purge victims were gradually released and rehabilitated, conservatives around Antonin Novotny (1904–1975) held on to power well into the 1960s. Conditions in the country seemed stable. Its industry, among the most advanced in the region before 1945, still provided a standard of living among the highest in the East bloc, and the distribution of wealth was the most egalitarian. By the early 1960s, however, it was clear that productivity was stagnating and that reforms were necessary if the economy were to compete in Western markets and continue to improve living standards. In 1963, the party began market-oriented reforms and, belatedly following their Soviet comrades, finally embarked on a more thoroughgoing condemnation of Stalin. This opening triggered an intense public discussion, and intellectuals such as Milan Kundera (b. 1929), Ludvík Vaculík (b.1926), and Václav Havel (1936–2011) subjected the Stalinist past to withering criticism in their writings and public statements. With Slovak dissatisfaction with Czech domination growing and student unrest over their living conditions generating open protest, Novotny's position grew increasingly tenuous. In January 1968, his colleagues in the leadership, with Brezhnev's blessing, replaced him as party chief (though not as president) with Alexander Dubcek (1921–1992), a leader from the Slovak branch of the party who the Soviets believed could maintain political stability while carrying out needed economic reforms.

They had misjudged their choice. Dubcek was not a radical, but, having criticized "coercive and despotic methods" even before his election, he now encouraged public debate on ending censorship, broadening press freedom, and a more thoroughgoing review of the Novotny leadership's role in the purges. By March, popular enthusiasm was growing, and the conservatives were in full retreat. Novotny gave up the presidency to General Ludvík Svoboda (1895–1979) on 22 March, and a few days later the Central Committee issued its "Action Program" demanding civil rights such as freedom of the press and assembly, the right to form voluntary organizations, freedom to travel abroad, independent courts, equal status and autonomy for Slovakia, and the rehabilitation of purge victims. In addition to the "democratization" of politics, which included a ten-year transition to genuine multiparty elections, the program called for major economic changes. In line with many of the ideas put forward by economist Ota Sik (1919–2004), indicative planning would replace rigid central planning, economic decision making would devolve to the enterprise level, and workers' councils would supervise management. Moreover, the trade unions, no longer mere "transmission belts of party policy," would be free to defend workers' interests.

This program to democratize bureaucratic collectivism was not an effort to return to liberal capitalism. It was, rather, a genuine and popular attempt to create what many came to call "socialism with a human face." Although working-class activists did not drive the reform process, its goals won their broad support. For many of the students, intellectuals, and rank-and-file party members who supported the reforms, the creation of democratic socialism was a realistic goal toward which society had been working between 1945 and 1948. There was now a chance to discard discredited Stalinism and renew the former movement, which would protect individual rights and pursue collective goals.

In May and June, the new government of Oldrich Cernik (1921–1994), buttressed by massive public demonstrations on May Day and other occasions, moved ahead with legislation abolishing press controls and creating a new federal state giving equality to the Czech and Slovak republics. The reform movement now began to build momentum. Never fully united on the scale and timing of proposed changes, some, such as Dubcek and Zdenek Mlynár (1930–1997), took a more cautious approach, but others, such as Vaculík, publicly demanded moving quickly toward a multiparty system and the creation of new citizens' committees that could also independently push for reforms. These demands, the emergence of new groups (such as the Club of Committed Non-Party People), and the proposed reestablishment of a Social Democratic Party intensified the Soviet government's fear that the KSC would lose its monopoly on power.

Dubcek repeatedly attempted to assure Brezhnev and other Warsaw Pact leaders that the situation was under control, but by mid-July the Soviets were warning the KSC that the situation was endangering the common interests of the socialist countries and that the party needed to rein in counterrevolutionary forces. Meeting with Brezhnev in Cierna, on the Czechoslovak–Russian border at the end of the month, Dubcek vainly tried to allay his fears. On 3 August, at a meeting of the Warsaw Pact in Bratislava, the Soviet leader proclaimed that "each Communist Party is free to apply the principles of Marxism-Leninism and socialism in its own country, but it is not free to deviate from those principles. . . . The weakening of any of the links in the world system of socialism directly affects all the socialist countries, and they cannot look indifferently upon this."[10] Following this not-so-veiled threat, Dubcek again attempted to convince Brezhnev that his concerns were unfounded, but he did not know that conservatives in the KSC, ensconced in the party apparatus and the de-

**Figure 6.2.   Alexander Dubcek in 1970 following his expulsion from the Czecho-
slovak Communist Party. Courtesy of the AsD and the Deutsche Presse Agentur.**

fense and security services and fearful of losing their posts, were at that
moment entreating the Soviets to intervene militarily. Fearing a complete
reformist victory at the KSC's upcoming party congress in September and
worried about the spread of the reformist infection, Brezhnev made his
decision on 18 August. Three days later, 500,000 Warsaw Pact troops
occupied Czechoslovakia.

The invasion—which the Czechoslovak government decided not to
oppose—brought the changes unleashed by the "Prague Spring" to an
end. There was widespread passive resistance to the invaders, but it did
not hinder the Soviets from forcing Dubcek and his colleagues, who were
arrested and then released, to reverse the reforms and begin the process

of "normalization." Humiliation trumped violence. There were no executions, but a massive purge removed hundreds of thousands from the party and even from their professions, relegating many to the margins of society. Replaced by Gustav Husák (1913–1991), who went on to head the party for eighteen years, Dubcek worked as a forester in Slovakia.

The impact of the invasion had ramifications far beyond the immediate situation in Czechoslovakia. To the Western powers, the "Brezhnev Doctrine" made clear that the USSR would allow no fundamental changes in its sphere of control. In Eastern Europe, it sent a clear message to erstwhile proponents of reform. Bureaucratic despotism would survive for many more years, but few now believed that it might be a starting point for the creation of a social order rooted in democracy, respect for the individual, and social justice.

Finally, the above examples of reform in the East show that politics lay at the heart of their failure. In each case, broad elements of the communist elite recognized that, once the basic industrial architecture of the economy had been established, changes were necessary to meet the rising expectations of populations becoming increasingly urban, better educated, and aware of how their lives compared with those of people elsewhere in the world. To legitimize the system, economic performance and living standards had to improve. Most of the proposed changes centered on the introduction of market mechanisms or, at a minimum, the decentralization of decision making to the lower rungs of the hierarchy more directly concerned with production. Such reforms resolved some economic problems and created new ones. Most importantly, however, they disconcerted many within the bureaucratic hierarchy, who feared losing control. As a result, reforms were often incomplete or were reversed. Ironically, most communist states then turned to the Western "class enemy" for credit and technology to reenergize their economies. The ruinous debts they amassed then helped undercut the system they hoped to preserve.

WESTERN SOCIALISM ON THE DEFENSIVE: THE NEW SOCIAL MOVEMENTS AND THE RISE OF NEOLIBERALISM

By the late 1960s, it was clear that the old "antisystem" parties in the West, Social Democratic and Communist, had become creatures of the system. While they still advocated for reforms on behalf of workers, sometimes used populist rhetoric, and may have hoped for socialism in the long run, both movements accepted the bourgeois parliamentary order. Indeed, following the Warsaw Pact's invasion of Czechoslovakia, Western communists condemned the action and insisted on the independence, sovereignty, equality, and autonomy of all parties. To outflank the socialists in electoral competition, they sought to broaden their support beyond the working class and, in the face of a revived nationalist right, were willing to form cooperative partnerships with other democratic forces. The Italian Communist Party, led by Enrico Berlinguer (1922–1984), offers an excellent example of this "Eurocommunist" approach. During the 1970s, Berlinguer advocated a "Historic Compromise" restoring the PCI's post-1945 coalition with the PSI and Christian democracy to achieve progressive reforms while also fending off left-wing terrorism and resurgent fascism. Eschewing the language of class struggle and distancing itself from the USSR, the PCI may have failed to unseat the DC, but in 1976 it won over 34 percent of the vote (the PSI won 11 percent) and ruled much of northern Italy. Like its counterparts elsewhere, it was now a part of the system.

While the Social Democratic and Communist parties, along with their trade union allies, dominated left-wing politics throughout Western Europe, new social movements, long in the making, challenged their hegemony virtually everywhere beginning in the late 1960s. Students, women, environmentalists, and peace activists, for example, mounted sharp criticisms of the institutionalized left's ideology and practice, organized grassroots movements of their own, and in some cases, such as that of the Greens, founded successful political parties. To some socialists, such as the philosopher Herbert Marcuse (1898–1979), these groups represented potential catalysts of anticapitalist revolutionary change that could replace or complement a working class that, lured by mass consumption and embedded in a universe of competition, had largely adopted capitalist consciousness as its own. Marcuse's hopes eventually proved too optimistic, but these "new left" movements fundamentally reshaped the ideological and political landscape of socialism and of their societies.

The origins of many of the new social movements often long predated World War II, but their emergence on a mass scale in the 1960s was, in part, a generational response to the post-1945 political and social order. By that time, the structures of the capitalist welfare states were well established and deeply embedded in the Western military alliance. Raised during the height of capitalist prosperity, many in the postwar generation scorned the materialism of their parents and of a system resting on endless growth despite enormous human and ecological costs. They rejected their society's (and the established left's) deeply patriarchal character, its oppression of ethnic minorities, and its economic exploitation of the underdeveloped "Third World." Chafing at the often unresponsive, top-down functioning of the bureaucratic welfare state, frustrated by social democratic support for the American war in Vietnam, and repelled by the Soviet system, the new generation cast about for alternatives.

Student unrest spread across Europe in the late 1960s for a variety of reasons. As rapid growth of the student populations led to widespread overcrowding and overtaxed facilities, frustrations deepened as the universities' archaic hierarchies of authority proved unresponsive to demands for change. Domestic concerns frequently triggered large-scale strikes, such as those in Italy in 1967, but students soon developed a much broader, indeed, global critique of society. In Germany, for example, student calls for the democratization of university governance and for a serious appraisal of the connections between the Third Reich and the postwar professoriate soon intersected with opposition to Western support for noncommunist dictatorships everywhere. In June 1967, after police in Berlin shot down a student protesting against the visiting Shah of Iran, over 100,000 students took to the streets across the country. This was a key step in the creation of an "extraparliamentary opposition" that aimed to confront the capitalist order. The April 1968 assassination attempt on the important student leader Rudi Dutschke (1940–1979), a massive student assault on the offices of the right-wing Springer press, and the government's passage of emergency laws to curb internal unrest marked the escalation of tensions between students and the state.

These tensions exploded in Paris in April and May 1968, when demonstrations for reform of the universities led to massive confrontations in which tens of thousands of students fought up to 20,000 policemen whose brutality, televised across the country, initially swung popular opinion behind the protesters. Student demands soon went far beyond alterations to university governance and encompassed calls for fundamental social change. Their slogans, such as "Be realistic: Demand the Impossible," "Commodities Are the Opium of the People," "Don't Negotiate with the Bosses: Abolish Them," and "Their Nightmares Are Our Dreams," reflected the widespread desire to question all established mores and institutions. Although the PCF and its allied trade union federation, the Confédération général du Travail (General Confederation of Trade Unions [CGT]), initially scorned student efforts to reach out to workers, by mid-May many rank-and-file unionists were joining student actions. On 13 May, the CGT reversed course, and student leader Daniel Cohn-Bendit (b. 1945) joined labor leaders in the front rank of a demonstration 800,000 strong. By the end of the month, 10 million workers had downed tools in a nationwide general strike. Many expected President DeGaulle to resign.

But PCF and CGT leaders were not interested in revolution. Indeed, aiming to protect the interests of their organizations within the system, they later prevented students from joining labor rallies and criticized the radicals. When Prime Minister Georges Pompidou (1911–1974) offered major concessions regarding wages and working hours, they took the deal despite the opposition of many workers. DeGaulle then outmaneuvered the isolated students by calling snap elections in mid-June that resulted in a sweeping government victory. It seemed that the radical moment had passed.

For many activists, however, the defeat meant only that the struggle had to be continued by other means. They were divided, however, on how to go forward. Some founded small and mutually hostile Leninist, Trotskyist, and Maoist communist parties aiming to mobilize the working class for revolution. Others withdrew from politics and mainstream society to form their own separate utopian communities. A third, more numerous group attempted to change society by transforming its institutions from within. Thus, in Germany, for example, tens of thousands joined the SPD's youth organizations in an effort to radicalize the party's politics. Finally, a tiny minority hoped to wake up the masses by using terrorist tactics to force the system to reveal its "fascist" nature via brutal repression. Small groups, such as the Red Army Faction in Germany and the Red Brigades in Italy, attempted to use the kidnapping and murder of elites to gain notoriety and support, but these actions only isolated the radicals; all eventually were defeated.

The year 1968 was also a moment of crystallization for the women's movement. As we have noted, although the socialist parties and unions had inscribed women's equality on their banners, in practice the male-dominated movement had relegated women's issues to the back burner. By the 1960s, women in most European countries had won the franchise, but legally they remained second-class citizens in the workplace, in public life, and even in their own homes. As it became clear that most males in the radical student and peace movements were no more respectful of women's contributions or concerns than those in traditional socialist and communist parties, feminists built organizations of their own while also working to transform established ones. In the realm of theory, feminist thinkers, such as Juliet Mitchell (b. 1940) and Sheila Rowbotham (b. 1943), engaged in wide-ranging debates about the relationship of patriarchy to class as forms of domination, while in the practical sphere, women formulated demands promoting concrete change in the workplace, in the family, and in politics. In all the European democracies, women called for equal pay; equal educational and job opportunities; access to day care, free contraception, and abortion; and equality in civil law, among other things. Women's consciousness-raising groups, large-scale demonstrations, publications, and local issue-oriented initiatives influenced public discourse both on the left and in the broader society, but the movement was also fractured by disputes concerning the degree to which it should be separatist, its attitude toward heterosexuality and lesbianism, and its view of political alliances. Attempts to build national organizations largely failed, and in many countries progress was slow in the face of deeply rooted social mores.

As was true of "first-wave" feminism in the 1920s, "second-wave" feminism in the 1970s initially had a limited impact on the parties and unions of the left. It took time to change the entrenched cultural and procedural norms of these institutions, and women activists did best at the local level, where socialist and communist governments could provide day care, legal aid, health care facilities, and adult educational opportunities. Institutional responses to feminism were very uneven and often opportunistic; many basic demands eventually made it into their programmatic documents, but women remained underrepresented in internal party posts, and this lack of clout meant fewer resources to address their concerns. Beginning with the Norwegian Labor Party in 1983, some parties, including the SPD and the British Labor Party, moved toward gender quotas in selecting party officers. Meanwhile, women's representation in socialist parliamentary delegations also varied greatly. By the early 1990s, women made up less than 10 percent of the Greek, Belgian, French, and British party delegations, 50 percent in Sweden and Norway, and between 18 and 35 percent in the remaining states.

The slow response of socialist and communist parties to the rise of the women's movement was repeated in the sphere of the environment. By the 1960s, growing awareness of the ecological damage wrought by industrialism made it an important political issue across the developed world. Echoing a powerful and widely read report from the Club of Rome, "Limits to Growth" (1972), writers such as E. F. Schumacher (1911–1977) and Andre Gorz (1923–2007) questioned the sustainability of an economic system based on endless accumulation and rising consumption and put forward ideas for a society based on different priorities. For the socialist movement, these ideas represented a serious challenge to their traditional support for economic growth, which translated into jobs and rising living standards for workers. At the same time, however, socialists had long recognized the dangers of industrial production for workers and surrounding communities. Their emphases on controlling production and economic planning gave them a degree of common ground with environmentalists, but it was difficult for them to envision an economy not centered on ever-increasing industrial productivity.

The socialists' slowness to prioritize ecological concerns was partly ideological, but it also reflected their practical dilemma as Western Europe's postwar economic boom ended in the early 1970s. In its place came a long period of "stagflation" characterized by slow growth, rapidly rising inflation, and growing unemployment. When Keynesian economic strategies failed to revive the economy, social democratic governments, such as Helmut Schmidt's in Germany, found it difficult to fulfill their commitment to full employment and to pay for escalating welfare costs. Viewing environmental issues as of secondary importance and often responding negatively to local citizens' initiatives, such as those opposed to nuclear energy, they alienated potential supporters and convinced many to found new "Green" Parties of their own. The Greens emerged out of local grassroots movements that attracted well-educated young people concerned about the environment, but they also drew feminists and peace movement activists who rejected socialists' support for NATO and its decision to deploy a new generation of intermediate-range nuclear missiles in the early 1980s. Between 1980 and 1991, Greens entered parliaments in ten states and put the movement on an international footing with the founding of the European Greens in 1983.

The rise of the Greens forced Europe's socialists to react, and by the end of the 1980s, especially in the wake of the 1986 Chernobyl disaster in Ukraine, they began to integrate environmental concerns into their programmatic agenda. By that time, however, the Greens were well established. Not only did their desultory responses to the concerns of students, women, and environmentalists cost them support, but the role of the Social Democrats in the Cold War also alienated many in the peace movement. Even more serious was the decline of the labor movement's traditional constituency. The rise of transnational capital and increasing global competition in the context of stagflation fueled the decline of heavy industry, the mechanization of the labor process, and the transfer of production to low-wage regions around the world. One consequence, rising unemployment, weakened the trade unions' bargaining power and placed labor on the defensive.

A second consequence, however, was existential. After reaching a peak in the late 1950s, the percentage of industrial workers fell precipitously. In England, for example, it declined from almost 50 to 30 percent by 1985, in Belgium from 48 to 29 percent, and in Sweden from 41 to 30 percent. In many regions, such as England's industrial north and Germany's Ruhr Valley, whole industries dried up, and many working-class communities virtually disappeared. These had been core communities of the socialist and communist movements, where the parties and unions had deep cultural roots and recruited much of their membership. Their decline, just beginning in the 1970s, was a fundamental threat. Of course, while the proportion of industrial workers declined, the number of dependent wage and salaried workers grew. But this "working class" was more variegated than ever in its lifestyles and consciousness, consisting of a wide range of white-collar employees, increasing numbers of women, and a vast array of skilled and unskilled service workers, and drawing them into the socialist movement was a major challenge.

The social democratic project rested on the assumption that, when well regulated, capitalism would produce the surpluses necessary to support the needs of capital, the welfare state, and rising living standards for the general population. During the postwar boom, this assumption seemed reasonable, but the onset of stagflation, falling profits, and the failure of the Keynesian response undermined it and opened the door to a renewed capitalist offensive aiming to roll back many of labors' gains and restore profits. Large segments of the transnational business elite and many middle-class critics of the welfare state adopted a neoliberal outlook centering on free trade, economic deregulation and privatization, and a radical reduction of the social state. British conservative Margaret Thatcher (b. 1925), who ousted a weak Labor government in 1979 and declared war on the workers' movement, best represented this radical reversal of the postwar consensus.

Supported by big business and the middle classes, Thatcher eviscerated the corporatist system by pushing through laws regulating union elections and decision-making processes, restricting their ability to strike, and narrowing the definition of collective bargaining. After making elaborate preparations, in 1984–1985 she precipitated a confrontation with the once-powerful coal miners' union and routed it, thus setting the tone for future labor relations in Britain. With unemployment at 13.2 percent in 1984, the density of union membership began to decline. After peaking in 1979 at 55 percent (13.5 million members), it slipped to 37.7 percent (9.9 million members) by 1990. While some countries, such as France, the Netherlands, Austria, and Italy, saw similar declines, others, such as Sweden and Belgium, saw union density increase. Local circumstances were important, but political power was crucial. In Britain, divisions on the left decisively weakened Labor. Prior to Thatcher's election victory, the Labor government's efforts to curb inflation via wage restraint infuriated many unions whose strikes undercut the policy. In 1980, the selection of left-wing leader Michael Foot (1913–2010) to head the party caused many on the right wing to quit and form a new Social Democratic Party. Thatcher never needed an absolute majority to win a parliamentary election because the opposition was always divided. Splits among unionists also weakened their cause as some leaders, thinking they could get a better deal by negotiating on a plant-by-plant rather than an industry-wide basis, undermined the postwar corporate bargaining system.

Thatcher envisioned a highly individualistic, competitive social order with the state's tasks limited to policing and foreign affairs. To that end, she privatized Britain's public industries (e.g., telecommunications and energy), deregulated the financial sector, ended subsidies to manufacturing firms, and sold off public housing. One-time sales temporarily filled the treasury but did not shrink the overall size of government, which now had to cover the costs of mass unemployment. While some sectors of the economy functioned more efficiently, the cost was widespread deindustrialization and social distress. Thatcher failed to gut the public health system or the schools, but she fundamentally altered the country's culture by elevating competitive individualism above all things and undercutting networks of social solidarity. When she left office in 1990, Britain was a much different place.

Neoliberalism's advance on the Continent was more tentative, but there is no question that social democracy was on the defensive everywhere, even where it held power. France provides of good example of the left's limited room for maneuver. After the demise of the SFIO in 1969, the Parti Socialiste (French Socialist Party [PS]) emerged, led by the charismatic François Mitterrand (1916–1996). Promoting the idea of workers' self-management and serving as a vehicle for Mitterrand's presidential aspirations, for about a decade the party maneuvered between the centrist left-radicals and the PCF, led by Georges Marchais (1920–1997). By aligning the PS with the communists via a vague but anticapitalist *Common Program*, Mitterrand attracted a part of the PCF's constituency to the PS. In 1978, the PS outpaced the PCF in a parliamentary election for the first time since 1945, and three years later he took the presidency in a runoff election in which the PS, the PCF, the Greens, and the Trotskyists backed him. A few weeks later, the PS swept the parliamentary elections, giving it full control of the government.

Mitterrand quickly abolished capital punishment, raised wages, reduced working hours, and lowered the retirement age. More important, he nationalized thirty-eight banks and financial houses and five of the country's largest industrial corporations. Thought substantial, these steps fell short of being "socialist," for they were not combined with efforts to empower workers or construct a new system of planning, investment, and redistribution that would have altered France's place in the international order. Nevertheless, France's business class wasted no time in moving capital abroad. This capital strike precipitated a crisis and within a year forced the government to retreat. Thus, instead of socialism, France got austerity and "modernization," in which many though not all of the nationalized enterprises were reprivatized. While it did not become another Britain, France, like most of the rest of Western Europe, became more integrated into an increasingly neoliberal EEC.

Thus, during the 1980s, social democratic Europe, while still intact, was on the defensive. With the demise of the postwar consensus, Christian democracy became the primary bearer of the neoliberal ethos in continental politics, though its version, tempered by Christian social teaching, was less rabidly individualistic than that of Thatcher's Britain. In addition to the political pressure of the right, Social Democrats and communists now found themselves facing new competition from the Greens, while their core constituencies shrank as the result of rapid economic, social, and cultural changes transforming the global landscape. Pressure from the new social movements pushed them to rethink their priorities, but this process was not yet far along when, like an unexpected earthquake, the implosion of the Soviet bloc and the reunification of Europe changed everything.

FROM BREZHNEV TO GORBACHEV: CRISIS AND REFORM IN THE USSR

If twentieth-century social democracy embodied modernity's closest approximation of the society envisioned by Condorcet and Paine, the Soviet Union and its satellites bore the nearest resemblance to the one envisioned by Babeuf. The USSR had abolished private ownership of the means of production and eliminated the capitalist marketplace in an effort to construct the material equality that Babeuf had insisted was necessary to make legal equality meaningful. A bold experiment that had fired the imagination of much of the world, many supported it even after its transformation into a bureaucratic collectivist tyranny. By the 1980s, however, the system's early dynamism had run into the sand, and the elderly leaders around Brezhnev best symbolized its stagnation. Unlike the youthful, dynamic, and often brilliant Bolshevik founders, this sclerotic gerontocracy was incapable of moving the country forward.

Much had changed since 1917. From a largely underdeveloped peasant society, the Soviet Union had developed into a modern, industrial one, and under Khrushchev and Brezhnev, the quality of life had gradually improved. By 1985, 65 percent of the people lived in cities, and only 15 percent remained on collective farms. Millions had gained access to new (if often cramped) low-cost apartments; between 80 and 90 percent of households owned televisions, refrigerators, and radios; and most had washing and sewing machines. Workers enjoyed full employment, and under Brezhnev their incomes rose faster than those of middle-class professionals. Few people owned cars, but public transport, along with basic consumer goods, was inexpensive. Although often of modest quality, public education and health care were free. By the mid-1980s, the USSR's large university system had produced over 15 million graduates in all fields, and the country could boast of real achievements in space exploration, in certain sectors of industry, and in the development of advanced weaponry of all types. Finally, the Soviet Union's military strength and its economic model made it an attractive ally for poor countries seeking alternative roads to development and to distance themselves from U.S. power.

These achievements show that central planning cannot simply be described as a failure inevitably doomed to collapse, but they also masked the system's weaknesses. With decisive power exercised from the top down, the vast bureaucracy ignored or was unable to respond to the desires of workers and consumers. Despite massive investments in science and technology, innovation in production methods and new products constantly lagged behind that of the capitalist countries, and with little public accountability, there was enormous waste, poor quality control, and few checks on the increasingly disastrous levels of environmental pollution. Crucially, the post-1965 political decision to match American military power absorbed as much as 25 percent of the country's gross domestic product (compared to 5 to 7 percent in the United States) and distorted the balance of economic growth. Housing, consumer goods, and many services (e.g., restaurants and repair shops) were often in short supply and of poor quality, and the state neglected essential infrastructure and devoted few resources to the important new technologies associated with computerization. Thus, as the return on investment in extensive growth dwindled, the state failed to shift adequate resources into new means of intensifying output. As a result, growth slowed to a halt in the early 1980s.

Economies of shortage fuel corruption. People at the top of the political hierarchy had the best access to goods and services as well as the opportunity to travel abroad. Average citizens often resorted to the illegal "second economy" to meet their needs, and those with connections or goods to barter at the repair shop or the butcher usually came out on top. Many people resorted to stealing materials from state construction sites to make repairs on their own homes. Worse yet, in order to accumulate foreign exchange for international purchases, the government set up so-called Intershops to sell high-quality and imported goods to foreigners and privileged party members with access to hard currency. Those without foreign cash thus became second-class citizens, stirring up much resentment.

Many of the older generation of Soviet and East bloc leaders and citizens were proud of their achievements, having overcome much of the crass poverty and insecurity that had characterized life prior to 1945. But their complacency overlooked the aspirations and criticisms of the younger generation, which had matured under very different circumstances. A large class of well-educated professional people had emerged that was well aware of the contrast between its living standards and social status and those of its counterparts in the West. Some chafed at the continued repression of political dissidents, at a system that often measured professional merit on the basis of political attitude, and at the privileges of the party bosses, but few contemplated radical changes to the system on which they depended. Workers, too, often grumbled about conditions in the "workers' state," but their lack of real power in the trade unions and the soviets engendered more cynicism than fervor for some kind of revolution. Meanwhile, in the realm of gender relations, a yawning gulf separated the egalitarian rhetoric and reality of Soviet life. By the mid-1970s, 90 percent of women were working or studying; they made up half of the industrial workers as well as two-thirds of the teachers and doctors. Yet the fields in which they worked were often lower paid, few made it into the higher echelons of the government or party, and, as a group, they bore primary responsibility for their households and children. Gender equality remained a distant dream. Thus, by the early 1980s, the gulf between the radical democratic and egalitarian promise of the Bolshevik Revolution and the realities of Soviet life was obvious to many, but it did not appear that radical change was in the offing.

Appearances do not tell the whole story, however, for attitudes toward the state were shifting, and people challenged the "totalitarian" order in a variety of ways. A thriving underground (*samizdat*) press allowed dissident intellectuals and academics, such as the Marxist historian Roy Medvedev (b. 1925), the liberal nuclear physicist Andrei Sakharov (1921–1989), and the Slavophile writer Alexander Solzhenitsyn (1918–2008), to criticize various facets of Soviet life and to challenge the government to live up to the international conventions on human rights that it had signed, such as the Helsinki Accords (1975). Some of their books and articles appeared in the West, making them well-known figures and thus constraining the government's ability to punish them, but publishing forbidden works was always risky, especially for lesser-known authors. In addition to such intellectual critics, many Soviet citizens avoided the state's control by participating in the black market and by reading and circulating banned literature, attending underground theatrical performances, and listening to music, such as Western rock and roll, that was regarded as out of step with the values of official socialist realism. These activities did not presage a coming revolution, but they marked a growing distance between a substantial portion of the citizenry and the Soviet system.

It was not popular unrest that initiated the transformation of Soviet society in the late 1980s. On the contrary, radical change was precipitated from above after Mikhail Gorbachev (b. 1931) was selected as general secretary of the Communist Party of the Soviet Union (CPSU) in 1985. Following Brezhnev's death in 1982, the party had chosen Yuri Andropov (1914–1984) to succeed him, but he died shortly thereafter, as did his elderly replacement, Konstantin Chernenko (1911–1985). Andropov, a veteran KGB chief known for his efficiency and disdain for corruption, had recognized that reform required replacing the gerontocracy with younger leaders. He had promoted Gorbachev, who had earned a reputation as a reformer, and advocated that he succeed him as party chief. After Chernenko's brief interregnum, Gorbachev got his chance.

Gorbachev was not a radical when he took office. Raised in provincial Stavropol, he studied law at Moscow State University, where he befriended Zdenek Mlynar (1930–1997), later one of the architects of the Prague Spring, and joined the CPSU in 1952. After serving as a leader of the Stavropol party youth organization, he specialized in agricultural issues and worked his way up until elected to the Central Committee at the age of forty-one. More cosmopolitan than his predecessors, Gorbachev's travels in Western Europe during the 1970s had impressed on him how far the USSR lagged behind. When he assumed power, the situation was worse. At a time when it desperately needed resources for its civilian economy, the USSR was bogged down in a rapidly accelerating arms race and a bloody war in Afghanistan. The invasion of that country in 1979 had given the Carter and Reagan administrations the political rationale they needed to ramp up arms expenditures, reduce trade with the East bloc, and aggressively assert U.S. power in the developing world. At the same time, with the price of oil (its most important export) falling, the

USSR had to pay for imports with increasingly large loans from Western banks, reaching $30 billion in 1986.

Gorbachev knew that these burdens were unsustainable if reform was to succeed. Like Andropov, he initially thought that instilling labor discipline and combating corruption would stimulate the economy, but as early as April 1985, he made clear that the overly centralized and unaccountable apparatus was the key problem. Based on the experience of earlier reform efforts in Eastern Europe, he knew that a part of the remedy lay in decentralizing decision making. But he also knew that without transparency and real (not falsified) information, reform could not succeed. Soon he was calling for honest public debate on systemic problems and for "socialist democracy" defined as "the self-government of the people." At the party's Twenty-Seventh Congress in February 1986, he stressed the need for economic restructuring (perestroika) while also asserting the importance of openness (glasnost) in criticizing the system's shortcomings. "Communists," he said," want the truth, always and under all circumstances."[11]

The government's initial efforts to suppress information about the Chernobyl nuclear disaster in 1986 made the need for glasnost doubly clear. Censoring information about environmental and other catastrophes, such as the destruction of the Aral Sea and the dumping of radioactive waste in the Arctic Ocean, was nothing new, but Chernobyl was an international debacle that forced the Soviets to open their system to scrutiny. It became clear that insiders had long known of the weaknesses of the Chernobyl facility, but the imperatives of secrecy had prevented any reforms. After Chernobyl, the drive to open up the system accelerated. The government relaxed press censorship, released political prisoners, allowed formerly banned books to appear, and ceased jamming foreign broadcasts. These actions led to the revival of public debate.

In order to push through perestroika, glasnost, and democratization, Gorbachev needed the support of the 19-million-member CPSU. He brought allies—such as Nikolai Ryzhkov (b. 1929), to lead the economic reform; Boris Yeltsin (1931–2007) as Moscow party chief; and Eduard Schevardnadze (b. 1928) as foreign minister—into the leadership and retired much of the old guard, but most of the party feared reform, and resistance emerged at all levels. Gorbachev faced an enormous challenge: he had to use the party to implement reforms directed against many of its own past practices, its privileges, and, ultimately, its monopoly on power. In the end, he could not pull it off.

Part of the problem was perestroika's vagueness. For example, the relationship of central planning to the newly empowered local enterprises remained unclear. The Law on State Enterprise implemented in 1988 foresaw "self-financing" enterprises operating on the basis of profits and losses, but no mechanism was put into place to reform the centrally controlled price system. Theoretically, enterprises now had more autonomy to decide what and how much to produce and to determine wages and prices, but central planners continued setting nonbinding production guidelines, to control resource allocation, and to place "state orders" for up to 85 percent of output, leaving only the remainder at the firm's disposal. A struggle arose between the center and periphery that worsened many long-standing problems, such as the hoarding of raw materials, and created some new ones, such as firms switching from essential but low-profit basic consumer goods to those bringing a higher return.

In the end, most large enterprises continued operating at a loss, and the state, fearful of mass closings, continued subsidizing them. In the arena of small business, matters were somewhat better, but here, too, contradictions abounded. A new law allowed the establishment of privately run "cooperatives," which increased from 8,000 enterprises with 88,000 employees in 1987 to 245,000 businesses employing 6 million workers in 1991. These firms essentially began to supplant the illegal "second economy." They supplied a wide range of goods and services to the private and state markets and paid relatively high wages, but they faced heavy regulation, high taxes, and much public resentment. Having been condemned for sixty years, such businesses enraged many people who regarded their high wages and prices as signs of criminal activity. They also encountered sabotage from state officials fearful of losing their authority. Bureaucratic and popular resistance was especially pronounced in the countryside, where efforts to lease land and equipment to small farmers stalled. After five decades of collective farming, few workers wished to face the daunting prospect of striking out on their own.

By 1989, perestroika had reduced the central planning apparatus from 1.6 million officials to 871,000 and substantially reduced its power, but the failure to create a functioning market deepened the crisis. State subsidies, financed largely through the printing press, kept firms' doors open but fueled rapidly rising inflation. Between 1985 and 1990, the budget deficit quadrupled, the foreign debt almost doubled to over $50 billion, and overall production actually declined. The delivery of basic goods became increasingly erratic, and many products ceased to appear at all. Although the reforms aimed to restore the vibrancy of the soviets, union autonomy, and the right to strike, workers' support was tepid in the face of declining real wages, shortages, and growing concerns about job security. In the summer of 1989, a strike involving 500,000 coal miners revealed their dissatisfaction and renewed strength as they forced the government to grant higher wages and to deliver basic goods worth over $5 billion.

As perestroika floundered, glasnost and democratization opened the floodgates of public expression and fueled the revival of civil society. Gorbachev did not initially envision establishing a multiparty democracy, but it was not long before powerful forces made that a likely outcome. Debates in the press about the full range of issues facing Soviet society raged, and the country's past came under sharp scrutiny. Not only were previously erased or vilified figures, such as Bukharin and Trotsky, restored to history, but also critical appraisals of Stalin were extended to include Marx, Lenin, and the Bolshevik Revolution itself. New independent organizations sprang up, such as Memorial, which aimed to raise public awareness of Stalin's victims, as did a range of political "clubs," including nationalist ones in the various republics. Religious life revived as the state ended its oppression of the Orthodox Church and looked to it as an ally in its efforts to fight corruption and gain legitimacy. Thus, as Gorbachev had expected, glasnost and democratization unleashed a vibrant discourse about the past and future course of Soviet society. Contrary to his hopes, however, these did more to weaken the legitimacy of communism than to strengthen it.

As the reforms went forward, conflict among CPSU leaders intensified. Egor Ligachev (b. 1920), for example, had been an early ally of Gorbachev but in 1987 began rallying conservatives aiming to stem the party's loss of authority and rein in the process of democratization. Ligachev encountered furious opposition from Yeltsin, who wanted to accelerate the reforms and, in front of the Central Committee, sharply criticized the leadership for dragging its feet and for its adulation of Gorbachev. Yeltsin's comments and his abrupt resignation from the Politburo (an unprecedented occurrence) angered his colleagues, who condemned his actions. Shortly thereafter, Gorbachev removed him from his remaining posts. This treatment caused a permanent rift between the two men. Over the course of the next four years, Yeltsin would become one of Gorbachev's principal opponents and ultimately would undermine his effort preserve the USSR.

Gorbachev's foreign policy also riled conservatives. Designed to complement the domestic reform process by freeing up resources and improving the Soviet Union's global position, his initiatives ended the USSR's hegemony in Eastern Europe, brought about its withdrawal from Afghanistan in 1989, and eventually ended the Cold War. These policies reflected fundamental "new thinking" among Soviet decision makers. Although Khrushchev had asserted that "peaceful coexistence" with capitalist states was possible, Soviet leaders had retained the idea of international class struggle and used it to justify their interventions abroad. Arguing that the advent of nuclear weapons in an increasingly interdependent world made such thinking obsolete, Gorbachev called for cooperation to solve "common human problems," such as environmental pollution, poverty, and nuclear disarmament. This decision to drop a core premise of Marxism was a radical step and raised many questions. If, for example, class struggle was no longer decisive, what did that mean for the future of communism? Gorbachev clearly aimed to alter the international political landscape, but the transformations he unleashed were larger and more contradictory than he had expected. Indeed, rather than shoring up the USSR, his policies in Eastern Europe sped up its dissolution.

THE END OF COMMUNISM IN EASTERN EUROPE

Soon after coming to power, Gorbachev urged communist leaders in Eastern Europe to adopt reforms. This move opened the door to opposition forces already present despite the "totalitarian" pretensions of the individual regimes. In Poland, for example, the Catholic Church, led after 1978 by a Polish Pope, John Paul II (Carol Józef Wojtyla, 1920–2005), had remained a potent independent force. In the summer of 1980, government mismanagement, falling living standards, and repression had sparked massive strikes as a result of which anticommunist Catholics, democratic socialist intellectuals, and radical workers had joined together to form Solidarity, a mass movement demanding better pay, improved health and retirement benefits, freedom of the press and assembly, workers' self management, and, most important, the right to form independent trade unions. Centered in the Lenin Shipyard in Gdansk and led by an electrician named Lech Walesa, Solidarity could challenge the state because of its broad support and the backing of the Catholic Church. By the end of August, the government agreed to allow Solidarity to set up new autonomous union organizations that would genuinely represent Poland's workers.

Fearing Soviet intervention, Solidarity drew back from openly challenging the PUWP's political monopoly, but its legalization represented a giant step in extending Poland's civil society and in creating a democratic space for workers. Initially, its demands were overwhelmingly in keeping with those of the labor movement, though it did not use the language or symbols of socialism, which Stalinism had delegitimized. Over the next year, 10 million Poles joined Solidarity, which pressured the state for further reforms, including free elections. In December 1981, the government of General Wojciech Jarulzelski (b. 1923) responded by declaring martial law, rounding up Solidarity's leaders, and driving the remnants underground.

Poland's communists held on to power but failed to resolve its economic or political crises. The next eight years consisted of a stalemate, as the opposition flourished in the underground and in the Church and the regime dug in its heels. Once Gorbachev was in power, however, the Polish government attempted to co-opt support for its austerity policies by putting them to a vote, but this softer approach also failed. Politically paralyzed and with no viable solution to the economic crisis in hand, by the end of the 1980s the communist leadership was ready to bargain. In February 1989, it opened "round-table" discussions with the opposition, and these led to an April agreement legalizing independent unions, spelling out economic reforms, and calling for new parliamentary elections. With about half the seats in the Sejm reserved for their own candidates, the communists did not intend to cede full power to Solidarity, but on 4 June, when the latter won ninety-nine out of 100 Senate races and every open seat in parliament, their defeat was total. After Gorbachev urged cooperation, further negotiation ensued. In September, Solidarity's Tadeuz Mazowieki (b. 1927) became prime minister with Jaruzelski elevated to the post of president. Mazowiecki had the stronger position and quickly moved ahead with plans for a market economy.

The demise of Polish communism was the result of a long process in which the government, never popular, had failed to live up to its own ideological principles or to meet the material needs of the people. Defeated in the realm of ideas and unable to effectively manage the economy, it resorted to repression, but by 1989 the regime had concluded that it could not continue down that road in the face of mass opposition. Bankrupt, the PUWP dissolved itself in January 1990.

Without Soviet support, Eastern Europe's communist regimes were unable to rely on sustained repression. Lacking ideological legitimacy and mired in economic crises, most communist elites opted to abdicate rather than fight. The circumstances of the break with communism varied appreciably from one country to another. If Poland's transformation could be characterized as a workers' revolution against the "workers' state," in Hungary the process unfolded largely within the Communist Party. In 1988, reformists unseated longtime party chief János Kádár and his allies and replaced them with a new leadership headed by Károly Grósz (1930–1996). Aware of events in Poland, the reformers embarked on a revolution from above that mixed market economics with political liberalization and nationalism. Reinterpreting the "counterrevolution" of 1956 as a popular uprising against Soviet domination, the government marked the shift by reinterring Imre Nagy's body in a massive public funeral. In the spring of 1989, it legalized independent opposition parties and announced new parliamentary elections, and in May, it took the monumental step of dismantling the fortifications along the border with Austria. Finally, in October, the communists renamed themselves the Hungarian Socialist Party. The Soviet-imposed order had come to an end.

Hungary's decision to demilitarize its border with Austria had decisive implications for East Germany, which had remained stable since the construction of the Berlin Wall in 1961 and even achieved a high level of prosperity by Eastern European standards. Under Erich Honecker, the GDR channeled considerable resources into new housing and consumer goods while registering respectable rates of economic growth, but by the 1980s, growth rates ebbed, debt to the West rose rapidly, and shortages became more frequent. The East German elite was fairly cohesive, and there were few signs of mass unrest, but the regime was increasingly paranoid. It routinely jailed or deported vocal dissidents, such as the scientist Robert Havemann (1910–1982), the communist critic Rudolf Bahro (1935–1997), and the singer Wolf Biermann (b. 1936), and its security service (the STASI) spied on about a third of the population of 16 million. Pockets of opposition, often sheltered by the churches, persisted among environmentalists (horrified at the country's severe pollution problems), peace activists, and democratic socialists, but they did not seriously threaten the regime.

Apparently impervious to change, Honecker enjoyed good working relations with West German Chancellor Helmut Kohl (b. 1930) and visited the Federal Republic in 1987. The SED played down changes in the USSR, ignored calls for reform, and in 1988 deported over 100 protesters for quoting Rosa Luxemburg's statement "Freedom is also the freedom of those who think differently" at a public demonstration honoring her martyrdom. In May 1989, the rigging of local elections was so blatant that an open protest ensued, even within the party itself. People also had a new means of expressing their fury: with Hungary's border to the West open, citizens could flee to West Germany, where they enjoyed instant citizenship. By September, 60,000 people had left the country.

Opposition forces also began to mobilize. In September, dissidents such as Bärbel Bohley (1945–2010) and Jens Reich (b. 1939) founded New Forum to promote free and open discussion, while others created a new Social Democratic Party and other openly political organizations to push for reforms. On 7 October, as Gorbachev visited East Berlin to honor the fortieth anniversary of the GDR's founding, large numbers of protesters shouting pro-perestroika and pro-Gorbachev slogans met with brutal force. When Gorbachev urged Honecker to embrace reforms, he refused to listen. Indeed, the onset of regular mass demonstrations in Leipzig and elsewhere convinced the old man that a "Chinese solution," like the massacre of demonstrators at Tiananmen Square in June, would be the best recourse. Fortunately, his subordinates thought otherwise. On 9 October, as security forces in Leipzig gathered to confront demonstrators, local officials convinced Honecker's deputy, Egon Krenz (b. 1937), to call off the action.

On 18 October, Krenz and his allies forced Honecker to resign and attempted to present themselves as reformers, but it was too late. On 4 November, over 500,000 people demonstrated for democracy in East Berlin, while every day thousands more left for the West. Within days, the entire government and Politburo had resigned, and Krenz formed a new government that included genuine reformers, such as Hans Modrow (b. 1928) from Dresden. It announced plans for electoral reforms and debated proposals to end restrictions on foreign travel. On 9 November, in a televised evening press conference, an East German official inadvertently precipitated the opening of the Berlin Wall by announcing that the new law would allow citizens the right to leave the country through any border crossing. Tens of thousands immediately headed to the border and by morning were flooding into West Berlin. By Christmas, almost 2.5 million had made the crossing. Most came back, but, to the SED's chagrin, opening the wall did nothing to ease the crisis gripping the country.

Indeed, the situation grew worse as people learned more about the GDR's massive foreign debt, the party's corruption, and the activities of the secret police. In December, the SED attempted to reinvent itself at an emergency congress. Now calling itself the Party of Democratic Socialism, it purged the old leadership, selected reformer Gregor Gysi (b. 1948) as new party leader, agreed to round-table discussions with New Forum, and scheduled free parliamentary elections. It was too late, however, to formulate a new program that might have reversed the GDR's fortunes. By January, democratic socialist intellectuals such as Bohley, Stefan Heym (1913–2001), and Christa Wolf (1929–2011) had lost the initiative to rising nationalist sentiment, and the cry of "we are the people" gave way to "we are one people." Scheduled for March, the elections became a referendum on reunification with West Germany in which the latter's major parties actively supported their "sister" or allied parties in the East. The result was a decisive victory for the CDU, which, in contrast to the more cautious SPD, advocated the most rapid route to unity. Within six months, East Germany, born of the Cold War as the antimodel to West German capitalism, would cease to exist.

By the end of 1989, communist governance in the remainder of former East bloc had disappeared. Either through party-imposed reforms from above, as occurred in Bulgaria, or through mass protests conducted by intellectuals, students, and workers, as was the case in Czechoslovakia, brittle communist regimes put up little resistance to the emboldened forces of change. Support for communist parties or their successors did not disappear completely, and in most of the new postcommunist systems, they continued to win at least 10 to 20 percent of the vote and even won the first free election in Bulgaria. But communist elites did not have the will to mobilize their minority of supporters to defend the old order with violence. Only in Romania was the transition a bloody one. There the megalomaniacal dictator Nicolai Ceauşescu (1918–1989) had no intention of yielding power, and his elite security forces remained loyal. In December, however, after a bloody confrontation between the latter and protestors angry at the repression of the country's Hungarian minority, matters spun out of control as demonstrations spread and an opposition faction within the party, the National Salvation Front, led by Ion Iliescu (b. 1930), moved to depose their chief. Rebels, backed by the army, quickly captured Ceacusescu and his wife, who were tried and executed for "crimes against the state" on Christmas Day. The National Salvation Front then legalized opposition parties and organized new elections, which Iliescu won in April 1990.

The end of communism in Eastern Europe meant the end of one-party states, the command economy, and the Warsaw Pact. For the most part, these attributes gave way to the democratization of political and civic life with free multiparty elections, parliamentary government, civil freedoms, and national sovereignty. Market economics followed, not always with salutary effects, but alternatives could at least be debated openly and the course changed. None of these transformations would have occurred had Gorbachev not radically revised Soviet regional policy after 1985, but, ironically, many in the USSR, especially among the 140 million non-Russians in the "autonomous" republics, now wondered why they, too, did not have the same options. Thus, as the democratization of the USSR moved ahead, it challenged Gorbachev's ability not only to reform the communist system but also to hold his country together.

THE COLLAPSE OF THE SOVIET UNION

Gorbachev's domestic reforms and Eastern European policy met increasing resistance within the CPSU, but conservatives also opposed his willingness in 1987 to sign an agreement with the United States limiting intermediate-range nuclear missiles, his support for an end to superpower rivalry in the Third World, and his call for a "common European home" from the Atlantic to the Urals. Dissatisfaction increased as glasnost and democratization allowed long-submerged ethnic nationalism to emerge, threatening the unity of the state.

The first major difficulties came in Lithuania, Latvia, and Estonia. In early 1988, people in all three states organized "popular fronts," which first demanded more cultural autonomy but later called for independence. In 1989, the Baltic communist parties withdrew from the CPSU, and huge demonstrations, such as a 2-million-person human chain spanning all three countries, made clear where most people stood. Nationalist movements also arose in Ukraine, Belarus, and Moldavia, but matters were particularly serious in Transcaucasia, where violence erupted in 1988 between Armenians and Azerbaijanis. In Georgia, too, a strong independence movement developed that, in turn, came into conflict with other local ethnic groups, such as the Osetins and Abkhaz. These situations placed the government in a quandary. Charged with maintaining order, it had to tread lightly since using force to quell disturbances (as occurred in Georgia) simply made the state a target of universal criticism. Even more vexing was formulating a response to peaceful supporters of independence. Suppressing them contradicted the thrust of the reform effort, but allowing them free rein threatened the country's future.

As he wrestled with these difficulties, Gorbachev decided to cut the Gordian knot of party intransigence by going to the people. In June 1988, the nationally televised Nineteenth Party Conference shocked the public, which for the first time witnessed the depth of the divisions within the party. In free and open debate, reformers and conservatives argued over the ongoing reforms. At the end of the largely fruitless discussions, Gorbachev pushed through a proposal to elect the Congress of People's Deputies, which would now be "the country's supreme body of power." It is likely that the conference delegates did not fully grasp the impact of their vote. In one stroke, Gorbachev had won agreement to set up a new democratic structure alongside the CPSU, suddenly no longer the sole power in the land.

In March 1989, the Soviet people elected the new Congress. It was not a completely democratic process, as the CPSU appointed one-third of the 2,250 deputies and remained the only legal party. Nevertheless, the remaining seats were contested as various organizations and municipalities nominated and supported candidates in open campaigns. Eighty-seven percent of the winners were CPSU members, but, freed from party discipline, they could speak their minds. The popular Boris Yeltsin, widely regarded as a scourge of the bureaucracy, got 90 percent of the vote in his Moscow constituency and soon established himself as a major figure on the national stage. Meeting in May, the televised Congress riveted the nation as Gorbachev presided over freewheeling debates in which a wide range of views, many critical of his leadership and of the CPSU, were aired. Gorbachev worked to push back conservative attacks while resisting demands by liberals, such as Sakharov, for deeper, more radical reforms. The Congress concluded by electing a new Supreme Soviet of 542 deputies chosen from its own ranks. A majority were CPSU members, but it was clear that a new political space had been opened for pluralistic politics.

Initially, Gorbachev did not favor sacrificing the Communist Party's monopoly on power, and, to the chagrin of many reformers, his public statements criticizing Stalin often simultaneously praised some of his policies along with the basic tenets of Leninism. By 1989, however, he was the de facto leader of a coalition that supported a multiparty democracy, a federated union in which republican governments had substantial power, and a CPSU that would revert to its social democratic roots. As chairman of both the Congress of Peoples' Deputies and the Supreme Soviet, he had substantial power, but it became increasingly difficult for him to assert it in the face of conservative resistance to change and radical impatience for deeper reforms. His apparent vacillation cost him substantial support among former allies on both sides, and his public popularity, especially in the face of the deepening economic crisis and rising nationalism, began to slip.

By early 1990, Gorbachev was losing control of the reform process. Under pressure from the radicals, in February the CPSU renounced Article 6 of the constitution, which had enshrined the party as "the leading and guiding force of Soviet society." Since the party structure had long bound the union together, as its authority waned, that of the once-moribund republics waxed. The Baltic States rejected Moscow's authority, and other republican legislatures also began to assert themselves. In March, the Russian Federation elected its own Congress of Peoples' Deputies, and shortly thereafter Yeltsin became its chairman. Looking toward Russia's own sovereignty, he declared, "If the center does not overthrow us in the next 100 days, Russia will be independent in everything." [12]

Although the Congress of Peoples' Deputies elected Gorbachev president of the USSR in March, he was unable to reassert the power of the national government. On the contrary, in June 1990, the Russian parliament proclaimed that republic's own sovereignty, a gesture that soon had substantive meaning in the economic realm. With production stagnating, shortages spreading, and inflation rising, the government proposed a five-year transition to a regulated market economy, but the radicals, including Yeltsin, supported a plan proposed by Stanislav Shatalin (1935–1997) to create a privatized market system within 500 days. Initially, Gorbachev leaned toward Shatalin but in the face of conservative opposition moved closer to the government's position. To the public, Gorbachev seemed to be a creature of conservatism, while Yeltsin rode the wave of nationalism and reform.

Gorbachev had shifted the fulcrum of governance away from the CPSU and toward the state, but he never broke with the party completely. By early 1991, he was seeking to recentralize his control by bringing more conservatives into his inner circle and halfheartedly adopting a harder line toward the independence movements. These efforts alienated wide segments of the populace, however, and after Soviet troops fired on protesting crowds in Lithuania and Latvia, the independence movements remained unbowed. As Gorbachev's popularity declined, Yeltsin's opposition to the "center" won him mass support. Gorbachev never ran in a contested election, but in June Yeltsin took the Russian presidency with 57 percent of the vote. He was now well positioned to oppose any effort to limit Russian independence.

Gorbachev hoped to regain the initiative by creating a new union treaty and reforming the CPSU. In March 1991, a strong majority of Soviet citizens voted in favor of preserving the USSR as a "renewed federation of equal sovereign republics," and armed with this mandate, Gorbachev set about negotiating new terms with the various republics. Meanwhile, he pushed a new and largely social democratic program through the Central Committee. For him, the ideal continued to be "a humane and democratic socialism," but now Scandinavian social democracy was the model.

Gorbachev's plans collapsed when conservative party leaders, many of them key figures in his own government, attempted to forestall the signing of the Union Treaty and to roll back the wheel of reform by launching a coup on 18 August 1991. The plotters arrested Gorbachev at his vacation home on the Black Sea, suspended the constitution, and sent tanks to the center of Moscow, but the coup was a fiasco. While a few leaders in the republics joined, most did not, nor did the elite forces in the KGB and army. The soldiers in the streets refused to fire on the crowds, and Yeltsin, seizing the moment, rallied massive crowds while waving the Russian flag from the back of a tank. After only three days, the coup fell apart. Gorbachev returned to Moscow and condemned the plot, but Yeltsin humiliated him in front of the Russian parliament and forced him to accept the CPSU's dissolution. Riding high, Yeltsin's government seized the party's assets.

The destruction of the party undermined one of the key pillars of the USSR. The succession of the individual republics delivered the coup de grâce. For several months, Gorbachev cherished the vain hope of creating a new federation, but the coup had precipitated a mass exodus from the union. By December, he headed a government whose institutional basis had dissolved, while Yeltsin presided over a mighty Russian Federation that now took the lead in creating a new Commonwealth of Independent States. Created on 21 December, this entity included Russia, Belarus, Ukraine, and eight other former Soviet republics and was very different from the model envisioned by Gorbachev. Since Gorbachev had no power, he was simply ignored. On 25 December, he drew the logical conclusion and resigned from the presidency of a country that no longer existed. The Soviet experiment had ended.

DOCUMENT 6.1. WHY SOCIALISM? (1949)

Albert Einstein

Best known for his theory of relativity, Albert Einstein (1879–1955) was one of the greatest scientists of the twentieth century. He spent much of his early career as director of the Kaiser Wilhelm Physical Institute and a professor at the University of Berlin. Sympathetic to social democracy and of Jewish background, he faced death threats following the Nazi seizure of power and migrated to the United States. There, he became a professor at Princeton, remained active in the cause of social justice, and applauded the founding of the independent socialist magazine Monthly Review *in 1949. This excerpt is drawn from an essay that appeared in that journal's inaugural issue.*

Man is, at one and the same time, a solitary being and a social being. As a solitary being, he attempts to protect his own existence and that of those who are closest to him, to satisfy his personal desires, and to develop his innate abilities. As a social being, he seeks to gain the recognition and affection of his fellow human beings, to share in their pleasures, to comfort them in their sorrows, and to improve their conditions of life. Only the existence of these varied, frequently conflicting, strivings accounts for the special character of a man, and their specific combination determines the extent to which an individual can achieve an inner equilibrium and can contribute to the well-being of society. It is quite possible that the relative strength of these two drives is, in the main, fixed by inheritance. But the personality that finally emerges is largely formed by the environment in which a man happens to find himself during his development, by the structure of the society in which he grows up, by the tradition of that society, and by its appraisal of particular types of behavior. The abstract concept "society" means to the individual human being the sum total of his direct and indirect relations to his contemporaries and to all the people of earlier generations. The individual is able to think, feel, strive, and work by himself; but he depends so much upon society—in his physical, intellectual, and emotional existence—that it is impossible to think of him, or to understand him, outside the framework of society. It is "society" which provides man with food, clothing, a home, the tools of work, language, the forms of thought, and most of the content of thought; his life is made possible through the labor and the accomplishments of the many millions past and present who are all hidden behind the small word "society."

It is evident, therefore, that the dependence of the individual upon society is a fact of nature which cannot be abolished—just as in the case of ants and bees. However, while the whole life process of ants and bees is fixed down to the smallest detail by rigid, hereditary instincts, the social pattern and interrelationships of human beings are very variable and susceptible to change. Memory, the capacity to make new combinations, the gift of oral communication, have made possible developments among human beings which are not dictated by biological necessities. Such developments manifest themselves in traditions, institutions, and organizations; in literature; in scientific and engineering accomplishments; in works of art. This explains how it happens that, in a certain sense, man can influence his life through his own conduct, and that in this process conscious thinking and wanting can play a part.

Man acquires at birth, through heredity, a biological constitution, which we must consider fixed and unalterable, including the natural urges, which are characteristic of the human species. In addition, during his lifetime, he acquires a cultural constitution, which he adopts from society through communication and through many other types of influences. It is this cultural constitution which, with the passage of time, is subject to change and which determines to a very large extent the relationship between the individual and society. Modern anthropology has taught us, through comparative investigation of so-called primitive cultures, that the social behavior of human beings may differ greatly, depending upon prevailing cultural patterns and the types of organization, which predominate in society. It is on this that those who are striving to improve the lot of man may ground their hopes: human beings are not condemned, because of their biological constitution, to annihilate each other or to be at the mercy of a cruel, self-inflicted fate.

If we ask ourselves how the structure of society and the cultural attitude of man should be changed in order to make human life as satisfying as possible, we should constantly be conscious of the fact that there are certain conditions which we are unable to modify. As mentioned before, the biological nature of man is, for all practical purposes, not subject to change. Furthermore, technological and demographic developments of the last few centuries have created conditions which are here to stay. In relatively densely settled populations with the goods which are indispensable to their continued existence, an extreme division of labor and a highly-centralized productive apparatus are absolutely necessary. The time—which, looking back, seems so idyllic—is gone forever when individuals or relatively small groups could be completely self-sufficient. It is only a slight exaggeration to say that mankind constitutes even now a planetary community of production and consumption.

I have now reached the point where I may indicate briefly what to me constitutes the essence of the crisis of our time. It concerns the relationship of the individual to society. The individual has become more conscious than ever of his dependence upon society. But he does not experience this dependence as a positive asset, as an organic tie, as a protective force, but rather as a threat to his natural rights, or even to his economic existence. Moreover, his position in society is such that the egotistical drives of his make-up are constantly being accentuated, while his social drives, which are by nature weaker, progressively deteriorate. All human beings, whatever their position in society, are suffering from this process of deterioration. Unknowingly prisoners of their own egotism, they feel insecure, lonely, and deprived of the naive, simple, and unsophisticated enjoyment of life. Man can find meaning in life, short and perilous as it is, only through devoting himself to society.

The economic anarchy of capitalist society as it exists today is, in my opinion, the real source of the evil. We see before us a huge community of producers the members of which are unceasingly striving to deprive each other of the fruits of their collective labor—not by force, but on the whole in faithful compliance with legally established rules. In this respect, it is important to realize that the means of production—that is to say, the entire productive capacity that is needed for producing consumer goods as well as additional capital goods—may legally be, and for the most part are, the private property of individuals.

For the sake of simplicity, in the discussion that follows I shall call "workers" all those who do not share in the ownership of the means of production—although this does not quite correspond to the customary use of the term. The owner of the means of production is in a position to purchase the labor power of the worker. By using the means of production, the worker produces new goods which become the property of the capitalist. The essential point about this process is the relation between what the worker produces and what he is paid, both measured in terms of real value. Insofar as the labor contract is "free," what the worker receives is determined not by the real value of the goods he produces, but by his minimum needs and by the capitalists' requirements for labor power in relation to the number of workers competing for jobs. It is important to understand that even in theory the payment of the worker is not determined by the value of his product.

Private capital tends to become concentrated in few hands, partly because of competition among the capitalists, and partly because technological development and the increasing division of labor encourage the formation of larger units of production at the expense of smaller ones. The result of these developments is an oligarchy of private capital the enormous power of which cannot be effectively checked even by a democratically organized political society. This is true since the members of legislative bodies are selected by political parties, largely financed or otherwise influenced by private capitalists who, for all practical purposes, separate the electorate from the legislature. The consequence is that the representatives of the people do not in fact sufficiently protect the interests of the underprivileged sections of the population. Moreover, under existing conditions, private capitalists inevitably control, directly or indirectly, the main sources of information (press, radio, education). It is thus extremely difficult, and indeed in most cases quite impossible, for the individual citizen to come to objective conclusions and to make intelligent use of his political rights.

The situation prevailing in an economy based on the private owner-ship of capital is thus characterized by two main principles: first, means of production (capital) are privately owned and the owners dispose of them as they see fit; second, the labor contract is free. Of course, there is no such thing as a *pure* capitalist society in this sense. In particular, it should be noted that the workers, through long and bitter political strug-gles, have succeeded in securing a somewhat improved form of the "free labor contract" for certain categories of workers. But taken as a whole, the present day economy does not differ much from "pure" capitalism.

Production is carried on for profit, not for use. There is no provision that all those able and willing to work will always be in a position to find employment; an "army of unemployed" almost always exists. The work-er is constantly in fear of losing his job. Since unemployed and poorly paid workers do not provide a profitable market, the production of con-sumers' goods is restricted, and great hardship is the consequence. Tech-nological progress frequently results in more unemployment rather than in an easing of the burden of work for all. The profit motive, in conjunc-tion with competition among capitalists, is responsible for an instability in the accumulation and utilization of capital which leads to increasingly severe depressions. Unlimited competition leads to a huge waste of labor, and to that crippling of the social consciousness of individuals which I mentioned before.

This crippling of individuals I consider the worst evil of capitalism. Our whole educational system suffers from this evil. An exaggerated competitive attitude is inculcated into the student, who is trained to wor-ship acquisitive success as a preparation for his future career.

I am convinced there is only *one* way to eliminate these grave evils, namely through the establishment of a socialist economy, accompanied by an educational system which would be oriented toward social goals. In such an economy, the means of production are owned by society itself and are utilized in a planned fashion. A planned economy, which adjusts production to the needs of the community, would distribute the work to be done among all those able to work and would guarantee a livelihood to every man, woman, and child. The education of the individual, in addition to promoting his own innate abilities, would attempt to develop in him a sense of responsibility for his fellow men in place of the glorifica-tion of power and success in our present society.

Nevertheless, it is necessary to remember that a planned economy is not yet socialism. A planned economy as such may be accompanied by the complete enslavement of the individual. The achievement of social-ism requires the solution of some extremely difficult socio-political prob-lems: how is it possible, in view of the far-reaching centralization of polit-ical and economic power, to prevent bureaucracy from becoming all-powerful and overweening? How can the rights of the individual be protected and therewith a democratic counterweight to the power of bureaucracy be assured?

Clarity about the aims and problems of socialism is of greatest significance in our age of transition. Since, under present circumstances, free and unhindered discussion of these problems has come under a powerful taboo, I consider the foundation of this magazine to be an important public service.

Source: Monthly Review 1, no. 1 (May 1949): 9–15.

————*ﾟﾟ*————

DOCUMENT 6.2. "WOMEN: THE LONGEST REVOLUTION" (1966)

Juliet Mitchell

Juliet Mitchell is a leading socialist feminist theorist and activist. An organizer of the Women's Liberation Conference held at Ruskin College in Oxford in 1970, she gave up an academic career to help build the British women's movement. Trained in English literature and psychoanalysis, she is the author of many books and articles on feminism. The following passage is from the conclusion to an essay that appeared in the New Left Review, *an important socialist journal. After analyzing the strengths and weaknesses of socialist theorists such as Fourier, Marx, Engels, and others on "the woman question," she argues that there are four interrelated structures of women's oppression: production, reproduction, sexuality, and socialization of children. These must be viewed as a totality and transformed simultaneously if women are to achieve full emancipation.*

It is only in the highly developed societies of the West that an authentic liberation of women can be envisaged today. But for this to occur, there must be a transformation of all the structures into which they are integrated, and an *"unité de rupture."*[1] A revolutionary movement must base its analysis on the uneven development of each, and attack the weakest link in the combination. This may then become the point of departure for a general transformation. What is the situation of the different structures today?

1. *Production:* The long-term development of the forces of production must command any socialist perspective. The hopes which the advent of machine technology raised as early as the 19th century have already been discussed. They proved illusory. Today, automation promises the *technical* possibility of abolishing completely the physical differential between man and woman in production, but under capitalist relations of production, the *social* possibility of this abolition is permanently threatened. . . .

2. *Reproduction:* Scientific advance in contraception could, as we have seen, make involuntary reproduction—which accounts for the vast majority of births in the world today, and for a major proportion even in the West—a phenomenon of the past. But oral contraception—which has so far been developed in a form which exactly repeats the sexual inequality of Western society—is only at its beginnings. It is inadequately distributed across classes and countries and awaits further technical improvements. Its main initial impact is, in the advanced countries, likely to be psychological—it will certainly free women's sexual experience from many of the anxieties and inhibitions which have always afflicted it.[2]

3. *Socialization:* The changes in the composition of the work-force, the size of the family, the structure of education, etc.—however limited from an ideal standpoint—have undoubtedly diminished the societal function and importance of the family. As an organization it is not a significant unit in the political power system, it plays little part in economic production and it is rarely the sole agency of integration into the larger society; thus at the macroscopic level it serves very little purpose.

The result has been a major displacement of emphasis on to the family's psycho-social function, for the infant and for the couple. . . .[3] The vital nucleus of truth in the emphasis on socialization of the child has been discussed. It is essential that socialists should acknowledge it and integrate it entirely into any programme for the liberation of women. . . . [T]here is no doubt that the need for permanent, intelligent care of children in the initial three or four years of their lives can (and has been) exploited ideologically to perpetuate the family as a total unit, when its other functions have been visibly declining. Indeed, the attempt to focus women's existence exclusively on bringing up children, is manifestly harmful to children. Socialization as an exceptionally delicate process requires a serene and mature socializer—a type which the frustrations of a *purely* familial role are not liable to produce. Exclusive maternity is often in this sense "counter-productive." . . .

4. *Sexuality:* It is difficult not to conclude that the major structure which at present is in rapid evolution is sexuality. Production, reproduction, and socialization are all more or less stationary in the West today, in the sense that they have not changed for three or more decades. There is moreover, no widespread demand for changes in them on the part of women themselves—the governing ideology has effectively prevented critical consciousness. By contrast, the dominant sexual ideology is proving less and less successful in regulating spontaneous behavior. Marriage in its classical form is increasingly threatened by the liberalization of relationships before and after it which affects all classes today. In this sense, it is evidently the weak link in the chain—the particular structure that is the site of the most contradictions. The progressive potential of these contradictions has already been emphasized. In a context of juridical equality, the liberation of sexual experience from relations which are

extraneous to it—whether procreation or property—could lead to true inter-sexual freedom. But it could also lead simply to new forms of neo-capitalist ideology and practice. For one of the forces behind the current acceleration of sexual freedom has undoubtedly been the conversion of contemporary capitalism from a production-and-work ethos to a consumption-and-fun ethos. Riesman commented on this development early in the 1950's: "there is not only a growth of leisure, but work itself becomes both less interesting and less demanding for many . . . more than before, as job-mindedness declines, sex permeates the daytime as well as the playtime consciousness. It is viewed as a consumption good not only by the old leisure classes, but by the modern leisure masses. . . ."[4] Bourgeois society at present can well afford a play area of premarital *non*-procreative sexuality. Even marriage can save itself by increasing divorce and remarriage rates, signifying the importance of the institution itself. These considerations make it clear that sexuality, while it presently may contain the greatest potential for liberation—can equally well be organized against any increase of its human possibilities. New forms of reification are emerging which may void sexual freedom of any meaning. This is a reminder that while one structure may be the *weak link* in a unity like that of woman's condition, there can never be a solution through it alone. . . .

What, then, is the responsible revolutionary attitude? It must include both immediate fundamental demands, in a single critique of the *whole* of women's situation, that does not fetishize any dimension of it. Modern industrial development, as has been seen, tends towards the separating out of the originally unified function of the family—procreation, socialization, sexuality, economic subsistence, etc. . . .

In practical terms this means a coherent system of demands. The four elements of women's condition cannot merely be considered each in isolation; they form a structure of specific interrelations. The contemporary bourgeois family can be seen as a triptych of sexual, reproductive and socializatory functions (the woman's world) embraced by production (the man's world)—precisely a structure which in the final instance is determined by the economy. The exclusion of women from production—social human activity—and their confinement to a monolithic condensation of functions in a unity—the family—which is precisely unified in the *natural part* of each function, is the root cause of the contemporary *social* definition of women as *natural* beings. Hence the main thrust of any emancipation movement must still concentrate on the economic element—the entry of women fully into public industry. The error of the old socialists was to see the other elements as reducible to the economic; hence the call for the entry of women into production was accompanied by the purely abstract slogan of the abolition of the family. Economic demands are still primary, but must be accompanied by coherent policies for the other three elements, policies which at particular junctures may take over the primary role in immediate action.

Economically, the most elementary demand is not the right to work or receive equal pay for work—the . . . traditional reformist demands—but *the right to equal work itself.* At present, women perform unskilled, uncreative, service jobs that can be regarded as 'extensions' of their expressive familial role. They are overwhelmingly waitresses, office-cleaners, hairdressers, clerks, typists. In the working-class occupational mobility is thus sometimes easier for girls than boys—they can enter the white-collar sector at a lower level. But only two in a hundred women are in administrative or managerial jobs, and less than five in a thousand are in the professions. Women are poorly unionized (25 per cent) and receive less money than men for the manual work they do perform: in 1961 the average industrial wage for women was less than half that for men, which, even setting off part-time work, represents a massive increment of exploitation for the employer.

Education

The whole pyramid of discrimination rests on a solid extra-economic foundation—education. The demand for equal work, in Britain, should above all take the form of a demand for an *equal educational system,* since this is at present the main single filter selecting women for inferior work-roles. At present, there is something like equal education for both sexes up to 15. Thereafter three times as many boys continue their education as girls. Only one in three "A"-level entrants, one in four university students is a girl. There is no evidence whatever of progress. The proportion of girl university students is the same as it was in the 1920's. Until these injustices are ended, there is no chance of equal work for women. It goes without saying that the content of the educational system, which actually instills limitation of aspiration in girls needs to be changed as much as methods of selection. Education is probably the key area for immediate economic advance at present.

Only if it is founded on equality can production be truly differentiated from reproduction and the family. . . . Traditionally, the socialist movement has called for the "abolition of the bourgeois family." This slogan must be rejected as incorrect today. . . . The strategic concern for socialists should be for the equality of the sexes, not the abolition of the family. The consequences of this demand are no less radical, but they are concrete and positive, and can be integrated into the real course of history. The family as it exists at present is, in fact, incompatible with the equality of the sexes. But this equality will not come from its administrative abolition, but from the historical differentiation of its functions. The revolutionary demand should be for the liberation of these functions from a monolithic fusion which oppresses each. Thus dissociation of reproduction from sexuality frees sexuality from alienation in unwanted reproduction (and fear of it), and reproduction from subjugation to chance and uncontrollable casuality. It is thus an elementary demand to press for free State provision of oral contraception. The legalization of homosexuality—which is one of the forms of non-reproductive sexuality—should be supported for just the same reason, and regressive campaigns against it in Cuba or elsewhere should be unhesitatingly criticized. The straightforward abolition of illegitimacy as a legal notion as in Sweden and Russia has a similar implication; it would separate marriage civically from parenthood.

From Nature to Culture

The problem of socialization poses more difficult questions, as has been seen. But the need for intensive maternal care in the early years of a child's life does not mean that the present single sanctioned form of socialization—marriage and family—is inevitable. Far from it. The fundamental characteristic of the present system of marriage and family is in our society is *monolithism:* there is only one institutionalized form of inter-sexual or inter-generational relationship possible. . . . Any society will require some institutionalized and social recognition of personal relationships. But there is absolutely no reason why there should be only one legitimized form—and a multitude of unlegitimized experience. Socialism should properly mean not the abolition of the family, but the diversification of the socially acknowledged relationships which are today forcibly and rigidly compressed into it. This would mean a plural range of institutions—where the family is only one, and its abolition implies none. Couples living together or not living together, long-term unions with children, single parents bringing up children, children socialized by conventional rather than biological parents, extended kin groups, etc.—all these could be encompassed in a range of institutions which matched the free invention and variety of men and women.

It would be illusory to try and specify these institutions. Circumstantial accounts of the future are idealist and worse, static. Socialism will be a process of change, of becoming. A fixed image of the future is in the worst sense ahistorical; the form that socialism takes will depend on the prior type of capitalism and the nature of its collapse. As Marx wrote: 'What (is progress) if not the absolute elaboration of (man's) creative dispositions, without any preconditions other than antecedent historical evolution which makes the totality of this evolution—i.e., the evolution of all human powers as such, unmeasured by any *previously established* yardstick—an end in itself? What is this, if not a situation where man does not reproduce himself in any determined form, but produces his totality? Where he does not seek to remain something formed by the past, but is the absolute movement of becoming?'[5] The liberation of women under socialism will not be 'rational' but a human achievement, in the long passage from Nature to Culture, which is the definition of history and society.

Source: Lisa DiCaprio and Merry E. Wiesner, *Lives and Voices: Sources in Women's History* (Boston: Houghton Mifflin, 2001), 559–64.

  1. See Louis Althusser, "Contradiction et Surdétermination" in *Pour Marx* (1965).

  2. Jean Baby records the results of an enquiry carried out into attitudes to marriage, contraception and abortion of 3,191 women in Czechoslovakia in 1959: 80 per cent of the women had limited sexual satisfaction because of fear of conception. *Un Monde Meilleur* (1964), p. 82n.

  3. See Berger and Kellner: "Marriage and the Construction of Reality," *Diogenes* (Summer 1964) for analysis of marriage and parenthood 'nomic-building' structure.

  4. Riesman, *The Lonely Crowd* (1950), p. 154.

  5. Karl Marx: *Precapitalist Economic Formations,* in *Early Writings,* trans. T. B. Bottomore (1963), p. 85.

DOCUMENT 6.3. PERESTROIKA (1987)

Mikhail Gorbachev

Within two years of his appointment as general secretary of the Communist Party, Mikhail Gorbachev realized that radical economic reforms would be necessary if the USSR were to deliver on the long-delayed promises of the October Revolution of 1917. The speech below outlines his early view of how the country needed to change and some of the obstacles he perceived.

The April [1985] plenary session and the 27th Party Congress opened the way for an objective critical analysis of the current situation in society and adopted decisions of historic importance for the country's future. We have irrevocably begun restructuring and have taken the first steps on this path. . . .

At the same time, we see that changes for the better are taking place slowly, that the task of restructuring has turned out to be more difficult that it had seemed to us earlier, and that the causes of the problems that have accumulated in society are more deep-rooted than we had thought. The more deeply we go into restructuring work, the clearer its scale and importance become; more and more new unsolved problems inherited from the past are coming to light. . . .

At a certain stage the country began to lose momentum, difficulties and unsolved problems began to pile up, and stagnation and other phenomena alien to socialism appeared. All of this had a serious effect on the economy and on the social and spiritual spheres.

Of course, comrades, the country's development did not stop. Tens of millions of Soviet people worked honestly, and many Party organizations and our cadres acted vigorously, in the interests of the people. All this restrained the growth of negative processes, but it could not prevent them.

In the economy, and in other spheres as well, the objective need for changes became urgent, but it was not realized in the political and practical activities of the party and the state.

What was the reason for this complex and contradictory situation?

The principle cause—and the Politburo considers it necessary to say this with total frankness at the plenary session—was that the CPSU Central Committee and the country's leadership, primarily for subjective reasons, were unable to promptly or fully appreciate the need for changes and the danger of the mounting crisis phenomena in society or to work out a clear-cut line aimed at overcoming them and making fuller use of the possibilities inherent in the socialist system.

Conservative inclinations, inertia, a desire to brush aside everything that didn't fit into habitual patters and an unwillingness to tackle urgent social and economic questions prevailed in both policy-making and practical activity.

Comrades, the executive bodies of the Party and the state bear the responsibility for all this. . . .

Lenin's theses about socialism were interpreted in an oversimplified way, and frequently their theoretical profundity and significance were emasculated. This also applied to such key problems as public ownership, relations among classes and nationalities, the measure of labor and the measure of consumption, cooperatives, methods of economic management, people's rule and self-management, the struggle against bureaucratic aberrations, the revolutionary-transformational essence of socialist ideology, the principles of instruction and upbringing, and guarantees of the healthy development of the Party and society.

Superficial notions about communism and various kinds of prophecies and abstractions gained a certain currency. This in turn lessened the historical significance of socialism and weakened the influence of socialist ideology. . . .

In point of fact, a whole system of weakening the economic instruments of power came into being, and a unique mechanism was forming for retarding social and economic development and holding back progressive transformations that make it possible to disclose and utilize the advantages of socialism. The roots of this retardation lay in serious shortcomings in the functioning of the institutions of socialist democracy, in outmoded political and theoretical principles that sometimes did not correspond to reality, and in a conservative mechanism of management.

Comrades, all this had a negative effect on the development of many spheres of the life of society. Take material production. Over the past three five-year plans, the growth rates of national income declined by more than 50 percent. For most indices, plans had not been fulfilled since the early 1970s. The economy as a whole became unreceptive to innovations and sluggish, the quality of a large part of output no longer met current demands, and disproportions in production became exacerbated. . . .

We have at the same time been unable to fully realize the possibilities of socialism in improving living conditions and the food supply, in organizing transportation, medical service, and education and in solving a number of other key problems. Violations of the most important principle of socialism—distribution according to work—appeared. The struggle against unearned income was waged indecisively. The policy of providing material and moral incentives for highly productive labor was inconsistent. Large sums of money were paid out in unwarranted bonuses and in various kinds of additional incentives, and reports were padded for the sake of personal gain. A dependent mind-set grew, and a "wage-leveling" mentality began taking root in people's minds. This hit at those toilers who were able and wanted to work better, while at the same time it made life easier for those whose idea of working involves little effort.

Violation of the organic tie between the measure of labor and the measure of consumption not only deforms the attitude toward labor, impeding growth in labor productivity, it also leads to the distortion of the principle of social justice, and this is a matter of great political importance.

The elements of social corrosion that emerged in recent years had a negative effect on society's spiritual temper and imperceptibly sapped the lofty moral values that have always been inherent to our people and in which we take pride—ideological conviction, labor enthusiasm and Soviet patriotism.

The inevitable consequence of this was falloff in interest in public affairs, manifestations of spiritual emptiness and skepticism, and a decline in the role of moral incentives to labor. The stratum of people, including young people, whose goal in life came down to material well-being and personal gain by any means increased. Their cynical position took on increasingly militant forms, poisoned the minds of those around them, and gave rise to a wave of consumerism. The growth of drunkenness, the spread of drug addiction and the increase in crime became indices of the falloff in social mores.

Instances of a scornful attitude toward laws, hoodwinking, bribe taking, and the encouragement of servility and glorification had a pernicious effect on the moral atmosphere in society. Genuine concern for people, their living and working conditions and their social well-being was frequently supplanted by political ingratiation—the mass handing out of awards, titles and bonuses. An atmosphere of all-forgivingness took shape, while exactingness, discipline, and responsibility declined. . . .

This was the situation, comrades, in which the question of accelerating the country's social and economic development and of restructuring was raised. In essence, what is involved here is a change in direction and measures of a revolutionary nature. We are talking about restructuring and related processes of the thoroughgoing democratization of society, having in mind truly revolutionary and comprehensive transformations in society.

This fundamental change of direction is necessary, since we simply have no other way. We must not retreat, and we have nowhere to retreat to. . . .

Today there is a need to state once again what we mean by restructuring.

Restructuring means resolutely overcoming the processes of stagnation, scrapping the mechanism of retardation, and creating a reliable and effective mechanism of accelerating the social and economic development of Soviet society. The main idea of our strategy is to combine the achievements of the scientific and technological revolution with a planned economy and to set the entire potential of socialism in motion.

Restructuring means reliance on the vital creativity of the masses, the all-round development of democracy and socialist self government, the encouragement of initiative an independent activity, the strengthening of discipline and order, and the expansion of openness, criticism, and self-criticism in all spheres of the life of society; it means respect, raised on high, for the value and worth of the individual.

Restructuring means steadily enhancing the role of intensive factors in the development of the Soviet economy; restoring and developing Leninist principles of democratic centralism in the management of the national economy, introducing economic methods of management everywhere, renouncing the peremptory issuing of orders and administrative fiat, ensuring the changeover of all elements of the economy to the principles of full economic accountability and to new forms of the organization of labor and production, and encouraging innovation and socialist enterprise in every way.

Restructuring means a decisive turn toward science. . . .

Restructuring means the priority development of the social sphere and the ever fuller satisfaction of Soviet people's requirements for good working, living, recreational, educational, and medical-service conditions. . . .

Restructuring means the energetic elimination from society of distortions of socialist morality, and the consistent implementation of the principles of social justice. . . .

The ultimate aim of restructuring is clear, I think—a thoroughgoing renewal of all aspects of the country's life, the imparting to socialism of the most up-to-date forms of social organization, and the fullest possible disclosure of the humanistic nature of our system in all its decisive aspects—economic, social, political and moral. . . .

On the political level, the matter at hand is deepening democracy in the electoral system and achieving the more effective and more active participation of voters at all stages of pre-election and election campaigns. . . .

It is quite natural that questions of expanding inner-Party democracy be examined within the overall context of the future democratization of Soviet society. . . .

. . . In improving the social atmosphere, it is also necessary to continue to develop openness. It is a powerful lever for improving work in all sectors of our construction and an effective form of control by all the people. . . .

. . . Here one cannot help saying regretfully that we continue to encounter not only hostility toward criticism, but also instances of persecution for it and the outright suppression of critical statements. Frequently this assumes such dimensions and scope, and takes place in such forms, that the Central Committee has to intervene in order to restore truth and justice and to support honest people who back the interests of the cause. . . .

. . . We want to transform our country into a model of a highly developed state, into a society of the most advanced economy, the broadest democracy and the most humane and lofty morality, where the working person will feel himself to be a full fledged proprietor and can enjoy all the benefits of material and spiritual culture, where his children's future will be secure, and where he will possess everything he needs for a full, meaningful life. We want to force even the skeptics to say: Yes, the Bolsheviks can do anything. Yes, the truth is on their side. Yes, socialism is a system that serves man, his social and economic interests and his spiritual elevation.

Source: Robert V. Daniels, ed., *A Documentary History of Communism in Russia: From Lenin to Gorbachev* (Hanover, NH: University Press of New England, 1993), 341–47.

Figure 6.3.   People's Power. Atelier Populaire, Paris, May 1968. Courtesy of IISH, Amsterdam.

Figure 6.4.   A British poster from 1976. Designed by A.B. The figures in the foreground are drawn from *The Fourth Estate*, a painting by Pelizzo de Volpedo, 1901. Courtesy of the IISH, Amsterdam.

NOTES

1. Quoted in Karl Dietrich Bracher, *The German Dictatorship: The Origins, Structure, and Effects of National Socialism* (New York: Praeger, 1970), 10.

2. Quoted in Dietrich Orlow, *Common Destiny: A Comparative History of the Dutch, French, and German Social Democratic Parties, 1945–1969* (New York: Berghahn Books, 2000), 27.

3. Donald Sassoon, *One Hundred Years of Socialism* (New York: Free Press, 1996), 84.

4. Quoted in Sheri Berman, *The Primacy of Politics: Social Democracy and the Making of Europe's Twentieth Century* (Cambridge: Cambridge University Press, 2006), 178.

5. *Aims and Tasks of Democratic Socialism. Declaration of the Socialist International Adopted at Its First Congress Held in Frankfort-on-Main on 30 June–3 July 1951*, http://www.socialistinternational.org/viewArticle.cfm?ArticleID=39.

6. Quoted in Lewis J. Edinger, *Kurt Schumacher: A Study in Personality and Political Behavior* (Stanford, CA: Stanford University Press, 1965), 42.

7. William Taubman, *Khrushchev: The Man and His Era* (New York: Norton, 2003), 11–14.

8. "Grundsatzprogram der Sozialdemokratischen Partei Deutschlands, beschloßen auf dem ausserordentlichen Parteitag in Bad Godesberg 1959," in *Programmatische Dokumente der Deutschen Sozialdemokratie*, ed. Dieter Dowe and Kurt Klotzbach (Bonn: J. H. W. Dietz, 2004), 326–27.

9. Jeffrey Kopstein, *The Politics of Economic Decline in East Germany, 1945–1989* (Chapel Hill: University of North Carolina Press, 1997), 47.

10. Quoted in Tony Judt, *Postwar: A History of Europe since 1945* (New York: Penguin, 2005), 443.

11. Quoted in Ronald Grigor Suny, *The Soviet Experiment: Russia, The USSR, and the Successor States*. New York: Oxford University Press, 1998, 452.

12. Geoff Eley, *Forging Democracy: The History of the Left in Europe, 1850–2000*. New York: Oxford University Press, 2002, 441.

SEVEN

Epilogue

The Retreat and Reemergence of Socialism, 1991 to the Present

The collapse of Soviet-style bureaucratic collectivism was a moment of world historical importance. With the dissolution of "communism" from Central Europe to Vladivostock, the bipolar Cold War world gave way to one dominated by liberal capitalism in which even "communist" China, once so scornful of Khrushchev's reforms, now set out on the capitalist road. Waxing triumphant, liberal thinkers reveled at the dawn of a new era with Francis Fukuyama boldly asserting that the Cold War's end marked "the end of history as such." "Mankind," he wrote, had reached "the end point of . . . ideological evolution and the universalization of Western liberal democracy as the final form of human government." Having vanquished communism and fascism, economic and political liberalism stood poised to "govern the material world." Conflicts would continue for a time, he conceded, but inevitably liberalism would usher in a "posthistorical" era in which "economic calculation and the endless solving of technical problems" would replace ideological struggle.[1] For Fukuyama, like Thatcher, there was no alternative.

Events over the past two decades have shown, however, that history has not ended. Capitalism reigns supreme but cannot escape its historical nature. As Marx once famously noted, "Men make their own history, but they do not make it just as they please . . . but under circumstances directly encountered, given, and transmitted from the past. The tradition of all the dead generations weighs like a nightmare on the brain of the living."[2] And so it is with capitalism, a socially constructed system that, even at its moment of supreme triumph, remains shot through with

295

contradictions that give rise to various forms of resistance. In this context, contrary to Fukuyama's expectations, socialism has remained an important force in the postcommunist world. It is not the unified, confident movement of the early twentieth century that expected to usher in the new age as a matter of historical inevitability. That movement, we know, crumbled in the wake of 1914, leading to the establishment of rival social democratic and communist currents.

Since the Cold War's end and the creation of the European Union, social democrats and communists have struggled to reorient themselves within radically changing environments. What has emerged is a variegated set of movements and institutions that, though much changed from their predecessors, are still capable of giving expression to those who desire a different world.

THE CRISIS OF SOCIALIST IDENTITY

Two contradictory tendencies divided Europe in the early 1990s. On the one hand, the Continent was clearly drawing together. In 1992, the Maastricht Treaty transformed the eleven-member European Economic Community (EEC) into the European Union (EU), a confederation of states linked together in a single market and by a supranational government empowered to coordinate policy and, within certain limits, to pass legislation on social, economic, juridical, and environmental matters as well as on foreign affairs. Other states soon joined, including most of those in Eastern Europe, so that by 2012 it consisted of twenty-seven members. Building this European polity was not without problems, but it nonetheless knitted the Continent together in unprecedented ways by facilitating the free movement of goods and people and making war among member states seem like a fantastic prospect.

On the other hand, post–Cold War Europe also was divided between a wealthy West and a relatively poor East and by explosive ethnic conflict, especially in the Balkans. Once heralded as a modestly successful experiment in workers' self-management and in balancing the interests of many ethnic groups, Yugoslavia gradually disintegrated after Tito's death in 1980. Economic and political crises fueled by enormous foreign debts, inflation, rising unemployment, and intensifying nationalism, especially in Serbia and Croatia, unleashed in 1991 civil war and ethnic cleansing that ended only following NATO's intervention in 1999. Similar tensions in other parts of the Balkans and Transcaucasia made it more difficult for states in these regions to create workable democratic institutions, slowed their transition to capitalism, and delayed their joining the EU.

The emergence of the EU took place within the broader context of late twentieth-century capitalist "globalization," a process in which governments reduced obstacles to trade and facilitated the mobility and power of capital through deregulation and privatization. Aided by advances in technology, such as electronic communication, capital's increased mobility allows it to quickly restructure the division of labor within and between states as transnational firms pursue "comparative advantages" that bring higher profits. After 1980, the capitalist powers of Western Europe relentlessly promoted neoliberal economic policies both at home and abroad. At Maastricht, conservative forces shaped the agreement largely along neoliberal lines. Once embedded in this international treaty, it became difficult for opponents to change its terms or implement contrary policies on the national level.

The existence of the Soviet system after 1945 had forced capital to make substantial concessions to labor in the form of collective bargaining, economic regulation, wage increases tied to rising productivity, and a generous welfare state. Communism's demise and the pressures of global competition emboldened capital to increase its effort, under way since the 1970s, to roll back those gains. Under "normal" circumstances, social democrats and communists would have strongly resisted such policies and offered alternatives. But circumstances were no longer normal. With the exception of the Czechoslovak Communist Party and the Communist Party of the Russian Federation, founded in 1993 as the successor to the Communist Party of the Soviet Union, most of the reformed parties in Eastern Europe now identified themselves as social democratic and, as we will see, when they returned to power sought to guide their states toward capitalism and EU membership. Meanwhile, the majority of Western communist parties, often torn between reformers and traditionalists, struggled to remake themselves into credible electoral parties. Most succeeded, but the process took time, and some, such as the French Communist Party, shrank in size and influence. By contrast, the Italian Communist Party joined the social democratic camp in 1991. Rechristened as the Party of the Democratic Left (PDS), it soon won power despite its left wing's departure to form the Party of Communist Refoundation.

While communists debated their identity and role in the "new world order," Social Democrats did the same. Out of power in most places in the early 1990s, parties such as the German Social Democratic Party (SPD), the British Labor Party, and the French Socialist Party all shifted to the right on economic matters while simultaneously seeking to attract women, middle-class people, environmentalists, and other groups whom they had earlier neglected. The Spanish Socialist Party (PSOE), in power from 1982 to 1996, led the way. Banned during the Franco dictatorship, the PSOE emerged from illegality in 1977 led by a youthful radical, Philipe González (b. 1942). Armed with a broadly anticapitalist program, it won the 1982 elections and proceeded to create a framework for the welfare state, but it also pursued austerity and "modernization" via the privatization of hundreds of state-owned enterprises and membership in the EEC. These policies and Spain's entry into NATO alienated many workers and traditional socialists, but González attracted enough cross-class support to win reelection three times.

During the mid- to late 1990s, Social Democrats across Europe replicated the PSOE's move toward the "center." In Italy, following the dissolution of Christian democracy and the Italian Socialist Party amidst corruption scandals, the PDS led a broad alliance of left forces (including the Greens and the Party of Communist Refoundation) to victory in the 1996 elections. In 1997–1998, British, German, French and the Scandinavian Social Democrats, sometimes in coalition with the Greens and other left parties, returned to power. Finally, in Eastern Europe, following an initial interlude during which anticommunist parties dominated the field, former communists won office as Social Democrats in Poland, Hungary, and elsewhere. Thus, within a decade after communism's fall, Social Democrats were in power in thirteen of the EU's fifteen member states.

What factors made this shift possible? Part of the left's success in the West was based on the exhaustion of the center-right parties after long years in power. In scandal-ridden Italy, the PDS was the last "man" left standing after the collapse of its rivals. In France, Gaullist President Jacque Chirac's efforts to cut civil service workers' benefits, reduce farm subsidies, and resist labor demands for a shorter workweek and earlier retirement united the left opposition. In Germany, Kohl's sixteen-year tenure leading a Christian Democratic Union government ran out of steam as the costs of reunification mounted, incomes stagnated, and unemployment remained high. Finally, British voters grew tired of the Conservatives as slow growth, sex scandals, and divisions over the EU undercut the party's credibility.

Meanwhile, drawing from the example of Bill Clinton's "New Democrats" and their slogan "It's the economy, stupid," youthful, energetic, and articulate Social Democrats, such as Tony Blair in Britain and Gerhard Schröder in Germany, charted a "new" political course, or "Third Way," that aimed to "modernize" their societies in accordance with the demands of the global marketplace while maintaining, with adjustments, the basic protections of the welfare state.[3] Criticizing their socialist forebears for equating justice with equality, for overreliance on the bureaucratic state to solve problems, for elevating rights over responsibilities, and for undervaluing the importance of entrepreneurship and the market for promoting growth, they argued that social democracy must abandon outdated doctrines and address the issues that concern people experiencing rapid change. Such an approach meant rewarding risk taking and work by reducing taxes on profits and wages, increasing the "flexibility" of the labor market by making it easier to fire workers, making new investments in "human capital" to prepare people to work with new technologies, reorienting social security away from welfare and toward work, reordering the tasks of government and shrinking its size, providing more support for families, and prioritizing the fight against crime. They also stressed the need for quality public services, including health care, and for opportunity for all regardless of race, gender, or age.

By the late 1990s, most social democratic parties had adopted elements of this agenda, which aligned business and labor policies with the logic of the market, retained some commitments to the welfare state, and reached out to different social groups, especially in the middle classes. Pragmatic party leaders were also ready to form coalitions with some once-scorned left-of-center rivals, such as the Greens. In Germany, for example, after experimenting at the provincial level, the SPD and the Greens formed a national government in 1998. For rank-and-file party members, however, the meaning of these shifts in outlook was not always clear. In Britain, matters were quite plain. Labor moved sharply rightward after three consecutive defeats between 1979 and 1993. Blair's selection as leader, the removal from the party program in 1995 of the long-cherished goal of nationalizing industry, and a vote of the membership on his "New Life for Britain" manifesto left few doubts about the party's direction. In Germany, by contrast, Schröder ran an anti-neoliberal electoral campaign and selected Oscar Lafontaine, vocal leader of the SPD left wing, as finance minister. His postelection change of heart, clearly out of step with the party's program, stunned many members and resulted in Lafontaine's departure from the government.

Although many social democrats, especially in the trade unions, were uncomfortable with the new neoliberal rhetoric, it was unclear what new policies would emerge. After the long conservative interregnum, however, most socialist voters stuck with their parties, which also attracted new supporters concerned with high unemployment, transparent government, resurgent nationalism, environmental problems, and the marginalization of immigrant minorities and the poor. As a result, social democracy returned to power in much of Western Europe.

In the East, the situation was different. There, the social democrats won power largely because many voters in these new democracies quickly became disenchanted with the impact of growing insecurity and the corruption that came with the market and privatization. In Poland, for example, Solidarity's leadership in 1989 offered a very different alternative from that of 1980–1981, when its demands for workers' self-management placed it squarely in the socialist tradition. By the time they emerged from the underground, the leaders, much influenced by Western social democratic and U.S. advisers, supported radical, free market reforms. In January 1990, Prime Minister Mazowiecki implemented a "shock therapy" program designed to replace the state-controlled economy with a privatized, market-oriented one. The result hit workers hardest. In the first year, gross domestic product fell almost 12 percent, unemployment rose from 0 to 6 percent (peaking at 16 percent in 1994), and inflation hit 500 percent. It was no wonder that, in a 1992 poll, 92 percent of Polish workers supported a strong welfare system, 80 percent wanted full employment and subsidized housing, and 70 percent wanted subsidized, cheap food. Because the government's policies devastated Solidarity's trade-union constituency, the movement collapsed and provided an opening for the successor party to the Polish United Workers' Party, the Social Democracy of the Republic of Poland (SdRP) and the former communist union organization the All-Polish Alliance of Trade Unions. Along with a group of smaller left-wing parties, the SdRP formed the Polish Democratic Left Alliance (SLD), which called for easing the transition by slowing privatization, maintaining industrial subsidies, and increasing investment in health care, education, and pensions. With support among workers, the unemployed, pensioners, small business people, and former state officials now turned entrepreneurs, in 1993 the SLD emerged as the Sejm's largest party and formed a government with the Polish Peasant Party. In 1995, SdRP leader and longtime communist Aleksander Kwasniewski (b. 1954) defeated Lech Walesa, the incumbent, to become Poland's president.

The SLD did not aim to reverse the transition to capitalism. On the contrary, it was at odds with other socialist groups, such as the Union of Labor, whose stronger opposition to sweeping privatization would have prevented the SLD from securing an International Monetary Fund loan. Thus, while the SLD drew much of its support from the "losers" in the transition process, it adopted an economic viewpoint similar to that of Blair's "New Labor" Party in Britain and Schröder's SPD. Such a strategy, which did relatively little to protect workers' interests, was risky over the long haul, as many traditional adherents would became disillusioned with their parties' approach.

THE "THIRD WAY" IN PRACTICE: BRITAIN AND GERMANY

Once back in power, Western Social Democrats carried out a range of reforms, some quite in keeping with their traditional support for the welfare state and the extension of democracy. New Labor, for example, doubled the budget of the National Health Service and invested large sums in education, transport, and policing, substantially improving their performance. As promised, Blair devolved some of the central government's powers to regional and local bodies, reestablished the Scottish parliament (abolished in 1707) and introduced a new assembly in Wales, and allowed, for the first time, the direct election of London's mayor. Labor eliminated most hereditary peerages in the House of Lords, and women occupied an unprecedented one-quarter of the party's 419 seats in parliament. Concomitantly, in France, Prime Minister Lionel Jospin (b. 1937) introduced the thirty-five-hour workweek, expanded the provision of health care, raised the minimum wage, and passed legislation allowing civil unions for gays, while in Germany Schröder's coalition announced a retreat from nuclear energy and also allowed civil unions.

Paralleling these changes, however, were social democracy's efforts to pressure unemployed workers to reenter the labor market by reducing unemployment and welfare expenditures. The latter were part of a larger attempt to shrink the size of the state by privatizing services and reducing outlays. As long as the economy grew fast enough to absorb the unemployed, as occurred in Britain, the government could go forward without generating much opposition, but in France and Germany, where unemployment remained high, resistance was fierce. In 1999, for example, when Jospin announced the privatization of state firms and public spending cuts, mass demonstrations and warnings from his Communist and Green allies forced him to back down.

In Germany, the government was more tenacious. After a lackluster first term, Schröder narrowly won reelection in 2002 primarily because, unlike Blair, he refused to join the American crusade against Saddam Hussein in Iraq. Once returned to office, however, he failed to reverse Germany's economic decline as near-zero growth and over 10 percent unemployment strained social insurance and pension systems and diverted resources from education and research. In 2003, with virtually no discussion in his party, the Red–Green coalition imposed a tough new course—Agenda 2010—sharply reducing unemployment and welfare benefits for the long-term unemployed, deregulating the labor market, and easing firms' ability to fire workers. It also began restructuring the social insurance system by raising workers' share of the financial burden, cutting health care and pension benefits, and pushing people to seek private insurance. These policies did little to ease the ongoing crisis and, by attacking the party's traditional constituency, caused a firestorm. After peaking at over 900,000 in 1990, SPD membership, like that of all German parties, had been steadily declining as part of a larger shift in the political culture. Between 2002 and 2006, however, it fell precipitously from around 694,000 to around 561,000. Public trust evaporated. In 1999, almost 60 percent of voters said they trusted the party's commitment to social justice, but by December 2003, only 24 percent did so. In 2005, Schröder tried to cut his losses by calling early elections, which he lost.

That the SPD remained in government as the junior partner in a grand coalition with the Christian Democratic Union was a testament to its "centrism" under Schröder, but to many members, it consummated the betrayal of the principles embedded in its Berlin Program of 1989 (updated in 1998). Rather than accommodating capitalist competition, the program charged party leaders with promoting a "counterweight" to global capitalism by organizing regional communities of states and by encouraging union organizing across national borders. It called for the expansion of workers' power in the workplace, improvements in their social security, and redistributing work in a highly productive economy in ways that promote full employment. In short, it demanded an environmentally sustainable economy with democratic control over the economic power of capital and strong unions. When the leaders elected to ignore these principles, many rank-and-file members left to organize a new Electoral Alternative for Work and Social Justice. Primarily active in western Germany, this group merged in 2007 with the Party of Democratic Socialism, the reformed successor to the Socialist Unity Party, which frequently won 20 to 30 percent of the vote in state elections in eastern Germany but had not been able to establish itself in the west. The newly formed Left Party could now compete on the national level and won almost 12 percent of the vote in the parliamentary elections of 2009. Its emergence as an alternative was part of a broader pattern across Europe, as surviving communist parties and new left parties filled the political void created by social democracy's shift to the center.

FINDING THEIR NICHE: FORMER COMMUNIST PARTIES AND PARTIES OF THE "FAR LEFT"

Confounding expectations, most of Western Europe's communist parties survived communism's fall. A few, such as the always miniscule Communist Party of Great Britain, dissolved, but most regrouped and, after shedding their right wing, reemerged as more democratic, flexible parties capable of challenging social democracy from the left. Spain provides one of the earliest examples of this development. With only 4 percent of the vote in the1982 elections, the Spanish Communist Party (PCE) clearly failed to compete effectively against the PSOE (with 46 percent), but as the latter moved to the right, the PCE gained ground. In 1986, it joined a coalition of left forces as part of a mass movement to block Spain's entrance into NATO. Although the effort failed, a part of the coalition stayed together to form the United Left, in which the PCE played a major role. Over the next decade, the United Left's anticapitalist, proenvironmental, socially inclusive platform, as well as its opposition to the formation of the EU and to Spanish support for the Gulf War, earned it increased support. After peaking at 10.6 percent in the 1996 elections, support slipped by more than half, but in 2011 the party rebounded, winning 7 percent. With 70,000 members and over 2,700 elected officials around the country, it remains a significant force.

Sweden, too, provides a good example of how former communist parties successfully adapted. In 1998, when the Swedish social democrats sustained their worst election result in 70 years (falling from 45.3 to 36.6 percent), the former communist Swedish Left Party doubled its share of the vote to 12 percent, and its parliamentary support became crucial to the survival of the Swedish Workers' Party (SAP) government. With the

SAP having tilted rightward, the explicitly feminist Left Party found its niche by opposing privatization of state services and Sweden's participation in the Euro zone while favoring increased welfare spending and the thirty-five-hour workweek. In 2006, however, Left Party support slipped back to under 6 percent, as the SAP suffered a decisive defeat due to squabbling within the coalition government, scandal, and center-right opponents perceived as moderate, fresh, and effective.

With the major exception of France, where the PCF gradually faded into insignificance, developments were similar in Greece, Portugal, Italy, and, as noted above, Germany. Levels of voter support fluctuated widely, but most of the reformed communist parties have been able to hold the allegiance of a substantial portion of the electorate. They were joined by a number of other "far-left" parties, such as the Red-Green Alliance in Denmark, the Socialist Left Party of Norway, the Socialist People's Party in the Netherlands, and the Coalition of the Radical Left in Greece, which formed from a variety of different left-wing forces, such as small Trotskyist and Maoist parties and other groups. These parties, along with the Greens, now have a firm foothold in European politics both nationally and as part of new transnational political organizations (see below).

Programmatically, there is substantial agreement among the reformed communist and new left parties. Virtually all oppose privatization and deregulation while supporting the thirty-five-hour workweek without loss of pay, greater union rights, democratization via use of the referendum and devolution of power to the local level, controls on international trade, taxes on international financial transactions, and nuclear disarmament. Resisting imperialist wars, such as the recent U.S.-led interventions in the Middle East, and viewing NATO as a Cold War anachronism, they favor strengthening the role of the Organization for Security and Cooperation in Europe and the United Nations to promote peacekeeping and call for the abolition or reform of the International Monetary Fund and the World Bank. Some, such as the former communists, are more class focused and less concerned with libertarian issues, such as gay rights, drug decriminalization, and nuclear power. Others tend to stress more populist themes, stressing the national interest rather than class.

Most of these parties view themselves as anticapitalist alternatives to social democracy. The New Anti-Capitalist Party in France (founded in 2009), for example, favors overturning capitalism by "revolutionizing" society" through class struggle and fighting for internationalist, feminist, antiracist, and environmentalist goals. It calls for a program that "challenges capitalist ownership of the means of production, attacks capital and profits, increases wages, pensions, [and] minimum incomes, and meets the needs of the population." Gains in these spheres would pave the way for "transitional demands" establishing workers' control over the economy and a new state.[4] Stressing many of the same principles, the German Left Party also calls for a "great transformative process that will lead toward democratic socialism in the twenty first century." At its core, such a change would require the radical expansion of democracy, giving citizens a say in their economic future, and the creation of an economy that includes large-scale public ownership, cooperatives, and private ownership of small enterprises.[5]

However militant their language, virtually all these parties are committed to participation in parliamentary politics. Parties operating within systems that use proportional representation, such as in Spain, Sweden, and Germany, have easier access to parliament than those using plurality-voting systems, such as in England and France. Most of the far-left parties have been hindered by splits over key issues, such as their opposition to the EU and their relationship to social democracy, but unlike the era of the Cold War, almost all of them have been willing to participate in national governments, usually as junior partners, when reasonable opportunities have arisen. Such moments have not always served them well, for they require willingness to compromise and take responsibility for the outcome of government policies. Moreover, while participation undercuts the arguments of critics who view the far left as a threat to the democratic order, it also illustrates the limits of their identity as opponents of the system.

As Luke March has noted, generally support for far-left parties stems from three overlapping groups. One is a "far-left subculture" that includes ideologically convinced supporters and activists long engaged in the activities of radical parties, student groups, unions, and nongovernmental, feminist, and environmental organizations. The communist and former communist parties also attract many still attached to the "womb-to-tomb" services of the former East bloc societies and local services provided in Western Europe where communists were strong. A second group consists of disaffected Social Democrats, and a third is drawn from protest voters, such as those upset about their country's entrance into the EU. The latter group has also strengthened the radical nationalist right, which in several countries, such as France, has successfully exploited widespread fear of immigration (from other EU states and from non-European countries) to draw workers away from both social democracy and its left-wing rivals.

While the communists and former communists tend to have stronger working-class and trade union ties (especially in the East), their clientele also is older and more socially conservative than that of their democratic socialist counterparts. Like the Greens, the latter tend to attract more left-libertarian supporters who are younger, white collar, better educated, and female. All of these parties tend to identify the "working class" much more broadly than in the past, but it is difficult to define them as "working-class" parties. Massive changes to Europe's economy and political culture have broken up many of the social and political communities that underpinned the labor movement in the mid-twentieth century, and electoral allegiances have become much more volatile. Although the social democratic parties' shift toward neoliberalism has raised tensions with their trade union allies, these have not yet led to large-scale defections to the far left.

It is important to note that in recent years, the far left and social democracy have made increased efforts to organize pan-European socialist institutions to compete for power at the European level. Historically, as capital has become increasingly mobile and transnational, it has become more important for labor to also organize across political boundaries. The construction of the EEC and its successor, the EU, created a continental economic and political framework that made it imperative for movements long focused on national politics to shift more attention to the international plane. The social democratic European Trade Union Confederation (ETUC), for example, began promoting workers' interests at the European level in 1973 and now represents over 60 million workers from eighty-five unions in thirty-six countries. Over the course of the past twenty years, most of the far-left parties have organized within the European Left Party, while Social Democrats are members of the Party of European Socialists. These formations work to develop joint political programs and to coordinate their campaigns. If European integration continues, international politics will increasingly supplant the centrality of the nation-state and enhance the importance of these organizations.

MOVING LEFT: SOCIALIST RESPONSES TO CRISIS OF 2008

The experience of the late 1990s showed that social democracy could attract enough cross-class support to win elections, but it soon became clear that holding power was something else. Parties sometimes lose power, of course, for noneconomic reasons, but as Ingo Schmidt has recently noted, social democracy's basic problem in the 2000s was rooted in its failed economic policy. As was true during the Keynesian "golden age" after 1945, social democracy's long-term political success depended on the economy generating enough growth to satisfy the job and security needs of its constituents. When the neoliberal model failed to deliver the required growth, social democracy's resort to austerity and "personal responsibility" alienated a substantial portion of its membership and electoral clientele. Many looked to other parties to represent their interests or simply decided to abstain from voting. The result was defeat in France (2002), in Germany (2005), and, after protracted decline, in Britain (2010).

The global financial meltdown of 2008 and the subsequent Great Recession demonstrated the bankruptcy of the neoliberal model pioneered in the United States and Britain and then adopted across Europe. The economic debacle also put the final nail in the coffin of the Third Way.

Just as the governments of George W. Bush and Barack Obama intervened with vast infusions of capital to prevent the complete collapse of the American (indeed the international) banking system, so too did their European counterparts, regardless of political orientation. Suddenly, all agreed on the need for state action to save the system from itself.

In general, Social Democrats have responded to the crisis by abandoning the language of Third Way politics and moving leftward programmatically. In the wake of the unfolding crisis, all of the major parties have called for stricter controls over financial markets and international coordination of economic and financial policies. Most have reemphasized the need for a "social Europe" that would end poverty, social exclusion, and discrimination while guaranteeing basic social security. To that end, they support a "Social Stability Pact," establishing European social and educational standards, a minimum wage, and strengthened workers' and consumers' rights. They also generally agree that the EU must lead the way in the transition to an environmentally and socially sustainable economy via common energy and industrial policies. Conscious of their sometimes competing national interests, there remain significant disagreements over the specific actions necessary to achieve these aims as well as over taxes, migration, and other matters, but the overall shift to a renewed recognition of the state's economic role and of the need for social security and solidarity is clear.

Where such rethinking will lead electorally is difficult to say. Contrary to widespread expectations, in the 2009 elections to the European parliament, both the Party of European Socialists and the European Left Party lost seats while the center-right gained ground. The following year, the Swedish Social Democrats and the Left Party again lost to a liberal-led coalition, and in 2011 the right unseated the PSOE as the Spanish economy collapsed. On the other hand, in the spring of 2012, French socialists won both the presidency and a parliamentary majority, while the presidential candidate of the radical Left Front scored a respectable 11 percent in the first round. Even more impressive was the rise of the Coalition of the Radical Left in Greece, where the mainstream parties, including the social democratic Panhellenic Socialist Movement, had led the country into depression. In the spring elections of 2012, it quintupled its popular support to become the second-largest party.

It is important to recognize that, although political parties and trade unions have been the most important bearers of socialist ideology over the past 150 years, socialism's future also depends on the continued vibrancy of extraparliamentary movements for radical change. These movements, such as the many grassroots efforts to promote gender and racial equality and gay rights, to restore and sustain the environment, to fight against imperialism and war, to secure the rights of labor, and to combat poverty at home and abroad, take many forms and may not be explicitly socialist, but they complement the extant socialist organizations, pressure them from the outside, and provide voter support and a recruiting ground for future members. The far-left parties have been particularly assiduous at building links with a wide array of single-issue groups and have been active in the "antiglobalization" movement. Along with the European Trade Union Federation, they participate in the European Social Forum, a biannual conference mobilizing social movements, unions, nongovernmental organizations, environmental, peace, and antiimperialist organizations working to combat neoliberalism and to show "that another world is possible."

In addition to these kinds of extraparliamentary organizations, contemporary socialism also can point to Europe's vibrant cooperative movement for alternatives to the corporate capitalist model. In Europe today, 123 million people are members of over 160,000 cooperatives employing over 5.4 million workers, demonstrating that it is possible for employees and consumers to jointly own and democratically manage their enterprises. Producing a wide variety of goods and services, modern cooperatives, like those of the early labor movement, operate within a capitalist framework and promote the goals of democracy, autonomy, and solidarity. Thus, just as their forebears struggled for self-determination and security at the time of industrial capitalism's emergence, contemporary workers seek many of the same aims.

SOCIALISM: PAST AND FUTURE

From its origins in the late eighteenth century, the European socialist movement has aimed to build a society based on the values of democracy, equality, and solidarity. During the nineteenth century, socialists were in the forefront of popular struggles against the growing insecurity, degradation, and physical danger that emerged with industrial capitalism. They fought to improve workers' living standards and demanded the same democratic and social rights for all. To achieve these goals, socialists created a rich array of social, political, economic, and cultural organizations that made their movement a formidable one and whose growth seemed to confirm that they were marching in step with history. Final victory seemed to be only a matter of time.

As we have seen, however, matters did not work out as many expected. Events such as the collapse of the Second International in 1914, the ensuing split in the movement that intensified after the Bolshevik Revolution, the rise of bureaucratic collectivism in the USSR, and its extension in the wake of World War II led to the creation of hostile "socialist" and "communist" camps. This division severely damaged the socialist cause. For many of those who experienced it, Stalinism perverted the language and substance of socialism to such an extent that it lost much of its legitimacy. Meanwhile, in the West, anticommunist socialists adopted

an openly reformist course in which the goal of taming capitalism replaced that of overthrowing it. The collapse of the bureaucratic collectivist order ended the division of the Continent and opened the prospect of
a new realignment for socialists. Although the movement did not reunite,
the contending currents are able to coexist and, under certain circumstances, to cooperate with one another. It remains to be seen if they will
draw closer together.

Despite the great harm wrought by Stalinism, there is no question that
democratic socialism has played a decisive and positive role in the shaping of contemporary Europe and the world. By asserting the political and
social equality of all citizens, socialists helped forge the modern constitutional order in which, at least in theory, every adult, regardless of wealth,
may participate. Moreover, their insistence that the creation of wealth
must serve the whole society rather than simply the owners of capital
laid the foundation for the welfare state. Western European socialists
failed to abolish capitalism, but after 1945 they tamed many of its most
negative features and created one of the world's most prosperous regions
in which wealth and opportunity were more widely shared than ever
before.

Even today, after decades of neoliberal attack, most of social democracy's post-1945 achievements remain intact. As scholars such as Richard
Wilkinson and Kate Pickett have shown, rich but unequal societies, such
as the United States and Britain, have far higher rates of violent crime,
drug usage, imprisonment, teenage pregnancy, and obesity; lower life
expectancy; widespread anxiety, fear, and mental illness; and poorer
school performance than countries with more equitably distributed
wealth. American workers typically labor 300 hours per year longer than
those in Norway and 400 hours more than those in the Netherlands, yet
the latter enjoy comparable if not superior living standards, on average,
due to easier access to public goods, such as high quality medical care.
Meanwhile, contrary to popular myth, social mobility is substantially
greater in the social democratic countries than in the United States.

Thus, social democracy's social achievements have had a major positive impact on the daily lives of Europeans for over half a century, and
even many conservatives accept a number of its features, such as socialized medicine, as a right of all citizens. Still, as we have seen, neoliberal
efforts have chipped away at the system, inequality is increasing even in
Scandinavia, and workers' living standards are under increasing pressure. Prescient observers such as Tony Judt are no doubt correct that
defending the gains of the past should be in the forefront of social democratic politics in the coming years, but given the nature of global capitalism, such an approach can be only a stopgap measure.

The great question for twenty-first-century socialists, whether social
democratic or on the far left, is whether they can really show that another
world is possible. Simply defending the gains of the past or even extend-

ing them substantially does not get at the basic contradictions of capitalism as a system predicated on inequality and the drive toward endless growth. It may be true that the welfare state and environmental regulation might ameliorate some of capitalism's consequences, but in a crisis-prone system of political economy resting on profit and perpetual accumulation, such gains are always limited in terms of space and time. Whereas the democratic socialists of the past, such as Bernstein, Hilferding, and Blair, repeatedly adapted their politics to the logic of capital accumulation, the challenge for future democratic socialists will be their ability to build a movement prepared to break with that logic. That requires confronting corporate power directly and doing so on a transnational basis. In effect, it means realizing the kind of internationalism that Marx favored when the system was in its infancy. Whether that is possible remains to be seen.

DOCUMENT 7.1. POLITICAL ACTION PROGRAMME OF THE PARTY
OF THE EUROPEAN LEFT 2011–2013

Motion of the EL-ExBoard to the EL 3rd Congress, Paris,
December 3–5, 2010

Agenda for a Social Europe
Joint Action Platform for resistance and alternatives in Europe

The 3rd Congress of the European Left is taking place as more and more
unbearable sacrifices are imposed on European people. Indeed, in the
vast majority of European countries, programmes of public spending
cuts, of super-austerity, of liberalisation of public services and the labour
market are being implemented. To generalise these policies, countries,
with the full complicity of their governments are being placed under
custody of the European Commission, the European Central Bank (ECB)
and other institutions such as the IMF.

These policies are presented as a necessary response to the financial
and economic crisis. But this is a crisis of capitalism, and of its current
globalised and financial form. This crisis also impacts on the environment, energy, food, cultural and moral values. Therefore this crisis finds
expression at all political levels and in all societies marked by the ruling
capitalist mode of production and similarly at the EU level with its recent
orientations, neoliberal policies and institutions.

The current debt problem constitutes a new phase of the protracted
crisis. It has its roots in the economic and political developments of the
last 30 years. Interlinking the multiple causes of the crisis, it is increasingly impacting on people's everyday lives.

We, the Party of the European Left, together with other socialist, communist and red-green parties and organisations—widely regarded as the
current plural European left, oppose these neoliberal policies and structures applied to the EU via successive treaties up to and including the
Lisbon treaty.

The responsibility for these policies lies with the coalition formed by
European, liberal and social-democratic parties that has dominated at the
European and national level. We seek to present a political alternative to
the neoliberal model. Given the widespread use of austerity, new resistance is developing across Europe. The major challenge facing the Left is
to set out alternatives, encourage this resistance, and mould from it a
movement for an alternative vision of civilisation committed to solidarity. We do this in the name of a social, ecological and peaceful Europe. . . .

. . . With the constructive will to formulate alternatives with which we
can enter into a broader dialogue with people—and to organise a common struggle—we present the following proposals. These proposals are

not simply to be taken or to be left, but are intended to evolve in an open debate among European people and movements.

1. It is time for a radical democratisation of European politics.

This crisis is also a crisis of democracy. . . . Too often crucial decisions are taken without working people. They experience the EU as a far off, incomprehensible and interventionist construction that ignores their demands and their hopes. Changing the foreign, environmental, social and economic policies of the EU and of the member states means instigating a new democratic process based on active participation by people, European and national parliaments via new participatory powers and rights. We stand for democratic republics with electoral laws that respect proportional representation. This democratic transformation process has to concern institutions as well as policies at the EU and national levels. . . .

2. We are not paying for your crisis!

The international financial and economic crisis washed like a wave over humanity's unsolved problems. In the last two years, the governments of the dominating powers, headed by the G 8, have kept the global financial system alive with enormous sums of public money. They have taken up their role as the rescuers of a collapsing global financial market. At the same time, they remain indifferent to growing poverty and the challenges of climate change. . . .

. . . Today, people are forced to pay for aid measures for banks whereas those who caused the crisis are spared. The belief that nationalisation of the banks is some kind of socialist profanity has been shaken. States have taken financial institutions under their wings, and some of them are already trading again and making respectable profits. However, government influence goes only so far as to rescue the banks, the bankers and their incomes. Equitably redistributing the wealth is not part of the programme. Governments are "nationalising" without ensuring democratic influence and control. They therefore are only nationalizing losses by increasing national debt, insufficient investment and higher charges. Thus they are already responsible for all kinds of unsolved social problems.

As previously, this "regulation" serves the interests of financial capital but not the interests of the majority. The prevailing political line knows only one answer to the crisis: plunder the public coffers and increase the exploitation of the workers. It participates in this class struggle from above and does not shy away from pitting low earners against people reliant on social welfare contributions and both against immigrants and refugees.

We are convinced that the majority of people can be won over to the campaign for socially fair, ecologically sustainable, democratic and peaceful European policies based on solidarity, and so we are publicising alternative solutions to the financial crisis.

2.1. Fight the crisis effectively—now!

The EU and European countries must move towards cooperation, and contribute to reforming the European and international monetary systems. Important strategic sectors, like the banking system, should be organized based on social ownership, democratic control and public access. . . .

The European Left proposes the following measures to reduce the power and influence of financial markets:

The European character of the debt crisis poses the urgent need for a European approach. We propose the annulation of part of the sovereign debt, in order to assist the indebted countries to develop policies for the restructur[ing] of their economies and avoid the destruction of social development.

- Against the so-called "Crisis Management or Orderly Default Mechanism," the establishment of a permanent protective mechanism of solidarity (and not of punishment) of states in difficulty. This Mechanism will cover also the states which do not belong to the Eurozone. This mechanism must be set in motion at the early stages of a crisis and not after it has completed its disastrous effects.
- Transformation of the mission of the European Central Bank. Through cash generation and based on social criteria, the ECB should extend low interest credit to member states to finance social development. . . .
- Taxation of all speculative transactions. EU institutions and member states should overhaul the architecture of global financial markets;
- New public revenues should be generated by taxing the income from financial assets and big capital, by means of a socially just tax reform aimed at stimulating the real economy. Domestic economies should be revitalised through structural policies and higher gross income;
- Abolition of tax havens established inside and outside European territory; banning—not only registration—of hedge funds and junk bonds;
- Creation of a European public rating agency. Countries can no longer be hostages to private rating agencies, which serve speculative interests;
- Issue of Eurobonds to allow member states to borrow at reasonable interest rates.

To fight wage and social dumping, and to strengthen social and ecological requirements, the following measures must be introduced or tested in all countries in coordination:

- Macroeconomic balance between states and a strong internal market;
- The introduction of standards which secure in all EU-countries—by law or by collective agreements—minimum wages at the level of at least 60% of the national average wage and always above the poverty threshold, with a high quality of social security for all;
- Restrictive regulation of subcontracted labour and the limiting of the number of short-term contracts. New regulations that make it illegal to employ foreign workers on a lower wage or worse conditions than those existing in the country where the work is done. The so-called Laval verdict and other rulings undermining the right to strike and work for better wages and working conditions must be annulled;
- Strengthened and binding collective agreements on working conditions and compliancy with required standards in the case of "posted workers";
- Modernise public services and infrastructure with an investment programme for the key areas of education, health and social care, research, transport and environmental technology. This will guarantee millions of new jobs in the future both in industrial and service sectors.

We want to lead the campaign for a global tax on financial transactions, for higher incomes, more protected and good jobs and humane working hours, secure pensions and better public infrastructure. We will do this together with trade unionists, social forums, women's, environmental and youth movements, migrant organisations and local authorities. We want to lead this campaign in our countries and at the European level. . . . Together with the trade unions we will lead the campaign for the establishment of a Social Progress Clause in European primary law. . . .

2.2. Action plan against unemployment, poverty and social exclusion 80 million people in Europe live below the poverty line.

The Left sees poverty as a social and political problem. We need development that places people in the foreground. For this reason, the fight against poverty will only be successful when this aim is the key component in all areas of EU and national policy. Europe needs a comprehensive safety net of high social standards. Homelessness and child poverty must end by 2015.

Overcoming poverty is closely linked to solving all other social and environmental problems in our society.

With these aims in mind, a Europe-wide action plan is urgently needed. The European Left proposes the following goals, which expand on the main aspects of the immediate battle against the crisis:

- A European-wide minimum wage of at least of 60% of the national average wage and the strengthening of collective agreements;
- An appropriate guaranteed minimum income for the unemployed, and those who do not have the means to sustain their livelihood;
- A decent income for students and people in professional training;
- A decent pension guaranteed for everyone at the age of 60 years;
- Concrete, regular working conditions and decent jobs;
- Shorter working hours without a drop in income;
- Higher investment in social security, health, public services, public housing and the public environment;
- Implementation of a programme for increased energy efficiency in private buildings using existing technology to guarantee warm accommodation to everyone, the housing expenses should not take more than 25% of an average household income. The taxing of capital gains and speculation businesses, the progressive taxation of incomes and a developed public sector represent the financial means for the implementation of this action plan. European policies that force national tax dumping on companies and demands higher contributions from the employed and socially disadvantaged must end. The European Left underlined in its platform for the 2009 European elections that the Stability and Growth Pact must be replaced by a new solidarity pact, focusing on growth, full employment, social justice and environmental protection.

3. For a new Development Model

The notion that ambitious and coordinated policies are necessary to face the challenges to humanity and the planet has spread. Nevertheless, the capitalist logic represents a major obstacle. The financial crisis, whose systemic nature has become obvious, reveals the extent of the waste generated by the current development approach. This is why all of the proposals that this document sets out reflect an alternative logic, of a new social development model democratic, sustainable and humane. These three dimensions are indissoluble: the social evidently includes the economic sphere, which should primarily be used to serve the needs and the aspirations of every individual. . . .

The Party of the European Left will continue its struggle for a consistent peaceful external and security policy for a world without weapons of mass destruction. . . .

- European development policy must oblige all EU member states to fulfill the Millennium Development Goals by 2015 by fulfilling the commitment reserve 0.7% of GDP for development aid. This requires a reorientation of the mode of production and consumption, which does not threaten the capacity of nature and where commodities and money are not the basis of appreciation. . . .

- The European Left works together with other forces for an energy revolution based on genuine renewable energy resources and energy savings. . . .
- We call for international cooperation to combat global warming. . . .
- We fight for individual civil liberties and the fundamental social and political rights of all EU citizens and immigrants based on the Charter of Principles for Another Europe. . . .
- Universal access to education, culture, media and the possibility to use one's own cultural forms of expression are essential for democratic dialogue in Europe and worldwide.
- We want to fight the financial crisis by regulating the markets, creating a consistent macro-economic orientation towards a social, ecological model of development and fighting against poverty. . . .
- The development of public services that serve the essential collective needs. . . . This means stopping the processes of liberalization and privatisation of public services and the massive private investment plans in these sectors.
- An active policy of job creation, accompanied by life-long learning systems.
- A new era of democracy on all levels, with new powers for employees and the elected representatives over the public funds allotted to large companies.

. . . The European Left stands for a vision of a radically different world, for democracy, peace and socialism. The European Left is open to everybody who wants to support this agenda. We aspire to a world of freedom, justice, and equality, without repression, exploitation, wars, hunger or need. We want to make this project a reality.

Source: http://www.european-left.org/english/3rd_el_congress/3rd_el_congress/.

DOCUMENT 7.2. PARTY OF EUROPEAN SOCIALISM DECLARATION OF PRINCIPLES

Adopted by the PES Council on 24 November 2011

Socialism and Social Democracy have a long and proud history of achievement. The welfare state, universal access to education and to health care, and the struggle for fundamental rights have improved the lives of countless individuals and created more equal, just and secure societies. In the 21st century, our movement continues to shape a better future for all.

Freedom, equality, solidarity and justice are our fundamental values. These universal values belong together. Democracy is a prerequisite to their full expression. Combined, our values form our moral compass to build progressive societies in today's world. These are societies in which individuals do not struggle against each other but work together for the benefit of all. These are thriving, trusting societies which take care of their environment now and as an investment for the future. These are societies in which each and every person is able to create the conditions for his or her emancipation.

Our values are being challenged. People, money, goods, information and ideas travel incessantly. But the reality of deregulated globalization provokes a more fragmented sense of living. Market forces, driven by finance and greed, are annexing huge amounts of power from democratic control. These forces serve the interests of a privileged few. Conservatives and neo-liberals, have deepened economic, geographic and social inequalities, promoting a system of short-termism, easy profits and loose rules that has led to the worst crisis in modern times.

We reject the politics of pessimism that claim that nothing can be done. We reject the language of hate that makes people, and whole communities, scapegoats for the ills in societies. Instead, we work to build inclusive societies and a better future for all. We need a new progressive global agenda to enable the fruits of globalization to benefit all. This is a matter of political choice and responsibility.

Our Principles for Action

1. Democracy must prevail in all areas of life to enable citizens to decide. Democracy must be pluralistic, transparent, truly representative of society's diversity and enable everyone to participate, with an open public sphere, an independent media and free access to internet. Freedom of speech is fundamental to a democratic society.

2. Strong public authorities all along the democratic chain, from the local, regional and national levels, to the European level of government, are essential. Together, they preserve the public good, guarantee the common interest and promote justice and solidarity in society. Good governance, the rule of law, accountability and transparency are the pillars of strong public authorities.

3. We want to shape the future so that people regain control over their lives. True freedom means that people are active citizens, not passive consumers, empowered to build societies which have a richness that goes beyond material wealth, so that each individual's fulfillment is also part of a collective endeavour.

4. Decent work is the keystone in ensuring people are the architects of their future. Giving back a real meaning, a real value and a real

continuity to work in life, is central to ensuring people's emancipation and sense of pride.

5. A society based on our values means a new economy that embodies them. Values-driven growth, means that environmental sustainability, human dignity and well being are fundamental to wealth creation. This new economy must foster social progress that raises living standards, secures homes and creates jobs. The public sector plays an essential role in this new economy.

6. Our politics work to preserve the planet's resources rather than exhaust them. Environmental sustainability means that we safeguard nature for present and future

7. Our renewed vision of solidarity is a joint investment in our common future. It means lasting justice and solidarity between generations. It means we preserve the planet, protect the elderly and invest in young people. Access to universal and free education is a cornerstone in ensuring our children and grandchildren have the means for emancipation.

8. A strong and just society is one that instills confidence and inspires trust. To guarantee this trust and confidence, we must ensure that the wealth generated by all is shared fairly. This collective responsibility embodies our conviction that we are stronger when we work together. It also reflects our determination to enable all people to live a dignified life, free of poverty. All members of society are entitled to protection from social risks in life.

9. We foster a sense of belonging based on a confident inclusion of all and not the fearful exclusion of some. An open and inclusive society values the individual and embraces diversity. This means the same dignity, freedom and equal access to rights, education, culture and public services for all, regardless of sex, racial or ethnic origin, religion or belief, disability, sexual orientation, gender identity or age. In this society, religion is separated from the State.

10. Building on the achievements of the feminist movement, we continue to fight for gender equality. This means that women and men equally share work, share power, share time and share roles, both in the public and in the private realms.

11. Our shared pride in society guarantees our shared security. A free, peaceful and just society is one in which people are safe as they go about their lives.

12. International solidarity means our political practice is always outward looking. Our solidarity goes beyond national borders. Ensuring long lasting prosperity, stability and above all, peace requires effective coordination in the international realm based on democracy, mutual respect and human rights.

To put our principles into action in a world of economic, social and cultural interconnection, new progressive politics linking local, regional, national and European levels are needed to regain democratic control. A comprehensive approach to policy making that integrates all levels of governance is the guarantee to making each and every individual's life more secure in the global, multipolar age. A progressive, democratic European Union, with solidarity between European people's and countries, reinforces democratic sovereignty on the national level on one side, and the international on the other.

Our commitment to European integration transcends competition between countries and reflects our determination to oppose the erosion of social rights. It embodies our pledge to build a European Union with lasting common political, social and economic realities, not only provisional cooperation between governments. There can be no political decision making without democratic control, no economic Union without a social Union, and no social Union without a common budget to support investment and reduce inequalities in the European Union. Alongside a political and economic European Union, an integrated Social Europe is crucial to improve the living conditions for citizens, in all countries indiscriminately. Our historical task is to work towards a progressive harmonization within a political Union, making it a tool for justice and emancipation.

A political voice that is truly progressive is needed in Europe. Unified action by the socialist, social democratic, labour and democratic progressive movement in the European Union and throughout Europe, and in cooperation with our partners within civil society and trade unions is required. The Party of European Socialists embodies these principles for action. Together, we will continue our political struggle in the European Union for progressive societies in the 21st century.

Source: http://www.pes.eu/en/about-pes/pes-documents.

NOTES

1. Francis Fukuyama, "The End of History," *The National Interest*, Summer 1989, 4, 18.

2. Karl Marx, *The Eighteenth Brumaire of Louis Bonaparte* (New York: International Publishers, 1981), 15.

3. Ingo Schmidt, "It's the Economy, Stupid! Theoretical Reflections on Third Way Social Democracy," in *Social Democracy after the Cold War*, ed. Bryan Evans and Ingo Schmidt (Edmonton: AU Press, 2012), 31.

4. Quoted in Dave Stockton, "The New Anticapitalist Party in France: A Historic Opportunity," *League for the Fifth International*, 30 July 2009, http://www. fifthinternational.org/content/new-anticapitalist-party-france-historic-opportunity.

5. *Program der Partei die Linke*, 2. Parteitag, 2. Tagung, Erfurt, 21. bis 23. Oktober 2011, 21.

Further Reading

GENERAL

Appleby, Joyce. *The Relentless Revolution: A History of Capitalism.* New York: Norton, 2010.

Azzellini, Dario, and Immanuel Ness. *Ours to Master and to Own: Workers' Control from the Commune to the Present.* Chicago: Haymarket Books, 2011.

Barclay, David E., and Eric D. Weitz, eds. *Between Reform and Revolution: German Socialism and Communism from 1840–1990.* New York: Berghahn Books, 1998.

Beaud, Michel. *A History of Capitalism, 1500–2000.* Translated by Tom Dickman and Anny Levebvre. New York: Monthly Review Press, 2001.

Berger, Stefan. *Social Democracy and the Working Class in Nineteenth and Twentieth Century Germany.* Harlow: Longman, 2000.

Braunthal, Julius. *History of the International.* 3 vols. Translated by Henry Collins and Kenneth Mitchell. New York: Praeger, 1967.

Brown, Archie. *The Rise and Fall of Communism.* New York: HarperCollins, 2009.

Cole, G. D. H. *The History of Socialist Thought, 1889–1959.* 5 vols. London: St. Martin's Press, 1953–1960.

Derfler, Leslie. *Socialism since Marx: A Century of the European Left.* New York: St. Martin's Press, 1973.

Eley, Geoff. *Forging Democracy: The History of the Left in Europe, 1850–2000.* New York: Oxford University Press, 2002.

Fried, Albert, and Ronald Sanders, eds. *Socialist Thought: A Documentary History.* Rev. ed. New York: Columbia University Press, 1992.

Gagnon, Paul A. *France since 1989.* Rev. ed. New York: Harper and Row, 1972.

Grebing, Helga. *History of the German Labor Movement: A Survey.* Warwickshire: Berg, 1985.

Harman, Chris. *A People's History of the World: From the Stone Age to the New Millennium.* London: Verso, 2008.

Joll, James. *The Anarchists.* 2nd ed. Cambridge, MA: Harvard University Press, 1979.

Kolakowski, Leszek. *Main Currents of Marxism.* Translated from the Polish by P. S. Falla. New York: Norton, 2005.

Lichtheim, George. *A Short History of Socialism.* New York: Praeger Publishers, 1970.

Lindemann, Albert. *A History of European Socialism.* New Haven, CT: Yale University Press, 1983.

Manuel, Frank E., and Fritzie P. Manuel. *Utopian Thought in the Western World.* Cambridge, MA: Harvard University Press, 1979.

Marshall, Peter. *Demanding the Impossible: A History of Anarchism.* Oakland, CA: PM, 2010.

Marx, Karl, and Friedrich Engels. *Collected Works.* New York: International Publishers, 1975–2004.

Miller, Susanne, and Heinrich Potthoff. *A History of German Social Democracy from 1848 to the Present.* New York: Berg, 1986.

Morton, A. L. *A People's History of England.* London: Lawrence and Wishart, 1979.

Moses, John A. *Trade Union Theory from Marx to Walesa.* New York: Berg, 1990.

Priestland, David. *The Red Flag: A History of Communism.* New York: Grove Press, 2009.

Sassoon, Donald. *One Hundred Years of Socialism: The West European Left in the Twentieth Century.* New York: New Press, 1996.

Stearns, Peter N. *The Industrial Revolution in World History.* Boulder, CO: Westview Press, 2007.

CHAPTER 2

Beecher, Jonathan. *Charles Fourier: The Visionary and His World.* Berkeley: University of California Press, 1986.

Beecher, Jonathan, and Richard Bienvenu, eds. *The Utopian Vision of Charles Fourier: Selected Texts on Work, Love, and Passionate Attraction.* Columbia: University of Missouri Press, 1983.

Berg, Maxine. *The Machinery Question and the Making of Political Economy, 1815–1848.* Cambridge: Cambridge University Press, 1980.

Condorcet, Antoine-Nicholas. *Sketch for a Historical Picture of the Progress of the Human Mind.* Translated by June Barraclough with an introduction by Stuart Hampshire. Westport, CT: Hyperion Press, 1979.

Cotlar, Seth. *Tom Paine's America: the Rise and Fall of Transatlantic Radicalism in the Early Republic.* Charlottesville: University of Virginia Press, 2011.

Deane, Phyllis. *The First Industrial Revolution.* 2nd ed. Cambridge: Cambridge University Press, 1979.

Forrest, Alan. *The French Revolution and the Poor.* New York: St. Martin's Press, 1981.

———. *The French Revolution.* Oxford: Blackwell, 1995.

Frank, Andre Gunder. *World Accumulation, 1492–1789.* New York: Monthly Review Press, 1978.

Gagnon, Paul A. *France since 1789.* 2nd ed. New York: Harper and Row, 1972.

Harrison, J. F. C. *Quest for a New Moral World: Robert Owen and the Owenites in Britain and America.* New York: Scribner, 1969.

Heller, Henry. *The Bourgeois Revolution in France, 1789–1815.* New York: Berghahn Books, 2006.

Hobsbawm, Eric. *Industry and Empire.* New York: Penguin, 1968.

———. *Workers.* New York: Pantheon Books, 1984.

Hunt, Lynne. *Politics, Culture, and Class in the French Revolution.* Berkeley: University of California Press, 1984.

Jones, Gareth Stedman. *An End to Poverty? A Historical Debate.* New York: Columbia University Press, 2004.

Katznelson, Ira, and Aristide R. Zolberg, eds. *Working Class Formation: Nineteenth Century Patterns in Western Europe and the United States.* Princeton, NJ: Princeton University Press, 1986.

Mantoux, Paul. *The Industrial Revolution in the Eighteenth Century: An Outline of the Beginnings of the Modern Factory System in England.* Forewords by T. S. Ashton and John Kenneth Galbraith. Chicago: University of Chicago Press, 1983.

Noble, David F. *Progress without People: In Defense of Luddism.* Foreword by Stan Weir. Chicago: Charles H. Kerr, 1993.

Owen, Robert. *A New View of Society.* 1818. Reprint, New York: AMS Press, 1972.

Paine, Thomas. "Rights of Man, Part II." In *Collected Writings,* edited by Eric Foner. New York: Library of America, 1995.

Rose, R. *Gracchus Babeuf: The First Revolutionary Communist.* London; E. Arnold, 1978.

Soboul, Albert, *The French Revolution, 1787–1799.* Translated by Alan Forrest and Colin Jones. London: NLB, 1974.

Thomis, Malcolm I., and Peter Holt. *Threats of Revolution in Britain: 1789–1848.* London: Archon Books, 1997.

Thompson, E. P. *The Making of the English Working Class.* New York: Vintage, 1966.

Thomson, David. *The Babeuf Plot: The Making of a Republican Legend.* 1947. Reprint, Westport, CT: Greenwood Press, 1975.

CHAPTER 3

Avineri, Shlomo. *Moses Hess: Prophet of Communism and Zionism*. New York: New York University Press, 1985.

Chase, Malcolm. *Chartism: A New History*. Manchester: Manchester University Press, 2007.

Cole, G. D. H. *Chartist Portraits*. London: Cassell Publisher, 1989.

Ehrenberg, John. *Proudhon and His Age*. Atlantic Highlands, NJ: Humanities Press, 1996.

Fischer, Ernst. *How to Read Karl Marx*. Introduction and historical notes by John Bellamy Foster. Commentary by Paul M. Sweezy. New York: Monthly Review Press, 1996.

Harrison, J. F. C. *Quest for a New Moral World: Robert Owen and the Owenites in Britain and America*. New York: Charles Scribner's Sons, 1969.

Hobsbawm, Eric. *The Age of Capital: 1848–1875*. New York: Scribner's Sons, 1975.

Hobsbawm, E. J., and George Rudé. *Captain Swing*. New York: Pantheon Books, 1968.

Hunt, Tristram. *Marx's General: The Revolutionary Life of Friedrich Engels*. New York: Metropolitan Books, 2009.

Johnson, Christopher H. *Utopian Communism in France: Cabet and the Icarians, 1839–1851*. Ithaca, NY: Cornell University Press, 1974.

McClellan, David. *Karl Marx. His Life and Work*. New York: Harper and Row, 1973.

Merriman, John M., ed. *1830 in France*. New York: New Viewpoints, 1975.

Moss, Bernard H. *The Origins of the French Labor Movement, 1830–1914: The Socialism of Skilled Workers*. Berkeley: University of California Press, 1976.

Pickering, Paul A. *Feargus O'Connor: A Political Life*. Monmouth: Merlin Press, 2008.

Sheehan, James. J. *German History, 1770–1866*. Oxford: Oxford University Press, 1989.

Thompson, Dorothy. *The Chartists: Popular Politics in the Industrial Revolution*. New York: Pantheon, 1984.

Wheen, Francis. *Karl Marx: A Life*. New York: Norton, 2000.

CHAPTER 4

Berger, Stefan. *Social Democracy and the Working Class in Nineteenth and Twentieth Century Germany*. New York: Longman, 2000.

Boxer, Marilyn J., and Jean H. Quataert, eds. *Socialist Women. European Socialist Feminism in the Nineteenth and Early Twentieth Centuries*. New York: Elsevier, 1978.

Callahan, Kevin J. *Demonstration Culture: European Socialism and the Second International, 1889–1914*. Leicester: Troubador Publishing, 2010.

Dolgoff, Sam, ed. *Bakunin on Anarchy: Selected Works by the Activist-Founder of World Anarchism*. New York: Alfred A. Knopf, 1972.,

Dominick, Raymond H. *Wilhelm Liebknecht and the Founding of the German Social Democratic Party*. Chapel Hill: University of North Carolina Press, 1982.

Evans, Richard J. *Comrades and Sisters: Feminism, Socialism, and Pacifism in Europe, 1870–1945*. New York: St. Martin's Press, 1987.

Gordon, Felicia. *Early French Feminisms, 1830–1940: A Passion for Liberty*. Cheltenham: Edward Eiger, 1996.

Grogan, Susan K. *French Socialism and Sexual Difference, 1803–1844*. London: Academic and Professional, 1991.

Guttsman, W. L. *The German Social Democratic Party 1875–1933*. London: George Allen and Unwin, 1981.

Kelly, Michael. *Modern French Marxism*. Baltimore: Johns Hopkins University Press, 1982.

Leier, Mark. *Bakunin: A Biography*. New York: St. Martin's Press, 2006.

Further Reading

Lidtke, Vernon L. *The Outlawed Party: Social Democracy in Germany, 1878–1890*. Princeton, NJ: Princeton University Press, 1966.

Lih, Lars T. *Lenin Rediscovered: What Is to Be Done? in Context*. Chicago: Haymarket, 2008.

Lopes, Anne, and Gary Roth. *Men's Feminism: August Bebel and the German Socialist Movement*. Amherst, NY: Humanity Books, 2000.

Naarden, Bruno. *Socialist Europe and Revolutionary Russia: Perception and Prejudice, 1848–1923*. New York: Cambridge University Press, 1992.

Rappaport, Helen. *The Making of a Revolutionary Conspirator: Lenin in Exile*. New York: Basic Books, 2010.

Sayers, Janet, Mary Evan, and Nannecke Redcliff, eds. *Engels Revisited: New Feminists Essays*. London: Tavistock Publications, 1987.

Shanin, Teodor, ed. *Late Marx and the Russian Road: Marx and the Peripheries of Capitalism*. New York: Monthly Review Press, 1983.

Slaughter, Jane, and Robert Kern, eds. *European Women on the Left: Socialism, Feminism, and the Problems Faced by Political Women, 1880 to the Present*. Westport, CT: Greenwood Press, 1981.

Stuart, Robert. *Marxism at Work: Ideology, Class, and French Socialism during the Third Republic*. Cambridge: Cambridge University Press, 1992.

———. *Marxism and National Identity: Socialism, Nationalism, and National Socialism during the French fin de Siécle*. Albany: State University of New York Press, 2006.

Traverso, Enzo. *The Marxists and the Jewish Question: The History of a Debate, 1843–1943*. Translated by Bernard Gibbons. Atlantic Highlands, NJ: Humanities Press, 1990.

Vincent, Steven K. *Between Marxism and Anarchism: Benoit Malon and French Reformist Socialism*. Berkeley: University of California Press, 1992.

Ward, Paul. *Red Flag and Union Jack: Englishness, Patriotism, and the British Left, 1881–1924*. Rochester, NY: Royal Historical Society, Baydell Press, 1998.

Wheen, Francis. *Marx's Das Kapital: A Biography*. New York: Atlantic Monthly Press, 2006.

Williams, Stuart. *Socialism in France: From Jaures to Mitterrand*. New York: St. Martin's Press, 1983.

CHAPTER 5

Alba, Victor. *The Communist Party in Spain*. Translated by Vincent G. Smith. New Brunswick, NJ: Transaction Books, 1983.

Applebaum, Anne. *Gulag: A History*. New York: Doubleday, 2003.

Atkinson, Dorothy, Alexander Dallin, and Gail Warshofsky Lapidus, eds. *Women in Russia*. Stanford, CA: Stanford University Press, 1977.

Beetham, David, ed. *Marxism in the Face of Fascism*. Manchester: Manchester University Press, 1983.

Berman, Sheri. *The Primacy of Politics: Social Democracy and the Making of Europe's Twentieth Century*. Cambridge: Cambridge University Press, 2006.

Chamberlain, Lesley. *Lenin's Private War: The Voyage of the Philosophy Steamer and the Exile of the Intelligentsia*. New York: St. Martin's Press, 2006.

Chase, William J. *Workers, Society, and the Soviet State: Labor and Life in Moscow, 1918–1929*. Urbana: University of Illinois Press, 1987.

Fainsod, Merle. *International Socialism and the World War*. 1935. Reprint, New York: Octagon Books, 1973.

Fitzpatrick, Sheila. *The Russian Revolution*. 2nd ed. Oxford: Oxford University Press, 2008.

Graham, Helen. *Socialism and War: The Spanish Socialist Party in Power and Crisis, 1936–1939*. Cambridge: Cambridge University Press, 1991.

Greene, Nathaniel. *Crisis and Decline: The French Socialist Party in the Popular Front Era*. New York: Cornell University Press, 1969.

Gruber, Helmut. *Red Vienna: Experiment in Working Class Culture, 1919–1934*. Oxford: Oxford University Press, 1991.

Haberkorn, E., and Arthur Lipow, eds. *Neither Capitalism nor Socialism: Theories of Bureaucratic Collectivism*. Alameda, CA: Center for Socialist History, 2008.

Hanson, Philip. *The Rise and Fall of the Soviet Economy: An Economic History of the USSR from 1945*. London: Longman, 2003.

Haupt, Georges. *Socialism and the Great War: The Collapse of the Second International*. Oxford: Clarendon Press 1972.

Hobsbawm, Eric. *The Age of Extremes: The Short Twentieth Century, 1914–1991*. New York: Vintage Books, 1996.

Lapidus, Gail Warschofsky. *Women in Soviet Society*. Berkeley: University of California Press, 1978.

Lewis, Jill. *Fascism and the Working Class in Austria, 1918–1934: The Failure of Labour in the First Republic*. New York: Berg, 1991.

Marples, David R. *Lenin's Revolution: Russia, 1917–1921*. Harlow: Longman, 2000.

McCauley, Martin. *Stalin and Stalinism*. Harlow: Pearson/Longman, 2003.

Mortimer, Edward. *The Rise of the French Communist Party, 1920–1947*. London: Faber and Faber, 1984.

Rizzi, Bruno. *The Bureaucratization of the World*. New York: Free Press, 1985.

Schapiro, Leonard, and Joseph Godson, eds. *The Soviet Worker from Lenin to Andropov*. 2nd ed. New York: St. Martin's Press, 1984.

Schorske, Carl E. *German Social Democracy, 1905–1917: The Development of the Great Schism*. New York: Wiley, 1965.

Sejersted, Francis. *The Age of Social Democracy: Norway and Sweden in the Twentieth Century*. Translated by Richard Daly with editing by Madeleine B. Adams. Princeton, NJ: Princeton University Press, 2011.

Service, Robert. *Lenin: A Biography*. Cambridge, MA: Harvard University Press, 2000.

———. *Stalin: A Biography*. Cambridge, MA: Harvard University Press, 2004.

Stites, Richard. *The Women's Liberation Movement in Russia: Feminism, Nihilism, and Bolshevism, 1860–1930*. Princeton, NJ: Princeton University Press, 1978.

Suny, Ronald Grigor. *The Soviet Experiment: Russia, The USSR, and the Successor States*. New York: Oxford University Press, 1998.

Tiersky, Ronald. *French Communism, 1920–1972*. New York: Columbia University Press, 1974.

Townson, Nigel. *The Crisis of Democracy in Spain: Centrist Politics and the Second Republic, 1931–1936*. Brighton: Sussex Academic Press, 2000.

Weitz, Eric D. *Creating German Communism, 1890–1990: From Popular Protests to Socialist State*. Princeton, NJ: Princeton University Press, 1997.

White, Dan S. *Lost Comrades: Socialists of the Front Generation, 1918–1945*. Cambridge, MA: Harvard University Press, 1992.

CHAPTER 6

Ash, Timothy Garton. *In Europe's Name. Germany and the Divided Continent*. New York: Random House, 1993.

———. *The Polish Revolution: Solidarity*. New Haven, CT: Yale University Press, 2002.

August, Frantisek, and David Rees. *Red Star over Prague*. London: Sherwood Press, 1984.

Birnbaum, Norman. *After Progress: American Social Reform and European Socialism in the Twentieth Century*. Oxford: Oxford University Press, 2001.

Bottomore, Tom. *The Socialist Economy: Theory and Practice*. New York: Guilford Press, 1990.

Fulbrook, Mary. *Anatomy of a Dictatorship: Inside the GDR 1949–1989*. Oxford: Oxford University Press, 1995.

Gaddis, John Lewis. *We Now Know: Rethinking Cold War History*. Oxford: Oxford University Press, 1997.

Gorbachev, Mikhail. *Memoirs*. New York: Doubleday, 1995.

Hanson, Philip. *The Rise and Fall of the Soviet Economy: An Economic History of the USSR from 1945*. Essex: Longman, 2003.

Hodos, George H. *Show Trials: Stalinist Purges in Eastern Europe, 1948–1954*. New York: Praeger, 1987.

Hosking, Geoffrey A. *The First Socialist Society: A History of the Soviet Union from Within*. Cambridge, MA: Harvard University Press, 1990.

Judt, Tony. *Postwar. A History of Europe since 1945*. New York: Penguin, 2005.

Kitschelt, Herbert. *The Transformation of European Social Democracy*. Cambridge: Cambridge University Press, 1994.

Kopstein, Jeffrey. *The Politics of Economic Decline in East Germany, 1945–1989*. Chapel Hill: University of North Carolina Press, 1997.

Lampe, John R. *Yugoslavia: Twice There Was a Country*. Cambridge: Cambridge University Press, 1996.

Larkin, Maurice. *France since the Popular Front: Government and People, 1936–1996*. Oxford: Clarendon Press, 1997.

Maier, Charles S. *Dissolution. The Crisis of Communism and the End of East Germany*. Princeton, NJ: Princeton University Press, 1997.

Moschonas, Gerassimos. *In the Name of Social Democracy. The Great Transformation: 1945 to the Present*. Translated by Gregory Elliott. London: Verso, 2002.

Naimark, Norman M., and L. I. A. Gibianskii. *The Establishment of Communist Regimes in Eastern Europe*. Boulder, CO: Westview Press, 1997.

Nicholls, A. J. *The Bonn Republic: West German Democracy, 1945–1990*. London: Longman, 1997.

———. *Freedom with Responsibility: The Social Market Economy in Germany 1918–1963*. Oxford: Clarendon Press, 1994.

Nove, Alec. *An Economic History of the USSR, 1917–1991*. New York: Penguin, 1992.

Orlow, Dietrich. *Common Destiny: A Comparative History of the Dutch, French, and German Social Democratic Parties*. New York: Berghahn Books, 2000.

Panitch, Leo, and Colin Leys. *The End of Parliamentary Socialism: From New Left to New Labor*. London: Verso, 1997.

Pérez Díaz, Victor. *The Return of Civil Society: The Emergence of Democratic Spain*. Cambridge, MA: Harvard University Press, 1993.

Sasson, Donald. *Contemporary Italy: Politics, Economy, and Society since 1945*. New York: Longman, 1997.

Sejersted, Francis. *The Age of Social Democracy: Norway and Sweden in the Twentieth Century*. Princeton, NJ: Princeton University Press, 2011.

Stokes, Gale. *The Walls Came Tumbling Down: Collapse and Rebirth in Eastern Europe*. 2nd ed. New York: Oxford University Press, 2012.

Taubman, William. *Khrushchev: The Man and His Era*. New York: Norton, 2003.

Tismaneanu, Vladimir. *Stalinism for All Seasons: A Political History of Romanian Communism*. Berkeley: University of California Press, 2003.

Valenta, Jiri. *Soviet Intervention in Czechoslovakia, 1968: Anatomy of a Decision*. Baltimore: Johns Hopkins University Press, 1991.

Wilde, Lawrence. *Modern European Socialism*. Aldershot: Dartmouth, 1994.

Williams, Allan M. *Southern Europe Transformed: Political and Economic Change in Greece, Italy, Portugal, and Spain*. London: Harper and Row, 1984.

Williams, Allan M., and Tom Gallagher. *Southern European Socialism: Parties, Elections, and the Challenge of Government*. Manchester: Manchester University Press, 1989.

Williams, Kieran. *The Prague Spring and Its Aftermath: Czechoslovak Politics, 1968–1970*. Cambridge: Cambridge University Press, 1997.

CHAPTER 7

Benaid, Daniel, Alda Sousa, Alan Thornett, et al. *New Parties of the Left: Experiences from Europe*. London: Resistance Books, 2011.

Hildebrandt, Cornelia, and Birgit Daiber, eds. *The Left in Europe: Political Parties and Party Alliances between Norway and Turkey*. Brussels: Rosa Luxemburg Foundation, 2009.

Hudson, Kate. *European Communism since 1989: Towards a New European Left?* New York: Palgrave, 2000.

Judt, Tony. *Ill Fares the Land*. New York: Penguin, 2010.

Leite, José Correa. *The World Social Forum: Strategies of Resistance*. Translated by Taci Romine. Chicago: Haymarket, 2005.

Panitch, Leo. *Renewing Socialism. Democracy, Strategy, and Imagination*. Boulder, CO: Westview Press, 2001.

Sassoon, Donald. *Social Democracy after the Cold War*. New York: New Press, 1997.

Schmidt, Ingo, and Bryan Evan. *Social Democracy after the Cold War*. Vancouver: University of British Columbia Press, 2012.

Wilkinson, Richard, and Kate Pickett. *The Spirit Level: Why Greater Equality Makes Societies Stronger*. Foreword by Robert Reich. New York: Bloomsbury Press, 2010.

Index

About the Author

William Smaldone is professor of history at Willamette University. He is the author of *Rudolf Hilferding: The Tragedy of a German Social Democrat* (1998) and *Confronting Hitler: German Social Democrats in Defense of the Weimar Republic* (Lexington Books, 2009). His current research interests include East German urban history and the history of Austro-Marxism. Active in a number of progressive and socialist organizations, from 1999 to 2002 he served as a city councilor in Salem, Oregon, where he lives with his wife and two children.